Language,

and Cl

,9.95

67p

MAR 1 4 1994
APR 1 9 1995

FEB 1 3 1996

APR 0 7 1998

FEB 1 7 2000
NOV 1 3 2000

OCT 0 2 2006

The 'Great Chain of Being' was a powerful verbal and visual metaphor for a divinely instituted universal hierarchy. This illustration, from Valades' *Rhetorica Christiana* (1579), shows the ordained ranking of all forms of higher and lower life – archangels, angels, humans, fowls, fishes, mammals, and plants – inter-linked by a great chain held in the right hand of God, who reigns on high with Christ. But the fallen angels, rebels against divine authority, fall from heaven, their wings shrivelling as they reach the Satanic underworld, where the damned are eternally tortured in the fiery pit of perdition.

(Reproduced by permission of the British Library, London)

Language, History and Class

Edited by

PENELOPE J. CORFIELD

Basil Blackwell

First published 1991

Basil Blackwell Ltd
108 Cowley Road, Oxford, OX4 1JF, UK

Basil Blackwell, Inc.
3 Cambridge Center
Cambridge, Massachusetts 02142, USA

British Library Cataloguing in Publication Data

A CIP catalogue record for this book is available from the British Library.

Library of Congress Cataloging in Publication Data

Language, history and class / edited by Penelope J. Corfield.
p. cm.
Includes bibliographical references and index.
ISBN 0-631-16732-3 : ISBN 0-631-16733-1 (pbk.)
1. Sociolinguistics. 2. Social classes. 3. Language and history.
I. Corfield, P.J.
P40.L296 1991
306.4'4--dc20   90-42447   CIP

Typeset in 10 on 12 pt Garamond by Photo·Graphics, Honiton, Devon
Printed in Great Britain by T. J. Press Ltd, Padstow, Cornwall

Contents

Preface

Analysis of language has provided both inspiration and controversy in twentieth-century intellectual life, especially in the humanities and social sciences. Critical dissection of linguistic communication has raised central questions about human conceptual powers and the nature of knowledge itself. Nothing is immune from scrutiny. Words and grammars, speech and speakers, texts and authors, readers and listeners: all are subject to fruitful probing. No doubt, too, in an age of iconoclasm, a sceptical dissection of the language of the physical sciences cannot be long deferred, and the traditional absolutism of an algebraic formula will be challenged by an insurgent pluralism of rival readings.

The study of history, a receptive discipline, has not remained immune from these intellectual currents. An awareness of the fertility and complexity of language and its importance in formulating and expressing meaning is having an increasing impact upon research. That has been particularly marked in social, cultural, and intellectual history, but by no means exclusively so. There is, for example, a growing interest in the role of political language in creating and defining the scope of political action. At the same time, the historian brings to these enquiries a countervailing concern with the dimension of time. If one strong tradition of thought in modern linguistic and literary studies has focused upon cross-sectional analysis of synchronized structures of thought and expression, historical interpretation stresses that every synchronic moment is always simultaneously part of a diachronic process – that is, time.

This collection of essays is grouped around one theme – out of the myriad dimensions of language and history – that has emerged from the common research interests of a number of historians. It is concerned with the broadly defined question of how past societies have been described and thought about by those living in them. The contributions range around the globe to discuss variously the languages of 'ranks', 'estates', and 'class'; the language of 'nobility'; the language of 'people' and power; the concept of 'society'; and the role of language itself as a social denominator. In addition, a sociolinguist interprets a modern source, with a discussion of the role of language analysis in the study of history.

Needless to say, these essays by no means exhaust the plenitude of issues. For example, the language of gender in relation to the language of social description is a promising area for further enquiry. Nor do these essays propound a uniform approach or viewpoint. Each contribution stands in its own right. Collectively, however, the volume offers a comparative range of studies, that point to conjunctions in the history of society, politics, ideas and semantics, and that suggest the importance not only of language in history but also of history in language.

Grateful acknowledgements go to friends and colleagues who have helped with advice and discussion, particularly Tony Belton, Ralph Fasold, Roger Fowler, Patrick Joyce, Evelyn Rawski, Francis Robinson, John Styles, Peter Trudgill, and the individual contributors to this volume. Above all, cordial thanks to John Davey at Basil Blackwell for vital editorial encouragement, and to Juliet Gardiner and Gordon Marsden, successive editors of *History Today*, who gave space and goodwill to this research in its early days, publishing short versions of the essays by Penelope Corfield, Geoffrey Crossick, Roger Mettam, Tony Thompson, and Keith Wrightson, which together formed a series on language and society entitled 'In So Many Words', in *History Today*, 37 (January–March 1987).

Acknowledgements

The essay by Philip Kuhn was initially published in *Class and Social Stratification in Post-Revolution China*, ed. J. Watson (Cambridge University Press, Cambridge, 1984), pp. 16–28, 241–3, and is reprinted by permission from Cambridge University Press. The essay by Penelope Corfield was first published in *History*, 72 (1987), pp. 38–61. Finally, the essay by William Downes reprints as an Appendix an extract from Paul Robeson's testimony from *Thirty Years of Treason: excerpts from hearings before the House Committee on Un-American Activities, 1938–68*, ed. E. Bentley (Thames and Hudson, London, 1972), pp. 770–4, with special thanks to Eric Bentley for permission to quote from this edition of the transcript.

P. J. C.
London

1

Introduction: historians and language

Penelope J. Corfield

Happy the lecturer whose students listen and take notes attentively and whose colleagues are able and willing to reconstruct the lecturer's systematic arguments from the surviving fragments. It occurs only rarely, but sometimes with famous results. It happened to Arnold Toynbee, half-teasingly dubbed the 'Apostle Arnold',[1] whose lectures on English economic history galvanized Oxford undergraduates in the early 1880s. After his premature death in 1883, two of his audience (one of whom later became one of the founding figures of economic history) consulted with their fellow students to devise a book from their collective notes and from Toynbee's own working papers.

The resultant study was published in 1884 as *Lectures on the Industrial Revolution of the Eighteenth Century in England*.[2] Toynbee's analysis

I am grateful to John Dinwiddy, Eckhart Hellmuth, Alice Prochaska, and John Williamson for their expert advice on specific points, and to Bill Downes, Sarah Richmond, John Styles, and Katie Wales for their critical readings of the general discussion.

[1] Arnold Toynbee (1852–83), tutor at Balliol College, Oxford, from 1878 until his early death, inspired many by his fusion of scholarship and passionate belief in Christian social reform. Toynbee Hall in London's Whitechapel was designed to promote contact between workers and academics as a tribute to his ideals. He should not be confused with his nephew and namesake Arnold J. Toynbee, author of the controversial world history entitled *A Study of History* (12 vols, Oxford University Press, London, 1934–61).

[2] See A. Toynbee, *Lectures on the Industrial Revolution of the Eighteenth Century in England: popular addresses, notes and other fragments* (Rivingtons, London, 1884), pp. xxx–xxxi, where Toynbee's widow thanked William J. Ashley (later Professor of Economic History at Harvard and Birmingham) and Bolton King for preparing the material for publication. An expanded 5th edition in 1908 included an appreciation of Toynbee by his close friend Alfred (later

immediately established its place in the literature of economic history, and was reprinted many times, most recently in 1969. But its greatest legacy was to summarize his central thesis in an evocative new term. He himself spoke of 'Industrial and Agrarian Revolution', but it was the simpler formulation of 'Industrial Revolution' in his title that gained widest currency. It confirmed that term as the accepted name for structural change in the English economy between *c*.1760 and the Great Exhibition of 1851,[3] eclipsing earlier interpretative phrases such as Southey's 'manufacturing system' or Carlyle's 'Age of Machinery'. Controversy followed and still continues: did an 'Industrial Revolution' really happen? Did something happen that needs a different name? Or did nothing happen, and was the 'Industrial Revolution' no more than a misleading metaphor, rashly adopted by Toynbee and unthinkingly perpetuated by scholars after him?[4] The vitality of the debate pays double tribute – to the alertness of Toynbee's students and to the analytical power of words.

A still greater rise to posthumous fame happened to another celebrated lecturer who also inspired others to reconstruct his ideas for publication. He was Ferdinand de Saussure, now generally known simply as Saussure. His specialism was the study of language itself. During his lifetime, he was not a celebrated 'apostle' in the public eye, but a relatively obscure teacher of philology, whose classes were rigorous in their methodology. Born in Geneva in 1857, he had studied linguistics in Germany and taught in Paris before returning to his birthplace as professor in 1891. There he lived quietly and published little, complaining in 1894 at 'the utter inadequacy of current terminology' for expounding his thought.[5] But in 1906–7, 1908–9, and 1910–11, the University of Geneva asked him to give a general lecture course on linguistics, and, after his death in 1913 at the age of 56, two of his colleagues put together an account

---

Viscount) Milner. For a critique, see D. C. Coleman, *History and the Economic Past: an account of the rise and decline of economic history in Britain* (Clarendon Press, Oxford, 1987), pp. 59–62, which, however, wrongly asserts that the *Lectures* were revised by Milner.

[3] A. Bezanson, 'The early use of the term Industrial Revolution', *Quarterly Journal of Economics*, 36 (1922), pp. 343–9, established that the phrase was in use in French from the 1820s onwards, in German from the 1840s, and that there were scattered uses in English before Toynbee.

[4] The term was attacked in the 1920s and 1930s, revived in the 1950s, but criticized anew in the 1970s and 1980s. For example, see M. Fores, 'The myth of a British Industrial Revolution', *History*, 66 (1981), pp. 181–98.

[5] J. Culler, *Saussure* (Fontana, London, 1976; rev. 1988), p. 15.

of his ideas, drawing on students' notes from the lectures and a few private jottings made by Saussure himself.[6]

Messrs Charles Bally and Albert Sechéhaye thereby played a crucial role in the genesis of a work that has eventually become a seminal text in modern cultural and linguistic thought, analysing the structures of language as the paramount human communication system. Their edition of Saussure's *Cours de linguistique générale*,[7] first published in Paris in 1916, was not an instant best-seller. It is awkwardly constructed, showing signs of its hybrid genesis. The initial reviews were patchy, claiming variously that its ideas were not new or, if new, not convincing.[8] Here there are parallels with the cautious first responses to Marx's *Kapital* in 1867 or to Freud's *Interpretation of Dreams* in 1899.[9] Works of stature, however controversial, are not always instantly recognized as such, instead gaining their reputation over the long term. But Saussure himself had confidence in the importance of his ideas. And 'great time', with the instrumental assistance of Saussure's two constructive colleagues, has endorsed that view.

Saussure himself lived in scholarly calm but not in cultural isolation. He was well versed in European and American research, including the work of his Parisian colleague Michel Bréal, whose *Essai de sémantique: science des significations* (1897) had already argued a case for language as a mind-made system.[10] Furthermore, both men were familiar with the ideas of Hyppolite Taine, the provocative French historian and

[6] It was not until 1967–74, with the publication of the students' unrevised notes, that scholars were able to examine the original organization of Saussure's lectures: ibid., pp. 17, 141.

[7] The *Cours* was translated into English as *Course in General Linguistics*, tr. W. Baskin (Peter Owen, London, 1960; McGraw-Hill, New York, 1966; Fontana, London, 1974); quotations are taken from this translation, unless otherwise indicated. For an introduction to this complex text, see R. Harris, *Reading Saussure: a critical commentary on the Cours de linguistique générale* (Duckworth, London, 1987).

[8] W. K. Percival, 'The Saussurean paradigm: fact or fantasy?', *Semiotica*, 36 (1981), pp. 33–49.

[9] See E. J. Hobsbawm, 'Dr. Marx and the Victorian critics', in idem, *Labouring Men: studies in the history of labour* (Weidenfeld, London, 1964), pp. 239–49; P. Gay, *Freud: a life for our time* (Dent, London, 1988), pp. 3, 132–3.

[10] On this, see H. Aarsleff, 'Bréal, "la sémantique", and Saussure', in idem, *From Locke to Saussure: essays on the study of language and intellectual history* (Athlone Press, London, 1982), pp. 382–98. But in his own comments on the history of linguistics, Saussure gave praise to the German *Junggrammatiker* or 'neogrammarians' and the American scholar W. D. Whitney: Saussure, *General Linguistics*, p. 5.

literary critic, whose reputation was at its zenith in the later nineteenth century. In his *De l'intelligence* (1870) he had suggested that people communicated ideas by means of 'signs', an idea that had earlier parallels in the speculations of John Locke in the 1690s and the Abbé Condillac in 1746.[11] Taine also sought to discover system within empirical diversity; and to achieve that, he had distinguished between the study of simultaneous and successive states ('*choses simultanées*' and '*choses successives*'). It was Saussure, however, whose trenchant analysis synthesized many of these strands into a new approach to the structure of language.[12] Bréal's name is now known only to experts; and Taine's reputation, once magnificent, plummeted after a devastating attack on his scholarly methods by a fellow historian in 1907.[13]

By contrast, Saussure rides serenely high. His work gave great momentum and intellectual excitement to his own subject. Furthermore, he did not view language in isolation. Instead, he argued that it should be incorporated into a much broader investigation into communication systems generally. He named this 'semiology' (others preferred 'semiotics') or the study of 'signs'.[14] That threw down an ambitious challenge which eventually had a long-term resonance well beyond the formal study of linguistics. Saussure therefore is known not so much as the founding-father of a closely defined school of thought or sect but rather as one of the seminal proponents of a new way of characterizing social analysis. He was an advocate of the distinctively European cultural 'modernism' of the early twentieth century. It was an approach that eschewed 'Victorian' assumptions about progressive linear growth, and cultivated instead a cool structural dissection. His influence has been compared with that of an array of formidable European thinkers: with

---

[11] H. Aarsleff, 'Taine and Saussure', in idem, *Locke to Saussure*, pp. 356–71, esp. pp. 63, 357, 361–2. For a cautious appreciation of Hyppolite Taine (1823–93), see S. J. Kahn, *Science and Aesthetic Judgement: a study in Taine's critical method* (Routledge, London, 1953).

[12] Saussure may have been alerted to Taine via Bréal; see Aarsleff, *Locke to Saussure*, pp. 387, 390, 392. In the absence of Saussure's working papers, his intellectual evolution remains conjectural; but see F. Godel, *Les sources manuscrites du Cours linguistique générale de F. de Saussure* (Société de Publications Romanes et Françaises, No. 61, Geneva, 1957).

[13] F. V. A. Aulard, *Taine, historien de la Révolution française* (Alcan, Paris, 1907).

[14] Saussure coined 'semiology' from the Greek *sémeîon* or 'sign' (see his *General Linguistics*, p. 16), and the term is current in many languages. But the alternative 'semiotics' (1880, *OED Supplement*) is usually preferred in Britain and America. Both words had had a prior history as technical terms for the study of medical symptoms: see *OED sub* semeiology, semeiotics.

Freud in psychology, Durkheim in sociology, and Wittgenstein in philosophy.[15] That exaggerates Saussure's immediate impact. But his ideas have proved to have intellectual longevity. References to his work multiply rather than abate; and, even if invocations are often totemic or sometimes hostile, this still indicates his centrality.[16] Furthermore, he had shown his own practical command of language by successfully launching into circulation a battery of new analytical terms, such as 'semiology', that replaced an older vocabulary whose inadequacies he had earlier lamented.

At the heart of Saussure's thought there is a marked binary, either/or structuration.[17] He was a disaggregative 'splitter' rather than a holistic 'lumper', to borrow another dichotomous, if inelegant, classification.[18] But Saussure's careful binary distinctions were made neither in pedantry nor in pursuit of an atomistic model of knowledge. On the contrary, he considered that languages worked only within structured linguistic systems. But to achieve analytical clarity, Saussure needed precise definition. Hence he bisected complex general concepts into their twofold components. There is an interesting analogy here with the binary notation that provides the basic building blocks for the sophisticated programming languages of modern digital computing.[19] Not that Saussure himself was a logician or a mathematician. But he held that definitional rigour was essential (one task of linguistics, he said, was to

[15] For Sigmund Freud (1856–1939) and Émile Durkheim (1858–1917), see Culler, *Saussure*, pp. 70–9; R. Bocock, *Sigmund Freud* (Horwood, Chichester, 1983); and A. Giddens, *Durkheim* (Fontana, London, 1978). For Ludwig Wittgenstein (1889–1951), see D. Pears, *Wittgenstein* (Fontana, London, 1971, 1985). For the early twentieth-century cultural context, see G. Lichtheim, *Europe in the Twentieth Century* (Weidenfeld, London, 1972, 1974), pp. 85–105.

[16] F. Gadet, *Saussure and Contemporary Culture*, tr. G. Elliott (Hutchinson, London, 1989), pp. 11–12, 111–55; and Culler, *Saussure*, pp. 90–131.

[17] Binary concepts persist in post-Saussurean semiotics. For Roland Barthes's comment on the binary also in the social sciences, see R. Barthes, *Elements of Semiology*, tr. A. Lavers and C. Smith (Cape, London, 1967), p. 12.

[18] For 'lumpers/splitters', see J. H. Hexter, *On Historians: reappraisals of some of the makers of modern history* (Collins, London, 1979), p. 242. More poetic are the 'hedgehogs' (holists) and 'foxes' (disaggregators) from an ancient Greek dictum that 'The fox knows many things, but the hedgehog knows one big thing': in I. Berlin, *The Hedgehog and the Fox: an essay on Tolstoy's view of history* (Weidenfeld, London, 1953, 1967), pp. 1–2.

[19] This does not imply that computational thought is directly analogous to human thought, merely that dichotomous contrasts can play a basic role in structured thought systems. For the continuing debate, see R. Penrose, *The Emperor's New Mind: concerning computers, minds, and the laws of physics* (Oxford University Press, Oxford, 1989), esp. pp. 392–449.

delimit itself), and upon that basis even as protean a phenomenon as language could be understood.

One central Saussurean dichotomy set out to establish the temporal frame of reference for analysis. He contrasted the state of affairs at any given point in time (the 'synchrony') with its existence through time (the 'diachrony'). Here he echoed Taine's distinction between the simultaneous and the successive, but with an original terminology.[20] The distinction did not deny history, but it made it easier to identify the abstract structural frame within the temporal flow. Hence linguists could focus upon the 'synchronic' state of a language without worrying about first tracing its origins and evolution from antiquity. It was analogous, Saussure suggested, to studying the rules of chess without first having to learn the history of the game. He accepted that each synchronic state existed in diachronic time. He further accepted – indeed stressed – that language was a product of the past.[21] But the two frameworks could be analytically disentangled. He pointed out that people use language spontaneously in the state they find it, without knowing anything of its past history. Therefore 'the linguist who wishes to understand a state must discard all knowledge of everything that produced it and ignore diachrony.'[22]

This proposition is as controversial as it has been hugely influential. There are crucial problems of definition. What is the duration of a synchronic moment: a decade, a year, a month, a day, a week, an hour, an atomically measured millisecond? How successfully can synchronic structures be studied without reference to the inexorable flow of space-time? Indeed, is the conceptual choice between the synchronic axis and the diachronic axis a false dichotomy? Historians tend to answer in the affirmative, although of course not unanimously. Furthermore, are linguistic systems really comparable with the rules of chess? Or does language have a much greater flexibility and historic adaptability in structure and usage, as well as an infinitely wider frame of reference? Again, many, including enthusiasts for the noble game of chess, answer

---

[20] 'Synchronic' in English dates from 1833, and 'diachronic' was a nonce-word in 1857. But their effective launch into circulation was Saussure's achievement: see G. Lepschy, 'European linguistics in the twentieth century', in *Studies in the History of Western Linguistics*, ed. T. Bynon and F. R. Palmer (Cambridge University Press, Cambridge, 1986), p. 191.

[21] Saussure, *General Linguistics*, pp. 79–100; Culler, *Saussure*, pp. 35–45, 84–6.

[22] Saussure, *General Linguistics*, p. 81.

this question in the affirmative.[23] Yet, despite these problems, Saussure's incisive approach proved immensely fruitful. The reception of his work tilted twentieth-century linguistics towards a descriptive and social-scientific study of language systems, an emphasis that still pervades the subject, although by no means universally.[24] The idea of a gradual linguistic 'progress' was dethroned, and analysis of relational systems elevated. There are strong parallels here with the yet more seismic impact upon modern thought of the contemporaneous development of relativity theory by another Swiss resident, the physicist Albert Einstein.[25] His analysis also dethroned the perception of time as absolute and uniform in measurement, and established instead its relativity to the point of observation.

Another of Saussure's binary distinctions then elucidated his subject-matter. He differentiated between *langue*, the language system in the abstract, and *parole*, which refers to the actual utterances of human speakers. Between them these form human linguistic communication in its widest sense, which he termed *langage*. Saussure agreed that *parole* remains variegated and personal: the 'executive' branch of the business. But *langue* provides the abstract framework, the structure that is not subject to individual whims and adaptations. Instead it is constructed socially as a self-contained whole. The linguist's task is therefore to differentiate between the two states and to analyse a *langue* as an integral system of signs.[26] The logical clarity of these definitions had great impact. Above all, they helped to disentangle the study of the theoretical mental computations of language systems from the applied diversity of words in action. Other linguists have contributed fresh interpretations of *langue/parole*. Scholars of the Prague school suggested code/message, while Noam Chomsky preferred grammatical competence/speech per-

[23] For a succinct critique of language as chess, see, e.g., M. Devitt and K. Sterelny, *Language and Reality: an introduction to the philosophy of language* (Blackwell, Oxford, 1987), pp. 213–14.

[24] The separate name for historical linguistics certainly implies that 'ordinary' linguistics has a synchronic focus. See T. Bynon, *Historical Linguistics* (Cambridge University Press, Cambridge, 1977); and S. Romaine, *Socio-histori-cal Linguistics: its status and methodology* (Cambridge University Press, Cambridge, 1982).

[25] For Albert Einstein (1879–1955) and theories of relativity, see A. Pais, *'Subtle is the Lord': the science and the life of Albert Einstein* (Oxford University Press, Oxford, 1982), pp. 17–24; and G. J. Whitrow, *Time in History: views of time from prehistory to the present day* (Oxford University Press, Oxford, 1988), pp. 172–6.

[26] Saussure, *General Linguistics*, pp. 9, 13–15, 17.

formance.[27] But none of these dichotomies has resolved all doubts. Are the two concepts really so distinct? Can *langue* be analysed without reference to *parole*? And, especially, how do long-term changes take place, if the state of a language at any given point in time is a self-contained system? But the general approach liberated enquiry; and indeed a Saussurean influence continues to pervade modern linguistics, even though the subject in practice has developed substantially since his pioneering approach to systematization.

Most significant was Saussure's dichotomous interpretation of 'signs'. He rejected the simplistic view that language is simply a list of names, each corresponding precisely to the object named. If that were so, it would be simple to translate from one language into another. Instead Saussure stated that each word is a double-sided linguistic 'sign', one side comprising the 'signifier' (*le signifiant*) and the other the 'signified' (*le signifié*). The first is the sound and expression of a word. Meanwhile the second represents not the 'real' object described but rather the concept signified. Hence 'cat' is not the exclusive term for a real feline quadruped, complete with fur, claws, whiskers, and tail. Instead, it signifies the idea or concept of such an animal, as expressed within one set of linguistic conventions. Language, in this view, does not simply hold a mirror to an autonomous 'real' world, but is itself a constitutive process that demarcates meaning via its own rules and conventions. Only thus can 'cat' make sense. Once established, the two sides of the sign are then inextricably united, like two sides of a piece of paper. 'Thought is the recto and sound the verso,' he wrote. 'We cannot cut one side without also cutting the other.'[28] Here was another resonant echo of Taine, who had earlier decided that the mental and the physical components of speech were 'like the verso and recto of a surface'.

On that basis Saussure pointed to the 'arbitrariness' of the sign within each linguistic culture. There is no intrinsic reason why one word should mean one thing rather than another. The link between each word and its signified concept is a matter of custom and practice.[29] But the 'arbitrary' sign does not mean the same as capricious usage: individuals cannot communicate by using language in a totally random fashion. If they unilaterally disregard all conventions and use an unknown termi-

---

[27] Gadet, *Saussure*, p. 140.
[28] Saussure, *General Linguistics*, pp. 65–7, 102–7, 111–22. This translation of Saussure comes from Aarsleff, *Locke to Saussure*, pp. 357–8, while Baskin offers 'Thought is the front, and sound the back', which is more homespun, albeit making the same point: *General Linguistics*, p. 113.
[29] Saussure, *General Linguistics*, pp. 67–70.

nology, they talk gibberish. They lack the absolute power of Humpty Dumpty, who famously explained to Alice: 'when I use a word, it means just what I choose it to mean – neither more nor less.'[30] But then he lived beyond the looking-glass. When using speech or writing to communicate successfully in this world,[31] individuals operate within the framework of at least one of the world's evolving stock of some five thousand or more languages.[32] People talk and listen, write and read, however creatively and imaginatively, within pre-existing linguistic communities. They use and develop languages that are socially constructed and socially negotiated. From that Saussure drew two different conclusions. On the one hand, he argued that the existence of *langue* is immutable, a fact of human life beyond individual decision making. But he also agreed that the rules and usages of language do in practice mutate over time.[33] There was therefore scope for eventual change, whether in grammar and pronunciation or in words and concepts, such as the new linguistic terms that he himself had so notably propounded.

There is more to Saussure, much more to modern language studies,[34] and more still to philosophical debates about the relationship of words to meaning. But these central definitions set the framework for a prolonged burst of research and scholarly debate. In a sense, both Saussure and, on a much lesser scale, Arnold Toynbee indicated the intellectual impact that can result from the successful crystallization of key concepts into a striking terminology which then continues to influence the thought of later generations. That does not mean that knowledge always grows incrementally; but it does mean that ideas, once communicated, are not

---

[30] L. Carroll, *The Annotated Alice: Alice's adventures in Wonderland; and through the looking-glass*, ed. M. Gardner (Penguin, Harmondsworth, 1960), p. 269.

[31] This does not deny the possibility of pre- and non-linguistic thought or of private languages. For discussion, see Pears, *Wittgenstein*, pp. 142–67; O. N. Jones (ed.), *The Private Language Argument* (Macmillan, London, 1971); and J. A. Fodor, *The Language of Thought* (Harvester, Hassocks, 1976).

[32] Estimates range between 3,000 and 10,000. For the problems of defining languages and dialects, see D. Crystal (ed.), *The Cambridge Encyclopaedia of Language* (Cambridge University Press, Cambridge, 1987), pp. 284–94.

[33] Saussure, *General Linguistics*, pp. 67–78.

[34] True to its synchronic emphasis, linguistics has not greatly cultivated historical analysis; but for European and Anglo-American traditions, see Aarsleff, *Locke to Saussure*; R. H. Robins, *A Short History of Linguistics* (Longman, London, 1967); G. Sampson, *Schools of Linguistics: competition and evolution* (Hutchinson, London, 1980); Lepschy, 'European linguistics'; and R. Harris and T. J. Taylor, *Landmarks in Linguistic Thought: the western tradition from Socrates to Saussure* (Routledge, London, 1989).

confined totally within one synchronic timespan. Indeed, the modern debate about all these issues has become notably prolonged. How do people learn and understand languages? How do they use them for expression and communication? How and why do languages persist or change? Are they really best understood as systems of signs, or is that too much a noun-centred view? What is the relationship of words to thought, and of both to meaning? How do language and thought relate to the past and present world? And does language itself create or control meaning? Some or all of these issues are confronted by linguists, literary theorists, semiologists, philosophers, feminists, anthropologists, sociologists, psychoanalysts, and psycho-biologists of speech, to name but a few. Indeed, an exploration of all the ramifications of language analysis would involve a substantial slice of twentieth-century intellectual history, as the modern quest for knowledge takes a 'linguistic turn'.[35]

Historians were certainly not the first who hastened to read Saussure's awkward masterpiece. Linguistics and history were not close neighbours on the intellectual map. Furthermore, Saussure's emphasis upon the importance of studying synchronic states of languages was not immediately appealing to those engaged in an intrinsically diachronic subject like history, even if the study of history certainly does not exclude a concern with structural analysis.

In fact, that specific term was initially associated in English historiography with a very different scholar. He was Lewis Namier, the controversial Polish emigré to England, whose two-volume study of *The Structure of Politics at the Accession of George III* (1929) shocked many of his fellow-historians through its uncompromising rejection of the traditional Whig stress upon the role of political parties.[36] Instead Namier scrutinized the personal and financial motivations of individual politicians. His approach clearly eschewed 'grand narrative', and emphasized synchronic patterning rather than the long-term trend. He promoted the close-focus study of what became known as 'high politics' (the politics of the power elite) plus the new technique of prosopography, or the reconstitution of group biographies. But, despite the title of his book,

---

[35] R. Rorty (ed.), *The Linguistic Turn: recent essays in philosophical method* (University of Chicago Press, Chicago, 1967). But there are critics of philosophic linguisticism: see, e.g., E. Gellner, *Words and Things: an examination of, and an attack on, linguistic philosophy* (Routledge, London, 1959, 1979) and C. W. K. Mundle, *Critique of Linguistic Philosophy* (Clarendon Press, Oxford, 1970).

[36] For L. B. Namier (1888–1960), see the hostile H. Butterfield, *George III and the Historians* (Collins, London, 1957) pp. 208–15, 288–93, and the judicious L. Colley, *Namier* (Weidenfeld, London, 1989), pp. 46–50, both rightly noting that traditional Whig views were already under siege before Namier's onslaught.

Namier was not concerned with persistent or institutional structures, other than as framework for the personal motivations of the governing elite. His view of society was an atomistic one, stressing the role of individual human nature rather than the structural power of ideology or party, let alone of class struggle or economic factors.[37] Hence, although his synchronic methodology was termed 'structural analysis', and although variants of his approach were adopted by others, it was not Namier and his followers who subsequently became identified as 'structuralists'. That was another school of thought, and besides its ambiance was French.

Controversy among historians is provoked most rapidly by new contributions within history, as the reception of Toynbee and Namier suggests. Nevertheless the organized study of the past is not only an accumulative and argumentative discipline, but it has also become increasingly eclectic and pluralist.[38] It continually absorbs new ideas and methodologies from other disciplines, which it then subjects to the historian's concerns with time, historical context, and a critical attention to the sources (sometimes disparaged as 'grubbing for detail' or 'source fetishism'). Intellectual borrowings have occurred both explicitly and implicitly, particularly from all the social sciences, including social anthropology.[39] And innovations have consistently promoted controversy, as over counter-factual economic modelling in the 'new' economic history[40] or over 'history from below' in the 'new' social history.[41]

[37] Namier's view of politics as elite competition rather than Marxist class struggle had affinities with the elitist philosophy of Vilfredo Pareto, under whom Namier had studied at Lausanne in 1906: see J. Namier, *Lewis Namier: a biography* (Oxford University Press, London, 1971), pp. 63, 92; Colley, *Namier*, pp. 24–5, 74; and, for Pareto, T. Bottomore, *Elites and Society* (Penguin, Harmondsworth, 1966), pp. 8–10, 12–13, 48–53.

[38] Historiology studies individual historians and/or distinctive traditions, as in H. J. Kaye, *The British Marxist Historians: an introductory analysis* (Polity Press, London, 1984), or G. G. Iggers, *The German Conception of History: the national tradition of historical thought from Herder to the present* (Wesleyan University Press, Middletown, Ct, 1968, 1983). But the modern internationalization of the discipline awaits a good history.

[39] See, e.g., P. Burke, *Sociology and History* (Allen and Unwin, London, 1980); L. Stone, 'History and the social sciences in the twentieth century', in idem, *The Past and Present Revisited* (Routledge, London, 1987); and C. Tilly, *As Sociology meets History* (Academic Press, New York, 1981).

[40] G. R. Elton and R. W. Fogel, *Which Road to the Past? Two views of history* (Yale University Press, New Haven, 1983).

[41] For a polemic against departures from traditional 'narrative history', see G. Himmelfarb, *The New History and the Old* (Belknap, Cambridge, Mass., 1987), who participates in the debates aired in 'AHR Forum: the old history

That being so, it is not surprising to find historians also investigating the 'linguistic turn'. No doubt it can be said that here again is nothing new. Historians have always been aware of the potential tyranny of words. Since the time of Thucydides they have been urged to test their evidence carefully, in order to avoid being 'misled by the exaggerated fancies of the poets or by the tales of chroniclers who seek to please the ear rather than to speak the truth.'[42] The fact that most sources survive in written form has always entailed close evaluation of language.

Yet the renewed debates have highlighted once more the analytical implications of linguistic usage. Indeed, in the excitement of decoding the structural assumptions built into old terminologies – such as, for example, those relating to women – there have been calls for a new epistemology or theory of knowledge itself. Certainly, the older positivist faith in the purity and neutrality of scientific method has long been questioned as the sole basis for understanding in the humanities and the social sciences.[43] Analytical rigour, definitional clarity, and fidelity to the sources remain cardinal principles for the study of history. But exemplary methods do not in themselves create knowledge. Nor do the sources alone reveal unproblematically to later generations history 'as it really occurred' (the Rankean 'wie es eigentlich gewesen').[44] Hence the continuing vigour of debate about the bases of knowledge, whether materialist, ideological, linguistic, and/or any combination of theories.

Three different but overlapping linkages make language cumulatively

---

and the new', *American Historical Review*, 94 (1989), pp. 654–98. Contrast also with the approach of contributors in F. Krantz (ed.), *History from Below: studies in popular protest and popular ideology* (Blackwell, Oxford, 1988).

[42] Thucydides, *The Peloponnesian War*, tr. B. Jowett (Bantam, New York, 1960), p. 33.

[43] The view that science displays a superior, value-free objectivity, proceeding from experiment to truth, has been challenged, e.g. by T. S. Kuhn, *The Structure of Scientific Revolutions* (University of Chicago Press, Chicago, 1962); and, although Kuhn's model of knowledge change via 'paradigm shifts' is also controversial, the nature of scientific knowledge is not beyond epistemological questioning. For a call for a more radical epistemology in feminist history, see J. W. Scott, *Gender and the Politics of History* (Columbia University Press, New York, 1988), p. 4.

[44] Leopold von Ranke (1795–1886), who inculcated new standards of accuracy, argued that 'strict presentation of the facts . . . is unquestionably the supreme law.' See L. Kreiger, *Ranke: the meaning of history* (University of Chicago Press, Chicago, 1977), pp. 4–5; plus A. Marwick, *The Nature of History* (Macmillan, London, 1970), pp. 34–8; and E. H. Carr, *What is History?* (Penguin, Harmondsworth, 1964), pp. 8–9, 119–20.

important to historians. First, all past speeches and writing are part of the past, and are therefore all part of the subject-matter of history. In the second place, much surviving information has been recorded either via oral transmission or, predominantly, in written form, so that the wordage produced at many past synchronic moments also constitutes a very large part (although not the totality) of the original evidence for diachronic analysis. Here it might be added that all intervening assessments by other historians or commentators also form part of the historian's source material, usually distinguished as 'secondary' authorities in contrast to the original, 'primary' sources. Thirdly, in common with the rest of humanity, historians themselves communicate via language, which mediates both the framing and the reception of their own views. These three linkages may be analysed separately, although they are not strictly demarcated from one another in practice.

Firstly, as a subject for investigation in its own right all language in history, including both Saussurean *langue* and *parole*, is of potential interest to historians. That, of course, provides a broad canvas.[45] Language is often considered generically, including: the evolution of grammatical rules and the changing stock of words;[46] the origins, evolution, and range of languages; how they are diffused and adapted; and the contribution of communal language use to racial or national identity.[47] At the same time, language is also viewed in diversity. That may include: variations of usage in differing circumstances, the changing meanings of words over time, the specialist practices adopted by specific social groups,[48] the extent or otherwise of gender differences in past *parole*

[45] A suggestive list of themes for investigation is given in P. Burke, 'Introduction', in *The Social History of Language*, ed. P. Burke and R. Porter (Cambridge University Press, Cambridge, 1987), pp. 4–13.

[46] For some case-studies, see S. I. Tucker, *Protean Shape: a study in eighteenth-century vocabulary and usage* (Athlone Press, London, 1967); M. Cohen, *Sensible Words: linguistic practice in England, 1640–1785* (Johns Hopkins University Press, Baltimore, 1977); and R. DeMaria, *Johnson's Dictionary and the Language of Learning* (University of North Carolina Press, Chapel Hill, 1986).

[47] See discussions in K. Deutsch, *Nationalism and Social Communication: an enquiry into the foundations of nationality* (MIT Press, Cambridge, Mass., 1953); and J. A. Fishman, *Language and Ethnicity in Minority Sociolinguistic Perspective* (Multilingual Matters, Clevedon, Avon, 1989).

[48] Rival political usages are documented in, e.g., J. T. Boulton, *The Language of Politics in the Age of Wilkes and Burke* (Routledge, London, 1963); and O. Smith, *The Politics of Language, 1791–1815* (Clarendon Press, Oxford, 1984). But the case for upper-class linguistic 'social control' is argued in J. Barrell, *English Literature in History, 1730–80: an equal, wide survey* (Hutchinson, London, 1983), pp. 110–75.

and the history of gender reputations in the use of language,[49] not to mention the problems of rivalry between different language-users in multilingual societies.[50] Meanwhile, underpinning all these discussions are important debates about the general cultural and intellectual impact of language upon any given society's thought and cultural perceptions.[51]

Historic speech utterances are, of course, particularly difficult to recover. The spoken content, tone of voice, and accompanying body language of most past *parole*, whether in the form of soliloquy or conversational exchange, have vanished virtually without trace. There is a corpus of modern verbal testimony to be audited via electronic recordings, which have their own constraints;[52] and oral traditions also transmit and adapt material such as proverbs, folk-tales, and songs. But in most cases the history of verbal utterances depends upon their being transcribed or referenced in some form of written record. That means that chatter and hesitation tend to be much less well documented than purposive locution, which in turn is often only incompletely recalled and obliquely chronicled.

However, there are sufficient transcriptions or re-creations of speech, as well as contemporary comments about speaking, to make it possible to study its history – for example, the role of oral communication in adapting and transmitting material from generation to generation,[53] the

---

[49] For changing patterns in accusations of defamation and scolding, see S. D. Amussen, *An Ordered Society: gender and class in early modern England* (Blackwell, Oxford, 1988), pp. 101–4, 118–20, 122–3; and for modern gender usages, see J. Coates and D. Cameron (eds), *Women in their Speech Communities: new perspectives on language and sex* (Longman, London, 1988).

[50] See R. Fasold, *The Sociolinguistics of Society* (Blackwell, Oxford, 1984), pp. 3–33, 303–5, for multilingualism and its educational implications.

[51] For discussion of the complex question as to whether and how far language – past or present – determines thought and social perceptions, see Burke, 'Introduction', pp. 11–17. And contrast B. L. Whorf, *Language, Thought, and Reality: selected writings of Benjamin Lee Whorf*, ed. J. B. Carroll (Wiley and Sons, New York, 1956) and G. W. Grace, *The Linguistic Construction of Reality* (Croom Helm, London, 1987), with R. Harris, *The Language Myth* (Duckworth, London, 1981), pp. 112–49, and M. Black, 'Some troubles with Whorfianism', in *Language and Philosophy*, ed. S. Hook (New York University Press, New York, 1969), pp. 30–5.

[52] On oral history both as subject and source material, see P. Thompson, *The Voice of the Past: oral history* (Oxford University Press, Oxford, 1978).

[53] See the discussion in R. Thomas, *Oral Tradition and Written Record in Classical Athens* (Cambridge University Press, Cambridge, 1989). The oral transmission/adaptation of songs and folklore is also analysed in R. Palmer, *The Sound of History: songs and social comment* (Oxford University Press, Oxford, 1988), pp. 1–6; M. Karpeles, *An Introduction to English Folk Song*, rev. P.

status of talking or of silence,[54] past styles in speech and rhetoric, the impact of 'secondary orality' in the modern electronic era of radio, television, and telephone,[55] and/or the changing conventions of inter-personal 'discourse', to use that term in its dialogic, conversational meaning. Here there is plenty of scope for fruitful interchange between historians and linguists, including not only the sociolinguists who study pragmatics or conversational dynamics,[56] but also the historical linguists who analyse – in a post-Saussurean rather than an anti-Saussurean spirit – diachronic continuities/changes in pronunciation, spelling, grammar, and word use.[57]

Furthermore, the relationships between written (scriptocentric) and spoken (phonocentric) modes of communication are themselves of historic interest. In contrast to speech, writing is much better documented via its own output, even though by no means the totality of that has survived. Historians thence analyse the diffusion of the written word,[58] the advent of print,[59] plus the history of the book and other forms of printed publication, and the wider cultural implications of literacy and

---

Kennedy (Oxford University Press, Oxford, 1987), pp. 2–11; I. and P. Opie, *The Lore and Language of Children* (Oxford University Press, Oxford, 1959); and R. B. Bottigheimer, 'Fairy tales, folk narrative research and history', *Social History*, 14 (1989), pp. 343–56.

[54] R. Bauman, *Let Your Words be Few: symbolism of speaking and silence among seventeenth-century Quakers* (Cambridge University Press, Cambridge, 1983).

[55] W. J. Ong, *Orality and Literacy: the technologizing of the word* (Methuen, London, 1982), pp. 3, 171; and debates launched by H. M. McLuhan, *Understanding Media: the extensions of man* (Routledge, London, 1964).

[56] On 'pragmatics' (not to be confused with philosophic 'pragmatism'), see, e.g., J. J. Gumperz, *Discourse Strategies* (Cambridge University Press, Cambridge, 1982); and G. Gazdar, *Pragmatics: implicature, presupposition, and logical form* (Academic Press, New York, 1979).

[57] See Bynon, *Historical Linguistics*; and for a detailed case-study using historical sources, see also M. Wakelin, *The Archaeology of English* (Batsford, London, 1988).

[58] See, e.g., J. Goody, *The Logic of Writing and the Organization of Society* (Cambridge University Press, Cambridge, 1986); Ong, *Orality and Literacy*, pp. 78–108; and, e.g., M. T. Clanchy, *From Memory to Written Record: England, 1066–1307* (Arnold, London, 1979).

[59] E. Eisenstein, *The Printing Press as an Agent of Change: communications and transformations in early-modern Europe* (2 vols, Cambridge University Press, Cambridge, 1979), and case-studies such as J. R. R. Ward, *The Printed Word and the Common Man: popular culture in Ulster, 1700–1900* (Institute of Irish Studies, Belfast, 1987).

the advent of a reading public.[60] The relationship of writing to the
recording and formal study of history itself may also prove a subject
worth further attention. Then the entire range of textual production is
open to investigation: from casual graffiti to official notices, from private
diaries to published dictionaries, from love-letters to business records,
from ephemeral news-sheets to great books. Again, every sort of writing
may be a subject for historical enquiry, whether generically or in terms
of individual items. That applies to all forms of written 'text', including
major and minor sources, fictional and non-fictional writing, literary
and non-literary productions, manuscripts and printed volumes, whether
written for public consumption or for private perusal. All have their
histories, as do their authors, readers, and historians.

'Text', incidentally, is a signifier that is gaining currency – in addition
to its religious connotation – to refer to all forms of written production.
It side-steps the problem of drawing precise boundaries between 'literature' and non-literary output.[61] The deployment of this term does
not, however, imply endorsement of the provocative dictum of the
philosopher-critic Jacques Derrida that 'there is nothing outside the
text.'[62] That appears to leave too little space for critics, let alone for the
scribblers who produce the words in the first place. But the concept has
rightly drawn attention to the intellectual and linguistic contents of
textual output. Hence, for example, a special focus on particular genres
of writing informs the contentious and fast-expanding fields of literary

[60] See H. J. Graff, *Literacy in History: an interdisciplinary research bibliography* (Garland, New York, 1981); J. Goody (ed.), *Literacy in Traditional
Societies* (Cambridge University Press, Cambridge, 1968); R. H. Finnegan,
'Literacy v. non-literacy: the great divide?', in *Modes of Thought: essays on
thinking in Western and non-Western societies*, ed. R. Horton and R. H. Finnegan (Faber, London, 1973); Ong, *Orality and Literacy*, pp. 78–138; B. V. Street,
Literacy in Theory and Practice (Cambridge University Press, Cambridge, 1984);
and, for examples, J. Brooks, *When Russia Learned to Read: literacy and
popular literature, 1861–1917* (Princeton University Press, Princeton, 1985);
R. A. Houston, *Scottish Literacy and the Scottish Identity: illiteracy and society
in Scotland and northern England, 1600–1800* (Cambridge University Press,
Cambridge, 1985); and I. Rivers (ed.), *Books and their Readers in Eighteenth-
Century England* (Leicester University Press, Leicester, 1982).
[61] On the difficulties of close definition, see T. Eagleton, *Literary Theory:
an introduction* (Blackwell, Oxford, 1983), pp. 1–16.
[62] Derrida's dictum *'Il n'y a pas de hors-texte'* (literally, 'there is no outside-
text') is cited in C. Norris, *Deconstruction: theory and practice* (Methuen,
London, 1982), p. 41. For a response from historians, see, e.g., 'Postlude –
what next with history?', in *History as Text: the writing of ancient history*, ed.
A. Cameron (Duckworth, London, 1989), pp. 206–8.

history, intellectual history, and the history of ideas. In addition, historians who are not specialists in language have nonetheless been encouraged to read past texts closely and to make them part of their subject-matter as well as part of their evidence. Thus many themes are illuminated by attention to their distinguishing 'languages' or synchronic communities of discourse (known as 'registers' in sociolinguistics): as in the 'languages of political theory', the 'languages of class', or the 'language of patriotism'.[63] But it is worth noting that all forms of linguistic communication, provided they are heard or read, and especially if they are recorded in writing, have a potential capacity to outlast their moment of production and to achieve a diachronic as well as synchronic significance.

Secondly, therefore, language, particularly written language, pervades the sources as evidence for the past whatever the subject under discussion. Historians spend a lot of time reading the written word. But not all their time. After all, they also work with statistics and quantitative data, and they draw upon a range of visual, tactile, auditory, and (unusually but not impossibly) olfactory evidence. But frequently it happens that these other sources of information are simultaneously webbed within a nexus of linguistic description or analysis – hence the importance for historians of debates about the understanding and interpretation of written texts, whether these are used as primary or secondary sources. Language is not a question simply for language experts but a matter of concern for all. Here advice arrives from many directions. Not only do literary theorists offer specialist perspectives; but there is a general input from modern Western cultural philosophies of knowledge,[64] which test and debate a growing corpus of ideas from anthropology, semiotics, linguistics, sociology, political economy, Marxism, hermeneutics, psychoanalysis, feminism, structuralism, post-structuralism, environmentalism, and so forth in an endless list. The abstraction of theory can prompt rejection and unease, especially from Anglo-

---

[63] See the case-studies in A. Pagden (ed.), *The Languages of Political Theory in Early-Modern Europe* (Cambridge University Press, Cambridge, 1987); G. Stedman Jones, *Languages of Class: studies in English working class history, 1832–1982* (Cambridge University Press, Cambridge, 1983); or H. Cunningham, 'The language of patriotism', in *Patriotism: the making and unmaking of British national identity – vol. 1: history and politics*, ed. R. Samuel (3 vols, Routledge, London, 1989), pp. 57–89.

[64] For post-1960s cultural ferment, see Q. Skinner (ed.), *The Return of Grand Theory in the Human Sciences* (Cambridge University Press, Cambridge, 1985), pp. 1–20; but there is as yet no good general history of twentieth-century Western cultural philosophy.

American empiricists who laugh nervously at the 'Gallic' pretentions of structuralism or the 'German' density of hermeneutics.[65] But the interdisciplinary ferment is creative, especially as no single orthodoxy rules. On the contrary, cultural pundits, such as Jean-Paul Sartre in the 1950s, Herbert Marcuse in the 1960s, or Louis Althusser in the 1970s often found that a sudden rise to the heights of fame and controversy has been as rapidly followed by relative intellectual eclipse.

From these continuing enquiries into the nature of knowledge have emerged insights into both the extrinsic and intrinsic study of written evidence. One intellectual tradition that has had considerable influence upon historical research and teaching is that of modern hermeneutics (or interpretative understanding), which encourages a deep immersion in the original sources. This approach was drawn from theories of knowledge rather than directly from textual exposition. It was inspired by the late nineteenth-century German philosophic rejection of scientific method as the basis of understanding in the humanities.[66] Historians cannot run experiments to test theories or to identify general laws of development. Instead, it was argued, they reconstruct the past via the process of *verstehen* (literally 'to understand'), which is translated as 'interpretation by empathic understanding' or simply 'empathy' (as distinct from personal sympathy or approval). It entailed recovering the totality of lived experience (*Erlebnis*) so that, as Jürgen Habermas has urged, historians

---

[65] In satirizing *mensonge* (= falsehood), M. Bradbury, *My Strange Quest for Mensonge: structuralism's hidden hero* (Deutsch, London, 1987), pokes fun at French theory and English qualms, while himself exemplifying the latter. See also J. H. Hexter, *The History Primer* (Basic Books, New York, 1971; Allen Lane, London, 1972), p. 352, who battles on behalf of 'common sense' against the abstract concept (in German = *Begriff*), with an inter-linguistic pun at the expense of '*begriffstricken* Germans'; see also ibid., pp. 16–20, 353–68.

[66] 'Hermeneutics' initially referred to Biblical interpretation as opposed to 'exegesis' or practical exposition: see R. J. Howard, *Three Faces of Hermeneutics: an introduction to current theories of understanding* (University of California Press, Berkeley, 1982), pp. xiv–xv, 1–3. The study of modern secular hermeneutics was inspired by Wilhelm Dilthey (1833–1911): see ibid., pp. 11–22; and M. Ermarth, *Wilhelm Dilthey: the critique of historical reason* (University of Chicago Press, Chicago, 1975). It now refers chiefly to the German-led tradition of philosophical enquiry into knowledge: see D. Held, *Introduction to Critical Theory: Horkheimer to Habermas* (Hutchinson, London, 1980), esp. pp. 308–11; but the term is sometimes used more loosely for any interpretative system, hence occasional references to, e.g., structuralist hermeneutics. The implications of new interpretations of understanding for teaching history are given practical exploration in A. K. Dickinson and P. J. Lee (eds), *History Teaching and Historical Understanding* (Heinemann, London, 1978).

learn to 'speak the language that they interpret.'[67] There are close parallels here with the Puritan stress upon experiential knowledge in religion, although hermeneutics itself remains a secular metaphysics.

Such an approach encouraged a cultural receptiveness towards the synchronic 'otherness' of past societies and a Maigret-like deep immersion in different ways of life, without the sins of present-day pride or modernist prejudice.[68] This aspiration, which had many progenitors, was readily absorbed by many historians. A similar point was made by Herbert Butterfield in his famous 1931 attack on the 'Whig interpretation' of history-as-progress.[69] He too urged his colleagues to shed present-mindedness and to view the past on its own terms. And the idealist philosopher and historian R. G. Collingwood went further. In *The Idea of History* (1946), he argued that the past was made comprehensible only by the mental re-enactment of past thought, bringing the past into the present rather than vice versa.[70] It was a formulation that also encouraged sensitivity to the historic record, although this view was not without its own problems, in that historians think about, rather than simply re-think, earlier events, and they also study aggregative, long-term, and non-human developments, as well as individual human thoughts and actions.

Nonetheless, the tenor of the hermeneutic debate generally enhanced understanding of the 'otherness' of the past, and it certainly discouraged a 'Whiggish' search for precursors of 'modernity'. It encouraged a precise attention to what people said, did, and wrote in their own historical context, rather than what a later generation might have expected or

[67] Habermas is cited in Held, *Critical Theory*, p. 300. For the interpretative terminology, see Howard, *Three Faces of Hermeneutics*, pp. 29–30.

[68] Georges Simenon's fictional sleuth Maigret relied only marginally upon scientific detection, but drew upon his own intelligence, empathy, and pertinacity, picking up the atmosphere of each case 'til he was so deeply steeped in it that the truth would stand forth of its own accord.' See 'Maigret and the Surly Inspector' (1947), repr. in G. Simenon, *Maigret's Christmas* (Penguin, Harmondsworth, 1981), p. 153, for expression of this approach, which recurs throughout the Maigret saga.

[69] H. Butterfield, *The Whig Interpretation of History* (Bell and Sons, London, 1931, 1950), esp. pp. 9–18. But Butterfield's wartime *The Englishman and his History* (Cambridge University Press, Cambridge, 1944) was deemed not to have lived up to these precepts: Carr, *History*, p. 42.

[70] Hence his claim that 'all history is the history of thought': see R. G. Collingwood, *The Idea of History*, ed. T. M. Knox (Oxford University Press, Oxford, 1946; in 1961 edn), pp. 215, 218, 282. And for interpretations, see Carr, *History*, pp. 20–30; and D. Boucher, *The Social and Political Thought of R. G. Collingwood* (Cambridge University Press, Cambridge, 1990).

demanded. Many areas of enquiry, such as the history of ideas, of popular culture, and of past *mentalités*, reflect this emphasis, which is widely shared across the ideological spectrum. For example, the liberal humanist Quentin Skinner stresses the need to study an author's works in the context of his or her own intellectual frame of reference and operative language as a guide to historical understanding of past political thought.[71] And a classic declaration of empathic intent has been penned by the heterodox Marxist E. P. Thompson, whose *Making of the English Working Class* (1963) explicitly set out 'to rescue the poor stockinger, the Luddite cropper, the "obsolete" hand-loom weaver, the "utopian" artisan, and even the deluded follower of Joanna Southcott, from the enormous condescension of posterity.'[72]

Respect for the sources, however, does not in itself offer a methodology for reading them; nor does 'immersion' provide a framework for analysis. Hence historians have also considered other philosophies and approaches. Among them, a close internal reading of texts has been encouraged not only by modern linguistic analysis but also by literary criticism[73] and its ideative counterpart, critical theory.[74] The principle of active cross-fertilization between history and literature would no doubt have pleased Taine, who was himself an expert in both. And certainly the development of interdisciplinary studies in the cultural interpretation of communication would have gratified Saussure. He had,

[71] See Q. Skinner, 'Motives, intentions, and the interpretation of texts', *New Literary History*, 3 (1972), pp. 393–408; and idem, 'A reply to my critics', in J. Tully (ed.), *Meaning and Context: Quentin Skinner and his critics* (Polity Press, Cambridge, 1988), pp. 232, 246–81.

[72] E. P. Thompson, *The Making of the English Working Class* (Gollancz, London, 1963; Penguin, Harmondsworth, 1968), p. 12.

[73] For the fecund linguistic contribution to text and discourse analysis see, e.g., R. Carter (ed.), *Language and Literature: an introductory reader in stylistics* (Allen and Unwin, London, 1982); and especially R. Fowler, *Linguistic Criticism* (Oxford University Press, Oxford, 1986). Meanwhile, introductions to traditions of literary criticism are found in R. Wellek, *A History of Modern Criticism, 1750–1950* (vols. 1–4, Cambridge University Press, 1981–3; vols. 5–6, Yale University Press, New Haven, 1986); F. Lentricchia, *After the New Criticism* (Athlone Press, London, 1980); and K. M. Newton, *Interpreting the Text: a critical introduction to the theory and practice of literary interpretation* (Harvester Wheatsheaf, London, 1990).

[74] For critiques of critical theory, see variously Eagleton, *Literary Theory*; C. Belsey, *Critical Practice* (Methuen, London, 1980); E. Goodheart, *The Skeptic Disposition in Contemporary Criticism* (Princeton University Press, Princeton, 1984); E. W. Said, *The World, the Text, and the Critic* (Faber, London, 1984); and P. Washington, *Fraud: literary theory and the end of English* (Fontana, London, 1989).

after all, argued that language should be studied not in isolation but within a wider semiology or science of 'signs', including customs and rituals.[75] One of the first responses had occurred in structural anthropology, where Claude Lévi-Strauss sought to identify a series of binary codes that structured meaning in so-called 'primitive' societies.[76] But gradually a very capacious area of enquiry, known as semiotics, has attracted scholarly interest, in an endeavour to establish not simply what communication systems say but particularly how they work as social codes and specialist 'languages'.[77]

Within this, 'structuralism' became influential as a school of thought, especially in French literary and philosophical circles in the 1960s and 1970s. That approach consciously continued the Saussurean project of focusing upon the synchronic structure of ideas in cultural space rather than their diachronic development over time. Indeed, the architectural ring to its name suggested its concern with the inner construction of a given text or source, as opposed to the external circumstances of its creation. Synchronic structures were formed by sudden disjunctures and ruptures in history, not by long-term trends of change or continuity.[78] In literary studies this viewpoint encouraged a reader- or critic-oriented analysis, in an approach playfully defined by Roland Barthes in 1968 as the 'death of the author'.[79] The focus falls not upon the context and

[75] Saussure, *General Linguistics*, p. 17.

[76] See, e.g., C. Lévi-Strauss, *The Raw and the Cooked: introduction to a science of mythology*, tr. J. and D. Weightman (Cape, London, 1970) Lévi-Strauss was influenced by the linguist Roman Jakobson, who was himself influenced by Saussure. See also critiques in E. Leach, *Claude Lévi-Strauss* (Fontana, London, 1974, 1976); and P. Pettit, *The Concept of Structuralism: a critical analysis* (Gill and Macmillan, Dublin, 1975).

[77] U. Eco, *A Theory of Semiotics* (Macmillan, London, 1977), pp. 9–14, lists nineteen areas of enquiry, comprising zoosemiotics (non-human communication systems), olfactory signs, tactile communication, codes of taste, medical semiotics, paralinguistics, kinesics (gestures), musical codes, formalized languages, written languages, natural languages, visual communication, systems of objects, plot structure, text theory, cultural codes, aesthetic texts, mass communications, and rhetoric. 'One would of course want to add anthropology and psychoanalysis to this list,' nonchalantly declares K. Silverman, *The Subject of Semiotics* (Oxford University Press, New York, 1983), p. 5.

[78] The best introduction is T. Hawkes, *Structuralism and Semiotics* (Methuen, London, 1977); and for theoretical exposition, see M. Foucault, *The Archaeology of Knowledge*, tr. A. M. Sheridan Smith (Tavistock, London, 1972), pp. 3–17; and idem, 'The order of discourse', in *Untying the Text: a post-structuralist reader*, ed. R. Young (Routledge, London, 1981), pp. 48–78.

[79] See G. R. Wasserman, *Roland Barthes* (Twayne Publications, Boston, Mass., 1981), p. 93. This dictum had antecedents in the teachings of both inter-

motives of the writer but upon the content and/or form of the text. Just as linguists analyse the systemic rules that make sense of spoken *parole*, so literary critics may seek to identify the signs and patterns in written 'discourse' (thereby stressing the term's modish second meaning to match spoken discourse). This acknowledges the power of words and discursive structures in helping to form meaning. It was taken up significantly in the fast-expanding field of women's studies. 'Language uses us as much as we use language,' a feminist analyst of language has declared.[80] It also emphasizes the role of the critical reader, who is able to decode and expose the hidden messages. 'Let us say, provisionally, that the critic, employing a new language, brings out a *difference* within the work by demonstrating that it is *other than it is*,' as one French expert has explained, albeit with less than Cartesian lucidity.[81]

Structuralist methodology in principle therefore contrasts very markedly with hermeneutic empathy as a method for discovering the past, although in practice historians often manage to combine ideas from both approaches. It is not the case that structuralism excludes the past. But it tends to view history as a series of successive synchronic states, each in itself static, rather than as a long-span diachronic process, whether of change or of continuity. Interestingly, this conflicts not only with 'Whig' views of progress, but also with a Tory stress upon the perdurance of deep traditions and, for good measure, with the Marxist revolutionary dialectic. Indeed, the Marxist tradition was particularly galvanized by the challenge to clarify the role of linguistic and cultural factors in its theoretical model of society. The most explicit structuralist engagement with history was undertaken by the French cultural philosopher Michel Foucault (although he found the structuralist label restrictive). In a series of substantial studies, he argued that madness, illness, criminality, and human sexuality are best understood not as timeless concepts but as socially constituted 'objectifications', produced by structures of knowledge and power and encoded in discursive practice, at specific moments in time.[82] This in itself provoked discussion and disagreement; and

---

war Russian formalism and post-war Anglo-American 'New Criticism': see Eagleton, *Literary Theory*, pp. 3–5, 48–9.

[80] R. Lakoff, *Language and Woman's Place* (Harper Row, New York, 1975), p. 3.

[81] P. Macherey, *A Theory of Literary Production*, tr. G. Wall (Routledge, London, 1978), p. 7.

[82] Michel Foucault (1962–84) eventually rejected the 'structuralist' label, although he is often so classified: see H. L. Dreyfus and P. Rabinow, *Michel Foucault: beyond structuralism and hermeneutics* (Harvester, Brighton, 1982), pp. vii–viii; P. Major-Poetzl, *Michel Foucault's Archaeology of Western Culture:*

structuralism in general has encouraged fresh debate as well as new studies of historical discourse,[83] although historians rarely manage that without some reference to the context of authorship. Furthermore, an awareness of written language has heightened perceptions of the textuality of texts, the intertextuality of meanings shed by one text upon another, and the intratextuality of implied meanings that may not have been consciously intended but may be 'read between the lines'. One example of such practice is the implication of normative male universality in the irritating habit, still maintained by some writers, of invariably referring to humankind (and the historian) as 'he'.

Hence the question remains as to the extent to which linguistic discourse itself exercises cultural control via its capacity to frame its users' thoughts and perceptions both consciously and unconsciously.[84] Does the 'arbitrary' signifier have arbitrary power? If so, that suggests an idealist determinism. But it also leaves many problems unexplained, including the origin of the signifier in the first place. Indeed, a pure structuralist appeal to the absolute authority of written discourse has wilted under critical fire.[85] Furthermore, it is far from clear that written discourse is best analysed as simply analogous to spoken discourse. Nor that deciphering discursive practice provides an unproblematic or value-free route to meaning. There are subjective elements in structuralist readings just as there are in empathic interpretations. As the fictional Morris Zapp explained pithily: '*Each decoding is another encoding.*'[86] Instead, literary critics have been alerted to what Mikhail Bakhtin termed the 'dialogic', or two-way, process of communication between speaker and respondent.[87] Hence the structuralist view, ultimately derived from

toward a new science of history (Harvester, Brighton, 1983), pp. 120–1; M. Poster, *Foucault, Marxism and History: mode of production versus mode of information* (Polity Press, Cambridge, 1984); and B. Smart, *Michel Foucault* (Routledge, London, 1985), pp. 15–16, 18–19, 28, 32. Foucault has achieved inclusion in *The Blackwell Dictionary of Historians*, ed. J. Cannon (Blackwell, Oxford, 1988), pp. 137–8; but see also A. Megill, 'The reception of Foucault by historians', *Journal of the History of Ideas*, 48 (1987), pp. 117–41.

[83] For a cautious summary, see P. Schöttler, 'Historians and discourse analysis', *History Workshop Journal*, 27 (1989), pp. 37–65.

[84] See references in fn 51 above.

[85] Eagleton, *Literary Theory*, pp. 106–26, criticizes literary structuralism.

[86] From Zapp's lecture to the literary disputants in D. Lodge, *Small World: an academic romance* (Secker and Warburg, London, 1984), p. 25 (and see pp. 22–3, 27–8, for arguments about Saussurean theories of meaning).

[87] The Russian critic Mikhail M. Bakhtin (1895–1975) stressed the dialogic nature of communication, invoking a pluralist concept of heteroglossia (*raznorecie*): see M. Holquist, 'Introduction', in M. M. Bakhtin, *Speech Genres*

Nietzsche,[88] that language works through domination, is open to challenge. The Linguistic communication may equally encompass cooperation, convergence, and community – let alone resistance, friction, and adaptation. 'Language control' can be powerful, but it is not absolute,[89] just as structuralist concepts of both language and society are too static. This recalls the very similar debates among historians about the notion of government as 'social control',[90] which was also justly criticized as too monolithic, timeless, and friction-free an account of political power.

Meanwhile, the rival polarities of content and context continue to generate argument. Some critics follow Jacques Derrida in the practice of 'deconstruction', which is post-structuralist in both name and intention. It accepts the structuralist concern for decoding content but does not confine its readings within a synchronic moment. Instead it bypasses all external referents, and deconstructs the 'sign' into perennial alternatives. Words form 'an endless chain of signifiers in which meaning is always deferred and finally absent.'[91] As that suggests, deconstruction can easily take the 'otherness' of subjective rereadings to the point

---

and Other Late Essays, tr. V. W. McGee (University of Texas Press, Austin, 1986), pp. ix–xxi. Amid the current plethora of competing theories and theorists, particularly following the intellectual eclipse of structuralism, may be detected the growing reputation of Bakhtin as a literary critic and linguistic philosopher: see V. N. Vološinov, *Marxism and the Philosophy of Language* (Moscow, 1929), a work that was probably substantially authored by Bakhtin, and M. M. Bakhtin, *The Dialogic Imagination: four essays*, ed. M. Holquist (University of Texas Press, Austin, 1981).

[88] Foucault summarized this provocative view, which has parallels with Nietzsche on will-to-power, without equivocation: 'there is no power relation without the correlative constitution of a field of knowledge, nor any knowledge that does not presuppose and constitute at the same time power relations' (quoted in Smart, *Foucault*, p. 76). For critical discussions of Foucault on power, see, e.g. J. Baudrillard, *Oublier Foucault* (Paris, 1977), rendered into the imperative as *Forget Foucault*, tr. N. Dufresne (Semiotext, New York, 1987); and J. Habermas, 'Some questions concerning the theory of power: Foucault again', in idem, *The Philosophical Discourse of Modernity: twelve lectures*, tr. F. Lawrence (MIT Press, Cambridge, Mass., 1985), pp. 266–93.

[89] For a warning to feminists against accepting the twin propositions that men control language and that language controls women, see D. Cameron, *Feminism and Linguistic Theory* (Macmillan, London, 1985), esp. pp. 134–61.

[90] See, e.g., critique by F. M. L. Thompson, 'Social control in Victorian Britain', *Economic History Review*, 2nd ser. 34 (1981), pp. 189–209.

[91] This definition is from D. Harlan, 'Intellectual history and the return of literature', *American Historical Review*, 94 (1989), p. 582. See also general discussions in Norris, *Deconstruction*, pp. 24–32, 91–108; Culler, *Saussure*, pp. 121–8; and essays in D. Attridge, G. Bennington, and R. Young (eds), *Post-structuralism and the Question of History* (Cambridge University Press, Cambridge, 1987).

of nullity, satirized by Bradbury as '*the age of the floating signifier*, when word no longer attaches properly to thing, and no highbonding glues can help us.'[92] But this has certainly sharpened debate about the status of written language, which has been joined particularly by historians of ideas, whose own subject-matter is vitally concerned with written texts.[93] By contrast, other literary critics have returned to context, striving to read items of literary output as they were first experienced. And a related school of thought analyses works of literature as 'interventions' at a specific historical moment. This latter approach is known as the 'new historicism',[94] although confusingly it has nothing to do with the old 'historicism' that was pungently denounced as teleology by Karl Popper. Here history's interest in literature meets with literary criticism's interest in history, although with rather different concerns and perspectives in the foreground of analysis.

Thirdly, and not surprisingly in view of these arguments, historians have also been alerted to their own linguistic practices as writers and teachers. Prompted by insights from literary criticism, there has been some research into the literature of written history.[95] This has included

[92] Bradbury, *Mensonge*, p. 5.

[93] For the debates about context/experience versus content/meaning, see review by J. E. Toews, 'Intellectual history after the linguistic turn: the autonomy of meaning and the irreducibility of experience', *American Historical Review*, 92 (1987), pp. 879–907; plus the exchanges between D. Harlan and D. A. Hollinger in *American Historical Review*, 94 (1989), pp. 581–626. For language and political thought, see also the general overviews by J. G. A. Pocock, 'Languages and their implications: the transformation of the study of political thought', in idem, *Politics, Language and Time: essays on political thought and history* (Methuen, London, 1972), pp. 1–41; and idem, 'The concept of a language and the *métier d'historien*: some considerations on practice', in *Languages of Political Theory*, ed. Pagden, pp. 19–38.

[94] See J. R. de J. Jackson, *Historical Criticism and the Meaning of Texts* (Routledge, London, 1989), esp. pp. 2–5, 71–4, 131–4, 147–51, 158–9; and H. White, 'The new historicism: a comment', in *The New Historicism*, ed. H. A. Veeser (Routledge, New York, 1989). For the celebrated attack on immanent theories of historical inevitability, see K. R. Popper, *The Poverty of Historicism* (Routledge, London, 1957).

[95] For studies in historical discourse, see, e.g., H. White, *Metahistory: the historical imagination in nineteenth-century Europe* (Johns Hopkins University Press, Baltimore, 1973); R. H. Canary and H. Kosicki (eds), *The Writing of History: literary form and historical understanding* (University of Wisconsin Press, Madison, 1978); P. Ricoeur, *Time and Narrative*, tr. K. McLaughlin and D. Pellauer (3 vols, University of Chicago Press, Chicago, 1984–8); L. Orr, 'The revenge of literature: a history of history', *New Literary History*, 18 (1986), pp. 1–22; S. Cohen, *Historical Culture: on the recoding of an academic discipline* (University of California Press, Berkeley, 1986); H. White, *The Content of Form: narrative discourse and historical representation* (Johns Hopkins

discussion of its characteristic tropes, or figures of speech, and its underlying narrative structures and discursive style. But the pluralism of the discipline makes its output very difficult to categorize into a single mode of representation. The study of the past can encompass narrative, description, interpretation, and/or analysis in any combination and at any degree of specialization. 'History' therefore ranges widely, from general works of synthesis to the methodological austerity of econometrics, the 'thick description' of much cultural history,[96] the detailed probing of post-Namierite 'high politics', the individual focus of biography, the aggregative calculations of demographic history, the visual documentation of art and architectural history, the theoretical expositions of intellectual history and the history of past concepts, the German *Begriffsgeschichte*,[97] and so forth, in all the modern diversity of the discipline.

For the same reason, historians may use, but do not depend upon, a specialist terminology. The language of written history is therefore as variegated as its subject-matter. It is generally considered important to define key terms. But perhaps the strongest professional code of good practice when analysing past times and places is to avoid imposing a conceptual terminology that is too obviously anachronistic. That acknowledges the importance of linguistic sensitivity, since later words, wrongly chosen, may obscure earlier realities. The disputes over Toynbee's popularization of the concept of an 'Industrial Revolution', for example, centred on precisely that issue. Yet it is not feasible to analyse the past wholly in the language of the past. Not only may historic usages themselves be diverse or contradictory, but historians cannot eliminate from their minds the entire intervening freightage of accumulative linguistic and intellectual change. Nor indeed can they themselves hope to communicate with their own readership without a creative recourse to the languages of their own times. In other words, diachrony, which creates history, also poses a fine linguistic challenge to historians.

University Press, Baltimore, 1987); A. Cook, *History/Writing: the theory and practice of history in antiquity and in modern times* (Cambridge University Press, Cambridge, 1988); H. Kellner, *Language and Historical Representation: getting the story crooked* (University of Wisconsin Press, Madison, 1989).

[96] This refers to Gilbert Ryle's concept as adapted by C. Geertz, 'Thick description: toward an interpretive theory of culture', in idem, *The Intepretation of Cultures: selected essays* (Hutchinson, London, 1975), pp. 3–30.

[97] See, e.g., the stimulating writings of R. Koselleck, *Futures Past: on the semantics of historical time*, tr. K. Tribe (MIT Press, Cambridge, Mass., 1985); and idem, 'Linguistic change and the history of events', *Journal of Modern History*, 61 (1989), pp. 649–66.

The essays that follow fruitfully develop these arguments via a sequence of historic and linguistic case-studies. Their collective subject-matter is the past of language in society, with reference not so much to the origin and derivations of words but to their creative use. Hence between them, these essays cut across the boundaries of cultural, intellectual, political, social, and economic history, as well as the history of past concepts. More specifically, the discussion is clustered around the theme of how various societies in the world post-1500 have been viewed and analysed by those living in them; as well as the political, social, and cultural consequences that flow from those perceptions.

'Class' thence comes under discussion, with all its controversial ramifications, as do alternative modes of social classification, such as by rank, caste, race, gender, religion, or political affiliation.[98] This returns the enquiry once more to the relationship of the 'signifier' to the 'signified', of words to 'things'. Does 'class' exist before it is named? If so, why is it not identified from the start but later 'discovered'? If, on the contrary, 'class' has no existence before it is named, how does naming create it, especially when some people refer to it while others do not? Can 'class' be made to go away if it is never mentioned at all, as some modern individualists clearly hope? And does the same apply to other forms of social classification?

Evidence from these essays interestingly points both ways: towards the creativity of words and concepts in use, and simultaneously to the context of social experience that is articulated. The variety of case-histories that are discussed here certainly suggests that the state of language is flexible and fluid. It is not a simple 'mirror' to a separate 'reality'. It is part of that reality, and therefore part and parcel of all its

---

[98] On historical applications and definitions of 'class', see P. Calvert, *The Concept of Class: an historical introduction* (Hutchinson, London, 1982); S. Ossowski, *Class Structure in the Social Consciousness*, tr. S. Patterson (Routledge, London, 1963); and other works cited in Select Bibliography, below pp. 298–303. For a study of differing modes of classification, see also O. C. Cox, *Caste, Class, and Race: a study in social dynamics* (Monthly Review Press, New York, 1948). In general, the historical evidence suggests that 'class' identity is less clear-cut, especially in application to specific individuals, than is often assumed in modern sociological and sociolinguistic theory. In particular, there are problems in allocating people by 'class' solely on the basis of the occupation of the (male) head of household, as this procedure ignores significant variations within occupations and completely prejudges the social position of the female half of the population: see A. P. M. Coxon and P. M. Davies with C. L. Jones, *Images of Social Stratification: occupational structures and class* (Sage, London, 1986); and P. Abbot and R. Sapsford, *Women and Social Class* (Tavistock, London, 1987).

complexities. These essays provide many examples. Social categories are often loosely defined, both in theory and in individual application; they may be adapted in parallel with social change, or not be adapted despite social change – indeed, contradictory concepts of society may coexist within the same community, and be used indiscriminately; at other times, one set of terms may be used for one purpose, with a rival set for other purposes. Speech itself is not usually understood only with strict literality, but derives meaning from the framework and implications of the communication. And entire societies may themselves be divided into contentious language groups, which in turn hold differing perceptions of key concepts. Furthermore, the concepts and language generated within one social tradition may subsequently be borrowed and adapted by another, while the concept of 'society' itself is socially defined. All this means that past communities do not neatly supply a single interpretative vision for later use by historians. Nor can language be viewed as an unproblematic by-product of an unproblematic socio-economic (or any other) context. 'For', as Marc Bloch commented, 'to the great despair of historians, men [sic] fail to change their vocabulary every time they change their customs'[99] – and, it might be added, fail to change their customs every time they adapt their vocabulary.

Yet, at the same time, a socially constructed and socially negotiated language implies a linguistic community to construct and use it, and in using it, to develop and re-create it. These essays also show a pluralist and not an atomistic process in action. Languages are used and articulated within historic contexts, as part of the complex experience of human society itself. Similarly the organizing concepts that describe communities are themselves not adopted or developed or borrowed completely at random. They relate to the full complexity – and not merely a single determinant – of their changing historical contexts. That can be seen, for example, in the way in which a term like 'class' became controversial in the course of usage, after its innocuous start. Concepts acquire meanings not simply in relation to other concepts but in reference also to contexts. That applies to all forms of information – to statistics as much as to language. It is right that the search for a physical 'thing' to match every 'word' has been abandoned. There is no corporeal 'jabberwocky' or 'heffalump' (or at least none found so far) – let alone a tangible 'if' or 'but'. Languages are much more complex than that. They are not simply compilations of nouns; and nouns themselves refer

---

[99] M. Bloch, *The Historian's Craft*, tr. P. Putnam (Manchester University Press, Manchester, 1954), p. 34.

to abstractions as well as to specificities. But all that is done interactively, by real language-users, deploying protean languages, within inexorable space-time.

Finally, therefore, language cannot evade history, nor historians language. There is comfort in a structured, timeless model of knowledge and the world, as the all-embracing cosmic hierarchy of the 'Great Chain of Being' implied (see frontispiece illustration). But even in heaven there are rebels. And certainly within the temporal universe, rules and structures are subject to time and the potential for change. Language therefore does not achieve perfect synchrony, even at its inception – let alone in the longer term. Like everything else, it is a matter for history, and submits to what Bakhtin termed 'the problem of *great time*'.[100]

[100] M. M. Bakhtin, 'Toward a methodology for the human sciences', in idem, *Speech Genres*, p. 170, concludes with a profession of faith and a problem for analysis: 'Nothing is absolutely dead: every meaning will have its homecoming festival. The problem of *great time*.'

2

Estates, degrees, and sorts: changing perceptions of society in Tudor and Stuart England

Keith Wrightson

The transition from a society of 'estates', or 'orders', to a 'class society' is one of the commonplaces of historical sociology. Medieval people, we are assured, conceived of society as being composed of three functionally separated but interdependent 'estates', or 'orders': those who pray, those who fight, and those who work. John Wycliff, for example, wrote of the 'thre statis: prestis, lordis, laborers'.[1] William Caxton described the three estates as 'clerkes, knyghtes, and laborers'.[2] Each estate had its God-appointed duties, and each also had its all-too-human failings or 'defections'. Social harmony and divine favour depended upon the proper performance of their duties by the members of each estate. As Caxton put it in the *Mirrour of the World* (1480):

> The labourers ought to pourveye for the clerkes and knyghtes suche thinges as were nedeful for them to lyve by in the world honestly; and the knyghtes ought to defende the clerkis and the labourers, that ther were no wronge don to them; and the clerkis ought to enseigne and teche these ii maner of peple and to adresse them in their werkis in such wise that none doo thinge by whiche he sholde displese God ne lese his grace.'[3]

From the eighteenth century, by contrast, there emerged a radically different perception of the basic structure of society which was to achieve

---

This essay is a much expanded version of an article which first appeared in *History Today*, 37 (1987), pp. 17–22.
[1] Quoted by R. Mohl, *The Three Estates in Medieval and Renaissance Literature* (Columbia University Studies, New York, 1933), p. 100.
[2] Quoted in ibid., pp. 16, 127.
[3] Quoted in ibid., pp. 126–7.

dominance in the early nineteenth century. Society was now conceived of, not in terms of 'estates' or 'orders', differentiated by social function, but in terms of 'classes' distinguished and evaluated primarily on economic criteria. These were sometimes perceived as many in number, sometimes reduced to two or three; sometimes regarded as firmly ordered in a pattern of authority and subordination, sometimes described as embodying the fundamental alignments of social conflict – 'one class of society united to oppose another class,' as William Cobbett put it in 1825.[4]

In the historical shift from the language of 'estates' to that of 'classes', then, we have more than a change in the conventional terminology of social description and analysis. We have a transformation of the very way in which people conceived of their social world, a conceptual displacement of vital significance in the making of 'modern' society. Yet, this process of changing social perceptions and identities is one which has been only partially explored. Much attention has been devoted to the development of the class identities of the nineteenth century and their associated terminology. Indeed, the emergence of class is one of the great themes, perhaps *the* great theme of modern English social history.[5] The long process of dissolution which overcame the concept and doctrine of the society of estates, however, has been largely neglected. We might all agree that such a transition occurred. We might guess that it took place over the period between the fifteenth century, when the terminology and philosophy of the three estates was still dominant, and the later eighteenth century, when the language of class became firmly established, and social theorists took up the task of explaining the origins and nature of classes. But what were the stages of this conceptual revolution? Were there intermediate terminologies of social description peculiar to what we call the early-modern period? If so, in what ways may they have been related to other processes of historical change? It is with these questions that this essay is concerned. We can begin to answer them by considering a little more critically than

[4] See P. J. Corfield, 'Class by name and number in eighteenth-century Britain', below, pp. 101–30; quotation taken from A. Briggs, 'The language of "class" in early nineteenth-century England', in *Essays in Labour History: in memory of G. D. H. Cole*, ed. A. Briggs and J. Saville (Macmillan, London, 1960), p. 47.

[5] For useful introductions to this extensive literature, see R. J. Morris, *Class and Class Consciousness in the Industrial Revolution, 1780–1850* (Macmillan, London, 1979); and R. S. Neale, *Class in English History, 1680–1850* (Blackwell, Oxford, 1981).

is usual the ways in which the people of Tudor and Stuart England described themselves and others.

Conventional vocabularies of social description can demonstrate remarkable inertia: they respond slowly to social and cultural change. Yet the sluggishness of the process whereby terminologies are rendered redundant and undergo replacement can be deceptive, implying a social stasis which is more apparent than real. Words may persist. Their meanings, however, undergo subtle shifts. Usages are modified. There are expansions and contractions of their range of significance, their resonances and implications. These simple facts are well borne out by consideration of the terms used by Tudor and early Stuart writers to describe their society. At first glance, there are ample grounds for supposing that the social commentators of the period continued to think in terms of a society of estates. Certainly they used the word frequently enough. Yet, significantly, they used it in a manner which implied a somewhat different conception of society than that embodied in the medieval theory of the three estates.

In the first place, they recognized not three, but a multiplicity of different estates. When the mid-sixteenth-century moralist Robert Crowley penned his *Voyce of the Last Trumpet*, he retained the traditional enough purpose of 'callyng al estats of men to the ryght path of their vocation', but he addressed not Caxton's 'clerkes, knyghtes and laborers', but 'twelve several estats of men': namely, beggars, servants, yeoman, priests, scholars, learned men, physicians, lawyers, merchants, gentlemen, magistrates, and women! Sir Geoffrey Fenton, in his *Form of Christian Pollicie* (1574), similarly undertook to teach 'the office of every estate', and dealt with those of magistrates, the clergy, schoolmasters, physicians, gentlemen, lawyers, merchants, tradesmen, and husbandmen. A generation later Sir Thomas Wilson, in his account of England *c.*1600, commented in detail on eight 'states', 'estates', or 'orders' of people: the 'common people' or 'commonalty' (comprising yeomen, copyholders, and cottagers), citizens, the nobility, knights, gentlemen, 'great younger brethren', common lawyers and civil lawyers.[6] While the language of estates persisted, the term was clearly being applied by these writers to almost any distinguishable occupational or status

---

[6] Mohl, *Three Estates*, pp. 187, 216–18; *The State of England Anno Dom. 1600. By Thomas Wilson*, ed. F. J. Fisher, Camden Miscellany, vol. 16, Camden Society, 3rd ser., 52 (1936), pp. 17ff. The relevant section of Wilson's account of England is reprinted in J. Thirsk and J. P. Cooper (eds), *Seventeenth-Century Economic Documents* (Clarendon Press, Oxford, 1972), pp. 751–7. Subsequent references will be to this version.

group. Indeed, in Wilson's case it also carried the connotation of a general condition of life as distinct from membership of a functional order of society.

Secondly, Tudor and early Stuart writers showed a marked tendency to couple the word 'estate' and the word 'degree'. Sir Thomas Elyot in his influential *Book Named the Governor* (1531) defined the 'publik weale' as 'a body lyvyng, compacte or made of sundry estates and degrees of men', and used the phrase 'estate and degree' repeatedly as a standard expression. Roger Ascham in *The Schoolmaster* (1570) wrote of 'every degree and state'. Robert Burton in his *Anatomy of Melancholy* (1621) viewed society as 'an inequality of states, orders and degrees'.[7] This common association of words was of some note, for it added to the *functional* differentiation of the estates of mankind an accompanying emphasis upon their *hierarchical* ordering.

Thirdly, while the writers who attempted to describe English society in the later sixteenth and early seventeenth centuries might continue to employ the term 'estate' on occasion, they abandoned the habit of conceptualizing society in terms of the three estates of medieval social theory and developed an alternative convention of social description derived from their preoccupation with 'degree'. Edmund Dudley in his *Tree of the Commonwealth* (1509–10) had addressed himself conservatively to the duties of the King and of the three estates of nobility, clergy, and commonalty, the last comprising 'all ye merchants, craftesmen and artificers, laborers, franklins, grasiers, farmers, tyllers and other generallie the people of this realme'. He was concerned, in the tradition of the literature of estates, to moralize about social, economic, and political roles, and for this purpose the conventions of the old categorization served well enough.[8] In contrast, the writers of the late sixteenth and seventeenth centuries who attempted to present the English to themselves in accounts of the polity, the commonwealth, or the topography of particular counties, were concerned less to moralize than to describe. And to this end they adopted the convention of depicting a *single* hierarchy of status and occupational groups. To be sure, some traces of the older classificatory conventions remained. The clergy, for example, were sometimes accorded separate discussion from lay society. Nevertheless, these writers did not rehearse the traditional tripartite distinction

---

[7] Mohl, *Three Estates*, pp. 156ff.; R. Kelso, *The Doctrine of the English Gentleman in the Sixteenth Century* (University of Illinois Press, Urbana, 1929), p. 70; P. Zagorin, *The Court and the Country: the beginning of the English Revolution* (Routledge, London, 1969), p. 24.

[8] Mohl, *Three Estates*, p. 150ff.

in their accounts of society. Instead they depicted a consolidated hierarchy of 'degrees'.

Thus, William Harrison in his influential *Description of England* (1577), having devoted an earlier chapter to the structure of the Church of England (though not to a clerical 'estate' as such), described lay society as a whole in a chapter entitled 'Of degrees of people in the commonwealth of England'. There he asserted that 'we in England divide our people commonlie into foure sorts,' namely 'Gentlemen' (a category including the titular nobility, knights, esquires, and 'they that are simplie called gentlemen'), the 'citizens and burgesses' of the towns, the 'yeomen' of the countryside, and lastly what he called 'the fourth sort of people' who had 'neither voice nor authoritie in the common wealthe, but are to be ruled and not to rule other' (a category which included 'daie labourers, poore husbandmen, and some retailers, . . . copie holders, and all artificers, as tailors, shomakers, carpenters, brickmakers, masons etc.'). Sir Thomas Wilson, in 1600, thought the subjects of the English realm could be divided in rank order into the nobility (greater and lesser), citizens, yeomen, artisans, and country labourers. He also broke down the walls of the medieval estates decisively by including bishops and 'chief ecclesiastical persons' among the greater nobility and 'lawyers, professors, and ministers, archdeacons, prebends and vicars', as well as all university graduates, alongside knights, esquires, and gentlemen, among the lesser nobility. A generation later John Hooker distinguished four 'degrees' in Devonshire society – gentlemen, merchants, yeomen, and labourers – while Robert Reyce in his *Discovery of Suffolk* listed seven 'degrees of callings': noblemen, knights, gentlemen, yeomen, townspeople, husbandmen, and the poor. And so we might continue through to Gregory King's famous table of twenty-six 'Ranks, Degrees, Titles and Qualifications', observable, as he thought, among the people of England in 1688, ranging from 'Temporal Lords' to 'Vagrants' and including along the way both 'Spiritual Lords' and two further clerical degrees.[9] Taken together, accounts of this kind provide the basis of what

---

[9] F. J. Furnivall (ed.), *Harrison's Description of England, Part I*, New Shakespeare Society, 6th ser., 1 (London, 1877), pp. 105ff.; Thirsk and Cooper (eds), *Seventeenth-Century Economic Documents*, pp. 751–2, 754–5, 780–1; V. Brodsky Elliott, 'Mobility and marriage in pre-industrial England' (unpublished Ph.D. thesis, Cambridge, 1978), pp. 24–5 (I am grateful to Vivian Brodsky for permission to cite her thesis); Zagorin, *Court and Country*, p. 24. For a useful account of such sources, see D. Cressy, 'Describing the social order of Elizabethan and Stuart England', *Literature and History*, 3 (1976), pp. 29–44. As is well known, two of the most familiar descriptions of England's social hierarchy, those by William Harrison and Sir Thomas Smith, are almost identical. Since it

historians have come to regard as the 'classical' hierarchy of estates and degrees in early-modern England: the titular nobility; knights, esquires, and 'mere' gentlemen; leading citizens and members of the learned professions; yeoman farmers; husbandmen; artisans; cottagers and labourers; servants; and paupers.

As might be expected, most of these developments had roots which can be traced back well before the sixteenth century. The concept of the three estates of mankind (which originated in the eleventh century) had long been inadequate as an account of a society of growing occupational complexity and subtler social differentiation. When English vernacular examples of the literature of estates emerged in the later fourteenth and fifteenth centuries, a tendency to discuss the duties and 'defections' not only of the three estates but of a more extensive catalogue of specific social groups was already apparent. Moreover, an early preoccupation with degree is evident enough both in the recognition of hierarchies of status within each of the three estates and in a more general concern with the question of precedence. The appearance in the fifteenth century of works in English like *The Copie of a Booke of Precedence of all estates and placing to ther degrees*, which dealt with the problem of precedence on public occasions and shuffled together the various degrees within each of the three estates into a single rank order of status, was both a response to the practical difficulties of public ceremonial and a sign of what was to come. One might point also to the sumptuary legislation which from the fourteenth century attempted to lay down in increasing detail the apparel considered appropriate to persons of different degree.[10] Given this long-term context, the contribution of the Tudor age can be seen as essentially an extension and consolidation of such trends, culminating in the eventual adoption of a new literary convention of social description which rendered redundant its medieval predecessor.

Crucial to these developments were perhaps two general influences: a growing nationalistic preoccupation with the English polity and the English nation, and a pervasive anxiety about the stability of both in a

---

now seems established that Harrison's was the earlier work, I have referred throughout to his *Description*. For the relationship between Harrison and Smith, see M. Dewar, 'A question of plagiarism: the "Harrison chapters" in Sir Thomas Smith's *De Republica Anglorum*', *Historical Journal*, 22 (1979) pp. 921–9, and G. J. R. Parry, 'William Harrison and Holinshed's *Chronicles*', *Historical Journal*, 27 (1984), pp. 802–3.

[10] Mohl, *Three Estates*, pp. 97ff., 114, 128–9; N. B. Harte, 'State control of dress and social change in pre-industrial England', in *Trade, Government and Economy in Pre-Industrial England: essays presented to F. J. Fisher*, ed. D. C. Coleman and A. H. John (Weidenfeld, London, 1976), pp. 132–65.

period of dynastic insecurity, religious strife, and socio-economic strain. The former led the writers of the Elizabethan period to lay aside a universalistic conception of social organization, delineated primarily for generalized moral purposes, in favour of the depiction of English specifics. It gave rise to the genre of patriotic descriptive works which W. G. Hoskins termed 'the discovery of England'.[11] And as the English dwelt upon the peculiarities of their own institutions, customs, and manners, they confronted also the distinctiveness of England's social structure. The latter fuelled their concern with order and degree, with authority and subordination. For as Sir Thomas Elyot opined, 'without ordre may be nothing stable or permanent; and it may not be called ordre, excepte it do conteyne in it degrees.'[12]

Against this general background can be placed a number of more specific developments which eroded the concept of the three estates and furthered the reconceptualization of England's social order. First among these was the abrogation of the clerical estate, a process described by Dr O'Day as a transition from 'estate to profession'. Prior to the 1530s the English clergy had been most emphatically a separate, legally constituted, estate. With the Reformation came not only the jurisdictional revolution of the royal supremacy but also a great reduction in the number of clerics and a narrowing of the range of clerical roles. The monasteries and chantries were suppressed. Minor orders were abolished. Many of those functionaries who had formerly been part of the clerical estate were reclaimed into lay society, while the remaining clergy of the Church of England were confined more to pastoral and ministerial roles. 'The clergy now ceased to be a vertical estate and became instead a group of men involved in a common occupation – that of the Ministry of the Word.' They became, in short, 'a profession – a hierarchically organized but occupational group which claimed status in society on the basis of the expert services which it offered the commonwealth'.[13] While the peculiar significance of the clerical profession was such that as late as the eighteenth century a number of writers continued to make passing reference to the distinction between laity and clergy in their accounts of the English people, there can be little doubt that the clerical estate effectively ceased to exist in the mid-sixteenth century. And it was

[11] W. G. Hoskins, 'The rediscovery of England', in idem, *Provincial England: essays in social and economic history* (Macmillan, London, 1965), pp. 209ff.

[12] Quoted in Mohl, *Three Estates*, p. 158.

[13] R. O'Day, 'The anatomy of a profession: the clergy of the Church of England', in *The Professions in Early Modern England*, ed. W. Prest (Croom Helm, London, 1987), pp. 28, 30–1.

recognition of this fact which led writers such as Wilson and King to incorporate clergymen of different degrees at appropriate points in their consolidated social hierarchies.

Of comparable significance was the erosion of the functional identity of the knightly, or noble, estate and the redefinition of the nature of that quality of 'gentility' which distinguished the lay elite from the mass of the commonalty. The noble estate, of course, had been defined originally in terms of its military function; and as late as the early sixteenth century, reality still bore some approximation to this theoretical role. While the actual feudal relationship (the provision of military service in return for title to land) had decayed in the course of the later Middle Ages, the assumption remained that the English nobility and their gentry retainers were still distinguished above all by their capacity to bear arms. They were perceived as a military elite in the final analysis, and the coincidence of theory and practice was demonstrated both in the Crown's recognition of the necessity of tolerating (under licence) the practice of indentured retaining and in the actual significance of baronial retinues in the forces fielded in time of war or rebellion. In the course of the later sixteenth and early seventeenth centuries, however, this military role was greatly reduced in significance. To be sure, high military rank long remained the prerogative of the nobility, while England's knights, esquires, and landed gentlemen remained familiar with the handling of horse and sword, and not a few (or their younger sons and brothers) still sought careers in arms. Yet technological developments in warfare both reduced the primacy of the mounted arm in the field, and demanded a more specific training of the would-be officer. The long Tudor and Jacobean peace provided fewer opportunities for the acquisition of military experience, and the introduction of the lieutenancy system and the 'trained bands' reduced the dependency of the state upon noblemen and their retainers. The profession of arms became increasingly the preserve of a minority of trained and experienced specialists and devotees, rather than the distinguishing characteristic (at least in potential) of an entire estate of the realm.[14]

---

[14] This was, of course, the culmination of a long process of development. For the increasing complexity and gradual differentiation of the noble estate in the later Middle Ages, the extension of the vocabulary of noble status from the battlefield to civilian society, and the development of the terminology of gentility up to the fifteenth century, see N. Saul, *Knights and Esquires: the Gloucestershire gentry in the fourteenth century* (Clarendon Press, Oxford, 1981), ch. 1. For the decline of the military role under the Tudors and Stuarts, see I. Roy, 'The profession of arms', in *Professions in Early Modern England*, ed. Prest, pp. 182–6, 190. Cf. L. Stone, *The Crisis of the Aristocracy, 1558–1641* (Clarendon

At the same time, however, the writers of the English Renaissance offered an alternative definition of gentility in place of the increasingly redundant chivalric ideal. Humanist moralists adapted the 'courtesy' literature of Italy to invest the concept of the 'gentleman' with a new meaning, derived ultimately from revived classical ideals of citizenship. In this new guise, the distinguishing mark of the gentleman became the possession not only of the wealth and leisure but also of the breeding and personal virtues necessary for government, for a more diffuse role of civic usefulness. Gentlemen were defined as governors, and true gentility as the quality and capacity to govern.[15]

This revised conception of the nature of gentility and of the essential role of gentlemen was, of course, perfectly compatible with the maintenance of the idea of a separate noble estate, albeit in a novel form; and indeed the distinction between gentlemen and the common people long remained the critical status distinction to be insisted upon in accounts of the English social hierarchy. To William Harrison, gentlemen as a whole were the first sort of people in the English commonwealth, notwithstanding their internal differentiation into the titular nobility, knights, esquires, and 'they that are simplie called gentlemen'. 'All the people which be in our countrie', wrote Richard Mulcaster in 1581, 'be either gentlemen or of the commonalty.' Sir Thomas Wilson distinguished both 'greater' and 'meaner' nobility, all of them gentlemen, from the commonalty in 1600, as did Edward Chamberlayne in 1669 and Guy Miège in the early eighteenth century.[16] Be this as it may, it was also the case from the reign of Elizabeth onwards that while some writers busied themselves with elaborating the ideal of the English gentlemen, others who were more concerned to describe English realities found themselves forced to acknowledge that in practice gentle status

---

Press, Oxford, 1965), ch. 5; P. Williams, *The Tudor Regime* (Clarendon Press, Oxford, 1979), pp. 111–29.

[15] For these developments, see Kelso, *Doctrine of the English Gentleman*, esp. pp. 37–40, 71, 81ff., 116–17. The transition is pithily summed up in J. S. Morrill, 'The northern gentry and the Great Rebellion', *Northern History*, 15 (1979), pp. 71–2. Gentlemen, of course, had long exercised the role of governors in practice. The humanist ideal was to render them fitter to perform such duties.

[16] Furnivall (ed.), *Harrison's Description* pp. 105–6; Cressy, 'Describing the social order', pp. 30–1; Thirsk and Cooper (eds), *Seventeenth-Century Economic Documents*, pp. 752–3, 755; G. Miège, 'The present state of Great Britain: an eighteenth-century self-portrait', in *Aristocratic Government and Society in Eighteenth-Century England: the foundations of stability*, ed. D. A. Baugh (New Viewpoints, New York, 1975), p. 42.

was accorded on quite different and less elevated criteria than those given emphasis by the theorists of gentility.

There were, of course, some clear and generally recognized criteria for membership of the gentle elite. Noble titles and from 1611 the novel title of 'baronet' were either inherited or conferred by the Crown. All noblemen were gentlemen, even though most gentlemen were not noblemen in the limited sense of that term used in England to indicate membership of the temporal peerage. Knights were created by the monarch for service in peace or war, those selected being most commonly 'chief men in their countries both for living and reputations', as Sir Thomas Wilson put it, adding waspishly 'though many of them know scarcely what knighthood means.' Esquires were prominent local gentlemen of ancient armigerous lineage, further defined by Wilson as men 'whose ancestors are or have been knights, or else . . . the heirs and eldest of their houses and of some competent quantity of revenue fit to to be called to office and authority in their country where they live.' The association of the addition 'esquire' with office and authority was further emphasized by its extension by courtesy to any holder of significant public office: to justices of the peace, for example, mayors, or comparable dignitaries.[17]

All this was perhaps clear enough and in accord with the notion of a gentle estate defined by virtue of its role in public service. The real problems came with the effective definition not of prominent but of 'mere' gentlemen, a social group which underwent marked numerical expansion in the course of the sixteenth and seventeenth centuries. William Harrison initially attemped to define such gentlemen as 'those whome their race and blood doo make noble and knowne': a gentility of birth and ancient prescription. But he was soon forced to insert 'or at least their vertues' into this formulation, in recognition of the possibility of achieving gentle status: and in the final analysis he was prepared, in a passage famous for its blunt realism, to accord gentle status to any man who could 'live without manuell labour and thereto is able and will beare the port, charge and countenance of a gentleman'. Gentility, then, was ultimately a matter of relative wealth and lifestyle, and any who could sustain the 'countenance' of a gentleman would be 'called master . . . and reputed for a gentleman' (firming up his claims 'good cheape', if he so desired, by purchasing a coat of arms from the heralds, who

---

[17] Furnivall (ed.), *Harrison's Description*, pp. 114, 128; Thirsk and Cooper (eds), *Seventeenth-Century Economic Documents*, pp. 755; Miège, 'Present state', pp. 42–6. For the late-medieval origins of the terminology of gentry, see Saul, *Knights and Esquires*, ch. 1.

would readily 'pretend antiquitie and service and manie gaie things' on his behalf). Nor was even landed wealth a necessary qualification for gentility, since Harrison was willing to extend the status to lawyers, university graduates, and physicians, as members of the learned professions, a matter on which Sir Thomas Smith and Sir Thomas Wilson agreed, the latter adding for his part the lesser clergy.[18]

The essential point is not so much that these writers frankly recognized the reality of social mobility into the gentle elite, though this was a matter of significance, as that they testify to the lack of functional or occupational homogeneity already apparent in the lower reaches of gentility. Already in the early part of the reign of Elizabeth the process which has aptly been termed the 'social flotation' of gentility was well under way.[19] By the end of the next century this process was so far advanced that landed gentlemen increasingly preferred the addition 'esquire' to distinguish themselves from the mass of claimants to a gentleman's rank. And shortly thereafter, Guy Miège, while conceding that gentlemen were 'those properly who, being descended of a good family bear a coat of arms without any particular title', also recognized approvingly that even trade no longer 'degraded' a gentleman. 'In short', he concluded, 'the title of Gentleman is commonly given in England to all that distinguish themselves from the common people by a genteel dress and carriage, good education, learning, or an independent station.'[20] Long before then, however, the status of gentleman, while retaining something of the dignity of a condition formerly associated with members of a discrete estate, had become, in effect, no more than a recognition of relative wealth displayed in an appropriate manner. Gentlemen still ruled England, but no unique occupational identity or functional role separated the lesser gentlemen of England from the commonalty. Gentlemen scored high in the social assessment of rank, but they were measured on the same scale. Gentility was now, quite literally, a matter not of estate but of degree.

The transition from the conventional conceptualization of society in terms of functional estates to its representation as a single hierarchy of

---

[18] Furnivall (ed.), *Harrison's Description*, pp. 128–9; Kelso, *Doctrine of the English Gentleman*, p. 26; Thirsk and Cooper (eds), *Seventeenth-Century Economic Documents*, p. 755. For an excellent brief account of 'the multiplication of the gentry, 1500–1640', see C. G. A. Clay, *Economic Expansion and Social Change: England, 1500–1700* (2 vols, Cambridge University Press, Cambridge, 1984), vol. 1, pp. 144–58.

[19] The phrase is P. J. Corfield's, used in discussion at the Anglo-American Conference on Comparative Social History at Williamsburg, Sept. 1985.

[20] Miège, 'Present state', pp. 46–7.

degrees, then, was furthered by the abrogation of one of the medieval estates of the realm and by the fraying of the collective identity of another. A final influence upon this conceptual shift was a heightened emphasis upon hierarchical ranking within the third estate, among the commonalty, those who worked. Inequalities, of course, had long been recognized among the common people of England. Such realities, however, were not the immediate concern of the authors of the literature of estates, whose principal emphasis fell upon the characteristic duties and 'defections' of specific occupations rather than upon their relative standing. The priorities of those who sought to describe English society in the late sixteenth and early seventeeth centuries were quite different. To be sure they were not greatly concerned to explore the full complexities of social stratification among the common people. Their fascination with the internal differentiation of the gentry was not matched by a subtle handling of the distinctions to be observed among those who enjoyed 'neither voice nor authoritie in the common wealthe'. Their contribution lay rather in singling out and repeatedly emphasizing the significance of certain key groups among the commonalty of town and country. Some largely urban-based professions, as we have seen, were elevated to gentle status by virtue of their associated education, wealth, lifestyles, and access to positions of authority. Harrison also accorded those citizens, who enjoyed the freedom of their cities and were 'of some likelie substance to bear office in the same', the 'next place to gentlemen' in the overall social hierarchy, and observed of wealthy merchants that 'they often change estate with gentlemen, as gentlemen doo with them, by a mutall conversion of the one into the other.' It was an accurate enough reflection of the fact that sons of the gentry were frequently apprenticed in the more prestigious urban companies, and that at least some of the most successful urban magnates established or re-established themselves on the land.[21] Among country people, the group repeatedly singled out as of especial significance was of course the yeomanry. Both Harrison and Wilson, conventionally enough, attempted to define the yeomen as substantial freeholders, holding their land 'by no base service of any lord or superior', though both also recognized that yeomen might also be tenants of gentlemen. What truly distinguished the yeomen in the eyes of these writers, however, was their relative wealth, the fact that they enjoyed a role in the 'government and maintenance' of the commonwealth, as officers in their parishes,

---

[21] Furnivall (ed.) *Harrison's Description*, p. 131. For the close connections between urban and rural elites, see K. Wrightson, *English Society, 1580–1680* (Hutchinson, London, 1982), pp. 27–30.

possessors of the county franchise, jurymen, and taxpayers, and finally
their position as potential aspirants – who might hope to achieve gentility, either directly or through the education and placement of their
sons. These characteristics gave them their 'certaine preheminance and
more estimation' among their neighbours, and the proud addition of
'yeoman' to their names in 'matters of law' rendered them 'exempt from
the vulgar and common sorts'.[22]

As with the withering away of the claims of the clergy to be regarded
as a separate estate and the broadening of the definition of gentility, this
emphasis upon the special position in the social order of both prominent
citizens and the rural yeomanry can be associated with actual social
change. It reflected those processes of enhanced economic and social
differentiation which have been described as 'the growth of oligarchy'
in sixteenth-century towns or 'the rise of the yeomanry' in the English
countryside.[23] For our immediate purposes, however, it is sufficient to
underline the fact that by stressing the close relationship of these groups
to the lesser gentry and by differentiating them so markedly from the
remainder of the commonalty, these accounts of the social structure of
the English commonwealth completed the conceptual transition from
the tripartite society of estates. Gentility and commonalty were linked
in a single continuous hierarchy of 'estates and degrees'. While it would
be foolish to assert that this alternative perception of society was entirely
new (for it clearly developed from long-established antecedents), it none
the less represented a significant reworking of traditional concepts in
the light of both changing preoccupations and priorities and a clearer
recognition of contemporary actualities. The Elizabethan hierarchy of
degrees was a perception of the social order which was concerned less

---

[22] Furnivall (ed.) *Harrison's Description*, pp. 132–3, 137; Thirsk and Cooper
(eds), *Seventeenth-Century Economic Documents*, pp. 752–3. For the fifteenth-
century origin of the term 'yeoman' as a status designation in rural society and
the difficulties of definition, see M. Campbell, *The English Yeoman under
Elizabeth and the Early Stuarts* (Merlin Press, London, 1960), pp. 10ff. and
ch. 2.

[23] For urban society, see P. Clark and P. Slack, *English Towns in Transition,
1500–1700* (Oxford University Press, Oxford, 1976), chs 8–9. For the emergence
and subsequent consolidation of the yeomanry, see, e.g., C. Dyer, *Lords and
Peasants in a Changing Society: the estates of the bishopric of Worcester, 680–1540*
(Cambridge University Press, Cambridge, 1980), chs. 8, 14; Z. Razi, *Life,
Marriage and Death in a Medieval Parish, economy, society and demography in
Halesowen, 1270–1400* (Cambridge University Press, Cambridge, 1980), ch. 7;
M. Spufford, *Contrasting Communities: English villagers in the sixteenth and
seventeenth centuries* (Cambridge University Press, Cambridge, 1974), chs. 2–5;
and Campbell, *English Yeoman*, *passim*.

with universal ideals than with present realities, less with function than with place, less with vocational and occupational differentials than with the bald facts of relative wealth, status, and power. The moral philosophy of the estates of the world retained its influence in the continuing conviction that the social order was God-ordained and that 'every degree of people . . . has appointed to them their duty and order.'[24] But the duties and 'defections' of particular estates had become subordinated to an overriding emphasis upon authority and subordination, upon what Elyot called that 'discrepance of degrees whereof procedeth ordre.'[25]

If the hierarchy of degrees described by Elizabethan and early Stuart writers was an attempt to impose intellectual order on a changing social reality, however, it enjoyed only limited success. Its adoption in influential accounts of English society certainly established a new convention of social description which rapidly displaced the medieval theory of estates and remained dominant throughout the seventeenth century. Its pervasive influence could be felt even in such mundane matters as the proper allocation of church seating, as when the churchwardens of Tisbury in Wiltshire were ordered by their diocesan chancellor in 1637 to place their parishioners 'according to ranks, qualities and conditions', or when those of West Walton were required by the vicar-general of Norwich in 1633 to reallocate their pews with 'especial regard to the degrees and qualities of the persons . . . to be removed, displaced and placed'.[26]

Yet, while it was widely accepted as an appropriate model for the conceptualization of the social order, the hierarchy of degrees remained problematic in that it was never authoritatively defined or sanctioned as a whole. Those who attempted to employ it found real difficulty in establishing hard and fast criteria of status, and were not infrequently driven into a morass of internal inconsistency. The outstanding example of such uncertainty, as we have seen, lay in the definition of gentility itself, an issue over which a vast amount of ink was spilt. But there was also a good deal of ambiguity and hesitancy about the correct hierarchical placing of certain other occupational and social groups. Were all members

---

[24] Quoting the Anglican 'Homily on Obedience' (1547), repr. in *The Tudor Constitution*, ed. G. R. Elton (Cambridge University Press, Cambridge, 1960), p. 15.

[25] Quoted in Mohl, *Three Estates*, p. 158.

[26] D. Underdown, *Revel, Riot, and Rebellion: popular politics and culture in England, 1603–60* (Oxford University Press, Oxford, 1985), p. 33; S. D. Amussen, *An Ordered Society: gender and class in early modern England* (Blackwell, Oxford, 1988), pp. 137–8.

of the learned professions gentlemen or not? Should leading merchants and urban plutocrats be assimilated to the gentry or accorded a separate, somewhat lower, grading of their own? What distinguished a lesser yeoman from a husbandman in practice; and should husbandmen, cottagers, and labourers be lumped together or carefully distinguished? Contemporaries came to different conclusions on such issues. The problem was that in the final analysis the 'degrees' conventionally distinguished lacked for the most part both fixity of definition and independent institutional reality. Relative status emerged from the interplay of a range of variables (of which wealth was the single most important), in a process of social assessment which was, and remained, largely informal. One consequence of this was that no two descriptions of the hierarchy of degrees were quite alike (save in cases of direct plagiarism). The neatness and fixity of what we conventionally think of as the 'classical' social hierarchy of early-modern England is in fact a creation of the interpretative decisions of historians. Contemporary authors certainly described what was recognizably the same society, but with significant individual variations which reflected their personal concerns and individual prejudices. However much they yearned after a neatly graded and immutable social order, the social system which they attempted to describe ultimately eluded them.

Perhaps for this very reason, it seems probable that the language of degrees remained very much a vocabulary of the study and the courts, of the scholar, the herald, and the scrivener. The graduated ladder of estates and degrees depicted by the writers of Tudor and Stuart England enjoyed a long life as a conventional mode of formal social description, and as such it has become familiar to generations of students of the period. Yet there is little enough evidence that it enjoyed great currency in the hurly-burly of daily life.

There were occasions, certainly, when the people of the time appended to their names their 'estate, degree, or mystery', notably in formal legal documents, some of which required such identification. For everyday purposes, however, people appear to have employed a much simpler, cruder, and more effective vocabulary to describe the essential distinctions of their social world. This informal terminology of social description, which can be gleaned from such sources as letters, depositions, pamphlets, and petitions, could be very variegated. It included the term 'gentlemen', as we might expect. But most other formal 'additions' were eschewed in favour of such terms as 'the common people', 'rich men', 'the poor', 'sufficient men', 'poor labouring people', 'the principal inhabitants', 'sufficient men', 'the multitude', 'mean personages', or 'the vulgar'. From the last third of the sixteenth century, however, when our evidence becomes more abundant, a specific vocabulary of informal social description emerges into prominence, a set of terms which can be called the language of 'sorts'. This development deserves especial consideration.[27]

As yet, the precise chronology of the emergence of the language of sorts remains uncertain. Instances of the use of the term 'sort' in social description can be found as early as the 1530s, as for example when Sir Thomas Elyot rejected the notion that all men could be 'of one degree and sort', or when the instructions to the Council of the North enjoined its members to defend the interests of poor people so that they would be able to live 'after their sorts and qualities'.[28] In this usage the word 'sort' appears to have been an essentially neutral term, implying no more than a category or type. By the last quarter of the sixteenth century, however, the vocabulary of sorts was enjoying a much wider currency, and the key to its development appears to have been the addition of a variety of resonant adjectives to the neutral term 'sort'. William Harrison's use of such language may reflect a transitional stage. He subdivided the 'degrees of people' in England into 'foure sorts', as we have seen, and also wrote of three 'sorts' of poor, a neutral usage. But he also alluded to 'the greater sort', 'the common sort', 'the vulgar and common sort', 'the wealthier sort', and 'the thriftlesse sort'.[29] It was through the emergence of a particular set of favoured and widely adopted linguistic couplings of this kind that the language of sorts gained the prominence which it was to enjoy in the English terminology of social description for a century and a half, and consideration of the adjectives involved provides useful clues to its development over time.

Under Elizabeth and the early Stuarts it appears to have been used primarily to express an essentially dichotomous perception of society. The crucial terms involved were the 'better sort', or less commonly the 'richer sort', as against the 'poorer', 'meaner', 'ruder', or 'vulgar' sorts of people. Thus, to Harrison the 'vulgar and common sort' comprised

[27] What follows is based upon a collection of examples of the informal language of social description assembled from primary sources and from dated quotations from such sources in the secondary literature. For the purposes of illustration I have selected examples readily available in print, where they can be consulted in context.

[28] W. R. D. Jones, *The Tudor Commonwealth, 1529–59* (Athlone Press, London, 1970), p. 14; M. James, *Family, Lineage and Civil Society: a study of society, politics and mentality in the Durham region, 1550–1640* (Clarendon Press, Oxford, 1974), p. 38.

[29] Furnivall (ed.), *Harrison's Description*, pp. 105, 106, 108, 137, 212, 213, 216.

all those below the rank of yeomen in his hierarchy of degrees. To the overseers of the poor in the parish of Strood, Kent, in 1598, 'the poorer sort of people' were the members of the sixty-one families 'which as yet are able to work and doth neither give nor take, but if husband should die are likely to be a parish charge,' as distinct from the eighty households whose heads were ratepayers and the handful of impotent paupers. To the authorities of Norwich in 1603 the 'better sort of people' were to be distinguished from the unruly 'ruder sort', while to John Rogers, writing in 1637, the parishioners of Essex were divisible into 'the meaner sort' and 'the richest'. The many letters which passed back and forth between the Privy Council in Westminster and the governors of the English counties during the dearth crisis of 1596–8 yield numerous instances of such usage. On the one hand were 'the richer sorte' of Cheshire, who were enjoined not to hoard malt and grain, and 'the better sort' of Durham and Northumberland, who were to be directed to relieve the poor. On the other were 'the poorer sort' of Buckinghamshire, who were oppressed by profiteering meal-dealers; 'the vulgar sorte' of Sussex, who were apt to riot (as were 'the common sort' of Suffolk); and, more generally, the 'poorer' and 'meaner' sorts of people throughout England, who lacked stocks of grain to see them through the crisis and bore the brunt of its privations.[30]

Such language clearly reveals a world of social meanings untapped by the formal social classifications of literary convention; and arguably it was so widely used because it was of greater practical significance. Its utility lay above all in the fact that it was a terminology of social simplification, sweeping aside the fine-grained (and sometimes contested) distinctions of the hierarchy of degrees and re-grouping the English into two broad camps which were evidently held to reflect the fundamental realities of the social and economic structure and the basic alignments of social relations. But it was more than just a useful classificatory terminology. It was a language of radical differentiation which was both economic and cultural, cleaving society into the haves and the have-

[30] Ibid., p. 137; P. Slack, *Poverty and Policy in Tudor and Stuart England* (Longman, London, 1988), p. 66; idem, *The Impact of Plague in Tudor and Stuart England* (Routledge, London, 1985), p. 306; W. Hunt, *The Puritan Moment: the coming of revolution in an English county* (Harvard University Press, Cambridge, Mass., 1983), p. 238; *Acts of the Privy Council, 1596–7*, 15 (11 Jul. 1596), 81 (3 Aug. 1596), 399 (26 Dec. 1596); *A.P.C. 1597*, 92 (5 May 1597), 97 (6 May 1597); *Cal. State Papers Domestic, 1595–7*, p. 420; *Cal. Border Papers, 1595–1603*, p. 413. I must thank Dr R. B. Outhwaite for making available to me his file on government correspondence during the dearth years of the 1590s.

nots, the respected and the contemned. Unlike the vocabulary of degrees, it was a language pregnant with conflict, aligning the 'richer' against the 'poorer', the 'better' against the 'meaner', 'vulgar', 'common', 'ruder', or 'inferior' sorts. And finally it was a language of dissociation, usually employed by those who identified themselves with the 'better' sort of people and stigmatized those whom they excluded from that company with a barrage of pejorative adjectives.

To appreciate the full significance of these terms, it is essential to grasp the fact that the distinction between the 'better sort' and the 'meaner sort' was not simply a distinction between gentlemen and the common people. The language of sorts was not at all confined to England's ruling elite in its currency. Its political sociology was more complex. For the 'better' and 'richer' sorts included also the local notables of England's towns and villages, those whose property gave them prominence in local life, and a growing part also in the government and administration of their townships and parishes. In 1576 George Gascoyne wrote of 'our gentrie and the better sort of our people' as distinct from 'mean personages'. Twenty years later it was suggested that 'the gentlemen of the country and some of the better sort' of Devon should keep hospitality, relieve the poor, and 'be at hand to stay the fury of the inferior multitude if they should happen to break out.' A London source of 1582 described a deputy alderman's widow as having been 'esteemed with the better sort'; and a Wiltshire source of 1633 speaks of 'farmers wives and others of the better sort'. The 'better sort' were those considered of appropriate standing to serve on juries at the assizes and quarter sessions. They were of sufficient prominence to be permitted burial within parish churches rather than in the common churchyard.[31] In short, the 'better sort' were a composite group of local notables distinct from both the greater gentry and the mass of the common people. They were those alternatively described as the 'substan-

<hr/>

[31] T. Watt, 'Cheap print and religion, c.1550 to 1640' (unpublished Ph. D. thesis, Cambridge, 1988), p. 340 (I must thank Dr Watt for permission to quote from her thesis); Historical Manuscripts Commission, *Somerset MSS* (London, 1898), p. 20; Slack, *Poverty and Policy*, p. 38; S. Wright, 'Churmaids, huswyfes and hucksters: the employment of women in Tudor and Stuart Salisbury', in *Women and Work in Pre-Industrial England*, ed. L. Charles and L. Duffin (Croom Helm, London, 1985), p. 109; P. Lawson, 'Lawless juries? The composition and behaviour of Hertfordshire juries, 1573–1624', in *Twelve Good Men and True: the criminal trial jury in England, 1200–1800*, ed. J. S. Cockburn and T. A. Green (Princeton University Press, Princeton, 1988), pp. 124–5; C. Gittings, *Death, Burial and the Individual in Early Modern England* (Croom Helm, London, 1984), p. 141.

tial men of the parish' or the 'principal' or 'chief inhabitants'.[32] They included such men as the minor gentry, clergy, farmers, and tradesmen of Orsett in Essex, who, as the self-defined 'better sort of the parish', petitioned in 1622 for the establishment of an oligarchical close vestry which would exclude 'the inferior or meaner sort' from parish government, or the persons of 'place, sufficiencie and estimation' in the clothing town of Braintree, who in 1611 sought the similar exclusion of 'the inferior and meanest sort of the parishioners and inhabitants'.[33]

Such examples could be greatly multiplied. They suggest that the language of sorts in its Elizabethan and early Stuart form may have developed as a way of expressing the essential identity of interest between England's ruling elite of gentlemen and the more prominent members of what the early Tudors called the 'commonalty'. It expressed a social alignment described in 1591 by the Essex labourer John Feltwell when he declared that 'the noblemen and gentlemen are all one, and the gentlemen and farmers would hold together one with another, so that poor men could get nothing,' and confirmed almost forty years later when Sir Thomas Fanshawe reported that the putting down of rioting cloth-workers at Maldon in 1629 and the trial and execution of their leaders had much satisfied 'the better sort of people' in the area.[34] To speak merely of gentlemen and the common people missed an essential social fact which the employment of 'the better sort' captured admirably and, for some, flatteringly. To this extent at least, the dichotomous social world encapsulated in the earlier manifestations of the language of sorts was directly related to a broader context of socio-economic change. It reflected not only the polarization of English local society produced by demographic expansion and economic change in the later sixteenth and early seventeeth centuries, but also the realities of power relations in the local community. It expressed clashes of interests and of values and shifts in collective identity. Indeed, since language does not simply follow social change but is in itself an influence on changing perceptions which can shape action, it may have helped in itself to further the social realignment of the age.

[32] For examples of such terms, see, e.g., C. Hill, *Society and Puritanism in Pre-Revolutionary England* (Secker and Warburg, London, 1964), p. 416; J. R. Kent, *The English Village Constable, 1580–1642: a social and administrative study* (Clarendon Press, Oxford, 1986), p. 66; Underdown, *Revel, Riot, and Rebellion*, pp. 27, 31, 261.

[33] D. G. Allen, *In English Ways: the movement of societies and the transferal of English local law and custom to Massachusetts Bay in the seventeenth century* (University of North Carolina Press, Chapel Hill, 1981), pp. 146–7, 148.

[34] Hunt, *Puritan Moment*, pp. 61, 241.

This dichotomous use of the language of sorts was to persist wherever it best expressed the social distancing of dominant local ruling groups from their 'meaner' neighbours. In the course of the early seventeenth century, however, a further term was added to the vocabulary of 'sorts', which was in widespread use by the 1640s. This was the 'middle sort', or 'middling sort', of people, a linguistic innovation which recast the language of sorts into a tripartite form.

Despite its popularity among historians of the early Stuart period, the origins of the term 'middle sort' have never been adequately traced. Early in the century Bacon referred to three tiers of society; the 'better sort', 'meane People', and 'middle People'; but the term seems not to have been widely employed before mid-century. It has been suggested that it may have been of urban, even metropolitan, origin, coined perhaps to describe the independent tradesmen and craftsmen who stood between the civic elite and the mass of the urban poor. This is a view which derives some support from the comments of the anonymous author of a late Elizabethan 'Apologie' for the City of London, printed by John Stow in 1603. Having divided its inhabitants into 'three sorts', or 'parts' – merchants, handicraftsmen, and labourers – he argued that most of London's retailers and artificers enjoyed a 'mean place', or 'middle place', in the metropolitan distribution of wealth, being 'neither too rich nor too poor', but living 'in the mediocrity'. It is implied also in William Prynne's attack upon the 'inequality' of ship-money assessments, written in 1637. In discussing rural taxpayers, Prynne distinguished only 'the richest knights or gentlemen', 'farmers', and 'poor men'. Writing of cities and corporations, he distinguished 'the richest' and 'the middle and poor sort of people'. If the term originated in the towns, however, it migrated gradually to the countryside. Indeed, one of the earliest cases of its use known to me was by a rowdy band of Wiltshire villagers who allegedly called out their opponents in a dispute at a revel held in 1620 with the cry 'Where are the middle sort of men in Tockenham?'[35]

This example, however, is unusual, and it seems probable that as a more broadly applicable term of social description the concept of the middle sort of people came into its own in the pamphlet literature and memoirs of the civil war period – above all, in defending the social basis

[35] Corfield, 'Class by name and number', p. 120; P. Laslett, *The World We Have Lost: further explored* (Methuen, London, 1983), pp. 46–7; J. Stow, *The Survey of London* (Everyman, London, 1956), pp. 492–3 (I am grateful to Dr V. Brodsky for bring this reference to my attention); B. Manning, *The English People and the English Revolution, 1640–49* (Heinemann, London, 1976), p. 154; Underdown, *Revel, Riot, and Rebellion*, p. 85.

of parliamentarian support against royalist accusations that the king's opponents relied heavily upon supporters drawn from the 'rabble'.[36] Thus William Lilly described London demonstrators against episcopacy in 1641 as 'men of mean or a middle quality', as distinct from both 'aldermen, merchants or Common Council-men' and 'the vulgar'. Parliament's supporters in Worcester were 'the middle rank of people'. In Birmingham, 'the middle and inferior sort of people' stood firm against Prince Rupert's advance, despite the defeatism of the 'better sort'. In Bristol, the king was supported by 'two extremes in that city', 'the wealthy and powerful men' and 'the basest and lowest sort'. But his cause was 'disgusted' by 'the middle rank, the true and best citizens'.[37] These examples indicate a continuing urban bias in application, which is reinforced by comparable accounts of parliamentarian support in rural areas, which frequently make the same essential propaganda point by referring to the goodwill or recruitment not of the 'middle sort', but of 'yeomen' or 'freeholders'.[38]

But at the same time some writers were extending the usage of 'the middle sort' to encompass countrymen as well as citizens, and indeed were applying it to the nation at large. In Gloucestershire, according to John Corbet, royalist support came from the rich and their dependents, 'the needy multitude', but parliament had the hearts of 'the yeomen, farmers clothiers and the whole middle rank of the people'. Similarly in Nottinghamshire, in Mrs Hutchinson's account, 'most of the middle sort, the able substantial freeholders . . . adhered to the parliament.' Richard Baxter wrote of the allegiance of 'tradesmen, and freeholders, and the middle sort of men'. An anonymous pamphleteer praised 'the middle sort of people of England and yeomanry' as the surest defenders of English liberties, while parliament itself appealed to 'the middle sort of people, who are the body of the kingdom.'[39]

Such an extension of the term 'the middle sort of people' was perhaps dictated by the demands of describing the participation of a heterogeneous body of people of intermediate status in both town and country in events of national significance. And to this extent the cataclysmic events of the 1640s made their own specific contribution to the ways in which the English perceived their society as a whole. For the new term

[36] Ibid., p. 3.
[37] Manning, *English People*, pp. 94, 160, 203, 205, 241; Underdown, *Revel, Riot, and Rebellion*, pp. 169–70.
[38] See, e.g., the many instances quoted in Manning, *English People*, pp. 238–9.
[39] Underdown, *Revel, Riot, and Rebellion*, p. 170; Manning, *English People*, pp. 235, 238, 240.

stuck, and in the later seventeenth and early eighteenth centuries 'the middle sort' was a firmly established mode of summing up, at both regional and national level, what Roy Porter has dubbed the 'stout midriff' of English society. Baxter wrote approvingly of 'a sober sort of men of the middle rank' to be found in 'most places' in England. Gregory King divided the population not only into twenty-six 'ranks' and 'degrees', but also into the 'better sort', 'poorest sort', and 'middle sort'. Daniel Defoe distinguished 'the Middle Sort, who live well', in his account of the social order, placing them between 'the rich' and 'the working trades'. Guy Miège discerned 'a middle sort' – specifically including yeomen or freeholders 'that have land of their own to a good value and husband it themselves' – between 'the degree of a gentleman' and the 'meaner' or 'inferior' sorts of people 'such as get their livelihood either in a mechanic, or servile way.'[40] In this development the informal language of sorts had once more proved adaptable, by means of its very resonant imprecision, to the task of capturing a process of social change. It provided the most appropriate appellation for the swarming world of petty tradesmen and manufacturers spawned by the commercial and industrial expansion of the seventeenth century, and one which could embrace also the substantial commerical farmers who were their rural counterpart.

By the second half of the seventeenth century, then, there were at least two current modes of social description in England, expressing alternative perceptions of a complex social reality. The hierarchy of degrees, jerry-built by the jobbing social analysts of Elizabethan England from the debris of the society of estates, lived on. Increasingly archaic, but remarkably resilient, it perpetuated the characteristic status designations of the sixteenth century, and provided, with its implications of oneness and order in a graduated ladder of dominance and subordination, a reassuring sense of stability and continuity in a transformed context. It was, indeed, the ghost of the Tudor regime, sitting enthroned upon the grave thereof.

Meanwhile, the informal language of sorts, a more authentic product of the social dynamism of the later sixteenth and seventeenth centuries, provided in its different forms an altogether more relevant everyday guide to the basic realities of social distance. Adaptable to context and

[40] R. Porter, *English Society in the Eighteenth Century* (Penguin, Harmondsworth, 1982), p. 363; Hill, *Society and Puritanism*, p. 243; Thirsk and Cooper (eds), *Seventeenth-Century Economic Documents*, p. 795; R. W. Malcolmson, *Life and Labour in England, 1700–80* (Hutchinson, London, 1981), p. 11; Miège, 'Present state', pp. 47–8.

responsive to change, it expressed the plasticity of social identity, the mutability of social alignments, the clash of interests, and the power relations of a dynamic society.

A period which began with a single conventional image of the social world, a single dominant construction of reality, ended with ambivalence. But it was an ambivalence in social perception which admirably encapsulated the fundamental ambiguities of both the social structure and the social relations of seventeenth-century England. Those ambiguities could be clarified and resolved only with the development of a vocabulary of social analysis, which could express both the continuing significance of the nice status distinctions of the language of degrees, and the basic realities of social distance and economic interest which resonated in the language of sorts, while at the same time provoking a re-evaluation of the very nature of social organization. Already by the year 1700 a handful of thinkers were beginning to experiment with just such a terminology: the language of class.

3

Hidalgo and *pechero*: the language of 'estates' and 'classes' in early-modern Castile

I. A. A. Thompson

Formal descriptions of society in Castile from the Middle Ages through to the eighteenth century were set, as they were everywhere in the West, within the framework of a tripartite structure inspired and sanctioned by the divine order of the heavens.[1] Those parts were spoken of usually as 'estados', sometimes as 'brazos', very occasionally as 'clases'. The language reflected three models of society coexisting in contemporary beliefs: the medieval concept of a society ordered by functions (*oratores*, *defensores*, *laboratores*); the organic concept of society as a *corpus mysticum*; and the Aristotelian concept of a society ordered by quality, power, and wealth (*mayores/ricos*, *medianos*, *menores/pobres*). Changes in the language of social description in Castile reflected the changing balance within the status system of those three principles of social classification: function, lineage, and wealth.

'Clase' was already in use as a term of stratification in Castile in the sixteenth century, much earlier, it seems, than in England. It is found both in a simple categorical sense,[2] and in the classical sense, as used by Servius Tullius for an ad hoc grouping of the population according to wealth for fiscal purposes.[3] But it also existed as a straightforward

---

[1] R. Pérez Bustamante (ed.), *La Villa de Santillana: estudios y documentos* (Santillana del Mar, 1984), p. 287, RC 8 Aug. 1445.

[2] A. Gónzalez Palencia (ed.), *La Junta de Reformación* (*Archivo Histórico Español*, vol. 5, Madrid, 1932), pp. 245–7.

[3] Instituto de Valencia de Don Juan, envío 45, caja 59, f. 453, Junta Grande, 20.2.1591: resolved on *empréstido* to 'repartir en tres clases todo el Reino, una de los grandes, prelados y Señores y cabildos eclesiásticos y ciudades; otra de

alternative to 'brazo' or 'estado'. Olivares in his *Gran Memorial* of 1624, having surveyed in turn the politics of the clergy, the various ranks of the nobility, and the 'people', concluded, 'having given Your Majesty an account of the classes of which these kingdoms are composed and of the manner in which Your Majesty should deal with each of them.'[4] This use of 'clase' may, however, have had a more specific, if latent, social connotation. Cobarruvias in his 1611 dictionary suggests that it was primarily an affectation of Latinists who 'divide peoples into three classes, "menores", "medianos" and "mayores".'[5] This Aristotelian division of society into 'mayores', 'medianos', and 'menores' was pervasive. It was already enshrined in the late-thirteenth-century *Partidas* of Alfonso the Wise, and expressed a view of the social order which, well before the end of the Middle Ages, was not specifically functional, and which was open to the application of general political, economic, and intellectual criteria to social stratification.[6]

The use of 'brazo' (literally 'arm', better rendered as 'member') was most often found in general considerations of the political system. This is the way Olivares used it in the *Gran Memorial*, for example.[7] Its importance lay in its metaphorical force. The analogy with the human body, so much more current in Spain as a theory of relationships than the Great Chain of Being, served to reinforce an organic and genetic, rather than a hierarchical, vision of the social order and to promote an

---

los caballeros y mayorazgos, y clérigos y hombres ricos; y otra de la demás gente del pueblo.' For the division of the population of Rome into tax bands by Servius Tullius, see P. Calvert, *The Concept of Class: an historical introduction* (Hutchinson, London, 1982), p. 13.

[4] 'Habiendo hecho relación a V. Majd. de las clases de que se componen estos reinos y del modo con que V. Majd. se debe gobernar con cada una': J. H. Elliott and F. de la Peña, *Memoriales y Cartas del Conde Duque de Olivares* (Madrid, 1978), vol. 1, p. 63.

[5] Sebastián de Cobarruvias, *Tesoro de la Lengua Castellana o Española* (1611), in modern edn (Madrid, 1979).

[6] E. Elorduy, *La idea del imperio en el pensamiento español* (Madrid, 1944), p. 466, 'Pueblo llaman el ayuntamiento de todos los omes comunalmente, de los mayores, e de los medianos, e de los menores. Ca todos son menester, e non se puede escusar, porque se han de ayudar unos a otros, porque puedan bien bivir, e ser guardados, e mantenidos': *Partidas*, II, 10, 1; Pérez Bustamante (ed.), *La Villa de Santillana*, p. 286.

[7] Elliott and de la Peña, *Memoriales y Cartas*, vol. 1, pp. 49–63: 'El brazo eclesiástico, que puede considerarse por la piedad de religión por el primero' (only uses 'brazo' for clergy); 'este brazo de la nobleza', p. 60; 'este brazo de la república', p. 61; 'los otros brazos', 'este brazo' (*sc.* 'el pueblo'), p. 61.

ideology of social harmony based on a functional network of reciprocal obligations and expectations.[8]

Neither 'clase' nor 'brazo' was in common use. Overwhelmingly, the preponderant idiom of social description was that of 'estados'. The language of 'estates' was ambivalent, however. Even by the early fourteenth century, when Don Juan Manuel's *Libro de los Estados* gave it its first, classic formulation, it had both an ordinal and an occupational sense, defining men not only in the mass ('all the estates in the world are comprised in three'), but also individually ('there are as many estates as there are men in this world').[9] Because of this ambivalence, the use of 'estates' was protean and imprecise. In its primary sense, 'estado' denoted a functional order with its own distinct way of life. It marked off the fundamental divisions of civil society into one or other of which a man must necessarily fall, 'since', as Moreno de Vargas put it, 'it would be an absurdity for one and the same person to be in two contrary estates.'[10]

Although the traditional, tripartite system of 'sacerdote', 'caballero', and 'labrador' survived in the literature of the sixteenth and seventeenth centuries and even into the eighteenth,[11] already during the later Middle Ages it was coming under increasing pressure from alternative perceptions of society deriving from the secular, social analysis of revived Aristotelianism and from the realities of economic and political change. With the growth of the market, urban culture, the legal profession, and a proto-bureaucracy, the language of 'estados' was having to be adapted to accommodate the development of more complex social formations than the simple functional presuppositions of the old society of orders could easily comprehend. One response was to make the functional system of the society of orders itself more complex. Enrique de Villena

[8] Closest to the idea of a 'Great Chain of Being', though very late (1781), is Antonio Javier Pérez y López: 'la sociedad es una cadena y no todos los eslabones deben ser iguales en consideración, pero los menores son dignos . . . y necesarios para la subsistencia del todo': see P. Molas, *La burguesia mercantil en la España del Antiguo Régimen* (Madrid, 1985), p. 143.

[9] 'Digovos que todos los estados del mundo se encierran en tres: al uno llaman defensores et al otro oradores et al otro labradores' (92); 'tantos son los estados que homes viven en este mundo' (83): from J. R. Araluce Cuenca, *El Libro de los Estados: Don Juan Manuel y la sociedad de su tiempo* (Madrid, 1976), pp. 54–5.

[10] J-M. Pelorson, *Les 'Letrados' juristes castillans sous Philippe III* (Le Puy-en-Velay, 1980), p. 224.

[11] J. A. Maravall, *Estado moderno y mentalidad social* (2 vols, Madrid, 1972), vol. 2, pp. 14–15.

in the fifteenth century conceived of society as divided into twelve 'estados', and in Diego Tovar y Valderrama (1645) there are not three basic social functions, but eight: those of the clergy, magistracy, army, nobility, agriculture, commerce, and the liberal and industrial professions.[12] Cobarruvias, in 1611, interposed the 'ciudadano' – 'he who lives in the city, and lives off his own capital, income, or property' – as 'an estate in the middle, between *caballero* or *hidalgo* and the artisan', which included 'the *letrados*, and those professing letters and the liberal arts.' In a number of places in the previous century an 'estado de ciudadanos', or 'mercaderes', actually existed as a separate estate of local government.[13]

Others responded by retaining the language of the three estates while depriving it of its traditional functional content, speaking, for example, of 'el estado de los medianos', 'el estado de la medianía', 'el mediano estado',[14] or, like Fernando Alvarez de Toledo in 1602, regarding the estates simply as degrees of wealth: 'There are considered to be three estates in the commonwealth: one of the rich, one of the poor, and one of those who have moderate wealth to get by on.'[15]

Both the 'ricos/medianos/pobres' schema and the Aristotelian 'mayores/medianos/menores' represent a more overtly hierarchical view of society than the traditional 'sacerdote/caballero/labrador' or the vulgar

---

[12] Ibid., vol. 2, p. 19: 'ca el mundo es partido de doze estados principales e más señalados, so los quales todos los otros se entienden': J. A. Maravall, *La philosophie politique espagnole au XVIIᵉ siècle* (Paris, 1955), pp. 109, 92. The 'cuerpo místico' concept was also particularly useful in permitting both greater complexity and imaginative flexibility in the description of social relationships. See, e.g., Juan Pablo Mártir Rizo, *Norte de Príncipes* (1626), ed. J. A. Maravall (Madrid, 1988), p. 18: 'Y porque toda República o comunidad es un cuerpo . . . podemos decir, y con razón, que el príncipe es la cabeza, los hombres sabios y prudentes, los ojos; los magistrados, jueces y otros ministros son los oídos que reciben las leyes, las constituciones del Señor, y las ejecutan. La lengua y boca, los letrados y abogados; las manos, la nobleza; los labradores, los pies, de quien se sirve este cuerpo así distribuido.'

[13] In Logroño, the three estates were 'hidalgos', 'labradores cristianos viejos', and 'ciudadanos': 'Nobiliario Riojano', *Berceo*, 2 (1947), p. 307. Of Herrera de Rio Pisuerga it was said in 1616, 'en la dicha villa hasta de algunos años a esta parte había tres estados, uno de hidalgos, otro de labradores, y otro de ruanos y mercaderes'; for which see Pelorson, '*Letrados*' *juristes*, p. 231.

[14] Gónzales Palencia (ed.), *La Junta de Reformación*, pp. 246, 247, 255.

[15] 'Tres estados se consideran en la República: el uno de ricos, el otro de pobres, y el otro de los que tienen moderado caudal con que pasar': J. L. Sureda Carrión, *La hacienda castellana y los economistas del siglo XVII* (Madrid, 1949), p. 165.

employment of 'estado' as a simple occupational category that one finds in village surveys: 'here there are people of all estates, farmers, *hidalgos*, artisans and labourers.'[16] The language of social description seems in general to have been less insistently vertical in Castile than it was elsewhere. Castilians spoke neither of first, second, and third estates;[17] nor did they oppose 'upper' to 'lower' in their general social classifications as commonly as the English. 'Upper' is little used. There are examples of generalized uses of 'bajo' or low – Cobarruvias, for example, defines 'Plebeyo' as 'el hombre baxo de la república que ni es cavallero, ni hidalgo, ni ciudadano' but 'lower' was usually applied more discriminatingly to specific individuals, groups, and occupations, rather than to the totality of the non-noble. However, Castilian social vocabulary was far from being entirely horizontal. Social mobility was usually described in terms of 'upwardness' (though less often in terms of 'downwardness'), and the natural/anthropological model was readily amenable to combining the ideals of harmony and interdependence with distinctions of quality and importance between the various members of the body.[18]

At the level of ordinary usage (as opposed to the theoretical formulations of the treatises) the impression is of a complete absence of coherence in the vocabulary of social description. Olivares, for example, uses 'brazo', 'estado', 'clase', 'lugar', 'jerarquía', 'grado', 'linaje' apparently indiscriminately to mean the same and different things. The nobility is spoken of variously as 'brazo', and 'clase'; but sub-groups within the nobility are also termed 'brazos' ('grandes') 'estados' ('los demás estados', 'tres estados' of *hidalgos*), 'clases' ('la cuarta clase de la nobleza'; 'divido también los caballeros en dos clases'), or they are a 'jerarquía de personas' (*señores titulados, caballeros*), a 'lugar' or station ('el segundo lugar de la nobleza', 'el tercer lugar de la nobleza'), a 'grado' or rank ('los hidalgos es el grado primero de la nobleza de Castilla'), or, in the case of the

---

[16] 'Hay de todos estados de gentes, labradores, hidalgos, oficiales e jornaleros': C. Viñas and R. Paz (eds), *Relaciones de los pueblos de España ordenadas por Felipe II: Ciudad Real* (Madrid, 1971), p. 580 (Villamayor).

[17] It is interesting that J. Lalinde in a recent contribution in J. Lalinde Abadía et al., *El Estado Español en su dimensión histórica* (Madrid, 1984), p. 43, translates Sieyès' 'tiers état' as 'estado llano'. Nevertheless, Olivares did use ordinal language in his *Gran Memorial*: 'El brazo eclesiástico, que puede considerarse por la piedad de religión por el primero' (p. 49), and 'El pueblo, señor, tiene el lugar tercero y inferior' (p. 61).

[18] Hierónimo Merola, *República Original sacada del cuerpo humano* (1587), 'tiene naturaleza partes viles y bajas cuyas partes son obedecer,' in P. de Vega (ed.), *Antología de escritores políticos del Siglo de Oro* (Madrid, 1966), p. 100.

'pueblo', 'este linaje de gente'.[19] This terminological promiscuity suggests that the words themselves were not particularly heavy with meaning, and that by this time the ordinary vocabulary of social description had become detached from its original associations.

The division of society into 'estados' did not, therefore, presuppose any particular scheme of social stratification: *eclesiástico/caballero/labrador, hidalgo/pechero, mayor/mediano/menor, rico/pobre*. Functional, economic, and legal definitions were frequently confused. An 'estado' could be an order, a status, an occupation, or a category of wealth. It merely denoted a distinct grouping of men with a way of life defined by some distinguishing feature which could be genetic or legal or functional or material – 'there are various estates in the community . . . gentlemen, burghers, craftsmen, husbandmen . . . each estate and way of life with its order and limits' (Cobarruvias) – and which varied from writer to writer and from place to place.[20] The use of 'estado' did not, by itself, make any statement about the nature of society; it did not necessarily connote the relational values of the society of orders; nor did it presume any consistent principle of status distinction.

Perhaps because of its flexibility, its conceptual ambivalence, its emphasis on function or occupation and on difference rather than hierarchy, the general vocabulary of social description in Castile does not seem to have responded very directly to changes in society. The language of 'estados' is the predominant idiom throughout the sixteenth and seventeenth centuries; and, despite increasing competition from alternative expressions in the eighteenth century, it remains so even at the end of our period. The changing balance within the status system of those three principles of social classification, function, lineage, and wealth, is reflected less in changing terminology than in changes in the meaning and the content of the words themselves. Those changes are best examined by

---

[19] 'El brazo eclesiástico' (p. 49), but also 'los otros estados más nobles' (p. 61); 'este brazo de la nobleza' (¿*hidalgos?* – not clear from text), 'los demás estados' (p. 60), 'este brazo de la república' (again not clear whether this is *nobleza* as a whole or *hidalgos*); references, to 'El pueblo, señor, tiene el lugar tercero y inferior' (p. 61), 'los otros brazos', 'este brazo', 'los otros estados más nobles' (p. 61), 'este linaje de gente' (p. 62); and quotation in fn 4 above: see Elliott and de la Peña, *Memoriales y Cartas*, vol. 1 pp. 49–63.

[20] In Villacastín (Segovia), for example, the graziers claimed to be 'el estado de señores de ganados': A. García Sanz, *Desarrollo y crisis del Antiguo Régimen en Castilla la Vieja* (Madrid, 1986), p. 366. In Bargas (Toledo) there was an 'estado de vecinos de Toledo' with its own reserved offices: C. Viñas and R. Paz (eds), *Relaciones de los pueblos de España ordenadas por Felipe II: Reino de Toledo*, pt 1 (Madrid, 1951), p. 122.

concentrating on one set of words, those which expressed the basic division within early-modern society, that between the noble and the non-noble.

There is no great problem in analysing what the learned have to say about society. More difficult to catch are the perceptions of those who lived the categories the learned thought. In this respect Spanish historians are supremely fortunate. Because of the peculiar importance of the lawcourts and the Military Orders as arbiters of nobility, they have available an exceptional body of materials expressive of the language of the ordinary, unlettered noble or commoner. The investigations for the Military Orders, entry into which required proof of nobility and purity of Christian blood on both sides for three generations, and the 'executive letters' (*cartas ejecutorias*) issued by the high courts of Valladolid and Granada in resolution of cases of disputed nobility between claimants and the towns and villages which challenged them generated a huge mass of documentation consisting largely of depositions of witnesses from all levels of society. No less than 30,000 'executive letters' survive in Valladolid alone. To these records can be added the justifications presented by the recipients of the hundreds of patents of nobility (*cartas de privilegio*) granted or sold by the Crown between the sixteenth and the nineteenth centuries and the responses to two national surveys, the so-called 'Topographical Relations' carried out in New Castile in the 1570s and the remarkable Ensenada *Catastro* of 1751/2 which runs to tens of thousands of manuscript volumes.[21] These unique records are only just beginning to be systematically exploited for the study of social history. Nevertheless, something can be said, albeit tentatively, about the social grammar of the 'vulgar', from whichever order of society they came, a grammar which is in many respects very different from that of the writers whose constructs have been relied upon rather too easily.

---

[21] See E. Postigo Castellanos, *Honor y privilegio en la Corona de Castilla: El Consejo de las Órdenes y los Caballeros de Hábito en el siglo XVII* (Junta de Castilla y León, 1988); A. Basanta de la Riva, *Archivo de la Real Chancillería de Valladolid. Sala de los Hijosdalgo: catálogo de todos sus pleitos, expedientes y probanzas* (4 vols, Valladolid, 1920); J. Fayard and M-C. Gerbet, 'Fermeture de la noblesse et pureté de sang en Castille à travers les procès de *hidalguía* au XVIᵉ siècle', *Histoire, Economie et Société*, 1 (1982), pp. 51–75; I. A. A. Thompson, 'The purchase of nobility in Castile, 1552–1700', *Journal of European Economic History*, 8 (1979), pp. 313–60; idem, 'Neo-noble nobility: concepts of *hidalguía* in early-modern Castile', *European History Quarterly*, 15 (1985), pp. 379–406; N. Salomon, *La campagne de Nouvelle Castille à la fin du XVIᵉ d'après les 'Relaciones topográficas'* (Paris, 1964).

The responses of the small-town and village elders to the questionnaires of the 'Topographical Relations' are probably the closest we can get to a coherent view of popular perceptions of the social order.[22] For them, too, society was divided into estates; on the one hand, 'el estado de los hijosdalgo' (the terms *noble* or *caballero* are not so commonly found) and on the other, a multiplicity of expressions, the most usual being 'el estado de pecheros', 'los hombres buenos pecheros', 'labradores, hombres buenos pecheros', 'hombres llanos pecheros'. What in the terminology of the 'Topographical Relations' distinguishes noble from non-noble is the *pecho*, personal taxation. The commoner was the taxpayer, the *pechero*; the *hidalgo* was the privileged, exempt from his share of the fiscal burdens of the community. To express the distinction noble/non-noble in the terms *hidalgo/pechero* was to highlight the fundamental conflict between *hidalguía* and the fiscal interests of the community ('they do not want to pay tax nor to contribute as the other householders do').[23] Ennoblement, therefore, was something to which the community was naturally hostile and resistant.[24]

Thus *hidalguía* in the 'Topographical Relations' was not defined by function, wealth, power, or lifestyle. The dichotomies rich–poor, powerful–weak, leisured–labouring existed, of course, and there are sometimes hints of their equation with status; but as often as not, the *hidalgo–pechero* axis bisected those poles. It is almost as if *hidalguía* in many communities was a social irrelevance. Indeed, when tax exemption was not at issue, communities were often indifferent to *hidalguía*, and might neither know nor care who was *hidalgo* and who was not.[25] In

---

[22] The surveys that survive have been published in C. Viñas and R. Paz (eds), *Relaciones histórico-geográfico-estadísticas de los pueblos de España, hechas por iniciativa de Felipe II: Provincia de Madrid* (Madrid, 1949); idem, . . . *Reino de Toledo* (3 parts, Madrid, 1951–63); idem, . . . *Ciudad Real* (Madrid, 1971); J. Zarco Cuevas, *Relaciones de pueblos del obispado de Cuenca* (Cuenca, 1983); J. Catalina and M. Pérez Villamil, 'Relaciones topográficas de España', *Memorial Histórico Español*, vols. 41–3, 45–6 (Province of Guadalajara).

[23] Zarco Cuevas, *Relaciones de Cuenca*, p. 512 (Tarazona de la Mancha).

[24] J. M. Diez Borque, *Sociología de la comedia española del siglo XVII* (Madrid, 1976), pp. 256–7.

[25] Viñas and Paz (eds), *Relaciones de Toledo*, p. 51: 'hay algunos vecinos de la villa de Talavera que viven en este lugar y pechan y contribuyen en la villa de Talavera y no se sabe si son hidalgos o no' (Alcaudete); p. 57: 'tres o cuatro están en este lugar en posesion de hidalgo, aunque no tienen ejecutoria, ni ellos saben si son hidalgos, ni si no' (Aldeanueva de Balbarroyo); Alcántara, 15 Apr. 1570: 'por ser esta villa libre de pechos . . . y no ser por esta causa del todo conocidos los hijosdalgo', AGS GA 73, f. 14; Valladolid, 18 Apr. 1570: 'el

Pastrana (Guadalajara), the respondents in 1575 did not know how many *hidalgos* there were in the town nor who they were, 'nor has it been of concern, as has, and still is, purity of blood, which is much esteemed. Hence the custom has been that no *converso* [of Jewish blood], nor anyone of Moorish race, be allowed as an official or deputy in its government.'[26] Equally, individuals might be content with their exemptions and indifferent to their status. When the *Corregidor* of Toledo tried to sell patents of nobility in the city, those he approached replied, 'that as they live in Toledo they have no need of any *hidalguía* beyond that bestowed by the privileges and liberties that past kings have granted to the householders living here in this city.'[27] The *hidalguía* of the 'Topographical Relations' was first and last a legal status that had little connection with any other scheme of values, and the language in which it was described was the language of the law. *Hidalguía* was spoken of as a property ('en propiedad y posesión de hidalgos', 'gozan de posesión') and as a legal right ('derecho adquirido'); and nobles were ranked not as *hidalgos* or *caballeros*, nor by 'sangre' or 'solar conocido' (although there are instances of such classifications), but by the judicial basis of their status – that is to say, whether they were accounted *hidalgo* by a judgement of the courts ('por executoria'), convention ('por posesión'), or royal patent ('por privilegio'), or whether their claims were still doubtful or in litigation ('dudosos', 'pretendientes'). It is the language of litigiousness and contention, in which *hidalguía* was often uncertain, subject to repeated challenge, and sustainable only so long as it could be successfully defended in the courts.

If the primary division was between noble and commoner, *hidalgo* and *pechero*, the dualism rich–poor was no less prominent in the 'Topographical Relations'. The fusion of status and wealth and the mass ennoblement of the rich has been seen by many historians as the central dynamic of the social history of the sixteenth and seventeenth centuries.[28]

---

pueblo es grande y libre, con dificultad se puede saber el que es hijodalgo, o no', AGS GA 73, f. 24.

[26] N. Salomon, *Recherches sur le thème paysan dans la 'Comedia' au temps de Lope de Vega* (Bordeaux, 1965), p. 82.

[27] 'Que biviendo en Toledo no tienen necesidad de más hidalguía que la que tienen por los previllegios y libertades que los Reyes pasados dieron a los vezinos desta cibdad que aqui biviesen': AGS CJH 23, f. 205, 24 Mar. 1557.

[28] M.-C. Gerbet, *La noblesse dans le royaume de Castille: étude sur ses structures sociales en Estrémadure de 1454 à 1516* (Paris, 1979), p. 132; A. Dominguez Ortiz, *La sociedad española en el siglo XVII*, vol. 1 (Madrid, 1964), pt 2, ch. 3; J. A. Maravall, *Poder, honor y élites en el siglo XVII* (Madrid, 1979).

The profits of growth and the financial problems of government enabled the rich, by buying offices, lands, and jurisdictions, to seize control of political and economic power in the communities and to engineer their own social elevation. It is not accidental that contemporaries used 'ricos y poderosos' as if they were one word; and it is undoubtedly true that wealth facilitated upward mobility, while poverty made difficult the preservation of status. As one speaker stated in the Cortes in 1624:

> The officials of the towns and villages will not dare list anyone in the tax rolls who is prepared to go to litigation, however notorious a *pechero* he is. Thus he is left exempted as if he were an *hidalgo*, and so becomes one. Contrariwise, if they list an *hidalgo* who is poor, he cannot litigate and loses his *hidalguía*.[29]

There was, of course, absolutely nothing unique about this challenge to the traditional system of orders from the pressure of new wealth in the early-modern period. Complaints about the devaluing of nobility by the power of money can be found in the fourteenth and fifteenth centuries no less than in the sixteenth and seventeenth. Moreover, the theoretical relationship between nobility and wealth was an ambivalent one. Almost all writers thought wealth an essential adjunct of nobility, while at the same time deploring the ennoblement of the rich. The difficulties of trying to reconcile socio-economic change with the tra-ditional tripartite structure of society can be seen in an anonymous paper of the early 1620s which bemoaned the breakdown of the balance between 'the poor', 'the middling' ('medianos'), and 'the truly rich', these last being equated with 'señores de título', 'caballeros', 'hidalgos', and 'nobles'. By taking from both 'ricos' and 'medianos' and by means of mortgages (*censos*), entails, and dowries, some men

> have become a special estate and separate kind [*género*] of person, neither of the rich, nor of the poor, nor of the middling, and have brought our society to the state of disorder that we see. In their ambition, those who would not have been out of place among the middling have wanted to join the rich, and others have become *caballeros* and *nobles* who would have been better in the business and the occupations that their fathers followed in their trades and *medianía*.

His solution to the diminution of the middling kind and to the rise of many low persons was to prevent access to 'el estado equestre' to anybody with less than the very considerable income of 4,000,000 *mara-vedís*; the rest could remain 'ciudadanos' or 'plebeyos'. Wealth could

---

[29] Salomon, *Campagne de Nouvelle Castille*, p. 300.

thus be made a quality of nobility precisely in order to check the ennoblement of the well-to-do.[30]

In effect, whatever social changes may have been taking place, the ideology of nobility was reluctant to accommodate the claims of the *nouveaux riches*. Conventionally, historians portray a noble hierarchy in Castile of *grandes*, *títulos*, *caballeros*, and *hidalgos*, graded by wealth. In general terms it was proably true that the average *grande* was richer than the average *título*, and so on; but there was no presumption in the language of status that this should be so. To be recognized as an *hidalgo* implied nothing about one's economic position – the 'Topographical Relations' abound in both poor and well-off *hidalgos*. Nor were contemporaries at all consistent in distinguishing *caballeros* from *hidalgos*, least of all in understanding the *caballero* to be a superior and wealthier kind of nobleman.

Just to take one example, in an account of 1570 a local official listed 142 'cavalleros hijosdalgo' in the town and district of Montanches (Extremadura), all of them 'poor, as are the people of this district in general.'[31] There was an economic difference between *caballero* and *hidalgo*, as Peñalosa wrote; for 'now, incorrectly, we call "caballeros" those noted *hidalgos* of ancient house and distinguished name who are of a more eminent and wealthy estate than other *hidalgos*.'[32] But the difference was not simply, or even principally, economic, but a difference of 'quality and estimation'. The epithets most characteristically associated with 'caballero' were not 'rico', nor even 'honrado', which were also applied at times to the *hidalgo*, the *labrador*, and the *mercader*, but 'principal', 'particular', 'calificado', 'noble'. In the city of Cáceres in the seventeenth century, when tax rolls were compiled, the 'caballeros notorios' and their descendants were noted as 'caballero hijodalgo', other nobles simply as 'hijodalgo'; and this was done 'as a clearer distinction and designation of the quality of each individual'.[33] Mme D'Aulnoy, though sometimes rather overcoloured in her descriptions of later-

---

[30] Gónzalez Palencia (ed.), *Junta de Reformación*, pp. 245–7.

[31] AGS GA 73, f. 46; at the same time, in Santo Domingo de la Calzada and the Merindad de Rioja no less than 942 'caballeros hijosdalgo' were listed, AGS GA 73, f. 60.

[32] Benito de Peñalosa y Mondragón, *Libro de las Cinco Excelencias del Español* (Pamplona, 1629), f. 87v.

[33] AHN Ordenes Militares, Calatrava, 1901, f. 23v., Calificación de la nobleza de D. Diego Antonio de Ovando, Cáceres, 26 June 1623: 'lo qual parece se haze para mayor distincion y declaracion de la calidad de cada uno.'

seventeenth-century Castile, got the tone right when she wrote, 'here it is not enough to be rich; it is necessary also to be of quality.'[34]

The language of the 'Topographical Relations' described the distinguishing marks of nobility; but it had nothing to say of its essence nor of the criteria by which the legal judgement of nobility was reached. *Hidalguía*, the generic term for nobility in Castile, was defined in the Middle Ages as 'the nobility which descends to men through their lineage.' It was not synonymous with knighthood (*caballería*). *Caballero*, at this time, was a functional term which did not necessarily denote hereditary nobility at all, but rather the personal grant of the privileges of nobility to townsmen of a certain level of substance, conditional on the maintenance of a horse and arms. During the fourteenth and fifteenth centuries, the tendency was for this 'caballería villana' of wealthy, sometimes *converso*, urban oligarchs to transform itself into hereditary *hidalguía*; and by the sixteenth century the semantic hierarchy had been reversed. The *hidalgo* had become the broad, base level of nobility, often rural and semi-proletarianized, and a new composite was emerging, the *caballero hijodalgo*, the term itself giving verbal expression to the fusion of lineage, wealth, and personal service to the king in war.[35]

The absorption of *caballería* into *hidalguía* had the effect of intensifying the militarist resonances of the language of nobility in the sixteenth century. Yet, at the same time, with the ending of the wars of the *Reconquista*, it was ceasing to be generally possible to move into the nobility through the half-way house of 'caballería villana'. The reign of Ferdinand and Isabella saw the last mass ennoblement in Castile for military service.[36] Ennoblement in the sixteenth century was overwhelmingly a civilian process effected through the courts and the phoney militarism of the Military Orders. More and more, nobility was being acquired by administrators, lawyers, financiers, and men for whom war was remote and foreign. There was a growing tension, therefore, as the sixteenth century progressed, between the social reality of the noble estate and the functional presuppositions of the society of orders.

Yet a functional view of nobility as the order of *defensores* persisted. It underlay the reimposition of military service on all *hidalgos* and

[34] Diez Borque, *Sociología de la comedia*, p. 201.
[35] Roger Boase, *The Troubadour Revival: a study of social change and traditionalism in late medieval Spain* (Routledge, London, 1978), pt 1; Gerbet, *La noblesse dans le royaume de Castille*, pp. 95, 125, 134.
[36] M-C. Gerbet, 'Les guerres et l'accès à la noblesse en Espagne de 1463 à 1592', *Mélanges de la Casa de Velázquez*, 8 (1972), pp. 295–326.

knights of the Military Orders in the mid-seventeenth century, as well as, for example, the opposition of the town of Fuente el Maestre to the exemptions of the Zambrano family on the grounds that such grants 'are always made for great and signal services in wars and battles, which neither they nor their father have ever done.'[37] The parvenu noble, therefore, compensated for his personal military deficiencies by an exaggerated adherence to a feudal-military ethos, translating his own administrative or financial services into the language of war and vassalage, and conjuring up deeds of valour by his family and forebears. A striking illustration of this sort of totemism is to be found in the complaint of two attorneys of Ubeda in 1600 against being listed as 'caballeros cuantiosos' and therefore required to present themselves at musters with horse and arms:

> They should not be obliged to maintain arms and a horse to go to the war when they are engaged in advocacy which is also fighting [*milicia*], for attorneys are justly called soldiers, and those who are actually practising that career and noble office, so necessary for Your Majesty's service and the good government of the commonwealth, have the same privileges, liberties and exemptions.[38]

More than four out of five of the justifications adduced for the grants of nobility sold in the seventy years after 1580 represented military services of one kind or another, but 70 per cent of those were surrogates, attributable to ancestors or relatives.[39]

The *hidalgo* ideal expressed in those justifications remained the 'defensor'. Yet the gap between the ideal and the reality, both in terms of social mobility (fewer and fewer of the new *hidalgos* had military services of their own) and in terms of the sociology of the military profession (which was proletarianized by conscription and deserted by the nobility), suggests that it is not enough to see the persistence of the language of the 'defensor' simply as a conservative force, buttressing an archaic, feudal ethos at the expense of progressive, 'bourgeois' attitudes. The petition of the Ubeda attorneys shows how conservatism of language could be used as a means of grafting groups with different values and backgrounds onto the stem of a historically sanctioned, and hence popularly accepted, status system without the need to compromise or deny those values, while at the same time holding together an elite of disparate origins under a common, unifying, ideological umbrella.

---

[37] AGS DGT Inventario 5, leg. 2, f. 72.
[38] Pelorson, *'Letrados' juristes*, p. 238.
[39] For the above, see Thompson, 'Neo-noble nobility', pp. 388–91.

With no reputable route to nobility by personal service alone, ennoblement in practice became almost exclusively a legal process of proving that one was already noble. To do that, it was necessary to prove affiliation in the male line to a recognized noble lineage, at least back to the grand-father, or a reputation as noble within the community by acceptance into the society of one's peers, through marriage, membership of noble confraternities, and a shared lifestyle. Until well into the seventeenth century, this took claimants back to a world of aural record, in which proof depended on the testimony of witnesses to their personal and hearsay knowledge of fact and repute, and in which the vulgar opinion of the community was the all in all. In effect, it was the community which was the arbiter of nobility. The endemic hostility of the community towards social promotion was, therefore, crucial in the definition of nobility in early-modern Castile. Nobility was defined as much by the concern to prevent escape from below as by the reluctance to allow access from above. What the community recognized, therefore, was not the accidentals of personal merit, virtue, learning, office, wealth, liberality, charity, and all the qualities so vaunted by philosophers and moralists, but the unchanging essence, blood and lineage. 'God forbid that I should be the vassal of someone baser than me,' expostulated one resident of Villalobón when he heard that Philip II's secretary of war was planning to buy the town.[40]

Elite designations of the commons frequently had connotations which were morally or politically pejorative: 'la gente común', 'el plebeyo', 'el vulgo', 'villanía'.[41] Most often the commons were defined in terms of qualities which were the antitheses of noble virtues: vicious, grasping, intemperate, inconstant, irrational, and cowardly.[42] The elite found it easier to maintain a unified vision of society and to hold nobility and commonalty within a single continuum of values. 'Since the beginning of the world there have always been some good and noble, and others evil and base,' wrote the Andalusian patrician Ferrand Mexia in 1477.[43] Against the

---

[40] AHN Pruebas de Santiago, exp. 2426, f. 10.

[41] 'Suena tan mal el nombre de labrador que es lo mismo que pechero, villano, grossero, malicioso', from Peñalosa, *Libro de las Cinco Excelencias del Español*; cited in L. Pfandl, *Cultura y costumbres del pueblo español de los siglos XVI y XVII* (Barcelona, 1929), p. 116.

[42] Cosme de Aldana's 1,000-line 'Invectiva contra el vulgo y su maledicencia' (1591), which begins 'Tramposo, desleal, Gente abatida,/ Gente manjar de horca, y de cuchillo./ Hambrienta Arpia, cruel fiera homicida,/ Hydra immortal . . . ,' is a nice example.

[43] *Nobiliario Vero*, bk 1, ch. 40, facsimile edn (Madrid, 1974). Mexia was a city councillor of Jaén and of an ancient noble family. His social attitudes were

tripartism of the formal models of society and the multiplication of estates in the late medieval and early-modern period, there was a counter-tendency to a polarization and a reduction to a unified scale of social values in which the dichotomies *noble–plebeyo, hidalgo–pechero*, rich–poor, *limpio–notado*, good–bad, handsome–plain, powerful–weak, ruler–ruled, would coalesce into the two poles of a single spectrum of honour and esteem.[44] The seventeenth-century mania for knighthoods of the Military Orders stemmed precisely from the fact that they were seen as demonstration of 'limpieza' in all four categories: lineage, office, race, and religion. Even in local government, those earlier instances of a third estate of 'mercaderes' or 'ciudadanos' seem to have disappeared. In the writing of the later sixteenth and seventeenth centuries, *noble–mayor–rico* were coming to be fused.

Conversely, the insistence on the particularity of 'estados' as referring to specific distinctions, as well as to a general partition of society, and the primacy of the purely legal *hidalgo–pechero* divide served to prevent the exclusion of the 'plebeyo' from the honour system. When the *hidalgo* graziers of Villacastín (Segovia) claimed the right to a half of all local offices as 'el estado de señores de ganado', they were denied by the town council on the grounds that

> sheep baron is not an estate with standing in the law, for there are also merchants, farmers and craftsmen, besides other occupations and ways of living, which are not 'estados' for the allocation of offices. . . . There are other townsmen who do not own sheep who are merchants, very rich and honourable men, very zealous for the public good . . . and they have no separate status nor personal distinctions amongst them.[45]

---

no doubt related to his bitter opposition to the favourite of Enrique IV, the populist upstart, the *Condestable* Miguel Lucas de Iranzo.

[44] Diez Borque, *Sociología de la comedia*, p. 261; B. Moreno de Vargas, *Discursos de la Nobleza de España* (Madrid, 1659), f. 42, cites the dictum 'no aver más de dos linajes en el mundo, que son ricos y pobres, juzgando aquellos por nobles, y a estos por plebeyos'; Merola, 'los plebeyos . . . como rudos, y de quien les mande como hombres cuyas partes son obedecer solamente,' in Vega (ed.), *Antología*, p. 105; *Actas de las Cortes de Castilla*, vol. 13, p. 78, 'está dispuesto aún por derecho divino que los nobles tengan el mando de los lugares, y los plebeyos los obedezcan, y se ocupen solo en servir para la provisión dellos' (4 Nov. 1593).

[45] 'Señores de ganado no es estado considerable en derecho, pues hay también mercaderes, labradores y oficiales, y otrosi dichos tratos y maneras de vivir, que no son estados para oficios . . . los demás vecinos que no tienen ganado son mercaderes, personas muy ricas y honradas y muy celosas del bien público . . .

The uniquely Spanish concept of 'limpieza de sangre' had something of the same function. The distinction between the 'limpio' and the 'notado', the pure and the impure of blood, was perhaps as fundamental a division of Spanish society as that between the noble and the commoner.[46] Indeed, in some ways 'limpieza' was the nobility of the commoner. According to an anonymous early seventeenth-century source:

> There are two kinds of nobility in Spain, a greater, which is *hidalguía*, and a lesser, which is *limpieza*, by which we mean 'Old Christian'. And although to have the former, *hidalguía*, is more honourable, it is more shameful to be without the latter, because in Spain we hold in more esteem a *pechero* who is *limpio* than an *hidalgo* who is not.[47]

'Limpieza de sangre', therefore, was at the same time a form of non-noble lineage honour, which the simple peasant 'labrador', uncorrupted by contact with the suspect urban civilization of the Moor and the Jew, enjoyed by virtue of the very anonymity of his ancestry, and a challenge to the honour of the noble lineage. Until the middle of the sixteenth century, when statutes requiring 'limpieza' spread throughout many of the most important institutions of Spanish society, *hidalguía* and *limpieza* had not necessarily been associated. The nobility, therefore, because of the very fame of its lineage, was vulnerable to the accusation of being tainted with Jewish blood. According to Jerónimo de Zevallos, writing *c.* 1635:

> by these means lowly men have set themselves against [the nobles], wanting through the investigation of their *limpieza* not merely to put themselves on the same plane but even to exceed them. . . . This so puffs them up with pride and arrogance that there is not a gentleman, noble, or lord whom they dare not try to discredit and defame as not *limpio*.[48]

---

y no hay diferencia de estados entre ellos ni cosa por la que hacer diferencia en las personas': García Sanz, *Desarrollo y crisis*, p. 367.

[46] The classic account of 'limpieza' is Albert A. Sicroff, *Les controverses des Statuts de 'Pureté de Sang' en Espagne du XVᵉ au XVIIᵉ siècle* (Paris, 1960). The centrality of 'limpieza' is stressed in contrary directions by J. I. Gutiérrez Nieto, as a form of class struggle of nobility versus bourgeoisie, in 'La estructura castizo-estamental de la sociedad castellana del siglo XVI', *Hispania*, 33 (1973), pp. 519–63, at p. 559; and as a form of anti-nobility, in 'Limpieza de sangre y antihidalguismo hacia 1600', in *Homenaje al Dr D. Juan Reglà Campistol* (Univ. of Valencia, Valencia, 1975), pp. 497–514. For J. A. Maravall, on the other hand, it is merely another barrier to the acquisition of nobility: *Poder, honor y élites*, p. 119.

[47] A. Domínguez Ortiz, *La clase social de los conversos en Castilla en la edad moderna* (Madrid, 1955), p. 229.

[48] 'Se han opuesto y oponen [a los nobles] por este medio los hombres bajos, queriendo no sólo igualarse pero aventajarse a ellos con un acto de limpieza, . . . y éste les llena de tanta soberbia y vanidad que ni hay caballero, noble ni

Limpieza was thus a form of anti-*hidalguismo*, a means by which the peasant could avenge himself on the pretensions of noble and urban wealth, and a form of compensation, a way for the *labrador* to counter his own social baseness. The *hidalgo*, in danger of being demeaned by his very status, was forced to react; and from the second half of the sixteenth century, *limpieza* too became an increasingly necessary prerequisite for nobility.[49]

The fact that the terminology of social description in Castile leant towards horizontality rather than verticality – that is employed a language that was not manifestly hierarchical in its categorization of the different social orders – may also have contributed to a sense of a common participation in the honour system. That the non-noble was not spoken of in the mass as the third estate, or the lower orders, but as 'el estado llano', 'el estado común', 'los hombres buenos', 'el estado de los pecheros', may have had something to do with what struck so many contemporary observers, right through the *ancien régime*, as the extraordinary social presumption of the Castilian commons, that punctilious lack of deference which persists still, and the relatively muted nature of social conflict in early-modern Castile, compared with other European societies.[50] The Frenchman Jean Muret, travelling in Spain in 1666, had imagined that the Spaniard's hypersensitive self-respect was only an amusing something that he had read about in *Don Quixote*:

> but I would never have believed that universally every Spaniard would have affected this ridiculous concern for his honour. It comes, sir, from that pride which is so natural to him and which makes them believe that all the other nations are as nothing in comparison with theirs. Indeed, you cannot see the meanest tramp who does not wear a sword. They imagine that to be Spanish is to be noble, as long as one does not descend from a moor, a jew, or a heretic.[51]

Castile seems to have been the only country in Europe in which the theatre did not portray honour as exclusive to the nobility, but allowed the ordinary peasant a genuine claim to honour and to the respect of the upper orders.[52]

---

señor a quien no se atrevan a desacreditar e infamar de no limpio': cited in Gutiérrez Nieto, 'Limpieza de sangre y antihidalguismo', p. 514, n. 37.

[49] Fayard and Gerbet, 'Fermeture de la noblesse', p. 65.

[50] For example, Bartolomé Joly (1603–4), Antonio de Brunel (1665), J. García Mercadal (ed.), *Viajes de Extranjeros por España y Portugal* (3 vols, Madrid, 1952), vol. 2, pp. 124, 412.

[51] Ibid., vol. 2, p. 717.

[52] D. R. Larson, *The Honor Plays of Lope de Vega* (Harvard University Press, Cambridge, Mass., 1977), p. 71.

For 300 years the 'executive letters' and the 'letters of privilege' are unwavering in deriving *hidalguía* first and foremost from the proven inheritance of a recognized, noble blood-line, a derivation encapsulated in the formula 'hidalgo notorio de sangre y solar conocido'. The assumptions of the claimants to nobility, of their witnesses, and, in so far as it is possible to judge, of the ordinary man adhered totally to the traditional definition of *hidalguía* as 'the nobility which descends to men through their lineage'. Indeed, although from the last decades of the sixteenth century, important changes are beginning to be visible in the language and the idioms of the 'executive letters' and the 'letters of privilege', they are changes that are tending to reinforce, rather than undermine, traditional values. Social differentiation itself becomes more extreme, more insistent, more verbalized. It is necessary to distinguish and to be distinguished. The title 'Don', once relatively uncommon, though beginning to be abused in the late sixteenth century, by the seventeenth century is sported by almost everyone of any social pretension whatsoever. City corporations, where in the sixteenth century, not one in five of the councillors would have been 'Don', are full – almost without exception – of 'Dons', knights of the Military Orders, *señores de vasallos*, even *títulos*.

Furthermore, nobility becomes more and more exclusively hereditary. The genetic language of blood, breeding, lineage, roots, trunks, branches ('sangre', 'casta', 'generación', 'raíz', 'tronco', 'rama') becomes more pervasive. The concept of purity of blood, unconnected with *hidalguía* in the earlier sixteenth century, becomes very much tied up with it by about 1570. That in turn brought the maternal line into the forefront of genealogical investigation. The genealogies, the ancestral memories, the family histories related in the proofs become longer, more remote, more glorious. Lineage connections are enshrined in a cascade of family names. In 1631, Juan Pérez Moreno de Mesa, the son of Juan Pérez Moreno de Mesa Cárdenas Alvarez Boorques y Gimeno and Doña Isabel de Montoya Palma y Marín, applied for *hidalguía*, and traced every single one of his parental lines.[53] The language of nobility becomes more profuse, more 'baroque'. Mere *hidalgo* is not enough; it has to be 'hombre noble caballero hijodalgo'. There is a proliferation of titles and of ranks; the *vizconde* appears, and three grades of grandeeship. There is a riffling turnover of titles as men rise from *señor* to *vizconde* to *conde*

---

[53] AGS DGT Inventario 5, leg. 2, f. 68.

to *marqués* and, not satisfied with one title, must become *Cardenal-Duque, Conde-Duque, Duque-Duque-Conde.*[54]

It is as if society was being de-individualized, the self dissolved into the family, the lineage, and the title, and personal characteristics erased by status. Graduates, who in the sixteenth century would always have called themselves *licenciado*, are in the seventeenth commonly using only the 'Don', and there are even army captains not using their titles. Wealth and poverty – mere accidents – seem also to be regarded with increasing indifference in the seventeenth century. This obsession with blood and lineage has been seen by historians as an aspect of 'refeudalization', a 'reaction of the society of orders' to a period of rapid social mobility and what has been called 'the social devaluation of *hidalguía*'.[55] It has been seen variously as an instrument of social exclusiveness, a 'closing of nobility', an attempt to shore up the social order by constructing a new justification for a demilitarized and unmilitary aristocracy, and the consequence of the collapse of the 'bourgeois alternative' in the sixteenth century.[56] It may also be related to the economic and moral crisis of Castile, one manifestation of a loss of confidence in the present and a flight back to past glories and traditional values. It could not have occurred, however, without the documentary revolution which took place from the middle of the sixteenth century or so. The reconstruction of ancient lineages became possible only when families could overcome the limitations of memory. The preservation of records of baptisms and marriages, notarial deeds of entail, marriage settlements and wills, the accumulation of 'executive letters', and the plethora of local and family histories and genealogies made it possible to prove affiliation documentarily and hence to escape the stranglehold of collective memory and public repute. Once fixed in the documents, the cult of lineage could overcome the vagaries of vulgar recognition and community acceptance; but it could do so only because it was itself the complete apotheosis of 'vulgar' values (Diego de Valera).[57]

By the end of the seventeenth century, this hypertension is showing

---

[54] A. Cánovas del Castillo, *Estudios del reinado de Felipe IV* (2 vols, Madrid, 1888–9), vol. 2, p. 372, of Medina de las Torres.

[55] Maravall, *Poder, honor y élites*, p. 73; Gutiérrez Nieto, 'Limpieza de sangre y antihidalguismo', p. 509.

[56] Fayard and Gerbet, 'Fermeture de la noblesse', p. 75; Maravall, *Poder, honor y élites*, pp. 102, 216; B. Bennassar, *Los Españoles, actitudes y mentalidad* (Barcelona, 1976), p. 123.

[57] 'Espejo de Verdadera Nobleza', *Biblioteca de Autores Españoles*, vol. 116, p. 100.

signs of subsiding, and in the eighteenth century a new and radically different social vocabulary begins to emerge.[58] First of all, the need to seek justification for *hidalguía* in feats of arms and service in war ceases to be so pressing. By the last third of the seventeenth century, nearly half of all applicants for *hidalguía* grants do not mention any military services at all; and after 1720, less than one in three offers any sort of military justification. Going too was the feudal language of the 'good and loyal vassal' that had characterized service until the mid-seventeenth century. Personal services to the king and his crown were no longer the only ones being used to justify ennoblement. In the eighteenth century it was also beginning to be possible to escape the obsession with blood and lineage. Whereas in the mid-seventeenth century, over 90 per cent had claimed association with a known, noble manor of the mountains of Cantabria ('solar conocido'), only one-quarter were doing so after 1720, and one-third made no pretence of any family connection with nobility whatsoever. The gaps left by the erosion of traditional values had to be filled by new values and new idioms, the 'bourgeois' virtues of 'unceasing work', 'diligence', 'application', 'integrity', education, and a new utilitarian ideology of service to the public ('la causa pública'), to one's neighbours and to the local community, manifested in public works, the provision of employment, or the paving of the streets and the planting of trees along the Valencia road that Don Manuel del Rio of Ocaña adduced in support of his ennoblement in 1783.[59] 'Utility' was the universal yardstick, measuring noble and commoner alike on a single scale of value; the census-takers of Arnedo in mid-century, for example, estimated that the *vecinos* of their city 'comprise, on the best judgement, the useful [*los útiles*], some $132\frac{1}{2}$; the useless and day-labourers [*los ynútiles y brazeros*], some 500.'[60]

Changes were also taking place in the relationship between the 'estados'. The polarity *hidalgo–pechero* seems to have faded. Instead, the *Catastro* and other censuses of the late eighteenth century and the 'cartas de privilegio' refer to 'el estado noble' on the one hand and to 'el estado general' or 'el estado de los hombres buenos' on the other. Not only is 'el estado pechero' relatively uncommon, but the emphasis on fiscal privilege and exemption from *pechos* as the distinguishing mark of the nobleman, though not entirely disappeared, is very much less prominent. Nobility was no longer being represented in terms that opposed it to

---

[58] For all that follows, see Thompson, 'Neo-noble nobility', pp. 392–5.
[59] AGS DGT Inventario 5, leg. 4, f. 315.
[60] F. Abad León, *Radiografía de Arnedo en el siglo XVIII* (Logroño, 1972), p. 65.

the interests of the community as a whole, and the ennoblement of the rich was no longer, almost by definition, a moral outrage. The correlative of this was the open acceptance of 'bienes de fortuna' as an explicit qualification for ennoblement in the last decades of the century. The wealthy, rather than being oblique and circumlocutory about their money, as in the seventeenth century, were now not ashamed to advertise their riches as a positive merit, and even to put hard figures on their incomes, thus bringing Castilian practice into line with what had been the norm in the Crown of Aragon even in the sixteenth century. Alongside that, it became possible, encouraged by royal legislation in 1783, to declare commerce and manufacturing as activities compatible with honour and as contributions to the public good worthy of honouring. Conditions of economic growth in the eighteenth century could enable the rich man to be seen not as anti-social but as a public benefactor.

The tendency to polarize society into rich and poor was, of course, nothing new to the eighteenth century, though eighteenth-century expressions of that polarization seem to be exceptionally stark – 'the rich are the masters and the poor the slaves.'[61] What is different in these years, in comparison with the predominant feeling of the previous 200 years, is the concern to increase the numbers of the nobility and the conviction that, for political and economic reasons, new wealth ought to be rewarded with noble status.[62]

In the eighteenth century, one has a sense of a realignment of social relationships. On the one hand, there is a rise in the status of the commons, recognized politically in the local government reforms of the 1760s and socially in the willingness of some new *hidalgos* to admit to 'honrado' and Old Christian, 'labrador' origins. On the other, there is a bridging of the gulf between *hidalguía* and 'el estado general' as

---

[61] Diego de Bohorquez to Campomanes, Granada, 27 Jan. 1766: 'estando en España tan mal repartidos los bienes con que Dios enriqueció la tierra, nos hemos vuelto unos polacos, que los ricos son los amos y los pobres los esclavos,' in M. Aviles Fernández and J. Cejudo López (eds), *Pedro Rodríguez de Campomanes: Epistolario, tomo 1 (1747–77)* (Madrid, 1983), p. 140.

[62] Ibid., p. 383, Rodrigo Ponce: 'Proyecto para multiplicar el número de gente noble en España,' 14 Sept. 1772; p. 385, Miguel de Muzquiz to Campomanes, 10 Oct. 1772; p. 401, Campomanes to Muzquiz, 26 Oct. 1772: 'Nunca conviene cerrar la puerta a la concesión de algunas hidalguías, porque hay hombres tan acaudalados en los pueblos, que conviene honrarlos, para que se establezcan solidamente y fomenten en ellos su industrial . . . Cuando una familia enriquece demasiado, posee un mayorazgo cuantioso y se halla con muchos renteros y colonos, no es fácil contener en la condición de los plebeyos a semejantes personas en una Monarquía, ni en una República Aristocrática.'

theoretically immutable distinctions of blood and lineage give room to individual achievement and purely personal criteria. In the personal listings of the *Catastro*, for instance, the courtesy title 'Don' is divorced from *hidalguía*; there are Dons who are not *hidalgos*, and many *hidalgos* (in some places a majority) who are not Dons. At the same time the language of 'estados' is beginning to weaken. It is difficult to draw up an accurate balance-sheet or a precise chronology, but there seems to be, first, an increasing use of historically neutral terms, such as *condición* ('condition'), and *calidad* ('quality' or literally 'sort'), and then, by the last quarter of the eighteenth century, a widespread use of 'clase'. Most often 'clase' was employed merely as a substitute for 'estado' or to designate a sub-grouping within an 'estado'; 'la clase de notorios hijosdal-go' (1774), 'la clase de caballeros' (1788), 'el estado y clase de ciudadanos' (1778), 'las clases llanas del vecindario' (1793), distinguishing 'comerci-antes en grueso' from 'las demás clases de plebeyos' (Puig); or, as when Melchor de Macanaz demanded in the reign of Philip V, 'that every man dress according to his class, so that one's dress proclaim one's profession and nobles not be confused with plebeians, nor the great with the middling'; or when Ramón Lázaro de Dou wrote in 1800, that 'In all times there has been debate about the compatibility of certain professions or activities with the estate of nobility which, in order to preserve the dignity which should pertain to persons of higher class [*clase superior*], has seemed to require that those who are in that class should abstain from sordid occupations.'[63] In the third edition of the influential *Diccion-ario de la Lengua Castellana*, published by the Royal Spanish Academy in 1791, 'estado' and 'clase' were defined almost interchangeably: 'estado' as 'El órden, clase, gerarquía y calidad de las personas que componen un reino, una república ó un pueblo; como el eclesiástico, el de nobles, el de plebeyos, etc.'; 'clase' as 'Orden ó número de personas del mismo grado, calidad ú oficio; como: la clase de los grandes, de los títulos, de los nobles, &.'[64]

---

[63] AGS DGT Inventario 5, leg. 4, f. 127, 18 Dec. 1774; f. 112, 6 Nov. 1788; f. 94, 25 Oct. 1778; Molas *Burguesía mercantil*, p. 160 (1793), p. 142 (Puig), p. 173 (Macanaz: 'que cada uno viste según su clase para que el vestido diga la profesión y no se confundan los nobles con los plebeyos, ni los grandes con los medianos'), p. 146 (Dou: 'En todos tiempos se ha disputado de algunas profe-siones o exercicios si podían compadecerse con el estado de la nobleza, la qual, para conservar el decoro en que deben estar las personas de clase superior, ha parecido exigir que los que se hallen en dicha clase se abstengan de ministerios sórdidos').

[64] It is interesting to see how definitions had changed since the first edition of the *Diccionario* some sixty years earlier: 'classe' (vol. 2, 1729) – 1. 'Orden

In all these cases, 'clase' introduces no new principle of stratification. On the contrary, 'clase' is frequently associated with quality or birth, as in 'the renown and class of those of our family name' (1778); 'some who are distinguished from the rest by their class and by the fortune of birth' (1801); 'there would be nothing more beneficial than a levelling of all classes and conditions, the result would be that no man would be accorded more virtue than is his due' (1786); 'Of what use is the illustrious class, a high descent, without virtue?' (Jovellanos).[65] It remains essentially a designation of status ('maintaining ourselves . . . with the honour, decency, and form appropriate to our class').[66] But by the end of the century it is beginning to be something more than that. In the 1790s, the enlightened reformer and civil servant Gaspar Melchor de Jovellanos, for one, is applying the term 'clase' to a binary social system based on relationship to the means of production:

> I shall divide the population into two classes: one which labours and the other which is leisured [these he later calls 'the opulent classes, who live of their own and are always at leisure']; I shall include in the former all

---

escogida en alguna materia en que hai diferentes individuos'; 2. 'Orden distinto de personas, que resulta de la division que se hace en las vecindades de alguna Ciudad, Villa o Poblacion, para el gobierno y conocimiento de los individuos, y vecinos que la componen'; 3. 'el grado o calidad que corresponde a la esphera de algunos individuos: como la classe de los Nobles, Hijosdalgo, Doctores, Maestros, Sabios, Politicos, &.'; 4. 'En las Universidades y Estudios se llama el Aula u orden en que se dividen los Estudiantes'; 'estado' (vol. 3, 1732) – 'Vale tambien comunmente la especie, calidad, grado y orden de cada cosa; y por esso en las Repúblicas se distinguen, conocen y hai diversos estados, unos seculares y otros Eclesiásticos, y destos los unos Clérigos y los otros Religiosos, y de los Seculares proprios de la República, unos Nobles y Caballeros, otros Ciudadanos, unos Oficiales, otros Labradores, &, y cada uno en su estado y modo de vivir tiene orden, reglas y leyes para su régimen.' By 1791, 'estado', though still retaining something of the broader sense of the genus (of which the 'clase' was the species), was explicitly conflated with 'clase', and had lost the connotation of a legally ordered way of life, distinguished by formal rules of conduct and prescriptions of the law.

[65] 'La buena memoria, y clase de los de nuestro apellido' (1778); 'algunos que distinguiéndose de los demás por su clase y por la casualidad del nacimiento' (1801); 'nada habría tan favorable como una igualación a nivel de todas las clases y condiciones, de donde resultaría que a ningún hombre se diese más valor que el que tuviera por si mismo' (1786); '¿De qué sirve La clase ilustre, una alta descendencia Sin la virtud?' (Jovellanos): AGS DGT Inventario 5, leg. 4, f. 94; Molas, *Burguesía mercantil*, p. 148; A. Dominguez Ortiz, *Sociedad y Estado en el siglo XVIII Español* (Madrid, 1976), p. 355.

[66] 'Manteniéndonos . . . con honor, decencia, y conveniencia correspondientes a nuestra clase': AGS DGT Inventario 5, leg. 4, f. 94.

the professions which live by the product of their daily work, and in the latter those which live by their rents or their safe investments . . . . It is true there will still be many people in the middle, but they will always belong to one class or the other, depending on whether their situation tends more or less towards occupation or idleness.[67]

Jovellanos's model of society is a long way from that of Cobarruvias, whose 'ciudadano' estate also lived off its rents, but which included the 'professions' and was distinguished as an 'estado medio', not only from 'los oficios mecánicos', but also from the 'caballeros' and 'hijosdalgo'. Jovellanos, much influenced by the writings of Cantillon, Turgot, Condillac, and, above all, Adam Smith, may be exceptional.[68] Given the general lack of new content in the word, it is uncertain what significance should be given to the adoption of the new idiom of 'clase'. The phenomenon has not been studied to my knowledge, or even noted. It may not be much more than a modish imitation of the French or the English. It is perhaps best, therefore, to take it to mark not so much a clear perception of a new social order as a mental retreat from the old. It is none the less interesting that the same terminological development occurred at much the same time in England, France, and Spain, societies of a very different nature which were undergoing very different experiences of economic and social change. The movement away from the language of 'estados' and 'brazos' was sometimes part of, sometimes merely the concomitant of, a radical critique of a social order that had been based on the ideal of a harmonious, organic community of interdependent, hereditary functions, distinguishing men in honour and respect by virtue of birth and lineage and embodying their status in legal rights and privileges. That society had never really been like that, never static nor closed to merit and mobility, did not mean that the new terminology was not part of a process of releasing individualist, competitive, self-made values from homage to the social ideals that the traditional vocabulary had enshrined.

What is not clear is how far and how quickly these linguistic changes

---

[67] 'Memoria para el arreglo de la policía de los espectáculos y diversiones públicas' (1790/96), in G. M. de Jovellanos, *Espectáculos y Diversiones Públicas Informe sobre la Ley Agraria*, ed. J. Lage (Cátedra, Madrid, 1977), pp. 117, 123.

[68] Gaspar Melchor de Jovellanos (1744–1811) was one of the most notable figures of the Spanish Enlightenment. An ecclesiastic, he was born of an ancient Asturian family with a modest estate, and followed a university and legal career as a high-court judge in Seville and Madrid, where he was closely associated with a team of enlightened aristocratic reformers in the government of Charles III, especially Campomanes and Floridablanca.

penetrated the society they were describing. There may well be regional and strata differences which it is not possible at the moment to identify. It is striking that many, though not all, the users of 'clase' are Valencian and Catalan. In the backwaters, away from the mainstream of industrial and commercial activity, society, values, and language may have been more resistant to change. That certainly was the opinion of the reformers themselves. The 'modernization' of honour was essentially a movement engineered from above by reformers and a reforming government intent on constructing a new social harmony, based on utilitarian functions to replace the natural harmony of the now largely defunct *corpus mysticum*.[69] The imposition of new values from above and the redrawing of the economic lines of social division upwards plutocratized nobility, and turned the entire institution of nobility into something alien to the traditional values of the community.

As the reformers themselves realized, the regeneration of Castile through the transformation of social values could not proceed against the conservatism of popular sentiment. 'The whole evil lies in the persuasion of the vulgar,' one complained in 1781.[70] 'Ideas have changed, it is true,' wrote another a few years later, 'but only among the writers . . . the people remains always immutable.'[71] In one sense, then, the failure of social reform, perhaps even the inconsistency with which it was pursued, was simply a recognition of the ineradicability of the 'vulgar' and populist conviction that regalist writers had been trying to combat for centuries: 'The king may make knights, but he cannot make gentlemen.'[72]

Clearly language is not something entirely divorced from its social context; but, equally clearly, words have lives of their own. For 500 years, and despite all the political, economic, and social changes that took place between the last centuries of the *Reconquista* and the ending of the *ancien régime*, the language of 'estates' remained the dominant idiom of social description in Castile. The language of 'class', lacking the residual, normative resonances of 'estados' and denoting a more

---

[69] Richard Herr, *The Eighteenth-Century Revolution in Spain* (Princeton University Press, Princeton, 1958), is still the fullest and best general English-language account of the reformers and reform in eighteenth-century Spain. Specifically on attitudes to nobility, W. J. Callahan, *Honor, Commerce and Industry in Eighteenth-Century Spain* (Harvard Graduate School of Business Administration, Boston, 1972) is particularly informative.

[70] J. Guillamón Alvarez, *Honor y honra en la España del siglo XVIII* (Madrid, 1981), p. 162, quoting Pedro Antonio Sánchez.

[71] V. Palacio Atard, *Los españoles de la Ilustración* (Madrid, 1964), p. 59.

[72] Valera, 'Espejo', p. 100.

material objectivity of classification, carried greater potential for the description of post-*ancien-régime* society, in the same way that 'caballero' survived the abolition of the legal privileges of nobility, whereas 'hidalgo', which was too specifically a legal concept, did not. Yet the rise of 'clase' antedated the decisive change in the nature of Castilian society, and did not initially carry the distinctive sense of a particular relationship to the means of production that it was to acquire. To put it another way, changing social realities did not so much create a new social vocabulary as expand the content of the vocabulary that already existed. Both 'estado' and 'clase' were able to contain different social circumstances through an expansion of meaning. Yet, at the same time, both were tied to the string of meanings they trailed behind them – hence the imprecision in their use but, at the same time, their adaptability and their survivability.

4

Definitions of nobility in seventeenth-century France

Roger Mettam

During the reign of Louis XIII, from 1610 to 1643, the definition of social groups was the principal topic in the Parisian and provincial salons frequented by the *beau monde*. Later in the century, many great nobles, both male and female, would pen their own observations on the nature of society, but in these earlier days it was more usual for them to commission men of lesser rank, who would present written arguments on current social issues. These documents would be read by, or read to, the members of a salon, as the starting-point for a civilized, courteous, but often passionate discussion. Writers of many kinds were employed to this end. Political theorists presented philosophical justifications, jurists expounded the long-term legal traditions, and playwrights dramatized the problems by weaving contemporary disputes into their classical and medieval plots. The passion in the ensuing *conversazioni* was engendered by the knowledge that new social forces were threatening the stability of the established hierarchical order.[1]

---

[1] The arguments about nobility and social status are discussed at some length in Davis Bitton, *The French Nobility in Crisis, 1560–1640* (Stanford University Press, Stanford, Calif., 1969) ; and in F. E. Sutcliffe, *Guez de Balzac et son temps: littérature et politique* (Paris, 1959). For the reign of Louis XIV, the best survey of social attitudes is contained in the more widely ranging book of Antoine Adam, *Grandeur and Illusion: French literature and society, 1600–1715*, tr. H. Tint (Weidenfeld, London, 1972). These three books are chiefly concerned with the opinions of writers – jurists, pamphleteers, poets, and playwrights – but occasionally nobles and members of other social groups voiced their own views at some length. One such instance is described by J. Michael Hayden, *France and the Estates General of 1614* (Cambridge University Press, Cambridge, 1974). Lastly, the lifestyles and priorities of this aristocratic age are vividly

The perceived dangers came from two different directions. First, the king and his ministers were subtly encroaching upon the corpus of aristocratic and clerical privileges, because these rights and liberties sometimes hampered the Crown in carrying out its tasks of protecting the realm, promoting order, giving good justice, raising adequate finance to sustain effective government, and stimulating certain kinds of economic activity.[2] The second threat came from below, because there was the problem of incorporating a new stratum of society into the traditional hierarchy of social categories. A novel but very influential group, the upper bureaucracy, whose members claimed to be noble and had already acquired the right to pass on their offices to their heirs, had to be assimilated. The old nobility, with its military origins and its emphasis on the chivalrous virtues of honour and valour, was not prepared to recognize these bureaucrats as equals, even though the offices they held did, in their own eyes and in those of the king, entitle them to be considered as noble.

In the early seventeenth century, the simplest and most generally accepted way of classifying French society was by recourse to the tripartite medieval division into estates of the realm. The First Estate was that of the clergy, underlining the superiority of the spiritual world over the temporal. The Second was composed of the nobility, and the Third included everyone who was neither a cleric nor a noble. The alternative term of the 'three orders' was also frequently used, but it carried no additional subtlety of meaning. The estates-general and the smaller *assemblée des notables* – the two institutions to which the king could summon representatives from all parts of the kingdom – also preserved the division into three estates. The *assemblée* did contain a fourth group, drawn from the upper levels of the judicial bureaucracy, but only a few of the publicists engaged by these office-holders were so bold as to suggest that this was indeed a Fourth Estate. The traditional estates were quick to refute such assertions. The estates-general was not called after 1614, until the revolutionary days of 1789, and the *assemblée* did not meet between 1626 and 1787. Even before the meeting of 1614,

---

revealed in Norbert Elias, *The Court Society*, tr. E. Jephcott (Blackwell, Oxford, 1983).

[2] See David Parker, *The Making of French Absolutism* (Arnold, London, 1983), pp. 1–96; Roger Mettam, *Power and Faction in Louis XIV's France* (Blackwell, Oxford, 1988), pp. 45–134; and on the financial problems of the Crown, Richard Bonney, *The King's Debts: finance and politics in France, 1589–1661* (Clarendon Press, Oxford, 1981), pp. 73–192.

the larger gathering had been called only infrequently, and the grievances and petitions which the nobility and the Third Estate presented to those meetings overwhelmingly reflected provincial concerns. These two orders had acquired no national sense of purpose, any more than the varied and disparate French provinces felt themselves to be part of a single nation. Only the clergy continued to meet more regularly in their *assemblées générales du clergé*, and even at those occasions the peripheral parts of the kingdom were not represented.

The provincial *états*, unlike the estates-general, did assemble annually or every few years in some parts of France, mostly those which had been incorporated relatively recently into the kingdom and were proud of their separate identity. They cherished their distinct traditions, customs, laws, privileges and in some cases their dialect or different language. These areas included the large and important provinces of Brittany, Burgundy, Languedoc and Provence. At most of these gatherings the three estates participated on equal terms, in the sense that either each had the same number of delegates or each had a single collective vote. Only in Languedoc were the meetings constituted in the manner ultimately to be adopted for the estates-general in 1789, whereby the Third Estate was doubly represented and, since the deputies voted as individuals, therefore equalled the combined voting strength of the nobility and the clergy.[3]

As categories to classify the whole of French society, each estate contained a wide variety of people. The First encompassed the regular orders of monks and nuns; the archbishops and bishops, who were usually drawn from leading aristocratic houses; and the lowly parish priests, who were often of similar background to their humble parishioners. Yet it was only the higher clergy which provided the delegates at meetings of estates and assemblies. The Second included all members of the *noblesse d'épée*, the sword-bearing nobles whose titles could be traced back, often over many centuries, to some outstanding act of service to the Crown and normally one of military valour. Here too there was a great disparity of wealth and rank, from the illustrious princely or ducal houses to the humble provincial noble. Nevertheless, membership of these two estates carried great privileges for everyone, not least exemption from paying most of the direct taxes. The socially

---

[3] The most detailed examination of these bodies is that of J. Russell Major, *Representative Government in Early Modern France* (Yale University Press, New Haven and London, 1980). The ecclesiastical assemblies are discussed by Pierre Blet, *Le clergé de France et la monarchie: étude sur les assemblées générales du clergé de 1615 à 1666* (2 vols, Rome, 1959).

ambitious bureaucratic nobility, so bitterly resented by the sword aristocracy, had no place in the Second Estate. Its only position in the traditional hierarchy was, to its indignation, among the motley members of the Third. Accordingly, on occasions such as the 1614 meeting of the estates-general, it preferred to voice its demands and opinions through the most prestigious tribunal within its own sphere of influence, the parlement of Paris, rather than join in the debates of the Third.[4]

The term *tiers état*, the Third Estate, had a variety of meanings according to the context in which it was used. In its broadest sense it included all laymen of non-noble status. At meetings of the provincial estates, its representatives were drawn exclusively from the bourgeois elite, usually the mayors of designated towns who had themselves been elected to their high municipal office by a narrow upper stratum of the citizenry. The word *bourgeois* was equally ambiguous. It might be used to describe all urban dwellers or only the more substantial townsmen or an even narrower elite which had been granted the privileges of *bourgeoisie* – notably the right of exemption from certain taxes. The Parisian bourgeois, in this most restricted sense of the word, claimed as one of his privileges that when he was involved in litigation, no matter where the dispute had arisen, the case could be heard only by the courts of the capital city which alone had jurisdiction over him, a piece of arrogance which was rejected by proud provincial tribunals. To the citizen who had acquired this high status of being bourgeois, it was an appellation of which he could be proud. Yet, when the duc de Saint-Simon described the ministers of Louis XIV as the sons of bourgeois – which the duke incidentally knew to be factually incorrect – he intended it to be a vile insult.[5]

If these imprecise terms presented few problems for the men of the time, because the context made the meaning clear, that did not prevent numerous squabbles among members of each estate and between estates about the criteria for evaluating social status and the exact order of precedence to be adopted on public and private occasions. The king was undeniably at the head of the French social pyramid, although the precise relationship between monarch and pope was a matter of dispute. Below this exalted level, there was less agreement about the precise configuration of the hierarchy. Cardinals and papal nuncios claimed a contro-

---

[4] See the references to the parlement of Paris in Hayden, *France and the Estates General*.

[5] See Louis de Rouvroy, duc de Saint-Simon, 'Lettre anonyme au roi', (Apr. 1712), in *Écrits inédits de Saint-Simon*, ed. M. P. Faugère (8 vols, Paris, 1880–93), vol. 4.

versial supremacy over all nobles who were not of the French blood royal. It was no coincidence that so many ministers – for example Richelieu, Mazarin, Dubois and Fleury – sought and received the red hat, which thereby gave them social as well as political superiority.

Among the nobility, problems of precedence were posed by the illegitimate members of both the Bourbon dynasty and the preceding house of Valois. Another focus for social controversy was the group of 'princes étrangers', 'foreign princes', great aristocrats who acknowledged the suzerainty of the king of France but who, because they came from families which had exercised sovereign power in the past or continued to do so in other parts of Europe, insisted on being ranked above all native French nobles of non-royal birth. Some of these princes, like those of the house of Lorraine, could demonstrate their relationship to a sovereign house without difficulty, although that did not make their demand for social pre-eminence any more palatable. Others could not even gain general acceptance for their claim, as in the case of the ducs de La Rochefoucauld, who insisted that their current ranking among the French dukes was incorrect and that they should be recognized as descendants of the sovereign princes of Marcillac.

Within the native nobility too, there were many disagreements about the relative status of individual families. There were conflicting theories about the criteria for assessing noble worth, and each house selected the arguments best suited to its own position and its past history. The duc de Saint-Simon, who as a *duc et pair* was on the highest rung of the French aristocratic ladder, preferred to stress the current rank of a noble in the hierarchy rather than the antiquity of his lineage, because his own family had been ennobled only in recent times.[6] Others, perhaps only *comtes* rather than *ducs* but with a direct line of noble succession stretching back to 1400 and beyond, insisted that the length of continuous nobility was a better test of worth than the titles and positions held by the latest generation of the family. The year 1400 was widely accepted as the date which conferred undoubted respectability on an aristocratic genealogy. Nevertheless, all these nobles agreed that the *noblesse* was a military elite in origin, and that the bearing of arms in support of the sovereign remained its principal function in the kingdom. Service in the bureaucracy could not be a qualification for ennoblement.

Many of the disputes about precedence and privileges, whether between members of the same or of different estates, led to prolonged

---

[6] Ibid., and Saint-Simon, 'Projets de retablissement du royaume de France', in *Écrits inédits*, vol. 4.

lawsuits and to the interminable lobbying of local dignitaries, royal ministers and great nobles, in the hope that they might lend their support to one of the parties in the quarrel. Often these battles could not be resolved, because both sides could produce convincing, if conflicting, evidence to support their pretensions, but the more important point was for them to be seen to be defending their rights and liberties against every challenge even though an ultimate victory was unlikely. Such rivalries also caused delays in the planning of processions and ceremonies, and perhaps disruption when these events took place. The participants – clerical, noble, judicial, municipal – might not agree on the order in which they should speak at a debate, sit in an assembly or enter a building.[7] Sometimes doorways had to be widened, the furnishings of rooms rearranged or new entrances constructed, so that rival elites did not have to concede superiority to others. On one occasion a corps of judges took clandestine action during the hours of darkness so that, when morning came and a procession was due to enter the assembly room, the provincial nobles found not only that the judges were sitting in the seats that they themselves intended to occupy, but that these intruders were locked behind a newly constructed iron grille and therefore could not be dislodged from their self-appointed position of precedence.

It was generally acknowledged by the social elites that an elected mayor or royal judge was given added status by the office he held, and had accordingly risen above the position in society to which he was entitled on personal and family grounds. It was the extent of that rise which remained a matter of contention, among both rival office-holders and other elite groups. Some historians have ridiculed these disputes, especially those that took place at the royal court, where courtiers of high birth competed for apparently trivial roles in the increasingly elaborate etiquette and ceremony. But such a verdict is unimaginative and unhistorical. These battles for precedence and ceremonial advantage were the outward manifestations of deep rivalries between individuals, families,

[7] See, e.g., the duc de Bourbon to Colbert, 18 June 1662, in *Correspondance administrative sous le règne de Louis XIV*, ed. G. B. Depping (4 vols, Paris, 1850–5), vol. 1, pp. 426–31. Sometimes these rivalries could erupt into violence, even among prelates; see letters from the archbishop of Toulouse to Colbert, 12 and 14 Feb. 1665 (ibid., pp. 182–9). The rivalries among the provincial elites are explored further in Roger Mettam, 'Power, status and precedence: rivalries among the provincial élites of Louis XIV's France', *Transactions of the Royal Historical Society*, 5th ser., 38 (1988), pp. 43–62.

clientèles and institutions, as they defended or sought to enhance their status, privileges and administrative powers.

Compared with these frequent and fervent altercations, which had a long pedigree in preceding centuries and were a familiar feature of *ancien régime* life, the problem posed by the new bureaucratic nobility, the *noblesse de robe*, was of an altogether more massive scale and significance.[8] It was not a disagreement about individual rights, but a fundamental challenge to the whole ethic of nobility. These *robins* had earned their noble titles and privileges by working in the administration, a criterion which no military *noble d'épée* could accept. There had always been occasional newcomers to the ranks of the sword, most of them acceptable because they had shown valour in battle, a few not so but nevertheless irresistible because they were royal ministers or favourites. That was very different from the inclusion among the nobility of a large group of office-holders, who lacked any military qualifications and virtues. Even more offensive was the fact that the bureaucrat could pass on his office to his heirs, so that all his descendants could also claim to be noble.[9] The old aristocracy was quick to denounce these men as *parvenus* and bourgeois, no matter how prestigious the offices they held. The only true source of *noblesse* was to be found in military prowess, displayed on one or more occasions. Such bravery led to the granting of the original title by the monarch, after which the whole family observed the traditional aristocratic ethic by pursuing further honour and glory. They thus built up a stock of cumulative virtue which was passed down the generations and might lead to additional royal patronage. The aristocrat was therefore under an immense obligation to be a worthy member of the Second Estate, and it was accepted that a noble who committed a base act should be punished more severely than a commoner guilty of the same offence. 'Noblesse oblige', and for a man to know virtue and then reject it was outrageous.

The bureaucratic nobles of the *robe* lacked not only military valour but also antiquity of lineage. Their detractors accused them of being unable to comprehend the notions of honour and virtue, and pointed out that most *robin* families had purchased their first office with money

---

[8] The standard work on the venal office-holders is still Roland Mousnier's substantial volume *La vénalité des offices sous Henri IV et Louis XIII* (Rouen, 1946), although some of the inferences he draws from his evidence would not now be accepted by everyone.

[9] For the purchaser, the hereditary element was vital if an office was to be regarded as a secure financial investment in a piece of 'property'.

acquired in the world of commerce and industry.[10] These activities, with their overtones of haggling in the market-place or of manual labour, however skilled, were forbidden by law to the nobility on pain of *dérogeance* – permanent loss of noble rank.[11] Although it was legally possible for an ennobled man to have been a merchant or a craftsman before he achieved his new status, provided that he did not continue to practise his trade or craft after his elevation, the military nobility asserted that this bourgeois lifestyle had left an enduring stain on the reputation of the family which could not be erased by royal grants of *noblesse*. Indeed, the king should never have honoured men of such base stock, and therefore their titles could not be considered as valid. Moreover, whereas the true aristocrat wore the *épée*, not only as a symbol of his military origins but as an indication of his right to defend his own honour on the duelling field, these office-holders were known as *noblesse de robe*, because it was their robes of office which had enabled them to rise into the nobility. This was trebly offensive to the families of the sword. It not only proved that these men lacked valour, but it revealed that they had worked for their living and continued to do so. It was considered totally inappropriate for any noble to work in order to earn money. The third grievance against the *robins* was that the senior judicial officials were eager to claim that they were the sole dispensers of justice in the realm, thereby challenging the privilege of the nobleman both to exercise his own seigneurial jurisdiction and to protect his honour in armed combat.

The members of the *robe* sought to avoid some of the censure heaped upon them by the *noblesse d'épée* through the device of changing their lifestyle. They tried to conform more closely to traditional aristocratic standards of behaviour, although they could not relinquish their offices and earnings. Most of them had abandoned the world of commerce and industry as soon as their family finances had permitted it, often long before their bureaucratic service was sufficiently distinguished to entitle them to noble rank. They purchased landed estates, built lavish town and country houses, and in every possible way portrayed themselves as 'vivant noblement', living nobly. The sword nobles were not impressed by this propaganda, knowing that external display could never compen-

---

[10] As in all these debates, there was an element of exaggeration in this statement, because many office-holders came from families which had acquired their initial fortune in the professions or the financial world, although it was true that a significant proportion had been involved in commerce or crafts at some time.

[11] See Gaston Zeller, 'Une notion de caractère historico-social: la dérogeance', *Aspects de la politique française sous l'ancien régime* (Paris, 1964).

sate for a lack of inner gentility. The *robins* were not slow to defend themselves against the scorn of the socially superior military nobility, some of whose members were impoverished landowners of little account. A literary war raged, conducted not only through the medium of short and pithy tracts, plays and poems, but also in authoritative histories of French institutions and society, compiled by partisan jurists who proclaimed their objectivity while subtly advancing the claims of either *robe* or *épée*.[12]

The upper levels of the bureaucracy, especially the judges of the parlement of Paris, which was the most prestigious appeal court in the kingdom, asserted not only that they were full members of the nobility but that they occupied a high position in the aristocratic hierarchy. The parlement, annoyed that its judges were not considered by the *épée* to be part of the Second Estate, went further, and insisted that it was superior to the entire estates-general, because it was traditionally the mediator between the king and all his subjects, whatever their rank. The *parlementaires* claimed that their court was the guardian of the 'lois fondamentales', a group of ancient laws so fundamental to the kingdom that even the king was bound by them. Included among them were the Salic Law, governing the succession to the throne, and the prescription that the monarch could not alienate or abandon part of his realm because it was not his to dispose of.[13] The Crown did not accept these limitations on its authority, and both sides stated their position fiercely in times of crisis. The parlements were equally swift in denouncing the pretensions of the First Estate of clergy, and this rival elite was also in their minds when they asserted their own superiority over the estates-general. The secular judiciary was frequently in dispute with the ecclesiastical courts, and the judges bitterly resented, and challenged whenever possible, the interference of the Holy See in the internal affairs of France. The *noblesse de robe* therefore reminded the Crown of its responsibilities, castigated the First and Second Estates as presently constituted, and disdained to be included in the ranks of the Third.[14]

[12] See, e.g., Antoine L'Oisel, *Institutes coutumiéres* (Paris, 1607); and Charles Loyseau, *Cinq livres du droict des offices avec la livre des seigneuries et celuy des ordres* (Paris, 1614). L'Oisel subtly defended the traditional aristocracy, whereas Loyseau combined an assertion of royal authority with a defence of the *épée* against its *robin* challengers.

[13] See J. H. Shennan, *The Parlement of Paris* (Eyre and Spottiswoode, London, 1968), pp. 151–254; and references to *parlements*, individually and collectively, in Parker, *Making of French Absolutism*.

[14] See Hayden, *France and the Estates General*, esp. pp. 133–7, 140–2, 144–5, 167–9.

The lively disputes between *robe* and *épée* about the nature of nobility did not prevent the two groups from working together on matters of common interest, especially in defence of social or provincial privileges against the encroachments of the royal ministers. Fraternization was also possible as long as the *robin* held a sufficiently prestigious post, although the sword noble would stress that he was inviting the man because of his office, not his *robe* nobility. In Paris society, it was generally agreed that the *présidents* of the parlement were men of immense prestige and status, who could properly be invited by the greatest aristocratic families to *soirées* and entertainments. As the judges were often highly intelligent and well read, it was also appropriate to ask them to the *conversazioni* on political, social and cultural issues which were held in the salons of eminent noble hostesses. Yet in a social milieu in which people received their equals and inferiors, but never visited families of lesser rank, it was extremely rare for a *parlementaire* to play host to a sword noble. The gulf between the two nobilities was also demonstrated geographically. The judges of the parlements undoubtedly built splendid town houses, as grand as those of many old aristocratic families, but they usually did so in a distinct area of the city. Thus in Paris the *épée* populated the *quartier* of the Marais, while the upper *robe* colonized the Ile Saint-Louis.[15]

If the sword nobility had to defend its pre-eminence against the pretensions of the office-holders, it regarded some of the policies devised by royal ministers, especially by Richelieu, as no less threatening. The Crown knew that nobles were essential in the army, where they provided the entire officer corps and were responsible for the recruitment of the soldiery. They were also important in helping to maintain order throughout the kingdom, although in times of crisis they might foment insurrection and behave disloyally. Richelieu made no attempt to undermine most of their cherished privileges, although the exemption of all nobles from most direct taxation made his task of financing lengthy wars an extremely difficult one. Nevertheless these rights and liberties were established in law, and the Crown could not have abrogated them arbitrarily without provoking a major revolt. Moreover Richelieu, him-

---

[15] The best study of a Parisian *quartier* is that of J.-L. Bourgeon, *L'Ile de la Cité pendant la Fronde: structure sociale* (Paris, 1963). Further evidence for the social geography of the Parisian elites can be readily gathered from Frédéric Contet (ed.), *Les vieux hôtels de Paris* (21 vols, Paris, 1908–37); Jean-Pierre Babelon, *Demeures parisiennes sous Henri IV et Louis XIII* (Paris, 1965); and Jean-Pierre Babelon, Michel Fleury, and Jacques de Sacy, *Richesses d'art du quartier des Halles, maison pour maison* (Paris, 1967).

self an aristocrat and a cardinal, did not even consider such a course of action, and indeed used the privileges of both nobility and clergy to build up the power of his own family.[16] Many of these rights were as precious to the *robe* as to the *épée*, because the bureaucratic elite was indisputably noble in the eyes of the law, whatever older military houses might say.

Richelieu therefore concentrated his attack on two fronts where he knew that not all nobles would unite against him. The first of these concerned the power of the princes, both of the French blood royal and from foreign sovereign houses. Their ambitions were particularly offensive to the Crown because, as their family power was based in more than one country, they needed to influence the foreign policy of Louis XIII and Richelieu. They were therefore the only group, apart from the clergy with its international allegiance to Rome, to demand a voice in an area of policy making which was regarded by the Crown as entirely within its own prerogative. Many Frenchmen, including the majority of nobles, welcomed this attack on these illustrious families, who at times destabilized the royal government, especially during the years when a king was a minor; who negotiated with the enemies of France; and who on occasion even encouraged foreign troops to invade French soil.

Yet the sword nobility as a whole, including these princes at one end of the scale and the humble seigneur at the other, was united in its opposition to another policy of Richelieu, the attempt to eradicate duelling. On this issue the *robe* nobles were on the side of the Crown, stressing that all subjects, however highly born, should submit to the authority of the judiciary. For the *épée*, the duty to defend their honour was one of their most cherished rights. Richelieu did not do all that the *robins* would have wished, for he had no intention of eroding the noble's right to exercise seigneurial justice in cases arising from disputes within his own estates, although he insisted that outside these narrow confines the noble should respect the powers of the royal, municipal and ecclesiastical courts. Duelling was more important because it was an issue on which the Crown could strike a symbolic blow against aristocratic independence, and the nobles were accordingly determined to resist such an attack. The edict forbidding the duel, which Louis XIII promulgated

[16] The policies of Richelieu as both minister and promoter of his family are well described in Joseph Bergin, *Cardinal Richelieu: power and the pursuit of wealth* (Yale University Press, New Haven and London, 1985); and Bonney, *King's Debts*, chs 3 and 4, gives a detailed account of the royal finances, with their wider ramifications for policy and government.

in 1626, was neither the first nor the last royal pronouncement on the subject because the practice could not be prevented throughout the realm, but each such decree provoked a vigorous argument between the supporters of the idea that the Crown was the supreme judicial power and the defenders of the traditional aristocratic ideology.[17]

In this, as in other debates about the nature of nobility or the role of the monarch and the configuration of the political and social hierarchy, the partisans did not attempt to examine the middle ground between their opposing positions, nor to establish precise boundaries between their respective rights and powers. Instead they stressed, in uncompromising terms, the fundamental principles on which their own arguments were based. Thus, in the debate about duelling, the sword nobility proclaimed the paramountcy of honour, and the royalists emphasized the total supremacy of the king. Neither side actually spelled out exactly what would happen when the monarch commanded a noble to act in a manner which seemed to him to be dishonourable. The defenders of the noble cause in this dispute enlisted eloquent literary evidence in support of their claims when they added the tragedy of *Le Cid*, by Pierre Corneille, to their propaganda. The great tragedian was in fact rather cautious in his remarks about honour, but the champions of aristocracy declared that the play was a ringing justification of their position. Richelieu too regarded the work as very anti-monarchical in tone, and it was with his support that Jean Desmarets de Saint-Sorlin quickly countered with his own play, *Roxane*, in order that the royalist cause could be presented to the theatre audiences of Paris. In *Le Cid*, Corneille had explicitly stated that 'for just vengeance there can be no punishment,' and had added: 'in order to preserve everything that I esteem, to disobey a little is not such a great crime.'[18] Desmarets, by contrast, asserted that 'anyone who attacks his king is guilty of parricide,' and commented: 'when one knows how to rule, one never allows past services rendered to mitigate a serious offence.'[19]

The author of *Roxane* belonged to the most austere of the groups which debated the fundamental nature of *noblesse* in the early seventeenth-

---

[17] 'Edit contre les duels', Feb. 1626, printed in F. A. Isambert (ed.), *Recueil général des lois anciennes françaises depuis l'an 420 jusqu'à la révolution de 1789* (29 vols, Paris, 1822–33), vol. 16, pp. 175–83; see also the edict of Louis XIV of Aug. 1679 on the suppression of duelling (Ibid., vol. 19, pp. 209–13).

[18] Pierre Corneille, *Le Cid*, act II, scenes 8 and 1 respectively. The play was first performed in Dec. 1636 or Jan. 1637.

[19] Jean Desmarets de Saint-Sorlin, *Roxane*, act V, scenes 3 and 8.

century French salons. He and his friends were much influenced by the neo-Stoic ideas which had been expounded most clearly by a priest, Pierre Charron. In his book *De la sagesse*, published in 1601, Charron had insisted that wisdom and human passions were contradictory. 'It is impossible even for Jupiter', he remarked, 'to love, to be angry, to be affected by some passion, and to be wise at the same time.'[20] Desmarets, in a commentary on Seneca, maintained that all grandeur was relative – 'a ship which seems large on a river is tiny when at sea' – and added that nobility was a term appropriate only to men who had a natural disposition towards virtue. 'It is man's spirit which ennobles him if, whether he comes from a cottage or a palace, it permits him to rise above his natural inclinations.'[21] Another neo-Stoic, Jean de Silhon, an early member of the Académie française and a secretary to Richelieu, began a discussion of war with a discourse entitled 'How it is that beasts of the same species do not make war on each other as men do. That uncontrolled passions are the cause of this disorder. That duels are against the law of man and especially against the authority of the prince.'[22]

Corneille was not alone in rejecting the austere creed that virtue could be achieved only by conquering passion. The Dominican bishop of Marseille, Nicolas Coeffeteau, approved of passions if they were used in conjunction with reason to attain desirable ends. He said that the desires of men differed according to their social status, and that the overriding passion of nobles was to seek honour and glory. They wished to enlarge their patrimony in order to bequeath it to their heirs, and the honours they achieved were a legitimate part of this legacy.[23] Jean-Louis Guez de Balzac, a friend of the bishop, glorified the emotions and rebuked the neo-Stoics for disregarding human weaknesses. He accused them of advocating a code of behaviour and a degree of knowledge which were so perfect that they were suited only to angels. True wisdom was rather to appreciate the real nature of man, and then suggest how he should conduct himself.[24]

Guez de Balzac and his friends did not discuss the origin of nobility but only its qualities. François La Mothe Le Vayer, a writer of slightly

[20] Pierre Charron, *De la sagesse*, p. 317 of the 1621 edn.
[21] Jean Desmarets de Saint-Sorlin, *Les morales d'Epictete de Socrate de Plutarque et de Sénèque*, 'Epistres de Sénèque', chs 34 and 36 of the 1653 edn.
[22] Jean de Silhon, *Le ministre d'estat avec le véritable usage de la politique moderne* (Paris, 1632), pt 2, bk 1, discourse 1.
[23] Nicolas Coeffeteau, *Tableau des passions humaines: de leurs causes et de leurs effects* (Paris, 1635), p. 599.
[24] [Jean-Louis Guez de Balzac], *Les oeuvres de Monsieur de Balzac* (2 vols, Paris, 1665), vol. 2, pp. 315–16.

more cynical mien, believed that 'noblesse' was not a natural condition but had been created by societies that wished to laud the virtuous man both when he was in this world and after he had left it. He therefore preserved the link between virtue and nobility, but insisted that virtue faded more rapidly than some apologists for aristocracy were wont to claim. Each generation would have to work very hard in order to maintain and increase the virtuous legacy passed down to it by its ancestors.[25] Even more offensive to the *noblesse d'épée* were the writings of Pierre Fortin de La Hoguette, one of the writers who sought to educate the young Louis XIV in the principles of good government. Fortin accepted the existence of a nobility without question, but advocated the ennoblement of men from the Third Estate who, although they had not displayed military valour, had performed municipal service or had given financial assistance to the Crown.[26] He then launched a fierce attack against the lifestyle of the court aristocracy, listing their vices and castigating their obsession with games of chance.[27] This theme of courtly excess was much favoured by some of the distinguished preachers who delivered sermons before Louis XIV, during his personal rule. The courtiers had to listen to these denunciations from the pulpit of their excessive pride, their frequently corrupt behaviour and their lust for glory, which had caused the unnecessary prolongation of wars.[28] Yet the authors of these sermons, like Fortin, did not challenge the whole notion of a nobility. They accepted the concept of noble virtues, insisting only that they be pursued with moderation and without oppressing lesser men.

Most sceptical of all about the nature of *noblesse* was a circle of writers closely or loosely associated with the Jansenist movement, whose leading spokesmen were Blaise Pascal, Pierre Nicole, and François, duc de La

[25] François La Mothe Le Vayer, 'De la noblesse', in his *Oeuvres* (2 vols, Paris, 1656), vol. 1, pp. 191–2, 197–8.

[26] Pierre Fortin de La Hoguette, *Les elemens de la politique selon les principes de la nature* (Paris, 1663), ch. 19, pp. 361–8.

[27] Pierre Fortin de La Hoguette, *Testament ou conseils fideles d'un père à ses enfans* (Leiden, 1655), pt 2, ch. 27, pp. 175–83, and ch. 29, pp. 194–5.

[28] Notable among them were the Oratorian Jules Mascaron (see, e.g., his funeral oration on the maréchal de Turenne in his *Recueil des oraisons funèbres* (Paris, 1704)); the Jesuit Louis Bourdaloue, whose sermons refer frequently to these topics (see his *Oeuvres* (3 vols, Paris, 1837)); and Jean-Baptiste Massillon, bishop of Clermont, especially the two sermons in his *Oeuvres* (3 vols, Paris, 1856), vol. 2, 'Petit carême', pp. 202 and 246.

Rochefoucauld.[29] Their views on the social elites followed from their attitude to human beings in general. Man was a 'bizarre' creature: credulity and incredulity, rashness and timidity, every pair of contradictory feelings was to be found within him. As for the noble virtues such as the pursuit of honour and glory, these were nothing more than manifestations of vanity and self-esteem. The grandeur of the aristocracy was also a deception, although it undoubtedly deceived both the nobles themselves and those who looked up to them. In the words of La Rochefoucauld, 'nothing flatters us so much as when an aristocrat takes us into his confidence, because we imagine it to be a recognition of our own merit, whereas it is usually a sign of his own vanity or his inability to keep a secret.'[30] Pascal noted that the status enjoyed by a noble rested on a considerable element of chance – not only on accidents of birth and on the marriages made by his ancestors, but also on the decision of the Crown to permit inheritance of rank when it need not have done so. Nevertheless the concept of nobility, although it had no moral justification, was of practical use in society. When ordinary people regarded an elite group with respect, they behaved with humility towards it. Social hierarchies, however spurious their origins, were an effective way of restraining the irresponsibility of the masses. The nobles must therefore play the role which was expected of them, and among their duties should be to dispense in the form of charity the riches which they too often squandered on self-glorification.[31] The worst offenders were the great courtiers, and Nicole remarked that, 'just as the monastic life was devised by the saints as a way to reach Heaven more easily, so the life led by the grandees at court is a means of gaining readier access to Hell.'[32]

These three writers were untypical of their age in that they made references to the poorer strata of society, even if in an unflattering

[29] The classic history of Jansenism remains that of Augustin Gazier, *Histoire générale du mouvement janséniste depuis ses origines jusqu'à nos jours* (2 vols, Paris, 1922); a briefer introduction may be found in the collection of texts by René Taveneaux (ed.), *Jansénisme et politique* (Paris, 1965). There is also the stimulating, if controversial, interpretation by Lucien Goldmann, *The Hidden God: a study of tragic vision in the* Pensées *of Pascal and the tragedies of Racine*, tr. P. Thody (Routledge, London, 1964).

[30] François, duc de La Rochefoucauld, *Reflexions ou sentences et maximes morales* (Paris, 1671), p. 90, no. 239

[31] The first discourse from Blaise Pascal, 'Trois discours sur la condition des grands', 1659/60; published in his *Opuscules et lettres* (Paris, 1956), p. 168.

[32] Pierre Nicole, *De l'education d'un prince* (Paris, 1670), pp. 190–220.

manner. Most social theorists did not mention them at all. The poor sometimes appeared in administrative documents, usually in connection with the foundation of poor-houses. Such institutions were normally founded and maintained, not for charitable motives, but because these potentially seditious members of urban society had to be incarcerated in establishments from which they could not escape. The rural poor would often be cared for in their villages, although they might form roaming bands of vagabonds or seek opportunities, often illusory, for employment in the towns.[33] Occasionally there are documents which categorize impoverished townsmen by their present or former occupations, if these were relevant to the context, but usually bureaucrats used more general terms such as 'la lie du peuple' (the dregs of the people) or, if there had been sedition, riff-raff, rabble, *canaille*. Only Christian thinkers like St François de Sales, St Vincent de Paul and some of the great preachers seriously addressed the problem of the poor, considering these unfortunates as souls in their own right. They emphasized the social teaching of Christ and, in common with Pascal, exhorted the rich to spend their wealth on alleviating the plight of the needy rather than wasting it on worldly vanity. Bourdaloue vividly described the lot of the poor, men weighed down with disease who have no means of regaining their strength, parents watching their children die of hunger or abandoning some of them to a freezing death in order to save a little bread for the others, and girls exposed to the ultimate misfortune. Worst of all were the conditions of galley-slaves and prisoners, miserable creatures confined, and then forgotten, by the rich. Each prison was 'a valley of tears, amidst whose frightening shadows figures burdened with chains turn towards you faces which are the very image of death.'[34]

In the years after 1661, when Louis XIV took personal control of the government on the death of cardinal Mazarin, the fierce arguments about the new and old nobilities died away. *Robe* and *épée* learned to live more harmoniously together, and they had discovered, during the civil wars of the Frondes in 1648–53, that they had many interests in

---

[33] The history of the peasantry in this period is best approached through the book by Emmanuel Le Roy Ladurie, *The French Peasantry, 1400–1600*, tr. A. Sheridan (Scolar Press, Aldershot, 1987), in which he provides a résumé of research by recent scholars.

[34] Bourdaloue, *Oeuvres*, 'Exhortations': an exhortation on charity towards the poor, based on St Luke 8:11: 'semen est verbum Dei'.

common.[35] Yet the main reason for the reduction in tension between the two groups was the determination of Louis XIV to discourage social mobility. Earlier in the century, favoured men had been elevated to high social rank, and, even if they had been very few in number, these social promotions had caused great offence to those who had either been overtaken by *parvenus* or found these intruders entering their own stratum. This practice now ceased, because the king both wished to avoid further provocation of the existing elites and knew that the rapid advancement of some individuals made others equally ambitious. He therefore determined, as he clearly stated in his own *mémoires*,[36] that henceforth all favours would be distributed evenhandedly among meritorious candidates, and that no one should ever be given a post for which he was socially unqualified. Excessive mobility ceased, and most leading members of society were pleased that, although their own opportunities for enhancing the status of their families were curtailed, they were unlikely to be overtaken in the hierarchy of rank and precedence by an inferior house. Louis ensured that examples of this new stability were there for all to see. Thus his trusted ecclesiastical adviser, Jacques-Bénigne Bossuet, remained bishop of Meaux because he lacked the degree of nobility which was essential for promotion to one of the great archbishoprics.[37]

Only the small circle of royal ministerial families received greater rewards than their social origins would have justified, but here too Louis refused to sanction the extravagant promotions seen in earlier reigns. None of the minsters during his personal rule became either a duke or a cardinal. Moreover, these close advisers were always very much at the mercy of the king because, if they fell from grace, their families would lose much of the prestige associated with ministerial power. A truly aristocratic house had its own prestige, acquired through valour, the careful planning of marriages and the grants of high offices and titles by the Crown over many generations. It hoped that the king would honour it further, but even if it forfeited royal favour, no monarch could take

[35] The best book on the Frondes remains that of E. H. Kossmann, *La Fronde* (Leiden, 1954). The detailed course of the civil wars is well summarized by A. L. Moote, *The Revolt of the Judges: the parlement of Paris and the Fronde, 1643–52* (Princeton University Press, Princeton, 1971).

[36] Louis XIV, *Mémoires for the instruction of the Dauphin*, introduction, translation, and notes by Paul Sonnino (Free Press, New York, 1970), pp. 24–5, 30–6.

[37] See Aimé-Georges Martimort, *Le gallicanisme de Bossuet* (Paris, 1953); Augustin Gazier, *Bossuet et Louis XIV: étude historique sur le caractère de Bossuet* (Paris, 1914).

away its illustrious name and status. Louis XIV knew that it was better
to play off the powerful nobles against each other, and to try to retain
their allegiance by spreading his patronage among them all. The alternative was to rely heavily on some of them and ignore the others, in which
case the latter group might make common cause against his government.
It was a lesson he had learned from studying the reign of his grandfather,
Henri IV, who had adhered to a policy of balancing factions, and the
subsequent ministry of Richelieu, who had departed from it. His own
successor, Louis XV, would not continue his policy, and factional
struggles would increase as a consequence, because those who were
denied influence sought ceaselessly to dislodge those in favour. As Louis
XV seemed prone to sudden changes of heart, any great noble house
could hope that one day it might gain the ultimate prizes.[38] Under Louis
XIV it was made clear that no single faction would ever achieve such
dominance.[39]

Although much had been written in the years 1600–61 about the
undesirability of rapid social advance, actual instances of it were always
fewer than the fierce tone of the denunciations might suggest. In particular, the passionate condemnations by aristocrats and their publicists of
mésalliances – marriages between impoverished *épée* and wealthy *robe*
houses – imply that the practice was widespread, whereas it was always
rare and became more so under Louis XIV. No matter how sparse the
funds in the royal treasury, the king could always find money to save
a sword family from the degradation of marrying into the bureaucracy.
Most marriages took place between spouses of remarkably similar backgrounds, the two families seeking to consolidate their position and
influence within their own stratum, rather than to enter a higher one.
These social groups were defined very narrowly so that, for example,
in a municipal elite where the councillors might be drawn from both
merchant and lawyer families, the marriages very seldom crossed the
divide between the mercantile and the professional.[40] Each house would
certainly try to be part of a wider network, with patrons in the upper
levels of society and clients in those beneath, but, if these numerous and

[38] See Peter Campbell, 'The conduct of politics in France in the time of the
cardinal de Fleury, 1723–43' (unpublished Ph.D. thesis, University of London,
1983).

[39] See André Corvisier, *Louvois* (Paris, 1983), esp. pp. 270–323; and Mettam,
Power and Faction, pp. 81–101, 175–203.

[40] See Barbara Diefendorf, *Paris City Councillors in the Sixteenth Century:
the politics of patrimony* (Princeton University Press, Princeton, 1983), pts 3 and
4; Sharon Kettering, *Patrons, Brokers and Clients in Seventeenth-Century France*
(Oxford University Press, Oxford, 1986).

rival clientèles stretched across the social strata, it was most uncommon for an individual drastically to change his own position in the hierarchy. Slow advance was possible, especially as a reward for long service or increased expertise, but the French aristocratic, judicial or municipal family and the extended clientèle were as much concerned to prevent rivals from rising as to improve their own fortunes.

On balance, a static society was safer for everyone. That did not prevent some very wealthy bourgeois from building grand town houses and playing at being noble. Such display may have impressed their own peer group, but it did not gain them entry into polite society. Much of the comedy in the plays of Molière rests on the stupidity of men who aspire to a higher social position than that for which their family background has fitted them. Whether it was mortals aspiring to be gods, valets changing places with masters, or the *bourgeois gentilhomme* attempting to acquire gentility, the message was always the same. The socially superior always outwit their inferiors, because they are more clever, though not necessarily more likeable, than those below.

Wealth was not a criterion in the delineation of social categories, although it was clearly useful to men of all ranks. The rich bourgeois could not buy himself into high society, although he could purchase an office and begin the slow ascent of his family through the bureaucracy until it ultimately became *noblesse de robe*. In the world of the sword nobility, it was generally agreed that the great aristocrats lived in a more lavish style than those lower down the noble hierarchy, and of course the king was the most splendid of all. This visual display was symbolic, and both monarch and aristocracy were quick to rebuke a lower noble whose ostentation was excessive for his rank. By contrast, when a family lacked the resources to sustain the appropriate lifestyle, it had to withdraw from society, in Paris or in the important provincial cities, and live quietly on its country estates until its finances improved. Yet it did not forfeit the lustre associated with its titles and offices. Its *soirées* and salons had ceased, but its prestige endured. As Antoine L'Oisel said earlier in the century, 'poverty is not a vice and does not disennoble.'[41] The First and Second Estates contained men of widely differing financial means, from the extremely rich to the severely poor. Even among the *robe*, for whom money had been essential in purchasing their ennobling offices, there were families of greatly varying fortunes. Among the bourgeois, the municipal administrative elites were the most prestigious but were not always the wealthiest. In seventeenth-century French social

---

[41] L'Oisel, *Institutes coutumiéres*, bk 1, title 1, no. 16 (15).

theory there was no group which was defined in terms of its monetary resources.

In the final decade of the century, some new ideas began to be voiced by a circle of writers who were themselves noble, although their proposed reforms were not welcomed by most members of the privileged orders. Hereditary aristocratic rights were questioned, especially exemption from direct taxation, and it was suggested that all subjects should pay taxes in proportion to their wealth. Noble birth was still to be regarded as important, but merit was also to be essential for advancement – for aristocrats as for everyone else. Policy-making and high administrative posts were to be the exclusive preserve of the upper *noblesse d'épée*, but men were to be selected from that narrow elite on the basis of their talents and not because their family had a long-standing tradition of filling certain positions. These reforming writers also praised the bourgeoisie for its pursuit of financial rewards. Monetary success was to be lauded, not despised, and hard work was to be honoured. Idleness, whether aristocratic or monastic, was a vice. Military prowess and the search for *gloire*, so dear to the nobility, were responsible for the proliferation of wars and much consequential human misery. Indulgence in luxury was an evil, whereas the poor deserved to receive genuine help and consideration.[42] If these novel arguments found no favour with most nobles, they quickly attracted the attention of royal ministers and were developed by a number of eighteenth-century thinkers. These ideas are therefore better regarded, not as the closing stage of the seventeenth-century debate on *noblesse*, but as the first steps towards the political and social theories of the so-called 'French Enlightenment'.

Despite turbulent periods in the relationship between the Crown and its leading subjects, as well as considerable tensions between or within the three estates, the terminology of social debate in seventeenth-century France did not change in any significant way. The First and Second Estates succeeded in preserving their status and their privileges, while both *épée* and *robe* sought to maintain the corpus of aristocratic rights and liberties even though they could not agree about the claim of office-

[42] These writers included the duc de Saint-Simon, the maréchal de Vauban, the comte de Boulainvilliers, and Fénelon, archbishop of Cambrai, all of them members of the circle around the duc de Bourgogne, grandson of Louis XIV and father of Louis XV. For the development of these ideas in the eighteenth century, see *The French Revolution and the Creation of Modern Political Culture*, vol. 1, *The Political Culture of the Old Regime*, ed. Keith Michael Baker (Pergamon, Oxford, 1987).

holders to be classed as noble. The aristocratic ethic remained dominant, although some wished to widen its scale of values to include non-military virtues. None would have denied that virtue and honour were essential attributes of the noble elite, although there was much disagreement on the precise qualities implied by these terms. Ascent into the *noblesse* was still the goal for the wealthy bourgeois, however slow that process might be, and even those thinkers in the 1690s who refused to despise the pursuit of financial rewards did not suggest that wealth conferred social respectability. The problem of whether the *noblesse de robe* could be regarded as true nobles had been posed when the first ennobling offices had been instituted long before the seventeenth century. It was only the scale of this mobility which had changed, as the Crown created numerous offices to solve its financial difficulties. The vocabulary of this debate had therefore been devised many years earlier, and it suited the members of the *robe* to claim that they possessed the traditional aristo-cratic virtues, even though they redefined them, rather than to suggest new criteria for assessing nobility. The social theorists therefore wrote and talked at length about the origins of *noblesse* and its qualities, but they did not seek to devise a more stratified table of social status. The *robe* were not willing to be a second-class nobility, and the *épée* were not prepared to accept them as nobles in any sense. Nor did the theorists attempt to stratify the bourgeoisie, or the Third Estate in general. These vague terms remained in general use, because there were no burning issues which could have been resolved by making the language more precise.

In the seventeenth century, when the Académie française was attempting to prescribe a uniform language for use throughout the kingdom to replace the many provincial dialects and languages which were dominant in extensive regions of France, linguistic variations there-fore became part of the weaponry in the passionate disputes between the provinces and the centre. The proudly separatist areas far from the capital had no intention of accepting a courtly and Parisian language in preference to their own. Yet the vocabulary of social classification did not become entangled in these debates. The definitions of the terms might vary from one province to another – for example, the Norman noble could participate in commerce without permanent loss of rank, whereas the rest of the nobility could not – but the terms themselves were accepted and understood everywhere. The meetings of the estates-general expressed this unanimity very clearly. All delegates accepted the criteria for membership of the First, Second and Third Estates. It was for groups or individuals to prove that they had the necessary qualifi-cations to move from one order into another.

The fiercest public debates were therefore about the rights and privileges of provinces *vis-à-vis* the court and capital or about the demarcation of conflicting jurisdictions.[43] More secretively, but no less passionately, networks of clients and patrons jostled for position in ceaseless rivalry. If these clientèles contained men from different social strata, working together for common or compatible purposes, they felt no impulsion to change the traditional way of classifying society. The line dividing nobles from commoners was sufficiently clear that an ennobled bourgeois had no difficulty in demonstrating that he had crossed it. On the other hand, the disagreements about the criteria of aristocratic worth – whether antiquity of lineage counted for more than the high rank and offices currently held by a family – permitted patrons and clients to claim superiority over a rival clientèle simply by adopting the interpretation most suited to their status and history. Their opponents would never concede victory, of course, and Louis XIV had no desire to arbitrate. He preferred to distribute his patronage skilfully, among all aspirants, so that no one felt affronted but none had triumphed. Everyone could therefore hold his head high, confident that his own arguments justified his claim to a particular place in the social hierarchy.

[43] Many of the linguistic disputes were concerned with the titles of provincial offices. For example, the government referred to the French municipal authorities as mayors and councillors. Toulouse proudly insisted that it had no such officials. It had *capitouls*, and its town hall was the *capitole*, a reminder of its foundation by the Romans, long before Paris and the northern French kingdom had been established. Lyon shared with Paris the distinction of having a *prévôt des marchands* instead of a mayor. If this enabled the Lyonnais to claim that their city was in every way the equal of the capital, they went even further, boasting, accurately, that their archbishop was still the *Primat des Gaules* and, more speculatively, that as a tribute to the pre-eminence of Lyon the name of its Roman founder, Lugdus, had been gallicized as 'Louis' and adopted by fourteen French monarchs.

5

Class by name and number in eighteenth-century Britain

Penelope J. Corfield

'Every nation has its Custom of dividing the People into Classes,' it was observed in 1753.[1] Nor was this claim advanced by a social radical or intellectual innovator. Its author was James Nelson, a London apothecary, whose tract on education and child-rearing was profoundly derivative. There is no suggestion in his text or its reception that he was writing in anything other than stock terms and concepts in circulation in mid-eighteenth-century Britain. He itemized five classes: '*England*, a mix'd Government and a trading Nation, have the Nobility, Gentry, Mercantile or Commercial People, Mechanics, and Peasantry.'[2]

He permitted himself some variation in nomenclature. The same passage continued: 'Were we to divide the People, we might run it to an Infinity: to avoid Confusion therefore, I will select five Classes; *viz.* the Nobility, the Gentry, the genteel Trades (all those particularly which

Grateful acknowledgement for stimulating discussions is owed to research seminars at the Universities of Birmingham, Bristol, London, and Oxford and to the participants at the Anglo-American Conference on Comparative Social History at Williamsburg (Sept. 1985), at which this essay was presented under the title 'The two, the three, the five, and the seven: numbers and concepts of class in eighteenth-century Britain'. It has since been published in *History*, 72 (1987), pp. 38–61. Warmest thanks also to many friends for argument and references, especially to Christopher Hill and F. M. L. Thompson for advice and encouragement and to Tony Belton for judicious goading.

[1] J. Nelson, *An Essay on the Government of Children, under Three General Heads: Viz. Health, Manners, and Education*, (London, 1753), 1756 edn, p. 273. He also suggested that four main social groups were to be identified in France: the 'Quality', the *noblesse*, the artificers, and the peasantry.

[2] Nelson's social commentary came in his section on education, of which one reviewer simply observed, 'under the last head, that of Education, there are few peculiarities': *Gentleman's Magazine*, 23 (1753), p. 509.

require large Capital), the common Trades, and the Peasantry.' He
offered a further clarification of the last term, which, he explained,
referred not only to the guileless country 'Rustics', but also to their
artful urban counterparts, 'the lowest Class of People, in *London* particularly. These People possess indeed the Ignorance of the Peasants, but
they seldom equal them in Innocence.'[3] He detected both social gradations and social flux, summarizing the position in highly eclectic
phrasing: '*England*, a trading Nation, connects more closely the whole
body of the People; links them, as it were, in one continued Chain, and
brings them nearer to a Level.'[4]

The point is not to introduce James Nelson (1710–94) as an unsung
hero of the social sciences, but rather to consider the eighteenth-century
ferment in social terminology that he so well exemplified. It was a period
of expanding vocabulary, experimentation in usage, and fluidity of style
and expression. 'In the disorder of its expressions, we see a people
prepossessed with a range of liberty, which they extend even to their
diction, who would think themselves fettered, in submitting to any
restraints in their language, and enslaved, in subjecting their periods to
the rules either of logic or of grammar,' proclaimed the *Monthly Review*,
with a certain extravagance, in 1771.[5] The production of dictionaries
became a growth industry, albeit always lagging behind 'the boundless
chaos of a living speech', as Samuel Johnson admitted.[6]

There were many proposals for an academy to regulate and standardize
the language, as well as complaints at the intrusion of new words from
France and America.[7] Some people, by contrast, welcomed the flexibility
of an expanding vocabulary. Optimistically, the *Gentleman's Magazine*
in 1788 proposed that 'a proper person or committee be appointed, to
ascertain all such words as are wanting in our language, to convey clearly
and precisely such ideas as naturally arise in the mind of every man.'[8]
Prudently, it refrained from stipulating what those thoughts might be,
while awaiting the clarification of the appropriate neologisms (itself,
incidentally, a term coming into currency in the later eighteenth century).
In such a context, it is not surprising to find that linguistic fluidity

---

[3] Nelson, *Essay on the Government of Children*, pp. 365–6.
[4] Ibid., p. 317.
[5] *Monthly Review*, 43 (1771), p. 529.
[6] Preface to S. Johnson, *A Dictionary of the English Language* (1755), as cited
in M. Cohen, *Sensible Words: linguistic practice in England, 1640–1785* (Johns
Hopkins University Press, Baltimore, 1977), p. 92; see also pp. 88–94.
[7] S. I. Tucker, *Protean Shape: a study in eighteenth-century vocabulary and
usage* (Athlone Press, London, 1967), esp. pp. 33–48.
[8] *Gentleman's Magazine*, 58 (1788), p. 947.

interacted creatively with social changes, both promoting a new vocabulary and conceptual framework for the analysis and interpretation of society itself.

'Class', a powerful organizing concept, then came into use. Contrasting with its later combative and contentious resonance, its arrival was simple. It glided into the language, and for some time it was deployed alongside older terms, sometimes almost interchangeably with them. Increasingly, however, both its sense and its contextual usage began to diverge from the specifications of 'rank and order'. An endless debate about the number and nature of social classes began. And, with that, there developed also a new set of qualifying adjectives, as 'upper, middle, and working' and all their many permutations gradually challenged 'higher, middling, and lower' and their many variants.[9] Social language became, as it has remained, a matter of some sensitivity. An enlightened curate, for example, was depicted, in an undistinguished novel of 1813, as one who always spoke of his *'industrious neighbours, for it was by that appellation, and not as the poor, that he was wont to designate the labouring class of his parishioners.'*[10]

Clearly, many others continued to think and write in highly traditional terms. Numerous variations of the Great Chain of Being were invoked. A well-ordered sequence of ranks and degrees in human society was deemed part of a divinely ordained hierarchy that embraced the whole of creation. None put it more cheerily than Soame Jenyns, who admired the 'wonderful Chain of Beings; . . . from the senseless Clod to the brightest Genius of Human Kind,'[11] although this was in fact rather a heterodox and modern formulation, since traditionally the angels had been placed at the apex. Belief in catenation was reassuring. It offered a model of an interlinked society, in which all components had an allotted role, of equal importance to the grand design but not necessarily of equal power, wealth, or prominence in terrestrial terms. There could

[9] The bibliography is extensive; for a compact general survey, see P. Calvert, *The Concept of Class: an historical introduction* (Hutchinson, London, 1982) and works cited there. The *locus classicus* for English usage is A. Briggs, 'The language of "class" in early nineteenth-century England', in *Essays in Labour History: in memory of G. D. H. Cole*, eds A. Briggs and J. Saville (Macmillan, London, 1960), pp. 43–73: it is illuminating on nineteenth-century formulations, but underestimates the precedent debate in the eighteenth century.

[10] A. Plumptre, *The History of Myself and my Friend: a novel* (London, 1813), vol. I, p. 19.

[11] S. Jenyns, *Disquisition on Several Subjects* (1782), in *The Works of Soame Jenyns, Esq. in Four Volumes*, ed. C. N. Cole (4 vols, London, 1790), vol. 3, p. 179.

be no scope for envy, explained Johnson, for there were 'fixed, invariable, external rules of distinction of rank, which create no jealousy, as they are allowed to be accidental' (i.e. beyond human intervention).[12] The formula applied as much to the political as the social order, soothing Boswell, who had had doubts about a philosophical basis for belief in monarchy.

This cosmography had an ancient lineage, with solid theological backing and a rich imagery.[13] It could also be given a secular and utilitarian gloss. John Trusler argued in 1790 that 'A poor man is equally respectable in society also, if he is a useful member of it; and his equality with the rich is shown and seen by his usefulness. As the servant cannot do without a master, so the master cannot do without a servant. . . . They are equal in point of utility, as members of the same society and subjects of the same state.'[14] That suggested a new caution, from the author of *The Way to be Rich and Respectable* (1766), but even such a mutedly egalitarian emphasis could encourage the very radicalism it sought to allay.

The Great Chain might turn into 'chains', with very different implications. Many traditionalists therefore tended to agree with Jenyns, that belief in the system depended rather upon trust than upon close scrutiny. Ignorance, he had strikingly averred in 1757, was the 'opiate' of the people: 'It is a cordial administered by the gracious hand of providence, of which they ought never to be deprived by an ill-judged and improper education.'[15] In the 1790s, Hannah More, in the guise of 'Will Chip, a country carpenter', comforted the poor man for his lowly condition with the thought that his wife was below him in social ranking, and consoled the wife with her superiority over her children.[16] Any challenge

[12] F. A. Pottle (ed.), *Boswell's London Journal, 1762–3* (Heinemann, London, 1950), p. 320.

[13] The Great Chain or Golden Chain were among the most frequently cited images; Jacob's Ladder was the main alternative, but that was going out of fashion by the eighteenth century, as the notion of ascent to heaven was taken less and less literally. See A. O. Lovejoy, *The Great Chain of Being: a study in the history of an idea* (Harvard University Press, Cambridge, Mass., 1936); and discussion in W. F. Bynum, 'The Great Chain of Being after forty years', *History of Science*, 13 (1975), pp. 1–28.

[14] J. Trusler, *Three Short Letters to the People of England* (London, 1790), p. 6. This book was written specifically in response to events in France, counselling the English people against radicalism and discontent.

[15] S. Jenyns, *Free Inquiry into the Nature and Origin of Evil* (London, 1757), in *Works*, vol. 3, pp. 49–50. His essay was reviewed critically by Samuel Johnson, who pointed out logical problems in notions of a strictly graded hierarchy of beings throughout the universe.

[16] [H. More], *Village Politics, Addressed to all the Mechanics, Journeymen, and Day Labourers in Great Britain, by Will Chip, a Country Carpenter*, 8th

to universal hierarchy was deemed futile. 'Believe me, Sir, those who attempt to level never equalise!', exhorted Edmund Burke in a famous phrase, also written in 1790. He elaborated: 'In all societies, . . . some descriptions must be uppermost,'[17] although he did not therefore draw the conclusion that social conservatives should never worry.

Composed and finite, the vision of the Great Chain of Being refuted the pressures and tensions within the system; but it could not give a very satisfactory account of their provenance, other than by appeal to original sin. Worryingly, such tensions seemed to be found in some abundance in eighteenth-century Britain. There were many references to a palpable sense of social mutability. It was not expressed simply, or even chiefly, in terms of case-histories of individual mobility, but rather in very generalized terms. Often stressed were innovations in dress and deportment, 'externals' that were of significance for rapid social assessment in an emergent mass society, in which individuals were not necessarily known to one another by birth and background.[18] A common eighteenth-century ballad version of the traditional popular satire 'The world turned upside down' related to the mutabilities of fashion. Susanna Blamire's poem, written c.1776, rehearsed what had become a familiar theme:

> All things are changed, the world's turned upside down,
> And every servant wears a cotton gown.[19]

---

edn (London, 1793), in idem, *Works* (6 vols, London, 1833/4), vol. 2, p. 227. It follows a fictional exchange between Tom Hod (a mason), who asserts, 'I say all men are equal. Why should one be above another?' and Jack Anvil (a blacksmith), who replies, 'If that's thy talk, Tom, thou dost quarrel with Providence and not with the Government.'

[17] E. Burke, *Reflections on the Revolution in France* (London, 1790), 1979 edn (Penguin, Harmondsworth), p. 138.

[18] See references in P. J. Corfield, 'Walking the city streets: the urban odyssey in eighteenth-century England', *Journal of Urban History*, 16 (1990), pp. 132–74.

[19] S. Blamire, *Stoklewath: or, the Cumbrian village* (written c.1776?; publ. 1842), in *The New Oxford Book of Eighteenth-Century Verse*, ed. R. Lonsdale (Oxford University Press, Oxford, 1984), p. 647. The satirical tradition of 'The world turned upside down' or 'the world turned topsy-turvy' had long been represented in European popular song and prints, associated with ideas of inversion and misrule (prints showed a horse riding a man, a baby nursing its mother, etc.), and had some currency in eighteenth-century Britain, including use as an inn-sign: see G. Böhmer (ed.), *Exhibition Catalogue: Die Verkehrte Welt* (Goethe Institutes, London, Amsterdam, and Munich, 1985). The concept also had a sharper application in periods of political upheaval: see C. Hill, *The World Turned Upside Down: radical ideas during the English Revolution* (Temple Smith, London, 1972), p. 86 and *passim*. Reportedly, also, the tune of 'The world turned upside down' was played at the British surrender at Yorktown in 1781.

Difficulties in social recognition, especially in the crowded cities, led to a decline of 'hat honour' and a much attenuated public expression of inter-personal deference.[20]

Contemporary references to change are by no means conclusive. They could be exaggerated, whether consciously or unconsciously, or simply erroneous. It sometimes happens that new developments seem more momentous to those living through them than they do to subsequent generations and to the verdict of history. Furthermore, no doubt some people in eighteenth-century Britain considered that little or nothing had changed, although they tended to be less vocal. Yet the public mood pointed to innovation, whether endorsed as 'improvement' or denounced as 'moral degeneration'. And such viewpoints, however diversified in expression, were not alternatives to 'social realities' but an intrinsic part of them.[21]

Prominently emphasized were three developments. One related to the growing diversity in sources of wealth and status. Jonathan Swift, for example, lamented in the *Examiner* in 1710 that '*Power*, which according to an old maxim was used to follow *Land*, is now gone over to *Money*.'[22] His point was exaggerated, for land and landed titles retained a considerable allure as well as affluence; but, visibly, there were alternative avenues of advancement. Trade, commercial services (especially banking), some professions, government, and, increasingly, industry, were all admired in the eighteenth century for their potential power and riches. Diversity encouraged a notable social competitiveness. 'As soon as you mention anyone to them [the English] that they do not know, their first inquiry

---

[20] The wearing and doffing (or not doffing) of headgear was socially very sensitive, as witness the impact of the early Quakers' refusal to remove their hats in the presence of social superiors: Hill, *World Turned Upside Down*, pp. 198–9. In the eighteenth century, formal 'hat honour' seems to have been on the wane, at least in the towns: see references in P. J. Corfield, 'Dress for deference and dissent: hats and the decline of hat honour', *Costume*, 23 (1989), pp. 64–79.

[21] This approach therefore rejects any dichotomous sundering of 'perceptions' and 'realities'. Viewpoints, even if shown to be erroneous, are not thereby rendered 'unreal'. This is a key point: the discussion looks at interpretative concepts in their full historical context, without discounting either the importance of ideas and words or that of social configurations. For linguists' debates about diachronic analysis of language change, see T. Bynon (ed.), *Historical Linguistics* (Cambridge University Press, Cambridge, 1977), p. x, where the historian's approach seems closest to the 'transformational-generative' model.

[22] J. Swift, in *The Examiner*, 13 (1710), updating James Harrington's proposition that 'such . . . as is the proportion or balance of dominion or property in land, such is the nature of the empire', *Oceana* (London, 1659).

will be, "Is he rich?"' claimed de Saussure in 1727.[23] Landowners were not alone in social eminence or claims to gentility. 'We Merchants are a Species of Gentry, that have grown into the World this last Century,' quoth Steele's merchant Sealand in a play of 1722/3. 'And [we] are as honourable, and almost as useful, as you landed Folks, that have always thought yourself so much above us.'[24] Indeed, by this period, the concept of the 'gentleman' had already begun its famous social peregrination, losing its oldest connotations of 'gentle' birth and 'idle' living, so that, in the later eighteenth century, individual vintners, tanners, scavengers, potters, theatre managers, and professors of Divinity could all claim the status, publicly and without irony.[25]

At the same time, there were perceptions of change in the distribution of wealth in the wider society. Not only was it argued that the nation as a whole was becoming more affluent, besotted by 'luxury', but in particular the gulf between rich and poor was filled by the increasingly numerous and socially visible 'middling' interests, later denounced inventively as the 'middlocrats'. In a celebrated letter on his business policy, Josiah Wedgwood in 1777 explained the value of noble patronage as the key to another equally important consumer market: 'The Great People have had these Vases in their Palaces long enough for them to be seen and admired by the Middling Class of People, which class we know are vastly, I had almost said, infinitely superior in Number to the Great.'[26]

[23] Mme Van Muyden (ed.), *A Foreign View of England in the Reigns of George I and George II: the letters of M. César de Saussure to his family* (John Murray, London, 1902), pp. 207–8.

[24] R. Steele, *The Conscious Lovers* (1722/3), in *The Plays of Richard Steele*, ed. S. S. Kenny (Clarendon Press, Oxford, 1971), p. 359. The nature of the interplay between landed and non-landed sources of wealth and status is discussed in L. and J. F. Stone, *An Open Elite? England, 1540–1880* (Clarendon Press, Oxford, 1984); see esp. pp. 281–92 for elite/bourgeois cultural assimilation.

[25] As listed in later eighteenth-century urban directories; from a survey by P. J. Corfield, 'Urban occupations in Britain in the early Industrial Revolution', funded by the Economic and Social Research Council, 1982–5 (detailed reports available). 'Gentleman' had always had a certain ambivalence between a moral and a social definition, and a growing chorus began to stress the former at the expense of the latter: see, e.g., R. Steele, in *The Tatler*, 207 (1710): 'The Appellation of a Gentleman is never to be affixed to a Man's Circumstances but to his Behaviour in them'. See also S. Letwin, *The Gentleman in Trollope: individuality and moral conduct* (Macmillan, London, 1982), and H. J. Shroff, *The Eighteenth-Century Novel: the idea of the gentleman* (Arnold-Heinemann, New Delhi, 1978).

[26] Quoted in N. McKendrick, 'Josiah Wedgwood and the commercialization of the Potteries', in N. McKendrick, J. Brewer, and J. H. Plumb, *The Birth of a Consumer Society: the commercialization of eighteenth-century England* (Europa,

It may well be that the collective affluence of this group was exaggerated, particularly as a result of their new social visibility in the fast-growing towns. Contemporaries faced difficulties in the precise assessment of long-term shifts in the ownership both of capital and of disposable income.[27] Many, however, agreed with Wedgwood, in detecting a newly extensive diffusion of wealth.

A sense of competitiveness and 'uppishness' was furthermore reported very generally, and among many 'degrees and conditions' of men. Social differentials had certainly not disappeared, nor poverty been abolished. But abjectness and fatalism were observed less often. 'Revolution' was specifically applied to changes in social mores, well before that term was applied to industrial innovation. Addison in 1711 observed it approvingly in 'behaviour and good-breeding' in the towns as opposed to the country-side.[28] In 1724 Daniel Defoe specified it as the decay of subordination: 'The Common People of this Country have suffer'd a Kind of general Revolution, or Change, in their Disposition, Temper, and Manners; . . . I say, they have suffer'd a general Change, such as I believe no Nation has undergone but themselves,' adding a conventional coda: 'I wish I could say it was a Change for the Better.'[29] Henry Fielding used very similar phrasing in 1751. Analysing the implications of Britain's rapid commercial expansion, he decided that economic growth 'hath indeed given a new Face to the whole Nation, . . . and hath almost totally changed the Manners, Customs, and Habits of the People, more especially of the lower sort.'[30]

London, 1982), p. 131; see also *passim*, as well as J. Sekora, *Luxury: the concept in Western thought, Eden to Smollett* (Johns Hopkins University Press, Baltimore, 1977), and J. Thirsk, *Economic Policy and Projects: the development of a consumer society in early modern England* (Clarendon Press, Oxford, 1978), esp. pp. 173–80.

[27] Historians have shared these difficulties, compounded by scarcity of reliable data and problems in defining social boundaries. Compare approaches in S. Pollard and D. W. Crossley, *The Wealth of Britain, 1085–1966* (Batsford, London, 1968), esp. pp. 169–73, 185–9; H. Perkin, *The Origins of Modern English Society, 1780–1880* (Routledge, London, 1969), esp. pp. 17–24; and W. Rubinstein, 'Wealth, elites and the class structure of modern Britain', *Past and Present*, 76 (1977), pp. 99–126.

[28] J. Addison wrote of 'a very great revolution' in *The Spectator*, 119 (1711); repr. in modern edn (8 vols, Everyman, London, 1950), vol. 1, pp. 362–3.

[29] D. Defoe, *The Great Law of Subordination Considered* (London, 1724), p. 50.

[30] H. Fielding, *An Inquiry into the Causes of the Late Increase of Robbers* (London, 1751), Preface, p. xxiii.

Journalists enjoyed the melodrama. 'We are a Nation of Gentry,' exclaimed *The World* in 1755. 'We have no such thing as Common People among us; between Vanity and Gin the whole Species is utterly destroyed.'[31] Pride and a taste for liquor were not the only culprits. Irreligion, education, and the growth of towns were also blamed. Some detected the hand of Eve. The dean of Gloucester was horrified to see women at Bath making advances to men, and concluded sombrely in 1783 that 'revolutionary principles are continually gaining ground.'[32] The sense of fundamental upheaval was reiterated, generation by generation. Southey in 1807 continued the litany: 'Perhaps no kingdom ever experienced so great a change in so short a course of years, without some violent state convulsion, as England has done during the present reign. . . . The alteration extends to the minutest things, even to the dress and manners of every rank of society.'[33] In other words, while social differentials still manifestly survived, it was difficult to assert that they were (as opposed to ought to be) timeless and unchanging in their structure and expression. Eighteenth-century England was a mobile and urbanizing society, in a commercial and industrializing economy. The static vision acquired its poignancy from the strong counter-currents of change.

Analytical responses to the 'confounding' of order and degree were correspondingly diversified. One major strand of thought embraced the whole of society, at least in theory, as 'the people', and tried to avoid reference to subordinate aggregations within the whole. The basic unit was the individual, in the context of, at most, a family This view had intellectual support, drawing upon the philosophical assumptions (if not conclusions) of Thomas Hobbes and, especially powerfully in the eighteenth-century context, of John Locke. It was fuelled by Enlightenment confidence in human rationality; and it matched an atomized view both of the universe, in which unitary elements were juxtaposed within

[31] *The World* (1755), as quoted in C. W. and P. Cunnington, *A Handbook of English Costume in the Eighteenth Century* (Faber, London, 1957), p. 21.
[32] G. Shelton, *Dean Tucker and Eighteenth-Century Economic and Political Thought* (Macmillan, London, 1981), p. 255.
[33] R. Southey, *Letters from England*, ed. J. Simmons (Cresset Press, London, 1951), pp. 362–3. Other changes included 'the invention of the steam-engine, almost as great an epocha as the invention of printing; the manufacturing system carried to its utmost point; the spirit of commerce extended to every thing; an Empire lost in America, and another gained in the East,' putting economic and imperial developments in close conjunction with social transformation.

a component whole,[34] and of the economy in which competing agents jostled in the market-place.

When formulated in legal and constitutionalist terms of individual claims as against inherited privilege and authority, its thrust was politically innovative: 'We hold these truths to be self-evident, that all men are created equal, . . . endowed by their Creator with certain inalienable rights.' The Declaration of Independence in 1776 gave immense authority to this approach in the emergent American consciousness. It also had a long provenance in English traditions of dissent, both secular and religious non-conformity appealing to the individual conscience. Meshing with the eighteenth-century belief in progress, it increasingly generated an air of expectation. 'It is an age of revolutions, in which everything may be looked for,' as Paine riposted to Burke. When the public demand for *The Rights of Man* (1791) was promptly matched by *A Vindication of the Rights of Woman* (1792), an agitated Hannah More essayed sarcasm to stem the tide: 'It follows, according to the natural progression of human things, that the next influx of that irradiation, which our enlightenment is pouring in upon us, will illuminate the world with grave descants on the *rights of youth* – the *rights of children* – the *rights of babies!*'[35] (In fact, Spence's *Rights of Infants* followed in 1797.)

While iconoclastic towards inherited titles and authority and dynamic in its acceptance of change, however, individualism was much more ambivalent when faced with acquired wealth and elective political power. Analysis that focused chiefly upon unitary components had a relatively weak conception of wider social relationships, and therefore often contained many implicit assumptions. Indeed, just as the earlier Whig appeal to the 'people' had turned out to be much more restricted in practice

---

[34] Among an extensive bibliography, see C. B. MacPherson, *The Political Theory of Possessive Individualism: Hobbes to Locke* (Clarendon Press, Oxford, 1962); S. Lukes, *Individualism* (Blackwell, Oxford, 1973); and J. E. Crowley, *This Sheba, Self: the conceptualisation of economic life in eighteenth-century America* (Johns Hopkins University Press, Baltimore, 1974).

[35] T. Paine, *The Rights of Man* (1791/2), ed. H. Collins (Penguin, Harmondsworth, 1969), p. 168; H. More, *Works*, vol. 3, p. 100. For the pluralism and diversity of radical traditions in action, see G. B. Nash, *The Urban Crucible: social change, political consciousness, and the origins of the American Revolution* (Harvard University Press, Cambridge, Mass., 1979); M. and J. Jacob (eds), *The Origins of Anglo-American Radicalism* (Allen and Unwin, London, 1984); J. Brewer and J. Styles (eds), *An Ungovernable People: the English and their law in the seventeenth and eighteenth centuries* (Hutchinson, London, 1980).

than its generosity of language implied,[36] so too with many versions of the people's 'rights' in the eighteenth century.

Some sorts of intermediate associations, between the one and the nation, were unavoidable. Individuals functioned within complex mass societies, with many groups, associations, contacts, and loyalties. Indeed, for a theoretical scrutiny of social behaviour, some aggregative analysis is inescapable for generalization about literally millions of people, who cannot be summed painstakingly one by one.[37] Of course, these intermediate groupings have not always been interpreted in economic terms. Local and regional communities, religious allegiance, and racial origin have all proved powerful sources of identification, especially when expressed in opposition to a rival.

Within eighteenth-century Britain, strong feelings certainly centred around all these forms of association. Antagonisms between English, Scots, and Irish had lengthy traditions, as did, in different permutation, tensions between English and Scottish Protestants on the one hand and Irish Catholics on the other. Local and regional identifications were also deeply engrained and much enshrined in popular jests and sayings. Counties were commemorated, for example, for their mythic qualities: 'Norfolk wiles', 'silly Suffolk', and so forth. The fast-growing urban centres in the eighteenth century also became focuses for loyalty and an often mocking affection. These were all crucial perspectives upon sectional networks, even if some of the epithets were hotly contested. As general descriptive terminology, however, they do not seem to have been as predominantly and as persistently used in eighteenth-century

[36] C. Hill, 'James Harrington and the people', in idem, *Puritanism and Revolution* (Secker and Warburg, London, 1958); H. T. Dickinson, *Liberty and Property: political ideology in eighteenth-century Britain* (Weidenfeld, London, 1977).

[37] Harriet Martineau disputed this point with Coleridge in the 1820s, claiming to envisage society purely as an 'aggregate of individuals'; but in her writings she used a number of collective nouns, including 'Capital', 'Labour', the 'middle class' (which she specified as her own), and 'workies', which she proposed as an affectionate version of 'working class': H. Martineau, *Autobiography* (2 vols, London, 1877), 1983 edn, vol. 1, p. 396; vol. 2, pp. 115, 306–7; see also her *Illustrations of Political Economy* (London, 1834), vol. 1, pp. xiv–xv. A tradition of not referring explicitly to social class is continued today in some political circles, especially among economic liberals; but it is still difficult to avoid some aggregative groupings, such as 'ordinary people/top people' or providers of 'essential services/others with special gifts': see, e.g., M. Thatcher, *Let our Children Grow Tall: selected speeches, 1975–7* (Centre for Policy Studies, London, 1977), p. 35.

Britain as were, by contrast, religious and racial designations in the much more heterogeneous society of nineteenth-century America.

Much discussion therefore centred around social labels. As already stressed, eighteenth-century usage was highly eclectic. Among the older terms, 'ranks', 'orders', 'degrees', and 'stations' were still deployed, all having relatively static implications, particularly the last, which ultimately found a still more permanent use with the railways and then dropped from social discourse. Other terms with some currency were 'sorts' (frequently found in the seventeenth century), 'parts', and 'interests',[38] the last often in the modern sense of a 'lobby' for a special interest group that might include more than one tier of society: for example, on occasion, groups of textile towns lobbied government in the textile 'interest' on behalf of both work-force and employers.

'Ranks' and 'orders' were used in the most general terms, but they had implications of social status as conferred primarily by birth. Individuals could be ennobled by grant from a higher power, but that was thought of as exceptional. In a mobile society in which origins and eventualities did not invariably match, 'sort', 'part', and, increasingly, 'class' were used instead. They were classificatory terms, referring to generic socio-economic position, into which an individual could rise or fall, rather than to lineage. 'Sort', the first newcomer, but a rather amorphous word, was outclassed by 'class', which was pithy and adaptable as noun, adjective, and verb. It was known in the language at least by 1656, when it appeared in Blount's *Glossographia*, majestically subtitled *A Dictionary interpreting all Such Hard Words . . . as are now used in our Refined English Tongue*. At that time, its major application was specified as scholastic, which it continued to retain; but it had the meaning also of 'an Order or Distribution of People, according to their several Degrees', as an Anglicization of the Latin *classis*, or tax group.[39]

---

[38] 'Commercial', 'trading', 'manufacturing', and 'monied' interests were all referred to in the eighteenth century, as well as the 'landed' interest, the last appealed to with subdued sarcasm in J. Tucker, *An Humble Address and Earnest Appeal to those Respectable Personages in Great Britain and Ireland, who, by their Great and Permanent Interest in Landed Property, their Liberal Education, Elevated Rank, and Enlarged Views, are the Ablest to Judge and the Fittest to Decide, whether a Connection with, or Separation from the Continental Colonies of America, be most for the National Advantage and the Lasting Benefit of these Kingdoms* (Gloucester, 1775).

[39] T. Blount, *Glossographia* (London, 1656); see also brief comments in Calvert, *Concept of Class*, pp. 12–13. Some seventeenth-century writers in Latin, including Milton, used *classis* (plural, *classes*), subsequently translated as social

Scattered usage followed in the late seventeenth and early eighteenth centuries. Defoe, a great language innovator, was one of the earliest to use the word, conflating the educational and social in 1698 with the announcement: 'In the Commonwealth of Vice, the Devil has taken care to level Poor and Rich into one Class, and is fairly going on to make us all Graduates in the last Degree of Immorality.' Others used the term to express general categories within society. Readers of the *Spectator* in 1712 may have been amused by 'Hotspur's' allocation of women into their 'distinct and proper classes, as the ape, the coquette, the devotee'; and they could certainly enjoy Addison's account of his London club that catered for all 'ways of life' and 'classes of mankind'.[40]

By the 1740s, and certainly the 1750s, specific references to social structure were couched in the new terms: Nelson's five 'classes' of 1753 have already been quoted; in 1749 Josiah Tucker wrote of 'classes of society', and identified the 'lower class of people'; in 1756 Massie's *Calculations of the Present Taxes Yearly Paid by a Family of Each Rank, Degree, or Class* was eclectic in its title, and in its text referred to 'gentlemen' and 'middling and inferior classes'; and in 1757 Jonah Hanway also noted the 'lower classes'. Within two decades, such applications were commonplace, although probably still a minority usage. Interestingly, this development paralleled the popularization of the term by the Methodists with their 'class system' for study of the Bible.[41] The social application of the term does not seem confined to any particular group or clique of authors or speakers, although spoken forms are, of course, much more difficult to trace. Certainly, the younger Pitt in 1796 was not intending to be controversial when he referred in Parliament to the 'labouring poor' as a 'class', in context of a speech explaining that

class or classes; but this, although comprehensible, is anachronistic in terms of usage in seventeenth-century English.

[40] Compare D. Defoe, *The Poor Man's Plea, in Relation to all the . . .* Acts of Parliament . . . for . . . suppressing Immorality in the Nation (London, 1698), p. 19; 'Hotspur', *The Spectator*, 354 (1712); and Addison, *The Spectator*, 34 (1711), Everyman edn, vol. 1, pp. 101–2, and vol. 3, p. 107, respectively.

[41] Nelson, *Essay on the Government of Children;* J. Tucker, *A Brief Essay on the Advantages and Disadvantages which Respectively attend France and Great Britain with Respect to Trade* (London, 1749); J. Massie, *Calculations of the Present Taxes Yearly Paid by a Family of Each Rank, Degree, or Class* (London, 1756), pp. 1, 8; J. Hanway, *A Journal of Eight Days Journey* (London, 1757), vol. 2, p. 264. A scan of eighteenth- and early nineteenth-century literature for social terminology has to take into account other applications of 'class': e.g., [J. Burton, attrib.], *The Class System Vindicated and Recommended* (London, 1843), is a tract in favour of the Methodist study groups for religious education.

nothing could be done by government to alleviate their hardships. By contrast, Charles James Fox, retaining the Whig tradition, usually spoke of the 'people'.[42]

New terms could be employed in new ways. The mutual relationship of one 'class' with another was conceptually much more fluid than those of 'ranks', which were 'serried', or 'orders', which were neatly aligned.[43] Certainly, the Great Chain did not envisage structural contest or competition within society. 'Rank struggle' would have been a contradiction in terms. 'Class', on the other hand, contained a potential for change, whether by cooperation, competition, or conflict. It also encouraged a much more conscious scrutiny of human society, in parallel with scientific 'classification' (another new term) of the animal and vegetable kingdoms. 'Through the extravagance of the last thirty years, a new mode of thinking has been adopted, and a revolution has taken place in the fashions of the mind,' affirmed *The British Tocsin; or, proofs of national ruin*, in 1795: 'The British Nation, once the adorer of prejudice, now invents queries . . . and pries into . . . abuses, with an inquisitorial nicety.' Among the questions posed by the poor man, it added, was 'Who reaps the produce of his labour?'[44]

There are many uncertainties as to what were the significant bases of social division. Attributions purely by birth ceased to be very helpful for explaining social and economic structures as a whole. Detailed hand-

---

[42] Spoken usage from the eighteenth century is, of course, only recorded through the written word, although some forms of transcripts, dialogues, and plays did attempt to record or re-create actual speech. Printed versions of Parliamentary oratory were almost certainly edited after the event, and thus usage should strictly be dated by publication: see W. Pitt, *The Speeches of the Rt. Hon. William Pitt in the House of Commons*, ed. W. S. Hathaway (4 vols, London, 1806), vol. 2, p. 365; also C. J. Fox, *The Speeches of the Rt. Hon. Charles James Fox in the House of Commons*, ed. J. Wright (6 vols, London, 1815), vol. 2, p. 174: 'It was the best government, where the people had the greatest share in it.'

[43] This comment refers to contextual meanings rather than formal definitions, since dictionaries from Johnson's *Dictionary* of 1755 to the current *Oxford English Dictionary* habitually define 'rank' as 'class', and vice versa. It was not strictly necessary for the words to change for meanings to mutate, as there are many examples of old words turned to new usages over time. The fact that terminology did change substantially, however, suggests in itself an emphatic process, generating new concepts of society and new vocabularies *pari passu*. Social conflicts and transformations in earlier periods have not infrequently been associated with similar linguistic challenge.

[44] Anon., *The British Tocsin: or, proofs of national ruin* (London, 1795), pp. 8, 21. This was a radical tract, published by Daniel Isaac Eaton, calling for liberty and revolution.

books to rankings and their formal status continued to be published for titled society: *Of the Several Degrees of Gentry and their Precedency* (1719) was one of many such compilations. Showing perhaps an under-tow of anxiety, it listed the ten degrees of highest rank (four excellent; six 'noble'), including the gentlemen among whom there were nine degrees of gentility, enabling the attentive reader to distinguish between gentlemen 'of ancestry' and gentlemen merely 'of blood'. These people formed an upper tier, set apart from the 'vulgar'. At once intricate on lineage and insouciant of the rest of society, this approach had its limitations. It was satirized by Addison, who asked whether in the 'Commonwealth of Letters', the author of a folio volume should rank above the author of a quarto, and both above a mere pamphleteer? The country squires, who were 'the illiterate Body of the Nation', thus fell 'into a Class below the three learned professions.'[45]

In the wider eighteenth-century enquiry into social classifications, there was fascination as well as imprecision over numbers. Serious economic analysts tended towards pluralism. One of the earliest writers to consider socio-economic groupings was the ever-fertile Defoe.[46] ''Tis plain', he wrote in 1705, 'the Dearness of Wages forms our People into more Classes than other Nations can show.' And in 1709 he propounded a seven-fold categorization:

1 *The Great, who live profusely*
2 *The Rich, who live plentifully*
3 *The middle Sort, who live well*
4 *The working Trades, who labour hard but feel no want*
5 *The Country People, Farmers, etc. who fare indifferently*
6 *The Poor that fare hard*
7 *The Miserable, that really pinch and suffer want*

Clearly not concerned with pre-ordained social rank, this was an attempt at establishing actual differentials, based on types of occupation and income levels, as well as consumption patterns. He offered very little detailed elaboration, but suggested that the fourth sort could be taken for a medium, such as carpenters, smiths, weavers, whether rural or

---

[45] Anon., *Of the Several Degrees of Gentry and their Precedency* (London, 1719), pp. iii, vii. 'Excellent' were prince, duke, marquis, and earl; 'noble' were viscount, baron, baronet, knight, esquire, and gentleman, among which last 'calling' there were nine gradations. Addison poked fun at disputes over precedence: *The Spectator*, 529 (1712), Everyman edn, vol. 4, pp. 168–9.

[46] D. Defoe, *A Review of the State of the British Nation*, vol. 6, no. 36 (25 June 1709); idem, *A Review of the Affairs of France*, vol. 2, no. 18 (14 Apr. 1705).

urban, from north or south. Here was a view of nation-wide horizontal groupings, in a modernizing terminology.

Another complex formulation was provided by Massie in 1756. Writing to disabuse the British people of their belief that they paid too much in taxation, he was not concerned primarily to establish social structure, and his conceptualization of society was very fluid. At times, he used a threefold designation (as already noted), but his detailed tabulation considered notional family expenditure for thirty different income groups. They were named under seven socio-occupational categories, although they were not systematically specified into classes by Massie himself:

1 *Noblemen or Gentlemen*: landed income between £4,000 and £20,000 p.a.
2 *Gentlemen*: landed income between £200 and £2,000 p.a.
3 *Freeholders*: landed income between £50 and £100 p.a.
4 *Farmers*: expending between £40 and £150 p.a.
5 *Tradesmen* in London and Country: expending between £40 and £300 p.a.
6 *Manufacturers* in London and Country: earning between 7/6d and 12/- p.wk.
7 *Labourers and Husbandmen* in London and country: earning between 5/- and 9/- p.wk.

The fascinations of his intricate tables are manifold, not least the shift in his data, which obviously stemmed from the nature of information then available, from landowners' rentals to traders' consumption levels to workmen's weekly earnings.[47] Even with incomplete information about commercial and industrial capital, Massie showed that old 'ranking' was no guide to actual wealth.

Something of that need to accommodate social diversification also underpinned Nelson's five-fold classification in 1753, which (as already cited) offered its own variants in terminology:

---

[47] Massie, *Calculations*, pp. iii–iv, 13–42 [interpolated pagination]; and P. Mathias, 'The social structure in the eighteenth century: a calculation by Joseph Massie', in idem, *The Transformation of England: essays in the economic and social history of England in the eighteenth century* (Methuen, London, 1979), pp. 171–89. Massie's figures can be adapted for comparison with the income/expenditure tables for different ranks and occupations compiled by Gregory King (1688) and Patrick Colquhoun (1803); but grouping of their data into social classes is more problematic: compare Mathias, 'Social structure', pp. 186–9, and Perkin, *Origins of Modern English Society*, pp. 20–1.

1 *Nobility*	1 *Nobility*
2 *Gentry*	2 *Gentry*
3 *Mercantile or Commercial People*	3 *Genteel Trades* (with large capital)
4 *Mechanics*	4 *Common Trades*
5 *Peasantry*	5 *Peasantry* (also rustics/lowest class)

It held a continuing notation of social hierarchy, with landowners firmly at the head and a 'peasantry' at the foot; but it incorporated evident awareness of non-landed affluence, as well as diversification of occupation and way of life among 'lower' social groups. Not to be outdone, in the climate of social scrutiny, *The Cheats of London Exposed* (c.1770) joined in with four light-hearted 'classes' of theatre audience:[48]

1 *The Nobs*
2 *The Citizens and their Ladies*
3 *The Mechanics and Middling Degrees*
4 *The Refuse*

Analytical aggregation in terms of five or seven had, however, considerably less appeal than notation in terms of two or three. These were much the most popular groupings. Two had a certain simplicity, an attractive directness. Its graphic immediacy was much used in journalism and reportage. 'In England, . . . in the daytime the lower classes get intoxicated with liquor and beer, the higher classes in the evening with Portuguese wines and punch,' remarked de Saussure, in a much relished dictum. *One half of the World knows not how the other half live*, trumpeted *Low-Life* in 1752, in an equally memorable dualism.[49] Again, the terminology was very various. Dichotomous classifications included high/low, upper/lower, superior/inferior, head/foot, great/mean, few/many, gentle/base, gentry/plebeians or, alternatively, gentry/common people, as well as rich/poor, the latter focusing upon wealth as well as status.

This represented a simplification of the fine gradations of the Great Chain, but it still retained a clear sense of dominance/subordination. It was often favoured by those at the traditional apex of society, who

---

[48] Anon., *The Cheats of London Exposed* (London, n.d., ?1770), pp. 66–7.
[49] Van Muyden (ed.), *Letters of Saussure*, p. 192; Anon., *Low-Life: or one half of the World knows not how the other half live, being a critical account of what is transacted by people of almost all religions, nations, circumstances, and sizes of understanding, in the twenty-four hours between Saturday night and Monday morning* (London, 1752; 2nd edn, 1754; 3rd edn, 1764).

tended to view all those below them as uniformly disfavoured. A string of disdainful epithets made it possible to refer to the 'vulgar', 'rabble', 'clowns', 'bumpkins' (usually rural), or Burke's 'swinish multitude'; yet such phrasing seems to have been comparatively cautious in its public expression, and certainly hostile status terminology was rarely used in direct parlance between 'freeborn Englishmen', however socially unequal.[50] The political expression of the few/many dichotomy was also adopted explicitly by some advocates of strong central government. Some patricians found it attractive, especially once the dangers of absolute monarchy had been curtailed. That argument recurred in the American debate after the War of Independence, as enunciated, for example, by Alexander Hamilton in 1787: 'All communities divide themselves into the few and the many. The first are the rich and well born, the other the mass of the people, . . . [who] seldom judge or determine right.' The claims of the few could be asserted in terms of power, whether of birth or of wealth, or, indeed, of intellect. A youthfully confident John Stuart Mill later promulgated in 1829 the dictum that 'The intelligent classes lead the government, and the government leads the stupid classes';[51] but brainpower proved notoriously difficult to fit into a social hierarchy.

In economic terms, the rich/poor dualism was also an ancient division, pointing to obvious differentials in incomes, assets, and way of life. It could promote fatalism, 'for the poor always ye have with you.' Some writers argued that a twofold classification was intrinsic to all forms of economic organization, and specified its origin in a division of ownership/labour. Thomas Malthus, for example, explained in 1798:

> A society constituted according to the most beautiful form that imagination can conceive, . . . would, from the inevitable laws of nature, and not from any original depravity of man, in a very short period degenerate into a society constructed upon a plan not essentially different from that which prevails in every known state at present: I mean, a society divided into a

---

[50] A common salutation 'even to the poor' was '*Honest Man*': F. M. Misson, *Memoirs and Observations in his Travels over England* (Eng. translation, London, 1719), p. 221. On the other hand, Englishmen were not slow to abuse the Scots directly, as Boswell often complained: see, e.g., Pottle (ed.), *Boswell's London Journal*, p. 72.

[51] A. Hamilton, speech of 18 June 1787, in *The Mind of Alexander Hamilton*, ed. S. K. Padover (Harper, New York, 1958), p. 114; and J. S. Mill, *Collected Works*, ed. F. E. L. Priestley (Routledge, London, 1963), vol. 12, pp. 27–8.

class of proprietors, and a class of labourers, and with self-love the mainspring of the great machine.[52]

Fielding's Jonathan Wild had in 1743[53] postulated a rather similar schema: 'Mankind are . . . properly to be considered under two great divisions, those that use their own hands, and those who employ the hands of others,' this being the basis of his resolve to become great by employing a gang of thieves.

A binary vision could, indeed, become a spur to action, not only to individuals but also to collective protest. If the rich/poor dichotomy was translated from have/have-nots into exploiters/exploited, drones/workers, oppressors/oppressed, then a powerful sense of grievance could be generated. Not surprisingly, the younger Pitt in 1795, for example, hastened to reject the dissenter William Smith's prototype of two groups, the 'useful' (commercial) and the 'useless' (landed) class. Equally strongly, political radicals on occasion in the 1790s stressed the charge of exploitation. Tom Paine denounced the coercive demands of aristocratic government: 'There are two distinct classes of men in the nation, those who pay taxes, and those who receive and live upon the taxes'; and Thomas Spence attacked the unfair privileges of the 'grand, voluptuous nobility and gentry, living on wealth', which was generated by 'the toil of the Labouring classes'.[54]

Yet, while a Manichean either/or interpretation continued to hold a strong appeal, particularly in times of confrontation, it was under continuing assault in the course of the eighteenth century from a tripartite classification. More complex and subtle than two, the 'three' was yet finite enough to be readily comprehensible. It evidently held much attraction. There were parallels in triadic constitutional forms, as in trinitarian theology. Indeed, it has been argued that a conceptual trifunctionality lies at the core of all Indo-European thought systems,[55] perhaps an excessively tidy-minded viewpoint.

---

[52] T. Malthus, *Essay on the Principle of Population* (London, 1798), 1970 edn (Penguin, Harmondsworth), p. 144.

[53] H. Fielding, *The History of the Life of the Late Mr. Jonathan Wild the Great* (1743), Everyman edn (London, 1976), pp. 41–2.

[54] Pitt, *Speeches*, vol. 3, p. 3; T. Paine, *Complete Writings*, ed. P. S. Foner (Citadel Press, New York, 1969), vol. 2, p. 478; H. T. Dickinson (ed.), *The Political Works of Thomas Spence* (Avero, Newcastle upon Tyne, 1982), pp. 50, 53.

[55] For a critical elaboration of Georges Dumézil's approach, see G. Duby, *The Three Orders: feudal society imagined* (Paris, 1978), tr. A. Goldhammer (University of Chicago Press, Chicago, 1980). In medieval times, three orders were invoked: 'those who fight, those who pray, and those who work'; rendered

In the English tradition, there were familiar triads in 'king, lords, and commons', or, alternatively, 'nobility, gentry, and commonalty'. As social distinctions, however, they were unhelpful, since so much of the population fell into the residual third category. Gradually, a more complex classification was adopted. It can certainly be identified in some seventeenth-century usages, albeit usually casually rather than systematically applied. Francis Bacon, for example, had referred to three tiers of society, with the 'better Sort' and the 'meane People' alike contrasting with the 'middle People', who made the best soldiers. Richard Baxter had other battles in mind, when he too wrote of a 'sober sort of men of the middle rank, that will hear reason, and are more equal to religion than the highest or the lowest usually are.'[56]

A number of early eighteenth-century economic writers and pamphleteers, including Davenant, suggested a threefold classification. Terminology remained very flexible, with references to an intermediate social group, conveyed in phrases such as 'middle sort/state/set/part/people/ condition/life', all less strictly hierarchic, as well as the older 'order/ rank/station'. 'Citizen' or 'Cit' also had some currency, but 'bourgeois', which can be found, did not Anglicize very successfully. The three formations were taken by some to represent different characteristics and lifestyles. Samuel Butler, in a private memorandum written in the 1670s, had resolved 'to have nothing to do with men that are very Rich or Poore, for the one sort are commonly Insolent and Proud, and the other Meane and Contemptible; and those that are between are commonly the most agreeable.' Later, Daniel Defoe was an advocate for the 'middle State'. As Robinson Crusoe's father explained, individuals so situated were 'not exposed to the miseries and hardships, the labour and sufferings of the mechanic part of mankind; and not embarrassed with the pride, luxury, ambition, and envy of the upper part of mankind.'[57]

In one instance, there was legislative endorsement of a tripartite schema, in a differential tariff of fines for public cursing and swearing (which was a behavioural characteristic of all levels of society). The

---

into more civilian mode in 1610 by C. Loyseau, *Traité des ordres*, as nobility, clergy, and the Third Estate.

[56] F. Bacon, 'Of Seditions and Troubles' and 'Of the True Greatness of Kingdoms', in *Essays* (repr. London, 1941), pp. 51, 54, 109–10; also R. Baxter, *The Poor Husbandman's Advocate*, as cited in C. Hill, *Society and Puritanism in Pre-Revolutionary England* (Secker and Warburg, London, 1964), p. 251.

[57] S. Butler, *Prose Observations*, ed. H. de Quehen (repr. Clarendon Press, Oxford, 1979), p. 14; D. Defoe, *The Compleat English Tradesman* (1725–6), 1841 edn (London), vol. 2, pp. 89–90; idem, *The Life and Strange Adventures of Robinson Crusoe* (1719–20), 1840 edn (London), vol. 1, p. 3.

earliest statute in 1624 had contented itself with a single tally of 1/- per offence for all offenders if charged within a given time span. Upon re-enactment in 1695, a higher fine of 2/- was introduced for all those specified as above the rank of a day-labourer or a common soldier and seaman. In the Profane Oaths Act of 1746, one further tier of penalty was inserted. Day-labourers were still fined 1/-; all others, above the labourers but below the rank of a gentleman, 2/-; but gentlemen and higher ranks (royalty not excluded) were now charged 5/- per offence.[58] The Act thus envisaged hierarchy in a definite threefold manifestation, indicated partly by occupation and partly by status (although what constituted a gentleman was not defined). Its effect upon the curbing of profanity was, however, widely agreed to be negligible.

Meanwhile, the public analysis of triadic society gradually incorporated the terminology of 'class'. As it did so, there emerged a parallel and key mutation in the qualifying adjectives to accompany the new noun. The 'higher', 'middling', and 'lower' classes, which were current concepts by the 1750s and 1760s, almost immediately began to be reinterpreted in some quarters, as 'upper', 'middle', and 'industrious', or eventually 'working' classes.[59] It is notable that those who used the new adjectives almost invariably paired them with the new noun. Hybrids, such as 'labouring ranks' or 'working ranks' were comparatively rare once 'class' had come into currency.

The contrasts showed most vividly in changing perceptions of the 'lower orders'. Yet the new vocabulary had a subtle effect at all levels. The vertical axis and the immobile construction of the Great Chain were under conceptual challenge. A gradual verbal shift from 'higher ranks' to 'upper class' was relatively undramatic. It shed the notion of a purely titled qualification, and could embrace a monied as well as a landed

[58] 21 Jac. I, cap. 20 (1624); 6 & 7 William III, cap. 11 (1695); 19 Geo. II, cap. 21 (1746): as the fines were raised in successive codifications, so the period of prosecution time was progressively shortened, from 20 days to 10 days to 8 days. Thomas Turner, *The Diary of a Georgian Shopkeeper*, ed. G. H. Jennings (Oxford University Press, Oxford, 1979), p. 37, observed that had all offending vestrymen been charged with their offences against this legislation, 'there would be no need to levy any tax to maintain our poor.'
[59] The noun shift can be found in other languages (French: *états* to *classes*; German: *Stand* or *Schicht* to *Klasse*), although their usage did not change as early or as prominently as it did in England, where the changing adjectival emphasis was particularly notable. See for comparison W. H. Sewell, *Work and Revolution in France: the language of labor from the Old Regime to 1848* (Cambridge University Press, Cambridge, 1981); and for a brief overview of English applications, R. Williams, *Keywords: a vocabulary of culture and society* (Croom Helm, London, 1976).

aristocracy. On the other hand, it still retained a sense of 'altitude'. But it was much more cautious in its expression, and was certainly less laudatory than older terms that referred to social 'superiority' which had connotations of better as well as higher status.

A growing chorus of public praise for the 'middle class' was still more assertive of a new social dispensation. The mid-point on the scale could traditionally be viewed as a mere half-way house. An aristocratic republican, in a poem on *The Equality of Mankind* (1765), had enjoyed teasing the social nervousness of the middle groups, depicting them as 'motley Beings':

> Who, dragged by Fortune into Middle Life,
> That vortex of malevolence and strife,
> Envying the Great and scoffing at the Mean,
> Now swol'n with pride, now wasted with chagrin.
> Like Mahomet's unsettled ashes dwell,
> Midway suspended between Heaven and Hell.[60]

This perception was, however, contrasted with an alternative celebration of the central equipoise, greeted in positively Aristotelian vein as the new 'Golden Mean'. The middle 'sort' or 'class' were singled out for their 'elegance' (1770); their state of life was 'undoubtedly the happiest' (1782); they fostered 'all the arts, wisdom, and virtues of society', and were the true preservers of freedom (1766); they were 'comfortable, modest and moderate, sober and satisfied, industrious and intelligent' (1800); indeed, they were 'the most virtuous, the most enlightened, the most independent part of the community' (1790). Thereupon, Joseph Priestley proposed that political office should be restricted to those of moderate fortunes, as they were generally 'better educated and have consequently more enlarged minds and are . . . more truly independent than those born to great opulence.'[61] These views were certainly not unbiased, but they were strongly affirmative. They tended, incidentally,

---

[60] M. Woodhull [sometimes Wodhull], *The Equality of Mankind* (Oxford, 1765); there are a number of variant readings in different editions.

[61] See variously J. Shipley, *Works* (London, 1792), vol. 2, pp. 143, 273; O. Goldsmith, *The Vicar of Wakefield* (London, 1766) 1982 edn (Penguin, Harmondsworth), p. 116; J. Larwood, *Erratics: by a sailor* (London, 1800); J. Aikin, *Address to the Dissidents of England* (London, 1790); J. Priestley, as cited in R. V. Holt, *The Unitarian Contribution to Social Progress in England* (Allen and Unwin, London, 1938), p. 86. The intellectual ancestry of this viewpoint can be found in Aristotle, *Politics*, Bk 4, ch. 11. For a modern survey of definitional problems, see G. D. H. Cole, 'The conception of the middle classes', in idem, *Studies in Class Structure* (Routledge, London, 1955), pp. 78–100.

to be voiced by members of the professions (clergymen, doctors, authors) rather than by the less vocal shop-keeping middle class.

The transformation of the 'lower orders' into 'workers', however, marked the clearest and most direct refutation of traditional hierarchy of 'high' and 'low'. This, too, had a lengthy tradition. The earliest reference, so far identified, to the 'working class' as such dates from 1789,[62] a symbolically notable year. But many variants had been in currency since at least the 1760s. For example, a petition from the Corporation of Norwich in 1763 referred to the 'industrious class'; Sir John Steuart in 1767 to the 'industrious classes'; John Gwynn in 1766 to the 'useful and laborious classes'. The *Monthly Review* had earlier, in 1751, referred to 'a class of all others the most necessary and useful to all, yet the most neglected and despised; we mean the labouring part of the people.'[63] The common emphasis was a rejection of verbal 'lowliness' and a recognition of the economic and social significance of toil.

By the 1780s and 1790s, 'labouring' or 'laborious' tended to supersede 'industrious': William Hutton wrote in 1781 of the 'laborious class', John Thelwall in 1796 of the 'laborious classes', and a correspondent to the *Monthly Magazine* in 1797 of the 'labouring classes', both variants being used by Thomas Spence; and Frederic Eden's *State of the Poor* was subtitled *A History of the Laborious Classes* (1797). These references were all made respectfully, some with specific radical purpose, as in the case of Thelwall and Spence, while Paine also proposed 'the industrious and manufacturing Part'.[64]

An incoming alternative usage was 'working class', first used by a

---

[62] Dictionary datings are all liable to revision in the light of fresh work on the eighteenth century: communication from *Oxford English Dictionary*, which welcomes new research findings. Grateful acknowledgement is due to the editor, Robert Burchfield, for generous help with references and datings.

[63] Norfolk Record Office, Case 16c, Petition for Bill to regulate burden of Poor Rate, etc., 1763; J. Steuart, *An Inquiry into Principles of Political Economy* (2 vols, London, 1767), vol. 1, p. 334; J. Gwynn, *London and Westminster Improved* (London, 1766); *Monthly Review* (Jan. 1751/2), reviewing H. Fielding, *Inquiry into the Causes of the Late Increase of Robbers*. 'Industrious' was also used generically, however, for many 'middling' manufacturing occupations, as well as those of the 'lower sort'.

[64] W. Hutton, *An History of Birmingham* (Birmingham, 1781), p. 50; J. Thelwall, *The Rights of Nature* (London, 1796), vol 2, p. 83; *Monthly Magazine*, 4 (1797), p. 109; Dickinson (ed.), *Political Works of Spence*, pp. 53, 55–6, 99; F. Eden, *The State of the Poor: or, a history of the laborious classes* (London, 1797); T. Paine, *The Poor Man's Friend: an address to the industrious and manufacturing part of Great Britain* (London, 1793).

Scottish writer, John Gray, in 1789, and echoed by John Aikin, describing a visit to industrial Lancashire in 1795. In the same year, a radical ballad, sardonically entitled 'Wholesome Advice to the Swinish Multitude', placed the words in close but not total juxtaposition, as it enquired melodiously:

> You lower class of Human Race, you working part I mean,
>   How dare you so audacious be, to read the works of Paine . . . ?[65]

These were relatively unusual formulations in the 1790s; but within two decades the new term had become quite widely used (sometimes in the singular, sometimes in plural form). From the start, it had connotations of political and social combativeness, to which ideological controversy was rapidly added, from Robert Owen's *New View of Society* (1813) onwards.[66]

The language of 'work' and 'labour' fused a number of emergent traditions in the course of the eighteenth century. Economic writers had observed the positive input from the toiling masses. Defoe again wrote of the importance of the 'working manufacturing People of England' (1725), sometimes simply described as 'working People' (1713, 1736); while others referred approvingly to the 'labouring and industrious Families', (1719), 'industrious People' (1731), 'manufacturing Work-

---

[65] J. Gray, *Some Reflections intended to Promote the Success of the Said Society*, in G. Dempster, *A Discourse containing . . . Proceedings . . . of the Society for Extending the Fisheries and Improving the Sea Coasts of Great Britain* (London, 1789), p. 50; J. Aikin, *A Description of the Country from Thirty to Forty Miles around Manchester* (London, 1795), p. 262; 'Wholesome Advice to the Swinish Multitude' (1795), in *Later English Broadside Ballads*, ed. J. Holloway and J. Black (Routledge, London, 1975), pp. 278–9.

[66] R. Owen, *A New View of Society* (London, 1813), new edn (London, 1817), pp. 17, 26, 48, 59, 176. This book was very eclectic in social terminology, contrasting the 'privileged classes' with variously the 'inferior situations in life', 'lower classes', 'working classes', 'lower orders', and 'poor and lower orders'. The pithiness of 'working class' commended its adoption; but it rapidly became controversial, and those of conservative cast of mind often preferred the plural form, to disavow notions of class struggle. However, even among radicals, usage remained very various; and their social critique was often couched in political rather than purely economic terms: for a highly fertile discussion, see G. Stedman Jones, 'Rethinking Chartism', in idem, *Languages of Class: studies in English working class history, 1832–1982* (Cambridge University Press, Cambridge, 1983), pp. 90–178.

folk' (1755), or, unvarnishedly, to 'Working/Labouring Men'.[67] These usages also converged with a long awareness in Poor Law policy formulation that the lower orders could not simply be described or treated in aggregate as the universal 'poor'. In practice, there were many gradations of living standards, even among the socially vulnerable on low incomes. Hence, from at least the later sixteenth century, the distinction had been made between the generality of the 'labouring poor' and the much smaller numbers actually in receipt of parish relief.[68] That bespoke a practical realism, especially given the habitual caution of ratepayers. Thus, while many in the eighteenth century continued to refer loosely to the 'poor', as though they were all equally impoverished or even all 'paupers', Poor Law policy had long recognized otherwise.

Affirmation of the common interests of labour also recurred in industrial disputes in the eighteenth century. Particularly given the perennial difficulties of framing a coherent organization, both within and certainly between trades, an emphasis on shared 'work' could foster a shared campaign. 'No Lowering Wages of Labouring Men to 4d. a Day and Garlick', an unmistakably English crowd demanded at Bristol in 1754. Legislation against various forms of industrial combination indicated official concern at the possibilities of united action from the work-force. A magistrate explained in 1759 that 'such Confederacies would have occasioned the greatest Confusion between the lowest Class of People and their Superiors, in all Trades and Occupations, in every Manufactory

---

[67] D. Defoe, *Compleat English Tradesman*, vol. 1, p. 252; anon., *The British Merchant: the cost of living* (London, 1713), vol. 1, p. 237; D. Defoe, *Letters from a Moor* (London, 1736), p. 168; anon., *A Second Humble Address from the Poor Weavers and Manufacturers to the Ladies* (London, ?1719); anon., *Case of the Petitioners against . . .* a New Workhouse in Manchester (London, ?1731); J. Clayton, *Friendly Advice to the Poor* (Manchester, 1755), pp. 13, 14. For changing economic interpretations, see also D. Coleman, 'Labour in the English economy in the seventeenth century', *Economic History Review*, 2nd ser., 8 (1955/6), pp. 280–93; and C. Hill, 'Pottage for freeborn Englishmen: attitudes to wage labour', in idem, *Change and Continuity in Seventeenth-Century England* (Weidenfeld, London, 1974), pp. 219–38.

[68] Gregory King's often misunderstood binary division (1688) between those 'increasing' and those 'decreasing' the wealth of the nation did not imply that the latter 50 per cent were equally 'poor', and certainly not that they were all 'paupers', as his detailed figures made clear: see M. D. George, *England in Transition* (Penguin, Harmondsworth, 1964), pp. 150–1. For the continuance of the debate, see G. Himmelfarb, *The Idea of Poverty: England in the early industrial age* (Faber, London, 1984).

and in every Employ,'[69] although in practice trade union activity faced many difficulties in sustaining such an organized 'Confusion'.

Rejection of hierarchical explanations of immanent inequality led to examination of the civil and economic bases of social differentiation. Enlightenment philosophers in Britain and France investigated systems of classification in society as well as the sciences. Furthermore, analysis was put into a framework of historical change, notably in the works of a trio of Scottish professors. Adam Ferguson's *Essay on the History of Civil Society* saw history as a moving process, advancing towards science and enlightenment. Social 'classes' and distinctions of 'rank' (he used both terms) came with the development of property and with increasing economic specialization ('Thinking itself, in this age of separations, may become a peculiar craft'). His analysis veered between emphasis upon change and dependence upon some degree of 'permanent and palpable subordination'.[70] In 1771, John Millar's *Observations concerning the Distinction of Ranks in Society* also detected innovation and specialization. History showed the 'gradual advancement of society in civilisation, opulence, and refinement'. With that, 'money becomes more and more the only means of procuring honours and dignities,' while the 'labouring part', also termed the 'mechanics and labouring people', became liberated from the grossest poverty.[71] Both accounts were determinedly secular,

[69] 1754 slogans of a Tory crowd, cited in L. Colley, *In Defiance of Oligarchy: the Tory party, 1714–60* (Cambridge University Press, Cambridge, 1982), p. 155; magistrate Sir Michael Foster, reported in *Manchester Mercury* (3 Apr. 1759) and cited in A. P. Wadsworth and J. de L. Mann, *The Cotton Trade and Industrial Lancashire, 1600–1780* (University of Manchester Press, Manchester, 1931), 1965 edn, p. 367. For general discussions of problems of industrial organization and the extent or otherwise of labour consciousness, see C. R. Dobson, *Masters and Journeymen: a pre-history of industrial relations, 1717–1800* (Croom Helm, London, 1980); and especially J. Rule, *The Experience of Labour in Eighteenth-Century Industry* (Croom Helm, London, 1981), and R. W. Malcolmson, 'Workers' combinations in eighteenth-century England', in M. and J. Jacob, *Anglo-American Radicalism*, pp. 149–61.

[70] Adam Ferguson, *An Essay on the History of Civil Society* (Edinburgh, 1767), 1768 edn, pp. 56, 161, 217, 249, 304. Ferguson (1723–1816) agreed with Montesquieu that 'Man is born in society, and there he remains' (p. 27), accepted that some subordination was 'natural' but not in conflict with 'natural rights', and attacked both despotism and slavery (pp. 103, 161, 308–9 respectively). For the European debate in the mid-eighteenth century, and particularly for the important contribution of the French physiocrats, see Calvert, *Concept of Class*, pp. 19–25.

[71] John Millar, *Observations concerning the Distinction of Ranks in Society* (London, 1771), esp. pp. 37, 184, 187, 232–3. Millar (1735–1801) used the term

relativistic about social forms; both were diffuse studies, hesitant about the ultimate destination of change.

Adam Smith synthesized their belief in the 'natural progress of opulence' with his own newly systematic study of economics. He argued that the division of labour in commercialized and urban societies was the source of growth and technical innovation. He also specified a tripartite classification, derived from the specialist means of production. The enterprise of freely competing individuals generated three great economic interests, or functional polarities. One was based upon rent; one upon profits of stock or capital; one upon wage labour. 'These are the three great, original, and constituent orders of every civilised society, from whose revenue that of every other order is ultimately derived,' he wrote famously, in the *Wealth of Nations* (1776).[72] Again, his social language was traditional, although diverse; but it was the distinctive triad of land, capital, and labour that found resonance. Those competing economic interests were subsequently taken by some radicals as constituting momentum for change. Charles Hall suggested in 1805 that 'Wealth consists not in things, but in *power* over the labour of others,' but he was melancholic that the process of growth and 'civilisation' would lead to a widening gulf between two classes of rich and poor. By contrast, John Thelwall's social analysis in 1796 was uncertain about the origins of inequality, but buoyant in the confidence that 'Monopoly and the

---

'rank' in his text and title in a very generic sense; he also deployed descriptive synonyms for specific groups (pp. 184, 233, 237). In his next work, *An Historical View of the English Government, from the Settlement of the Saxons in Britain . . . to the Present Time* (London, 1787), republished posthumously in a much extended edn (4 vols, London, 1803), vol. 4, pp. 115, 118, 141, he wrote specifically of 'class' in a categorization of 'Landlords, capitalists, and labourers' derived from Adam Smith. The Scottish contribution to the British debate was notable; and Scottish traditions of social description might repay further examination.

[72] Adam Smith, *An Inquiry into the Nature and Causes of the Wealth of Nations* (1776), Everyman edn (2 vols, London, 1970), vol. 1, p. 230. See also p. 336, for 'progress of opulence'; and vol. 1, pp. 10, 70, 310–11, vol 2, p. 346, for his variegated social terminology. Like many fruitful syntheses, the writings of Adam Smith (1723–90) have influenced many later, different schools of thought, by direct descent, as in *laissez-faire* economics, and by dialectical extension: cf. Marx's comment 'No credit is due to me for discovering the existence of classes in modern society, or the struggle between them': letter to J. Weydemeyer, 5 Mar. 1852, in *Karl Marx: Selected Writings*, ed. D. McClellan (Oxford University Press, Oxford, 1977), p. 341.

hideous accumulation of capital in a few hands, like all diseases not absolutely mortal, carry in their own enormity, the seeds of cure.'[73]

Diversity of debate, fluidity of language, competing interpretations: the eighteenth century in Britain was not an era of social inertia or conceptual stasis. There was a belief in change and social mutability, rather than in a strictly graded or strictly denoted social hierarchy.[74] Specification of 'class' intersected, however, with the older language of 'rank and degree'. Many vocabularies intermingled the two,[75] as the old terminology became increasingly generic and decreasingly precise. Social judgements were flexible, often dependent upon 'externals' rather than on birth and parentage. As the flighty young heroine of another bad novel (1757) declared, in intended parody of contemporary style: 'Well, the age is come to nothing; the world is turned topsey-turvey – no taste, fashion, genius, or *bon goût* left. I'll go home and change my dress, for I hate to be seen above three hours in my own gown.'[76]

The atmosphere of social change was particularly characteristic in urban and commercial circles; but these were very much the new cultural lodestars. It was a commonplace that Britain was a maritime and trading power, well before the growth of its industrial might. 'I have been bred up to think that the trade of this nation is the sole support of it,' remarked the Duke of Newcastle (b.1693) in 1766. Edmund Burke later worried that 'Commerce, trade and manufactures' were instituted as 'the gods of our economical politicians'.[77] The pluralism of wealth, the

---

[73] C. Hall, *The Effects of Civilisation on the People in European States* (London, 1804/5), 1849 edn, p. 39; and Thelwall, *Rights of Nature*, vol. 1, p. 24.

[74] This argument therefore differs from the interpretation in Perkin, *Origins of Modern English Society*, p. 17, where English society is defined as 'an open aristocracy based on property and patronage'. It also diverges from the emphasis in E. P. Thompson, 'Eighteenth-century English society: class struggle without class?', *Social History*, 3 (1978), pp. 133–65; and idem, 'Patrician society, plebeian culture', *Journal of Social History*, 7 (1974), pp. 382–405. In particular, the emergence of a self-conscious urban middle class seems to be omitted from both these influential accounts, as well as the general sense of pervasive social change.

[75] Investigation of terminology in writings of some of the eighteenth-century's long-lived letter-writers and diarists shows individual flexibilities, especially in youth, with usage tending to become more stereotyped in later life. Much change was also intergenerational. Diverse and conflicting usage in eighteenth-century language makes it difficult for historians to describe society purely in the terms used at the time, as some authorities would prescribe.

[76] Anon., *The Sedan: a novel* (2 vols, London, 1757), vol. 2, p. 4.

[77] British Library, Add. Mss 32973, fols 432–3, for Newcastle; Burke, *Revolution in France*, p. 174.

visibility of the middle class, and the 'uppishness' of the once 'lower orders' were the corollaries of economic change. In 1774 Dean Tucker considered that the challenge to traditional hierarchy was the origin of 'that medley, or contradiction of characters, so remarkable in the English nation'. It antedated the advent of large-scale industrialism and factory production. Southey, who had identified the advent of the new manufacturing system, also explained in 1807 that 'The commercial system has long been undermining the distinction of ranks in society. . . . Mushrooms are every day starting up from the dunghill of trade.'[78]

New 'classes' remained difficult to define in detail. There were often individual misfits, as well as collective uncertainties as to the number of significant social alignments. Disputes between Manicheans and Trinitarians continued. There were also tensions within emergent social stereotypes, as between the ethos of the 'professional' and the 'shop-keeping' middle class. The specification of group 'consciousness' was not a simple response to new nouns and adjectives.[79] Lower-class organizations were faced with the task of coordinating an even greater diversity of trade and sectional interests. Yet the fierce anxiety in conservative defences of the 'old ways', especially in the political reaction of the 1790s, indicated the extent to which traditional power dispensations were held to be under threat. Reform, which many viewed as inevitable in the 1770s and 1780s, was halted by alarm and retrenchment, not by social inertia.[80]

British society in the eighteenth century was therefore increasingly experienced as mutable and combative. Power was resynthesized into

[78] Shelton, *Dean Tucker*, p. 177; Southey, *Letters from England*, p. 367.

[79] An immense area for debate about social/political 'consciousness' has been opened up by E. P. Thompson's challenging *The Making of the English Working Class* (Gollancz, London, 1963); see also references and discussion in R. S. Neale, *Class in English History, 1680–1850* (Blackwell, Oxford, 1981); R. J. Morris, *Class and Class Consciousness in the Industrial Revolution, 1780–1850* (Macmillan, London and Basingstoke, 1979); and much work in progress on the eighteenth century.

[80] In 1783, e.g., the younger Pitt had declared that every thinking man must agree that constitutional reform was 'absolutely necessary'; while in 1792 he feared 'great danger of anarchy and confusion' in the attempt: Pitt, *Speeches*, vol. 1, p. 75; vol. 2, p. 90. Some scholarly research has stressed the lack of social fluidity at the traditional apex of the peerage and the owners of large country houses: Stone, *An Open Elite?*, *passim*; and J. Cannon, *Aristocratic Century: the peerage of eighteenth-century England* (Cambridge University Press, Cambridge, 1984); but this focus has tended to isolate the titular elite, especially as the number of intermediary titles (knights, baronets) was in decline (ibid., p. 32). The alleged immobilism at the top certainly did not stem wider social change and demands for reform.

active terms, of acquisition, production, and display, rather than of inheritance, formal title, and ancient lineage. If earlier generations had devoted their calculations to the search for the 'number of the Beast', their successors had a fertile new field of enquiry into the nature and number of 'social class'.

6

The emergence of 'society' in eighteenth- and nineteenth-century Germany

James Van Horn Melton

In Western political thought, the concept of civil society underwent a fundamental transformation during the seventeenth and eighteenth centuries. The individualistic premises of seventeenth-century natural law and the articulation of an autonomous sphere of exchange in the emerging science of political economy had by the late eighteenth century produced a concept of civil society that distinguished between a public realm monopolized by the state and a private sphere within which individuals were free to pursue their interests. This distinction reflected the growing emancipation of labour and commodity exchange from political and seigneurial directives, a process that increasingly stripped social relations of their 'public' character and relegated them to a 'private' sphere free from state interference. At the same time, the rise of the territorial state since the late Middle Ages had served to demarcate a sphere of public authority within which political functions, previously diffused at a varietly of levels, were consolidated and exercised by the sovereign state. The result was the disjunction of the public and private spheres that was to form the precondition for the modern liberal state.[1]

I would like to thank Howard Kaminsky and Edgar Melton for their helpful comments on an earlier draft of this essay. My thanks go also to the Institute for Advanced Study, Princeton, where a fellowship enabled me to carry out the necessary research.
[1] On the emergence of civil society as a sphere of private autonomy, see Jürgen Habermas, *Strukturwandel der Öffentlichkeit: Untersuchungen zu einer Kategorie der bürgerlichen Gesellschaft* (Darmstadt and Neuwied, 1962), pp. 94–101. See also John Keane, 'Despotism and democracy: the origins and development of the distinction between civil society and the state, 1750–1850', in *Civil Society and the State: new European perspectives*, ed. John Keane (Verso, London and New York, 1988), pp. 35–66.

The liberal disjunction of state and society ran counter to older traditions of political thought, dating back to Aristotle, that viewed social and economic relationships as embedded in and hence inseparable from the polity.[2] The identity of state and society was fundamental to Aristotelian political theory, and found classic expression in Aristotle's famous dictum that men were political animals, destined by nature for political association. Hence in the tradition of Aristotelian political thought, state and civil society – *polis* and *koinonia politike, res publica* and *societas civilis, Staat* and *bürgerliche Gesellschaft"* – were essentially synonymous. Utterly foreign to Aristotle, as one recent historian has written, was 'the peculiar division between a narrow public and broad private realm characteristic of bourgeois regimes'.[3] Aristotle's *polis* was a moral community and an end in itself, not an instrument for securing and promoting the private interests of individuals. Human association was the product neither of a fear of death, as Hobbes would later argue, nor of material self-interest, as Adam Smith was to contend. Human beings banded together because they were by nature political animals capable of concerted action directed towards a higher good. Hence community and polity, 'society' and 'state', were for Aristotle identical. This identity was implicit in his constitutional 'types' (monarchy, aristocracy, democracy), each an undifferentiated whole comprising both the 'public' and 'private spheres'.

Following the rediscovery and reception of Aristotle's *Politics* in the thirteenth century, Aristotelian categories became firmly entrenched in the political thought of late-medieval and early-modern Europe.[4] The conceptual conflation of state and civil society was in line with the fusion of 'public' and 'private' functions that had been the hallmark of European feudalism. The administrative, judicial, and fiscal functions that one associates with the modern state were shared at all levels by seigneurs, guilds, ecclesiastical corporations, and other 'private' individuals or corporations. Hence civil society was *de facto* political in character, while political authority

---

[2] On this tradition, see Otto Brunner, 'Das "ganze Haus" und die alteuro-päische "Ökonomik"', in idem, *Neue Wege der Verfassungs- und Sozialgeschichte*, 3rd edn (Göttingen, 1980).

[3] Paul Rahe, 'The primacy of politics in ancient Greece', *American Historical Review*, 89 (1984), p. 269. See also Jürgen Habermas, 'The classical doctrine of politics in relation to social philosophy', in idem, *Theory and Practice*, tr. John Viertel (Beacon Press, Boston, 1973), pp. 42–3.

[4] Quentin Skinner, *The Foundations of Modern Political Thought* (2 vols, Cambridge University Press, Cambridge, 1978), Vol. 1, pp. 49–51; Peter Petersen, *Geschichte der aristotelischen Philosophie im protestantischen Deutschland* (Leipzig, 1921), pp. 4–5.

was embedded in what we would call 'social' relations of dependence. Karl Marx recognized this aspect of 'old civil society', when he wrote:

> The character of the old civil society was *directly political*, that is to say, the elements of civil life, for example property, or the family, or the mode of labor, were raised to the level of elements of political life in the form of seigniory, estates, and corporations. . . . Thus, the vital function and conditions of life of civil society remained nevertheless political, although political in the feudal sense.[5]

Although the Aristotelian identification of state and civil society was commonplace in the political discourse in late-medieval and early-modern Europe, it proved particularly tenacious in Germany.[6] For in the Holy Roman Empire, social and political structures were constitutionally continuous to a degree not found elsewhere in Europe. This continuity is seen in the peculiar constitutional structure of the empire, fragmented as it was into hundreds of semi-autonomous principalities that included duchies, counties, bishoprics, imperial cities and knights, and the like. Although each of these territories was subject in varying ways to the emperor, its secular or ecclesiastical rulers exercised extensive rights of lordship (*Herrschaft*). Their rule emanated directly from the property rights and privileges they possessed as nobles, bishops, towns, or other corporations. Hence in the case of princely territories, as Leonard Krieger has written, 'the rights of aristocracy in the community were inextricably confused with the exercise of political rulership.'[7] Evocative of this 'confusion' was the fact that, as late as 1842, a Prussian nobleman could assert that 'the king is a large estate owner and landowner; the noble estate owner is a small king.'[8]

[5] Karl Marx, 'On the Jewish question', in Karl Marx and Friedrich Engels, *Collected Works* (New York, 1975), Vol. 3, p. 165.

[6] The standard English-language survey of German history during our period remains Hajo Holborn, *A History of Modern Germany* (Knopf, New York, 1959–69), vols 1–2. The more recent and concise study by Rudolf Vierhaus, *Germany in the Age of Absolutism*, tr. Jonathan B. Knudsen (Cambridge University Press, Cambridge, 1988), is valuable for the period from 1648 to 1763. Although technically not an introductory survey, Mack Walker's *German Home Towns: community, state, and general estate, 1648–1871* (Cornell University Press, Ithaca, 1971) is a broadly conceived and pioneering interpretative work.

[7] Leonard Krieger, *The German Idea of Freedom: history of a political tradition* (Beacon Press, Boston, 1957), p. 16.

[8] Quoted in Robert M. Berdahl, *The Politics of the Prussian Nobility: the development of a conservative ideology, 1770–1848* (Princeton University Press, Princeton, 1988), p. 54. Berdahl (p. 56) also notes that it was common for conservative Prussian nobles in the early nineteenth century to assert that estate ownership was an 'office' (*Amt*).

The term 'estate' was also illustrative of this fusion of the social and the political. 'Estate' (*Stand*, or *Stände* in the plural) was a category central to the social, political, and legal vocabulary of late-medieval and early-modern Germany. At the level of the empire, *Stände* referred to the plethora of territories or individuals who were directly subject to the emperor and who attended the imperial diet. At the territorial level, *Stände* designated those corporate groups (for example, nobles, burghers, or prelates) represented in the local diets. Finally, *Stand* also referred more broadly to an individual's social rank or occupation, as in *Adelstand* (nobility), *Bauernstand* (peasantry), or *Handwerkerstand* (artisanry), along with the juridical rights and privileges accompanying that status. In 1744, for example, Johann Heinrich Zedler's lexicon began by defining *Stand* as 'the quality of a person that distinguishes him from others, and which in view of this distinction, assigns him rights that are different from others.'[9] The protean concept of 'estate' shows the extent to which social, political, and juridical relationships were closely bound up with one another.[10]

To be sure, the consolidation of territorial absolutism in early-modern Germany ultimately pointed the way toward a more formal separation of public and private spheres. But initially, at least, German jurists and theologians had little difficulty assimilating the expansion of princely authority into traditional Aristotelian political categories. In this regard, the Protestant reformer Philip Melanchthon was a pivotal figure in the reception and popularization of the *Politics*. Faced with the task of institutionalizing the Reformation and concerned with the threat to Protestant unity posed by Anabaptism and Zwinglianism, Melanchthon drew on Aristotle in ceding to the prince a broad range of moral, religious, and social duties.[11] In so doing, Melanchthon helped to legitimate the growing intervention of territorial rulers in the lives of

---

[9] Johann Heinrich Zedler, *Grosses Vollständiges Universal-Lexicon* (64 vols, Leipzig and Halle, 1732–50) Vol. 39 (1744), p. 1093.

[10] On the concept of *Stand*, see Berdahl, *Politics of the Prussian Nobility*, pp. 11–13. For a brief but excellent discussion of 'estate' as a central concept of the late Middle Ages, see also Howard Kaminsky, *Simon de Cramaud and the Great Schism* (Rutgers University Press, New Brunswick, 1983), pp. 66–8.

[11] On Melanchthon and Aristotle, see Hans Maier, *Die ältere deutsche Staats- und Verwaltungslehre* (Neuwied, 1966), pp. 201–5; Petersen, *Geschichte der aristotelischen Philosophie*, pp. 42–52; Horst Dreitzel, *Protestantischer Aristotelismus und Absoluter Staat* (Wiesbaden, 1970), pp. 88–96. Melanchthon's educational reforms securely established Aristotle's *Politics* in Protestant university curricula, and his synthesis of Lutheran theology and Aristotelian philosophy established a tradition of political thought that prevailed at Protestant universities up to the eighteenth century.

their subjects. Epitomizing these interventionist tendencies was the proliferation of police (*Polizei*) ordinances that aimed at securing the moral, religious, and material well-being of the community. In early-modern Germany, 'police' denoted a far broader range of state activities than that implied in modern usage. *Polizei* ordinances attempted to regulate church attendance, the observance of religious holidays, the administration of poor relief, the spread of luxury, and other activities deemed important to the moral and spiritual life of the territorial community.[12] In this regard *Polizei* hearkened back to older conceptions of the state as an ethical community, and rested on an implicit identification of state and civil society.

In important respects the work of Samuel von Pufendorf (1632–94), the Saxon-born jurist, historian, and political theorist, broke with this tradition, and anticipated later conceptions of civil society as an autonomous sphere of exchange. Often regarded as a continental disciple of Hobbes, Pufendorf differed from the English philosopher in emphasizing the natural sociability (*socialitas*) of individuals. He attributed this sociability to the biological weakness of the human species: 'scarcely any other animal', he wrote, 'is attended from birth by such weakness. Hence it would be a miracle, if anyone reached mature years, if he had not the aid of other men.'[13] The inability of humans to survive on their own and their realization that security, the satisfaction of material needs, and the acquisition of goods were obtained more easily in commerce with others than in isolation, bound individuals together. 'They who unite in a body for promoting of Traffick, are led to it purely by Hopes of advancing their Goods more in Conjunction with others, than they could by their private Industry: and whatever disappoints or puts an end to these hopes, prevails with all, but Fools or Madmen, to put an end likewise to the Society [*societati*].'[14] Unlike the Dutch theorist Hugo

---

[12] On *Polizei* ordinances in early-modern Central Europe, see Marc Raeff, *The Well-Ordered Police State: social and institutional change through law in the Germanies and Russia, 1600–1800* (Yale University Press, New Haven, 1983), pp. 43–180, and Maier, *Die ältere deutsche Staats- und Verwaltungslehre*, pp. 130–84.

[13] Samuel von Pufendorf, *The Two Books on the Duty of Man and Citizen according to the Natural Law*, tr. Frank Gardner Moore (Oxford University Press, New York, 1927), Bk 1, ch. 3, sect. 3.

[14] Samuel von Pufendorf, *Of the Law of Nature and Nations*, tr. B. Kennet, 4th edn (London, 1729), Bk 7, ch. 1, sect. 2, as cited in Istvan Hont, 'The language of sociability and commerce; Samuel Pufendorf and the theoretical foundations of the "Four-Stages Theory"', in *The Languages of Political Theory in Early-Modern Europe* ed. Anthony Pagden (Cambridge University Press, Cambridge, 1987), p. 266. My account of Pufendorf's notion of sociability is taken from Hont's analysis, as well as that of Hans Medick, *Naturzustand und*

Grotius, Pufendorf did not consider society the result of any innate affection that humans felt for others. It was self-interest, not an 'appetite for society', that cemented the social bond. But unlike Hobbes, for whom untrammelled self-interest was a source of anarchy, Pufendorf viewed self-interest as constitutive society itself. Self-interest and sociability were not antithetical, but predicated on each other, an idea that was later to emerge in Adam Smith's theory of commercial society.[15]

Still, Pufendorf was careful to adapt his theory to the absolutist realities of his day. He believed that the growing complexity of civil society had in time required that its members surrender their natural freedom to a sovereign, to whom Pufendorf granted broad powers of intervention and regulation.[16] Here the contradiction between Pufendorf's absolutist conclusions and his 'proto-liberal' premises[17] reflected not only his political caution, but also the social and economic conditions that prevailed in Germany in the wake of the Thirty Years War.[18] As German princes faced the task of rebuilding and repopulating their territories, their policies became interventionist as never before. Absolutist police ordinances now sought to create the cultural and material preconditions for expanded production through measures like the promotion of technological innovation, improvements in transportation, and reforms in public hygiene and education.[19] In the process, the broadly interventionist policies of seventeenth- and eighteenth-century princes served further to encourage conceptions of the polity that subsumed 'social' relationships within it.

Naturgeschichte der bürgerlichen Gesellschaft. Die Ursprünge der bürgerlichen Sozialtheorie als Geschichtsphilosophie und Sozialwissenschaft bei Samuel Pufendorf, John Locke, und Adam Smith (Göttingen, 1973), pp. 40–63.

[15] In Pufendorf, writes Hont, 'the foundations of a theory of commercial society were already fully present': Hont, 'Language of sociability', p. 266.

[16] See Medick, *Naturzustand und Naturgeschichte*, pp. 60–3.

[17] It is by no means clear whether German readers of Pufendorf understood the 'liberal' implications of Pufendorf's concept of civil society. Even J. Weber, editor and translator of the 1711 Frankfurt edition of Pufendorf's *Law of Nature and of Nations*, added a footnote explaining that Pufendorf's use of the term 'civil society' referred to 'the ruling authorities [*Obrigkeiten*] and the subjects as bound together in an empire, republic, or the like'; quoted in Manfred Riedel, 'Gesellschaft, bürgerliche' in *Geschichtliche Grundbegriffe: Historisches Lexikon zur politisch-sozialen Sprache in Deutschland*, ed. Otto Brunner, Werner Conze, and Reinhardt Koselleck (5 vols, Stuttgart, 1972–84), vol. 2, p. 739.

[18] On the socio-economic consequences of the Thirty Years War, see Vierhaus, *Germany in the Age of Absolutism*, pp. 1–8, and Geoffrey Parker, *The Thirty Years' War* (Routledge, London, 1984), pp. 225–35.

[19] Raeff, *Well-Ordered Police State*, pp. 43–180.

These ideas found systematic expression in the work of Christian Wolff, the foremost representative of the early German Enlightenment, whose *Reasonable Thoughts on the Social Life of Man, and the Community in Particular* (1721) was known in its day as 'the German Politics'.[20] Defining society (*Gesellschaft*) as 'a means of promoting the common welfare',[21] Wolff made no sharp distinction between social and political institutions. His analysis of *Gesellschaft* examined not only institutions like marriage, the family, and the household, but also the various types of government.

Although Wolff was the last German philosopher to build a systematic philosophical edifice on Aristotelian foundations, the tradition he represented persisted throughout the eighteenth century. Beginning in the 1720s, the establishment of faculties of 'cameralistic science' (*Kameralwissenschaft*) at German universities also legitimated and systematized the interventionist policies of territorial absolutism. Cameralism (after *Kammer*, the chamber of the territorial ruler), which historians have often defined as simply a Central European variant of mercantilism, was in fact far more ambitious in its range of theoretical and practical concerns.[22] As a self-professed science of politics, cameralism sanctioned state intervention in virtually every sphere of social, economic, and cultural life. For Joseph Sonnenfels, the Austrian cameralist and official, political subordination and membership in civil society were inseparable: 'We cannot keep ourselves from looking to the head [*Oberhaupt*] of a society. . . . We perceive society, and we perceive ourselves as part of society, in the prince.'[23] While the term 'civil society' (*bürgerliche Gesellschaft*) appears often in

---

[20] See Hans Werner Arndt's introduction to Christian Wolff, *Vernünftige Gedanken von dem gesellschaftlichen Leben der Menschen und insoderheit dem gemeinen Wesen*. Here I have used the 4th edn (Frankfurt and Leipzig, 1736), repr. in Wolff, *Gesammelte Werke*, Pt 1, vol. 5 (Hildesheim and New York, 1975).

[21] Ibid., p. 3.

[22] On cameralism, see Walker, *German Home Towns*, pp. 145–51; Keith Tribe, *Governing Economy: the reformation of German economic discourse, 1750–1840* (Cambridge University Press, Cambridge, 1988), pp. 35–54; James Van Horn Melton, *Absolutism and the Eighteenth-Century Origins of Compulsory Schooling in Prussia and Austria* (Cambridge University Press, Cambridge, 1988), pp. 110–19.

[23] Joseph Sonnenfels, 'Über die Liebe des Vaterlandes', in his *Gesammelte Schriften* (Vienna, 1785), vol. 7, p. 120, as cited in Leonard Krieger, *An Essay on the Theory of Enlightened Despotism* (University of Chicago Press, Chicago, 1975), p. 50. On the absence of any fundamental distinction between state and society in cameralist thought, see Tribe, *Governing Economy*, p. 64.

eighteenth-century German treatises on politics, it did not denote a private sphere of social relations independent of the state and subject to its own laws. Even as the terms 'social' and 'society' gained widespread currency in France with the appearance of Rousseau's *Du contrat social* (1762), d'Holbach's *Système social* (1773), and the works of the physiocrats, German translations were just as apt to render 'social' as 'political'. The physiocrat G. F. Le Trosne's *On the Social Order* (1777), for example, was translated three years later by Christian Friedrich Wichmann as *The System of Political Order*.[24] As for the influence of Scottish moral philosophy, much has been made of the 'Smith reception' in Germany as a source of liberal economic thought. But while German translations of *The Wealth of Nations* appeared in 1776–8 and 1794–6, its *laissez-faire* implications do not appear to have been as obvious to eighteenth-century Germans as they are to us today. Indeed, eclectic cameralist writers like Sonnenfels or J. E. von Pfeiffer had little difficulty in selectively assimilating Smith's ideas into their own statist categories.[25]

During and after the French Revolution, the conceptual conflation of state and society persisted in German political discourse. Indeed, it is striking that it was the 1790s that witnessed the first German translations of Aristotle's *Politics*, those of the Badenese official Johann Georg Schlosser (1798) and the Silesian publicist Christian Garve (1799).[26] Schlosser, the brother-in-law of Goethe and a critic of the French Revolution, published his translation and commentary with the express purpose of reaffirming the importance of the *Politics* in the light of

[24] Le Trosne, *De l'ordre sociale* (1777); translated by Christian Friedrich Wichmann as *Lehrbegriff der Staatsordnung* (Leipzig, 1780). The tendency of German translators to render the term 'society' as 'state' persisted in the nineteenth century. Franz Josef von Buss, the Catholic social reformer, translated G. P. Hepp's *Essai sur la théorie de la vie sociale* (Essay on the Theory of Social Life) (Paris, 1836) as *Systeme der Staatswissenschaft* (System of Political Science) (Freiburg im Breisgau, 1839). In the text, Buss rendered 'social theories' as 'theories of the state', and 'individuals living in society' as 'individuals living in the state'. For these and other examples, see L. A. Geck, *Über das Eindringen des Wortes 'sozial' in die deutsche Sprache* (Göttingen, 1963), p. 10.

[25] See Tribe, *Governing Economy*, pp. 133–48. On German translations of Smith and other Scottish writers, see the useful appendix in Norbert Waszek, *The Scottish Enlightenment and Hegel's Account of Civil Society* (Kluwer Academic Press, Dordrecht, 1988) pp. 252–67.

[26] Johann George Schlosser, *Aristoteles Politik und Fragment der Oeconomik: Aus dem Griechischen übersetzt und mit Anmerkungen und einer Analyse des Textes versehen von J. G. Schlosser* (Lübeck and Leipzig, 1798); Christian Garve, *Die Politik des Aristotles* (Breslau, 1799).

1789.[27] Political theorists of the Restoration condemned the natural-rights tradition, which they blamed for the cataclysmic events of the revolutionary era, and adamantly rejected any distinction between state and society. A conservative defender of monarchical rule and noble privilege, Karl Ludwig von Haller vehemently denied that civil society could have existed prior to the state. Haller's major work, appropriately entitled *The Restoration of Political Science* (1816–20), insisted that dominion had always existed in nature: 'Just as nature unites individuals through their mutual needs and diverse endowments, so, by necessity, has nature established relations of dominion and dependence, freedom and subjection, without which any kind of association is impossible.'[28] The fallacious idea of civil society as a sphere of freedom and equality, he argued, stemmed from a wilful distortion of the republican forms of speech that had characterized Roman political language. Natural-rights theorists had adapted terms like *societas civilis* and *res publica* to their own ideological agenda, thereby positing a sphere of natural equality that was prior to, and hence independent of, the state. The resulting disjunction, a product of 'the celebrated tendency in more recent times to separate artificially everything that belongs together',[29] had produced revolution, undermined relations of dominion and dependence, and hence destroyed the natural bonds uniting individuals. The idea of civil society as an association of free and equal members had been particularly destructive in this regard, and Haller wished for nothing so much as its elimination from all political writing: 'It would be desirable if the expression *civil society*, a term originally imported from the Latin *societas civilis*, could be banned from learning altogether.'[30]

Haller's bitter polemic indicates that, despite the survival of the Aristotelian tradition in German political thought, the disaggregation of older conceptions of civil society had become clearly visible by the early nineteenth century. Already in the eighteenth century, the new forms of literary expression and bourgeois sociability that characterized the

[27] See Manfred Riedel, 'Aristoteles-Tradition am Ausgang des 18. Jahrhunderts: Zur ersten Übersetzung der "Politik" durch Johann George Schlosser', in *Alteuropa und die moderne Gesellschaft: Festschrift für Otto Brunner* (Göttingen, 1963), pp. 278–315; and idem, *Between Tradition and Revolution: the Hegelian transformation of political philosophy*, tr. W. Wright (Cambridge University Press, Cambridge, 1984), p. 134.

[28] Karl Ludwig von Haller, *Restauration der Staats-Wissenschaft* (2nd edn, 6 vols, Winterthur, 1820–5), vol. 1, p. 351.

[29] Ibid., vol. 1, p. 14.

[30] Ibid., vol 1, p. 461.

culture of the German Enlightenment[31] were helping to establish the conceptual foundations for the disjunction of the private and the public spheres. Paradigmatic of this process were the so-called 'moral weeklies', which arose during the second decade of the eighteenth century and reached the high point of their popularity in the 1740s. The moral weekly of the early eighteenth century was aimed at the commercial bourgeoisie in centres like Hamburg and Leipzig, where trade had begun to recover from its seventeenth-century slump by 1700.[32] Like the English *Spectator* and *Tatler*, on which they were originally modelled, moral weeklies like the Hamburg *Patriot* (1724–6) or the Leipzig *Biedermann* (1727–9) aimed at the moral edification of an educated, middle-class readership.[33] They were overwhelmingly apolitical, and articles rarely dealt with the world of diplomacy, courts, or administration. A contributor's comment in the *Patriot* in 1726 that 'I don't get mixed up in public matters, for that I haven't any vocation,' is highly characteristic of the genre.[34] The terms 'social' and 'society' appear repeatedly in the moral weeklies, but they refer not to the broader sphere of human relations but to a narrower, privatized world of family, friends, reading groups, and other such forms of bourgeois sociability. With their demonstrative abstention from politics and their self-conscious, almost philistine preoccupation with the private world of the *Bürger*, the moral weeklies implicitly affirmed a separation of the social and the political, the public and the private. Their deliberate abstinence from political discussion in part reflected the constraints of censorship. More positively, however, moral weeklies served to delineate a bourgeois sphere distinct from the sphere of the princely court. Although they abstained from any commentary on political matters, moral weeklies frequently contrasted the superficiality and ostentation of court life with the sobriety and propriety of the *Bürger*. In 1726, the Hamburg *Patriot* described the ideal *Bürger* in the following terms:

[31] On Enlightenment culture in Germany, see the standard work by W. H. Bruford, *Germany in the Eighteenth Century: the social background of the literary revival* (Cambridge University Press, Cambridge, 1959).

[32] On the commercial significance of eighteenth-century Hamburg and Leipzig, see Vierhaus, *Germany in the Age of Absolutism*, pp. 25–6. For Hamburg, see also Joachim Whaley, *Religious Toleration and Social Change in Hamburg, 1529–1819* (Cambridge University Press, Cambridge, 1985), pp. 10–11.

[33] On the moral weeklies, see the indispensable study by Wolfgang Martens, *Die Botschaft der Tugend: Die Aufklärung im Spiegel der deutschen moralischen Wochenschriften* (Stuttgart, 1968).

[34] Quoted in ibid., p. 334.

'Everything in his outer conduct is upright, proper, and of good taste, but also bourgeois [*bürgerlich*] in every regard. He knows and sets the borders between bourgeois prosperity and a noble or courtly style of living; balls, galas, soirées, and card-playing are not terms that can be found in his bourgeois dictionary.'[35]

As Reinhart Koselleck has argued, the remarkable popularity of Freemasonry in eighteenth-century Germany was also paradigmatic of a stricter delineation between the public and the private spheres.[36] In the beginning at least, Freemasonry explicitly eschewed political aims in favour of the moral improvement of its members. The masonic obsession with secrecy further reinforced a disjunction of a private, moral sphere from the public realm of politics. Implicit in the masonic cult of secrecy was the attempt to establish an autonomous, interior space within the state, free of political intervention, where social rank was not a criterion for membership.[37] The analogies between Freemasonry and the changing concept of civil society were noted by Gotthold Ephraim Lessing in his *Ernst und Falk* (1778–80), where the Freemason Falk proclaimed that 'by its very nature, Freemasonry is as old as civil society. Both could only originate together, if civil society is not itself the outgrowth of Freemasonry.'[38]

Also symptomatic of the emerging sphere of the private was the shift in the language of household and family that occurred in the eighteenth and nineteenth centuries. Prior to the eighteenth century, the use of the German word *Familie* was relatively rare; far more common was the term *Haus*, or household, which designated not only a kinship group but also the totality of individuals living under the authority of the *paterfamilias*. In seigneurial households this included peasant subjects, in peasant households the farm servants and 'hired hands', and in guild households journeymen and apprentices.[39] In this sense, *Haus* expressed

---

[35] Ibid., pp. 347–8.

[36] Reinhart Koselleck, *Kritik und Krise: Eine Studie zur Pathogenese der bürgerlichen Welt* (Freiburg and Munich, 1959), pp. 49–60. The first masonic lodge in Germany was established in 1737, and within five years additional lodges had cropped up in most major German cities. See Horst Möller, *Vernunft und Kritik: Deutsche Aufklärung im 17. und 18. Jahrhundert* (Frankfurt am Main, 1986,), pp. 217–18.

[37] Koselleck, *Kritik und Krise*, p. 57.

[38] Gotthold Ephraim Lessing, *Ernst und Falk* (1778–80), in *Lessings Werke*, vol. 12 (Stuttgart, 1890), as cited in Koselleck, *Kritik und Krise*, p. 57.

[39] On the concept of the household in 'Old Europe', see Brunner, 'Das "ganze Haus"'.

the fusion of public and private authority so characteristic of social and political relationships in early-modern Germany.

Only in the eighteenth century, when the French word *famille* was imported into German usage, did the use of *Familie* become relatively common.[40] Even then, the word initially retained the older and broader sense of *Haus*. In 1735, for example, Johann Heinrich Zedler's *Universal-Lexikon* defined *Familie* as 'as number of persons . . . who are subject to the power and dominion of the housefather [*Hausvater*].[41] In the course of the century, however, German definitions progressively narrowed. In 1775, Johann Christoph Adelung's lexicon defined the family as 'those persons, married couples and children, who make up the society of a household. . . . Occasionally this expression also includes the domestic servants and farm hands.'[42] In 1784, the *German Encyclopedia* restricted the term 'family' to a man's 'wife, children, and relatives, who live together in an undivided household; servants can be reckoned a part of the family only in a limited sense.'[43] In the Prussian General Code of 1794, the legal definition of the family was restricted to husband, wife, children, and, only in limited cases, to servants.[44] In practice, the Prussian state during the first half of the nineteenth century lacked the administrative resources and apparatus needed to police the countryside effectively, and continued to rely on the household as a unit of social and political control.[45] But in the early nineteenth century the narrower definition of *Familie*, seen in Hegel's conception of the family as a private domestic sphere of 'affective' relations,[46] had clearly begun to compete with older notions of the *Haus*. Writing in the wake of 1848, the conservative publicist and ethnographer Wilhelm Heinrich

---

[40] See Dieter Schwab, 'Familie', in *Geschichtliche Grundbegriffe*, vol. 2, p. 270.

[41] Zedler, *Grosses Vollständiges Universal-Lexikon*, vol. 9 (1741), p. 205.

[42] Quoted in Schwab, 'Familie', p. 277.

[43] Quoted in ibid.

[44] See Reinhart Koselleck, *Preussen zwischen Reform und Revolution*, 3rd edn (Stuttgart, 1981), pp. 62–77; and idem, 'Die Auflösung des Hauses als ständischer Herrschaftseinheit: Anmerkungen zum Rechtswandel von Haus, Familie, und Gesinde in Preussen zwischen der Französischen Revolution und 1848', in Neithard Bulst *et al.*, *Familie zwischen Tradition und Moderne* (Göttingen, 1981), pp. 112–15.

[45] Koselleck, 'Die Auflösung des Hauses', p. 121. See also Christiane Eisenberg, *Deutsche und englische Gewerkschaften: Entstehung und Entwicklung bis 1878 im Vergleich* (Göttingen, 1986), pp. 56–7.

[46] 'The family, as the immediate substantiality of mind, is specifically characterized by love': Georg Wilhelm Friedrich Hegel, *The Philosophy of Right*, tr. T. M. Knox (Clarendon Press, Oxford, 1942), para. 158.

Riehl lamented: 'Unfortunately our modern age recognizes only the "family", not the comprehensive household [*das ganze Haus*], that cosy and congenial concept that includes not only the biological family members, but also those bound to them through their labor and through bonds of spontaneous affection.'[47]

If the emerging sphere of the private served to transform the language of civil society in eighteenth-century Germany, so did new conceptions of the public realm. In sixteenth- and seventeenth-century Germany, the German term *Publikum* (derived from the classical Latin *publicus*) referred generally to those subject to a particular edict or decree issued by a ruling prince.[48] In the early eighteenth century, however, *Publikum* also acquired a meaning less political in nature, and referred particularly to an educated readership, the 'reading public', to whom a written work was addressed. In this sense *Publikum* (or its synonym *Öffentlichkeit*), reflected the growth of literary production associated first with moral weeklies and later with the dramatic expansion of political journalism beginning in the 1770s.[49] By then the term had become politicized, referring to an enlightened 'public opinion', which was independent of princely courts as well as of traditional corporate institutions and estates, and which represented the interests of society *vis-à-vis* the ruler.[50] In 1784 Friedrich Karl Freiherr von Moser, editor of the influential *Patriotic Archive for Germany* (Frankfurt), declared that the rise of political journalism served 'to arraign before the high court of the public [*Publikum*] the evil and brutal prince, those who oppress and deceive the land . . . without view of their person, estate, or title.'[51] The self-appointed spokesmen for this public – journalists like Moser in Frankfurt or August Ludwig Schlözer in Göttingen – found in 'publicity' (*Publicität*) their primary weapon. They identified *Publicität* with the free and open exchange of ideas, freedom of the press and freedom of speech. Johann Wilhelm von Archenholz, the Prussian-born journalist and Anglophile, waxed enthusiastically: '*Publicität*! That magical word now heard everywhere, the word to which even princely perukes and

---

[47] Wilhelm Heinrich Riehl, *Die Naturgeschichte des deutschen Volkes*, vol. 3: *Die Familie*, ed. Günther Ipsen (Leipzig, 1935), p. 202.

[48] See Lucian Hölscher, 'Öffentlichkeit', *Geschichtliche Grundbegriff*, vol. 4, p. 422.

[49] See the analysis and statistics in Hans-Ulrich Wehler, *Deutsche Gesellschaftsgeschichte*, vol. 1: *Vom Feudalismus des Alten Reiches bis zur Defensiven Modernisierung der Reformära, 1700–1815* (Munich, 1987), pp. 304–6, and Möller, *Vernunft und Kritik*, pp. 268–81.

[50] See Habermas, *Strukturwandel der Öffentlichkeit*, pp. 76–111.

[51] Quoted in Hölscher, 'Öffentlichkeit', p. 437.

heads of nations defer – pay heed!'[52] The term 'public opinion' (*öffentliche Meinung*), in the sense of an educated body of opinion representing the interests of society against the ruler, was borrowed from the French, and increasingly popularized during the Revolution. Writing after the defeat of Napoleon in 1814, the Rhineland progressive Joseph Görres called upon German journalists to be 'spokesmen for public opinion, tribunes who represent the majority, the mouth of the people and the ear of the princes'.[53]

After 1815, 'public opinion' became a catchword legitimizing the constitutional demands of the liberal bourgeoisie. Here 'public opinion' was synonymous not with the voice of the majority, but with that of the propertied and educated middle classes. In 1820, the *Brockhaus* lexicon defined the term as 'the prevailing views of the larger, more educated part of the public concerning the general affairs of mankind'; more concretely, the historian Leopold von Ranke wrote in 1832 that public opinion 'resides in the middling classes of the people.'[54] But for our purposes, what is significant about the term is not its social referent, but rather the way it served to crystallize the concept of a social sphere whose interests were not necessarily identical with those of the state. Predicated on a market-related model of free exchange, affirming the existence of a body of opinion representing the interests of society *vis-à-vis* the state, the category of public opinion helped to sharpen the distinction between the social and the political.

By the late eighteenth century, German political commentators had begun to draw such a contrast. In 1792 the Marburg cameralist Heinrich Jung-Stilling distinguished between 'state society' (*Staatsgesellschaft*) and 'civil society' (*bürgerliche Gesellschaft*), and a year later the Göttingen journalist and historian August Ludwig Schlözer similarly contrasted 'civil society without government' (*societas civilis sine imperio*) with 'civil society with government' (*societas civilis cum imperio*).[55] It was during the first half of the nineteenth century, however, that the concept of civil society as a private, autonomous realm came into its own. It was to be most systematically elaborated in Hegel's *Philosophy of Right* (1821) and, by extension, in the writings of Lorenz von Stein and Karl Marx. Hegel conceived of civil society as a discrete, intermediary realm between the family and the state. This sphere – and here Hegel's reasoning closely resembles that of Pufendorf and the Scottish philosophers –

---

[52] Ibid., p. 447.
[53] Ibid., p. 454.
[54] Ibid., p. 455.
[55] See Otto Brunner, 'Freiheitsbegriff', in idem, *Neue Wege*, p. 187.

ultimately arose out of the recognition by individuals that they could satisfy their needs more easily in commerce with others than in isolation. So while Hegel saw civil society as a sphere of 'particular wills' within which individuals pursued their private interests, he believed that the interdependence of human needs served to prevent civil society from collapsing under the weight of egoistic drives: 'In the course of the actual attainment of selfish ends, . . . there is formed a system of complete interdependence, wherein the livelihood, happiness, and legal status of one man is interwoven with the livelihood, happiness and rights of all.'[56]

Yet Hegel's vision of civil society was inspired by more than the abstractions of political economy. Although Hegel, like Adam Smith, saw civil society as bound together by a system of needs, he also saw it pulled apart by the contingencies of the market and the crises of overproduction that he recognized as an inevitable result of modern capitalism. While the household economy of the past had provided some degree of security and subsistence in times of dearth, civil society 'tears the individual from his family, estranges the members of the family from one another, and recognizes them as self-subsistent persons.'[57] The ominous consequences of this deracination could be found in England, whose impoverished 'rabble of paupers' Hegel viewed as 'one of the most disturbing problems which agitate modern society.'[58]

Although it took England as a model, Hegel's view of mass poverty as an affliction endemic to modern civil society anticipated the debate over 'the social question' that raged in Central Europe during the 1830s and 1840s. Here, as in France and England, the upheavals of 1830 sharpened the perception of *Pauperismus* as a uniquely modern phenomenon. Borrowed from English and French usage, the word *Pauperismus* came into vogue in the late 1830s. It was used to denote the mass of rural and urban poor who were propertyless, and hence without any apparent stake in the existing social order.[59] The social and economic roots of *Pauperismus* lay in the dramatic expansion of a landless, sub-peasant stratum of rural labourers that had occurred during the preceding century. Initially the problem was somewhat mitigated by the growth of 'proto-industrial' production in regions like northwest Germany, Silesia, and Bohemia. But by the 1830s, demographic growth in the countryside had begun to reach its Malthusian limit, while

[56] Hegel, *Philosophy of Right*, para. 183.
[57] Ibid., para. 238.
[58] Ibid., addition 149.
[59] Werner Conze, 'Proletariat, Pöbel, Pauperismus', in *Geschichtliche Grundbegriffe*, vol. 5, pp. 41–4.

competition from English textiles inflicted a devastating toll on Central European cloth production. The resulting crisis, which reached its peak in the famine of 1845–7, drove thousands of rural and urban labourers down to the barest subsistence level.[60]

The accompanying debate over the origins and nature of *Pauperismus* helped to transform the language of civil society in two fundamental ways. First, the more modern terms 'class' (*Klasse*) and 'proletariat' (*Proletarier*) rapidly gained currency in German political discourse, their usage now rivalling that of earlier terms like 'estate' (*Stand*) or 'rabble' (*Pöbel*).[61] The term *Klasse* had been used to characterize social groups since the late eighteenth century, but usually in a highly general way. In 1810, for example, the Prussian reformer Karl August von Hardenburg called on representatives from 'every class of the people' to support his fiscal reforms of 1810.[62] In the course of the *Pauperismus* debate of the 1830s, however, more specific modifiers were joined to the term as a way of distinguishing the propertyless from the propertied. Hence the 'lower classes' (*niedere Klassen*), 'poor classes' (*arme Volksklassen*), and 'proletarian class' (*Klasse von Proletariern*) were contrasted with the 'upper classes' (*höhere Klassen*) or 'educated classes' (*gebildete Klassen*).[63] It was also in the 1830s that 'Proletariat' (*Proletarier*), a word hitherto rare in German usage, became an established social category. To contemporaries, proletariat and *Pauperismus* went hand in hand: 'The proletariat', wrote the Prussian official Josef von Radowitz in 1846, 'looms like a giant, and with it pauperism, the festering wound of the age, is torn open.'[64]

Second, as a result of the debate over the 'social question' (*soziale Frage*), the term 'sozial', also rare prior to this time, had by 1840 fully entered the vocabulary of German publicists and politicians.[65] Particularly striking in this regard was the deliberate contrast now drawn between

---

[60] For a concise analysis, see Wehler, *Deutsche Gesellschaftsgeschichte*, vol. 2, pp. 281–96.

[61] For a discussion of this shift, see Werner Conze, 'From "Pöbel" to "Proletariat": the socio-historical preconditions of socialism in Germany', in *The Social History of Politics: critical perspectives in West German historical writing since 1945*, ed. G. Iggers (Berg, New York, 1985), pp. 49–80; James J. Sheehan, *German Liberalism in the Nineteenth Century* (University of Chicago Press, Chicago, 1978), p. 32; Wehler, *Deutsche Gesellschaftsgeschichte*, vol. 2, pp. 559–60.

[62] Cited in Wehler, *Deutsche Gesellschaftsgeschichte*, vol. 2, p. 559.

[63] Ibid., p. 560.

[64] Quoted in Conze, 'From "Pöbel" to "Proletariat"', p. 59.

[65] Geck, *Über das Endringen des Wortes 'sozial'*, p. 16.

social and political phenomena. In 1844, for example, the liberal writer Theodor Oelker distinguished between matters that were 'purely social' and those that were 'political'; that same year, his liberal compatriot Theodor Mundt warned of the 'seeds of discontent that threaten to lead not merely to political but also to social revolution.' In 1847, the literary historian and publicist Emil Weller observed that 'what we now designate with the word *social* was in the past rendered by the concept *political*.'[66]

With the outbreak of revolution in 1848, opponents, as well as supporters of revolution, emphasized its explicitly social character. Prince Metternich acknowledged despairingly that the crisis 'was no longer about politics [*Politik*], but the social question.' In Berlin, the radical republican Rudolf Virchow concurred: 'This revolution is not simply political; it is at heart social in character.'[67]

In 1855 Robert von Mohl, the South German liberal and professor of politics, wrote that 'in recent times it has come to be clearly recognized that the communal life of the individual in no way exists in the state alone. . . . The word "society" has finally been spoken.'[68] As Mohl noted, by the mid-nineteenth century the term 'social' had come to designate a sphere of activities and relationships conceptually distinct from the state.

Yet remnants of the older Aristotelian paradigm were to persist in German thought. German economic science in the nineteenth century retained a strong ethical component, and its leading representatives never questioned the interdependence of state and economy.[69] As Manfred Riedel has argued, a concept of the state rooted in the political categories of Greek antiquity was also a hallmark of nineteenth-century German historicism.[70] Here it follows that the first major critic of the

---

[66] Quoted in ibid., p. 42.
[67] Wehler, *Deutsche Gesellschaftsgeschichte*, vol. 2, p. 703.
[68] Robert von Mohl, *Die Geschichte und Literatur der Staatswissenschaften* (Erlangen, 1855), pp. 70–1.
[69] See Tribe, *Governing Economy*, pp. 5–6, and Edgar Salin, *Geschichte der Volkswirtschaftslehre*, 3rd edn (Bern, 1944), p. 37.
[70] Manfred Riedel, 'Der Staatsbegriff der deutschen Geschichtsschreibung des 19. Jahrhunderts in seinem Verhältnis zur klassisch-politischen Philosophie', *Der Staat*, 2 (1963), pp. 42–4. See also Wolfgang Hardtwig, *Geschichtsschreibung zwischen Alteuropa und Moderner Welt: Jakob Burckhardt in seiner Zeit* (Göttingen, 1974), pp. 328–31. On nineteenth-century German historicism, see Georg Iggers, *The German Conception of History* (Wesleyan University Press, Middletown, Ct, 1968; rev. edn 1983); and Leonard Krieger, *Ranke: the meaning of history* (University of Chicago Press, Chicago, 1977).

newly emerging discipline of sociology was Heinrich von Treitschke. Treitschke's 1859 polemic against Robert von Mohl, who in 1855 had called for a science of society (*Gesellschaftswissenschaft*) distinct from a science of politics (*Staatswissenschaft*), helped launch a debate that continued well into the next century.[71] Bemoaning what he saw as a disintegration of the older tradition of *Staatswissenschaft* into the modern disciplines of sociology and economics, Treitschke called for a return to the ancient ideal of the state as the core of all national life.[72] In viewing sociology as the historically contingent product of a civil society artificially disjoined from the state, Treitschke articulated what was to become a persistent theme in German conservative thought.[73] At the same time, Treitschke's invocation of the Greek *polis* epitomized an attitude towards state and society that would continue to pervade much German political discourse. Writing at the end of the nineteenth century, the historian Otto Hintze summarized this attitude when he wrote:

> When we [Germans] use the term 'state', we do not simply mean the government . . . but also the land and its people. In this respect, our usage does not entirely conform to that of the English and the French. For them, a population living together and united under a political organization is defined as a 'society', and they conceive of the 'state' more narrowly than we. But for us the state is concrete unity . . ., a totality comprising both 'state' and 'society'.[74]

Even today, remnants of this tendency to represent state and society as continuous spheres linger in the German term *Bürger*. Meaning both

---

[71] Mohl, *Geschichte und Literatur*, pp. 102–10; Riedel, 'Der Staatsbegriff', p. 51.

[72] Heinrich von Treitschke, *Die Gesellschaftswissenschaft: Ein kritischer Versuch* (Leipzig, 1859; repr. Halle, 1927), esp. p. 40. In Treitschke's essay, 32 out of a total of 169 footnotes are references to Aristotle's *Politics*. Treitschke later wrote to the economist Gustav Schmoller that 'my real teacher on politics was Aristotle': Treitschke, *Briefe*, ed. Max Cornelius (3 vols, Leipzig, 1913–20), vol. 3, p. 397.

[73] This theme was particularly prominent during the Nazi period, when it was further developed by the jurist E. R. Huber, the sociologist Hans Freyer, and the historian Otto Brunner. For examples, see Ernst Rudolf Huber, 'Die deutsche Staatswissenschaft', *Zeitschrift für die gesamte Staatswissenschaft*, 95 (1934), pp. 8–15; Hans Freyer, 'Gegenwartsaufgaben der deutschen Soziologie', *Zeitschrift für die gesamte Staatswissenschaft*, 95 (1934), pp. 117–30; Otto Brunner, *Land und Herrschaft*, 3rd edn (Brünn, 1943), pp. 124–34.

[74] Otto Hintze, 'Roschers politische Entwicklungstheorie', in idem, *Gesammelte Abhandlungen*, vol. 1: *Soziologie und Geschichte: Gesammelte Abhandlungen zur Soziologie, Politik und Theorie der Geschichte*, ed. Gerhard Oestreich (Göttingen, 1964), p. 41.

'bourgeois' and 'citizen', *Bürger* has a semantic field that includes both private members of civil society as well as citizens of a state. Here it is revealing that Hegel's Heidelberg lectures on natural law and politics (1817–18), where he first developed his celebrated distinction between state and civil society, resorted to the French *citoyen* and *bourgeois* in order to avoid the ambiguity implicit in the term *Bürger*: 'Here [in civil society] the *Bürger* is a *bourgeois*, not a *citoyen*.'[75]

It is worth pondering how this conceptual ambiguity may have shaped German attitudes toward 'bourgeois society' in the nineteenth and twentieth centuries. In the course of the nineteenth century, *bürgerliche Gesellschaft* increasingly came to mean not just civil society in the liberal sense, but also the more emotionally charged 'bourgeois society'. Here the term's negative rhetorical thrust was to characterize both socialist discourse on the left, as well as a tradition of radical conservative thought stretching from Wilhelm Heinrich Riehl in the 1850s to the sociologist Hans Freyer in the National Socialist era.[76] At both ends of the political spectrum, of course, hostility towards bourgeois society was a response to the new problems posed by industrialism, urbanism, and the apparent triumph of the cash nexus in social relations. But as we have seen above, these connotations also had an older lineage, one rooted in a classical language of politics that was antithetical to the presuppositions of modern civil society in the West.

---

[75] G. W. F. Hegel, *Vorlesungen über Naturrecht und Staatswissenschaft*, ed. C. Becker *et al.* (Hamburg, 1983), p. 112.

[76] See Riehl, *Die Naturgeschichte*. On Freyer's earlier hostility to bourgeois society, see the excellent study by Jerry Z. Muller, *The Other God that Failed: Hans Freyer and the deradicalization of German conservatism* (Princeton University Press, Princeton, 1987), esp. pp. 194–5. The radical conservative hostility to bourgeois society is also treated in the classic study by Fritz Stern, *The Politics of Cultural Despair: a study in the rise of the Germanic ideology* (University of California Press, Berkeley, 1961).

7

From gentlemen to the residuum: languages of social description in Victorian Britain

Geoffrey Crossick

When John Wade published his *History of the Middle and Working Classes* in 1833,[1] there was nothing new about such use of the language of class. Just three years previously a meeting to approve the setting up of the Birmingham Political Union had agreed that 'it is expedient to form a GENERAL POLITICAL UNION between the Lower and the Middle Classes of the people.'[2] Class terminology, emerging as an element in public language during the previous century, now became prominent in political debate. It came readily to the lips of a Lancashire weaver in 1841, who urged those gathered to protest at the new police force in his area. 'Who sent for the police?' He replied that it was: 'the middle class. The middle class chose the men who concocted and passed

I am grateful to Heinz-Gerhard Haupt and Peter Trudgill for their comments on an earlier version of this essay, and to Jürgen Kocka for a helpful discussion on some of its themes.

[1] J. Wade, *History of the Middle and Working Classes: with a popular exposition of the economical and political principles which have influenced the past and present condition of the industrious orders* (London, 1833). Readers unfamiliar with nineteenth-century British society will find useful introductions in the following works: F. M. L. Thompson, *The Rise of Respectable Society: a social history of Victorian Britain, 1830–1900* (Fontana, London, 1988); H. Perkin, *The Origins of Modern English Society, 1780–1880* (Routledge, London, 1969); G. Best, *Mid-Victorian Britain, 1851–75* (Weidenfeld, London, 1971).

[2] A. Briggs, 'Thomas Attwood and the economic background of the Birmingham Political Union', in *The Collected Essays of Asa Briggs* (2 vols, Harvester, Brighton, 1985), vol. 1: *Words, Numbers, Places, People*, p. 160.

the law empowering the police to become in society nothing but out-laws.'[3]

These were heady days in British political life, and such times of social and political crisis diffuse words which have spread more slowly in preceding years. By the end of the 1840s many witnesses before parliamentary inquiries spoke a language of class with increasing comfort; before the Select Committee that investigated public library provision in 1849, people of widely varying political opinions talked of 'lower classes', 'working classes', 'middle classes', 'middle and professional classes', and 'labouring classes'.[4] Much can be made of the different adjectives attached to the word 'class', and of whether the term was used in the singular or plural form. 'Middle class' became singular first,[5] as is neatly indicated by Cobbett's 1830 observation that 'we see, at last, then, the middle class uniting with the working classes',[6] but one can exaggerate the significance of such nuances in Britain. Jean Dubois found that the cleavage in France between *classes ouvrières* and *classe ouvrière* followed recognizable political lines in the three years of crisis that followed 1869, with the plural a descriptive term which implicitly denied the unity of workers, while the singular form assumed a measure of class antagonism and was most used by socialists.[7] However, no such political distinction can be discerned in Britain during those earlier years of political crisis. Nor does disagreement over whether to talk of 'working', 'labouring', or 'operative' classes seem to have followed any obvious political lines – the radical *Poor Man's Guardian* used most of them fairly indiscriminately. 'Lower' was perhaps the one adjective that evoked distaste among those to whom it was applied, as when the radical *Gorgon* as early as 1818 demanded reforms that would allow the productive energies of the people to prevail, so that they would no

---

[3] Quoted in R. D. Storch, 'The plague of Blue Locusts: police reform and popular resistance in northern England, 1840–57, *International Review of Social History*, 20 (1975), p. 71.

[4] Select Committee on Public Libraries, *British Parliamentary Papers*, referred to hereafter as *BPP*, 1849, vol. 17.

[5] The *Oxford English Dictionary* gives 1812 as the date of the first singular usage. The *Examiner* on 31 Aug. 1812 wrote of 'such of the Middle Class of Society who have fallen upon evil days.'

[6] Quoted by G. Himmelfarb, *The Idea of Poverty: England in the early industrial age* (Faber, London, 1984), p. 292.

[7] J. Dubois, *Le vocabulaire politique et social en France de 1869 à 1872* (Paris, 1962), pp. 18–23.

longer be 'lowest' but be properly named 'working classes'.[8] By 1849, according to Harriet Martineau, 'the term "lower class" or "lower classes" is gone out of use. The term is thought not complimentary to the democracy, and so we say "the working-class", which is less precise'.[9] The adjectives may have revolved, but 'class' became a commonplace of social vocabulary, so that by the end of the Victorian era one could not even begin to chart its usage: it was everywhere. When Blackburn Olympic beat the Old Etonians in the famous Cup Final of 1883, the Blackburn local paper exulted in the victory of 'Lancashire lads of the manual working class' over 'the sons of some of the best families of the upper class in the Kingdom'.[10]

Historians have often stopped there, and moved on to other matters. But does the diffusion of the language of class provide a measure of the spread of class itself? Asa Briggs suggested that changes in terms 'reflected a basic change not only in men's ways of viewing society but in society itself.'[11] Was language a mirror held up to Victorian society, capturing its changes?[12] In part that has to be so, or we would all be in Humpty Dumpty land; but historians have too readily taken the language at face value, for the words used by Victorians to describe their society were no mere reflection of external reality, but an intervention within it.[13]

This can be seen in the reluctance of the National Society, the Anglican educational organization, to use the language of social class when in

---

[8] S. Wallech, 'The emergence of the modern concept of "class" in the English language', (unpublished Ph.D. dissertation, Claremont Graduate School, 1981), p. 479.

[9] Quoted by Himmelfarb, *Idea of Poverty*, p. 291.

[10] Quoted by C. Andrew, '1883 Cup Final: "Patricians" v. "Plebeians"', *History Today*, 33 (1983), p. 24.

[11] A. Briggs, 'The language of "class" in early nineteenth-century England', in *Essays in Labour History: in memory of G.D.H. Cole*, ed. A. Briggs and J. Saville (Macmillan, London, 1960), p. 44. This typically pioneering essay remains the starting-point for discussions of the early nineteenth century.

[12] It should be stressed at the outset that in this essay I am not primarily concerned with the question of how far class is a helpful tool of historical analysis with which to approach nineteenth-century Britain. Though much of what I shall say about the language of social description bears upon that question, and though the language of contemporary social expression has contributed too little in any rigorous way to the debate on class in nineteenth-century Britain, this is an analytically distinct issue.

[13] Although not substantially concerned with social description, Gray's analysis of the language of the factory reform movement is a rare example of the analysis of what I have called 'language as intervention': R. Gray, 'The language of factory reform in Britain, c.1830–60', in *The Historical Meanings of Work*, ed. P. Joyce (Cambridge University Press, Cambridge, 1987), pp. 143–79.

1838 it set up a committee to consider 'the education of the children of
tradesmen and farmers and other persons standing in a similar relation
to the class more usually designated "poor"'.[14] Socially conservative
writers such as Southey and Disraeli similarly held to a language which
denied class, and posited an alternative society bound together by ranks,
orders, and obligation. The ambiguities of class intrude even here,
however; for the bishop of Norwich showed how a traditional Anglican
social vision could happily absorb the language of class into its older
conception of the social order. He told middle-class supporters of the
Ipswich Museum that they were 'links in that great chain by which the
higher classes of society and the lower are connected together.'[15] It must
be remembered that Victorians were a part of the society which they
were describing; and if the terms they used were an attempt to describe
the world, they were at the same time an attempt to shape it.[16] If
language held up a mirror to Victorian society, the resulting reflection
was by no means straightforward.

What did people actually mean when they described themselves and
others in terms of social class? A clear shift of emphasis can be detected,
from one eighteenth-century pattern in which class served as a synonym
for rank to a conception in which classes were determined by the relative
position of groups within the productive system. It was there already
in Adam Smith's argument that rent, profits, and wages each generated
what he saw as distinct social orders.[17] The early nineteenth century
then witnessed a critical transition in political economy as the settled
nature of Smith's three orders yielded, above all under the influence of
Ricardo, to the more relational conception of classes within a productive
system. Landlords, capitalists, and labourers transposed easily into
higher, middle, and lower classes, and political economy thus provided
a sense of class as relations that could somehow coexist with the eighteenth-century sense of class as a hierarchy. This conflation of relations

[14] Quoted by B. Heeney, *Mission to the Middle Classes: the Woodard Schools,
1848–91* (Church Historical Society with University of Alberta Press, London,
1969), p. 14.
[15] *Suffolk Chronicle*, 18 Dec. 1847. I am grateful to Philip Hills for allowing me
to draw on his researches on nineteenth-century Ipswich for this and subsequent
references from the *Suffolk Chronicle*.
[16] Quentin Skinner has correctly stressed the need to understand the way in
which 'our social vocabulary and our social fabric mutually prop each other up.'
See his 'Language and social change', in *The State of the Language*, ed. L.
Michaels and C. Ricks (University of California Press, Berkeley, 1980), p. 576.
[17] A. Smith, *An Inquiry into the Nature and Causes of the Wealth of Nations*
(1776; rept. 1871), Bk 1, Conclusion.

in economic and social space with position in a vertical hierarchy was to bedevil conceptions of the social order throughout the nineteenth century.[18]

Political economy's ability to influence parliamentary and public debate and to shape many of the arguments of those who opposed it gave it a central role in developing a more recognizably modern notion of class. Yet the language of class is a familiar one, and the familiar can seduce by the very ease with which it is recognized. There are the dual dangers that in posing the question in terms of the progressive advance of the terminology of class and the uneven retreat of older vocabularies, we not only find simply what we are looking for and then chart its advance, but we also assume that the meaning of the terminology of class is the meaning we expect. The historian is brought face to face with the need for caution when confronted by the plethora of apparently contradictory usages in early- and mid-Victorian writings. John Wade's book may have proclaimed classes in its title, but by the fourth page we read that nineteen-twentieths of the community make up 'the INDUSTRI- OUS ORDERS'.[19]

Even more striking is the almost random switching between the language of class and the language of ranks by a progressive writer such as J. D. Milne in his survey of the position of women. His mingling of rank, degree, and class was familiar in the eighteenth century,[20] but the supposed triumph of the language of class does not lead one to expect it in the middle of the nineteenth. Milne's chapters glide indiscriminately between 'middle ranks' and 'middle classes', 'labouring ranks' and 'labouring classes', while his conception of class itself ranges from class as an identity rooted in common concerns and class movements on the one hand, and class as a category, a mere section of society classified by the observer in an eighteenth-century sense but devoid of any larger social identity on the other.[21]

The terms we encounter thus need close attention. To peel away those layers of familiarity – to recognize, as L. P. Hartley put it, that the past is a foreign country[22] – requires a careful reading of speeches and writings

---

[18] For the role of political economy in ideas of class, see the thesis by Wallech referred to in fn 8 above, though Wallech's interesting work is flawed by his exaggeration of the importance of formal doctrines and his failure to recognize the complex and contradictory usages of class in early- and mid-Victorian Britain.

[19] Wade, *History of the Middle and Working Classes*, p. iv.

[20] Compare Smith, *Wealth of Nations*, Bk 1, Conclusion.

[21] [J.D. Milne], *Industrial and Social Position of Women, in the Middle and Lower Ranks* (London, 1857).

[22] L. P. Hartley, *The Go-Between* (Hamish Hamilton, London, 1953), p. 9.

in context, of the kind that Gareth Stedman Jones has given to the language of Chartism. His starting-point is a rejection of any automatic link between the language of class antagonism in radical political movements and the evidence of economic and social discontent to which historians have readily turned both to explain Chartism and to give meaning to its class rhetoric. Stedman Jones, by resisting the notion that the language of class merely reflected Chartists' economic and social experience, has drawn our attention to the lineage of the language they employed, to its context and meaning. He suggests that the critical divide expressed in the Chartist language of class was political rather than economic and social, a division rooted in an older radicalism which reached back to Wilkes and the Commonwealthmen and which saw the concentration of political power in the hands of the corrupt as the primary cause of the oppression of the people. It was in that political exclusion and oppression, rather than in the social divisions of industrial capitalist society, that their terminology of class found its meaning. Stedman Jones's close textual reading represents a major advance in understanding the political language of early-Victorian radical movements, although he so locks the language of Chartism into a single radical tradition that the ambiguities and the imprecisions of the ideas become submerged.[23] The new ideas and perceptions expressed in unchanging language need stressing just as much as do the older ideas expressed through new language. Nor were the new meanings articulated through words alone; when Feargus O'Connor insisted on dressing in fustian for the celebrations of his release from prison in August 1841, he was employing a symbol of class that gave the term a meaning distinct from that of the language of political exclusion.[24]

Our sense of a new language of social description in early-Victorian Britain comes partly from such movements as Chartism, for through much of the Victorian period the language of class was used most of all in political and public debate, and grew with political conflict. The Reform agitation between 1830 and 1832 and the Chartist upsurge a decade later both sharpened the terms used by those involved. Indeed, Hetherington's view, just two years after the Reform Act, the Act that

[23] G. Stedman Jones, 'Rethinking Chartism', in idem, *Languages of Class: Studies in English working class history, 1832–1982* (Cambridge University Press, Cambridge, 1983), pp. 90–178. For a thoughtful critique of Stedman Jones, see R. Gray, 'The deconstruction of the English working class', *Social History*, 11 (1986) pp. 363–73.

[24] P. A. Pickering, 'Class without words: symbolic communication in the Chartist movement', *Past and Present*, 112 (1986), pp. 144–62.

had served 'to detach the middle from the working classes, and to unite the former with the aristocracy, in common league against the producers,'[25] reveals the centrality of reform struggle to the spread of class language. The public language of class was therefore about far more than social description; it was itself an element in social and political action. When Lord Brougham announced in 1831 that 'by the people . . . I mean the middle classes, the wealth and intelligence of the country, the glory of the British name,'[26] or when Cobden asked Peel 'Do you shrink from the post of governing through the *bona fide* representatives of the middle class?'[27] they were more concerned with political rhetoric than with identifying a social group.

Historians nevertheless lean heavily upon such usage when pointing to class language, and that is why it is necessary to take care with it. When the Chartists argued that they were a working-class movement or the Anti-Corn Law League spoke proudly at times of its middle-class character, the terminology had real bite. Yet other terms remained prominent in political argument, and historians' quest for evidence of 'class' in a social sense can too easily allow alternative vocabularies of political assertion and social description to pass relatively unnoticed. Popular radicalism remained firmly rooted in an alternative critique which saw society divided between 'industrious' or 'productive classes' on the one hand and 'idle' or 'unproductive classes' on the other. French political discourse in these years embraced a similar dichotomy, with the concept of *oisiveté* (idleness) being attached by liberal critics of the Restoration order to the nobility and by Saint-Simonians to that section of the bourgeoisie whose income derived from non-productive investment. In neither country was this a conflict between capital and labour. In Britain, it was rooted in an older radical division, which would not fit any social divide on the basis of class that we might make, but was sharpened by the ideas of productiveness implicit in political economy. The title of the National Union of the Working Classes referred as much to that tradition as to a newer idea related to wage labour. This older terminology survived alongside the new, but subtle changes were under way. By the 1840s radicals were narrowing the term 'industrious' to mean wage-earners, as when Henry Vincent told an Ipswich meeting that 'the industrious classes and the more intelligent and independent of

---

[25] *Poor Man's Guardian*, 24 May 1834, quoted by Stedman Jones, 'Rethinking Chartism', p. 129.

[26] *Oxford English Dictionary*, *sub* 'middle class'.

[27] Quoted by Briggs, 'The language of "class"', p. 59.

the middle classes are beginning to think for themselves.'[28] Such terms remained charged with political power even in the decades that followed Chartism. E. W. Belbin, soon to become secretary of the Greenwich branch of the Reform League, praised emigration in 1865 on the grounds that England had not 'room enough for the proper development of the energies of the productive or labouring classes,'[29] while a few months later, at a reform meeting on Blackheath, G. T. Floyd moved that 'the time has arrived when the industrious classes of this country should be entrusted with the franchise.'[30]

'The people' was a closely related and powerful concept, whose lineage can also be traced to eighteenth-century radical ideas, and it too had narrowed its meaning by the 1840s. It never entirely shook off the sense of the cause of the people – whatever the source of their income – against their oppressors, even though it increasingly referred to a group centred on the working class. 'The people' could be evoked on the one hand as an alternative to class, in an attempt to draw together working class and bourgeoisie,[31] or on the other as an act of class assertiveness, universalizing the concerns of the working class by making their interests central to the nation, rather than locked within a marginal and sectional class position. There was no single usage of the word, and it is difficult to separate different contemporary implications of the term without close explorations of the kind which Tournier has presented for *le peuple* in the French Revolution of 1848.[32] There was no simple moment of transition when one meaning yielded to the other, for this was contested ground, as we can see in *The Voice of the West Riding*'s denunciation of many liberals in 1833 on the grounds that 'they use the word "people", but it is with the Whiggish Broughamic sense.'[33] The middle classes

[28] *Suffolk Chronicle*, 12 June 1847.

[29] *Bee-Hive*, 15 Apr. 1865.

[30] *Workman's Advocate*, 9 Sept. 1865.

[31] A good example is Thomas Attwood's use of the term 'masses' to refer to the working class, which became 'the people' when the productive element of the middle class was added. See C. Behagg, 'An alliance with the middle class: the Birmingham Political Union and early Chartism', in *The Chartist Experience: studies in working class radicalism and culture, 1830–60*, ed. J. Epstein and D. Thompson (Macmillan, London, 1982), pp. 59–86.

[32] M. Tournier, 'Le mot "peuple" en 1848: désignant social ou instrument politique?', *Romantisme*, 9 (1975), pp. 6–20.

[33] Quoted by Gray, 'Deconstruction of the English working class', p. 370. This Whig use of 'people' introduces a further ambiguity more common in Vormärz Germany, where *Volk* could in certain contexts designate not all the people or those outside government, but the politically responsible, educated,

were now being excluded by many popular radicals from their conception of the people. The *Northern Star* proclaimed 'the labouring classes – the real "people"' as early as 1838.[34] Yet in 1848 Joseph Morgan, a leading Greenwich Chartist, could still counterpose the people to traditional elites. Having offered to the Greenwich electors the alternatives of MPs drawn from the aristocracy, army, navy, government, and Church, he concluded that 'if you wish the people to be represented . . . return Samuel Kydd.'[35] The term's ambiguity was part of its political strength, and its lineage part of its political appeal. The Chartist demand was, after all, 'The People's Charter'. The language, less concerned with identifying a precise social group, reflected the politics for which it was used.

Similar ambiguities surrounded 'middle class' in the crisis years of the 1830s and 1840s. It was a term of pride in oppositional politics, whether against aristocratic government or working-class excesses, and referred less to a social group than to the right-thinking, morally upright core of British society, untainted by the corruption of the old order. 'We were a middle-class set of agitators',[36] Cobden observed of the Anti-Corn Law League, but it was by no means clear to whom his 'middle class' referred. Henry Vincent told an Ipswich audience that 'the middle classes were becoming more powerful, the commercial classes stronger.'[37] Was Vincent drawing a distinction here, or were the expressions synonymous in his mind? The term remained a vague one, whose centre of gravity lay somewhere between wage-earners and aristocrats, but whose essential purpose was not to pinpoint a social group. The temptation to interpret the terminology of political rhetoric as the carrier of primarily social meanings must be resisted, for what we find is a language of political dispute whose social content remains ambiguous.

Nowhere is this more true than in the case of the term 'capitalist'. As a neutral description, it was creeping into use, as when Samuel Smiles argued in 1839 that 'the interests of capitalists and labourers are identical;'[38] whereas writers such as Thomas Hodgskin were beginning to use

---

and propertied sections of the population. See J. J. Sheehan, 'Liberalism and society in Germany, 1815–48', *Journal of Modern History*, 45 (1973), p. 602.

[34] Quoted by Stedman Jones, 'Rethinking Chartism', p. 104.

[35] *Northern Star*, 5 Feb. 1848.

[36] Quoted by Briggs, 'The language of "class"', p. 59.

[37] *Suffolk Chronicle*, 12 June 1847.

[38] Quoted by R. J. Morris, 'Samuel Smiles and the genesis of *Self-Help*: the retreat to a petit bourgeois utopia', *Historical Journal*, 24 (1981), p. 100.

it as a term of socialist analysis.[39] Its principal use, however, lay in the mainstream of working-class radical argument between the end of the Napoleonic Wars and the Chartist years. It referred not to industrialists and factory owners (for whom interesting hybrids were coined, such as 'millocrats' and 'factory lords'), but to those whose essentially artificial wealth was a consequence of the political order: fund-holders, financiers, bankers, and middlemen. In other words, it described neither a social group nor part of the system of economic relations, but a parasitic and unproductive element which thrived only because of the corrupt political framework.[40] Even for Hodgskin and other early socialist economists, it was in their activities as middlemen, rather than as owners of the means of production, that employers became 'capitalists' and hence parasites living off an economic system to which they were extraneous. Those who go in search of a language of social description in the minefields of early-Victorian political conflict should beware. It is not just that the past is a foreign country; they speak a foreign language there too.

Historians are hardly assisted by the reluctance of Victorians to argue over systems of social classification, which never became a matter of serious public debate, in contrast to some of the other societies examined in this volume.[41] For societies which sought – even if they did not satisfactorily find – fixed conceptual frameworks for the social order, the historian must resist the temptation to read the society through those structures. Historians of sixteenth-century England or eighteenth-century France have learned to avoid that temptation and, indeed, to explore to good effect the distances between the social system as analysed by historians, the everyday social relations of the society, and the formal framework of social and legal designation. Eighteenth-century England saw the dissolution of what formal framework might still have been

[39] For the early socialist political economists, see N. W. Thompson, *The People's Science: the popular political economy of exploitation and crisis, 1816–34* (Cambridge University Press, Cambridge, 1984).

[40] For a more dispassionate account of the continuing strength of banking and commercial fortunes over those derived from manufacturing, see W. D. Rubinstein's essays collected in idem, *Elites and the Wealthy in Modern British History: essays in social and economic history* (Harvester, Brighton, 1988); though the excessive neatness of his distinctions between different sources of wealth at times matches that of early nineteenth-century radical analysis.

[41] Even in the context of the more fluid designations of eighteenth-century Britain, Corfield could observe that 'much discussion therefore centred around social labels': P. J. Corfield, 'Class by name and number in eighteenth-century Britain', above, p. 112.

employed and the emergence of the more chaotic world of social description which matured in the middle decades of the nineteenth century. Overlapping and often contradictory terminologies came to prevail, terminologies which rarely purported to offer a comprehensive description of the social order and which did not seek even theoretically to encompass the totality of the society's primary relationships. Here was the liberal perception come to fruition – one is reminded of Margaret Thatcher's comment that there is no such thing as society, only individuals. George C. Brodrick, writing in *Essays on Reform* in 1867, asked 'what is a "class" but a purely artificial aggregate, which may consist of hundreds, thousands, or millions, according to the fancy or design of its framer?'[42] Those with property and authority still sought a basis for stability and order; but they now found it in a morality and a rationality that was axiomatically available to all, rather than in a specific interrelationship of ordered groups within a social system.

What was lost by the nineteenth century was the metaphorical imagery (such as the Great Chain of Being) or the complex interacting hierarchy of older perceptions of the social system and of older languages of social description. Victorian Britain's language of social description lacked a perception of a system of relationships which the terminology purported to describe in its entirety. In this new liberal setting, for example, paternalism became essentially personal. Paternal relationships were once part of a larger symbolic order of dependency and responsibility, but the surviving relationships of paternal authority[43] did not link into some metaphorical social system of which they would have been merely a mundane expression. The daily process of social assessment was confusing in most societies, but what was special about Victorian liberal ideology was the absence of a public and formal conception of the social order. With the exception of some radical discourse at times of early-Victorian political crisis, the vocabulary of social description was far more concerned with aggregating individuals than with identifying the sections of a cohesive idea of the social order.

For a variety of reasons, then, historians of the language of social description are forced to look for evidence in more obscure places than public political and social debate. The nature of these sources, however, makes it no easy task to probe an everyday language. Where can we find people talking? Certainly in the evidence given to parliamentary

---

[42] G. C. Brodrick, 'The utilitarian argument against reform', in *Essays on Reform*, ed. Anon. (London, 1867), p. 7.
[43] The best study is P. Joyce, *Work, Society and Politics: the culture of the factory in later Victorian Britain* (Harvester, Brighton, 1980).

inquiries and Royal Commissions, which was meticulously recorded, question by question and answer by answer, and these reveal a more routine use of class terms by mid-century. Unusual social investigators – above all, Henry Mayhew in mid-century and Charles Booth and his collaborators in its last decade – recorded their interviews, and there too we glimpse people talking. What are so painfully lacking, however, are contemporary observers with the sensitivity to the nuances of language in daily speech shown by Stephen Reynolds, who wrote in 1908 of the Devon fishing village in which he had gone to live:

> In Under Town, I notice, a gentleman is always *gen'leman*, a workman or tramp is *man*, but the fringers, the inhabitants of the neutral zone, are called *persons*. For example: 'That *man* what used to work for the council is driving about the *gen'leman* as stays with Mrs Smith – the *person* what used to keep the greengrocery shop to the top of the High Street afore her took the lodging house on East Cliff.'[44]

Our sources therefore remain insistently literary, and anyone who reads widely in Victorian writings must be struck by the sheer diversity of the public language of social description that one encounters, almost a chaos of terminology. After the increasingly widespread usage of the language of class in the early-Victorian years, the mid-Victorian decades present a contrast in which the resonances of class terminology seem less powerful, and yield in public debate to a more eclectic vocabulary. That eclectic set of terms could not, however, conceal the essential leanness of Britain's three-class perception of the social structure. There was no place for peasants, master artisans, or *petits bourgeois*, all of whom were such significant elements in the languages of description elsewhere in Europe; nor were liberal professions perceived as a distinctive part of the social system as they were in both Germany and France. All these were incorporated into the three-class model, as were the state civil servants whose distinct names elsewhere (*Beamten, fonctionnaires*) signified a group perceived to have a distinct place in the social and legal system. That lean perception of the class system has none the less to be set alongside the profusion in the mid-Victorian years of vocabularies which bypassed a class language and proliferated other even more fragile categories: moral, occupational, even description by housing type ('villa middle class', 'slum-dwellers'). There is less talk of 'working class' and 'middle class', but more of 'deserving' and 'undeserving poor', of 'respectable artisans' and 'gentlemen', as a good proportion of society

[44] S. Reynolds, *A Poor Man's House*, 1982 edn (Oxford University Press, Oxford), p. 52.

(including much of the working class) came to concentrate on divisions which emphasized moral rather than economic criteria.

The 'intelligent and respectable artisan' became a commonplace of social discussion as politicians looked optimistically for signs of improvement in at least a section of the working class. Smiles had already told the public libraries inquiry that mechanics institutes were used by 'the upper class of artisans';[45] and by 1859, when the *Ashton Reporter* argued in favour of the enfranchisement of 'the industrious and intelligent artisans of our cities and manufacturing districts',[46] such a picture of working-class stratification was commonplace, above all in reforming circles. The existence of a responsible, intelligent, and respectable section of the working class which could safely be given the vote became central both to the reform movement and to the manoeuvrings in Parliament. The efforts to find a formula, above all a rating level, which fitted the dividing line within the working class proved unsuccessful, not least because this upper stratum proved too fragile to be pinned down by any of the formulas devised.[47] A language of social description thus became part of the politics of the crisis, and was strengthened by it. It was a view of social divisions within the working class shared by a good number of skilled workers, though they understood better the realities of working-class life and the fact that more than moral choices were involved.[48]

Against these 'respectable artisans', in the perfect symmetry of middle- and upper-class social analysis, stood their counterparts, 'the roughs'. Disturbances such as the Sunday trading riots, the Murphy riots, or the Tichborne demonstrations were regularly attributed to the bad behaviour of this group. The labels that were attached to social groups powerfully shaped perceptions of them. The idea of a 'submerged tenth', or more commonly 'the residuum', had an apparently greater precision than 'roughs', because it was used by those seeking to tackle urban social problems. Yet it, too, claimed to have identified a lower and self-perpetuating section of workers deemed a threat to the moral health of the rest of the working class. The language identified the problem, and

[45] Select Committee on Public Libraries, *BPP*, 1849, vol. 17, p. 128.

[46] Quoted by N. Kirk, *The Growth of Working-Class Reformism in Mid-Victorian England* (Croom Helm, London, 1985), p. 183.

[47] On the efforts to resolve these problems, see F. B. Smith, *The Making of the Second Reform Bill* (Cambridge University Press, Cambridge, 1966).

[48] For the meanings of respectability within the working class, see G. Crossick, *An Artisan Elite in Victorian Society: Kentish London, 1840–80* (Croom Helm, London, 1978), chs 7–9; P. Bailey, 'Will the real Bill Banks please stand up?', *Journal of Social History*, 12 (1979), pp. 336–53.

thus defined the solutions by which a delimited group could be regulated, segregated, perhaps persuaded (or compelled) to emigrate. In the debate following Andrew Mearns's *The Bitter Cry of Outcast London* (1883), the Rev. Brooke Lambert wrote of Whitechapel's 'large mass of the deplorable residuum',[49] and in that decade the term became established in journalism and social comment. 'It must be admitted that the residuum is hopeless,' a Charity Organization Society report bleakly observed;[50] and an article in *The Times* offered a three-tiered working class comprised of artisans, the poor ('a class which yet differs only in being poorer'), and below them 'a class with no traditions of honest independence and with no ties to the general scheme of society. . . . In a single word, it is the residuum.'[51] The middle of these categories introduces us to the 'respectable poor', another of these moral terms of social description. These were the people who had to be protected against the threat of the residuum; thus Lord Compton urged that 'the honest and deserving poor should be prevented from drifting into the workhouse class,'[52] while Ellice Hopkins feared 'the endless contamination of the children of the respectable poor.'[53]

Moral designations were vital to social description, above all from the mid-nineteenth century onwards, and the process went beyond discussions of the working class. Look at the term 'gentleman', which leaps up to perplex the historian reading newspaper reports of a charitable meeting or trying to make sense of town directories or poll books. They might simply be local men of standing or wealth, as when the town clerk of Warrington sought support for the museum library from 'gentlemen in the town';[54] but in the early-Victorian years wealth alone did not guarantee the status of gentleman. Independence was essential, which meant that people who lived off investments and property and those who had retired to do so more readily received the title. The mid-Victorian years,

[49] Rev. Brooke Lambert, 'Jacob's answer to Esau's cry', *Contemporary Review*, 46 (1884), p. 375.

[50] *Charity Organisation Review* (Mar. 1886), quoted by G. Stedman Jones, *Outcast London: a study in the relationship between classes in Victorian society* (Clarendon Press, Oxford, 1971), 1984 edn, p. 289.

[51] Quoted by J. Saville, 'The background to the Industrial Remuneration Conference of 1885', introduction to repr. edn of *Report and Proceedings of the Industrial Remuneration Conference* (Kelley, New York, 1968), pp. 34–5.

[52] Lord Compton, 'Distress in London: remedies', *Fortnightly Review*, 43 (1888), p. 151.

[53] Ellice Hopkins, 'The industrial training of pauper girls', *Contemporary Review*, 42 (1882), p. 152.

[54] Select Committee on Public Libraries, *BPP*, 1849, vol. 17, p. 109.

however, saw the term disintegrate as a description of social position. It became too vague to describe local elite position, in which urban leadership was now established by pluralistic public activity rather than by the office and rank of early-modern towns. In this new urban world, elites held their position as much by their place in voluntary associational activity as by their holding of municipal office.[55] No satisfactory term emerged to replace the now inadequate 'gentleman'; and the urban 'notables' in France, whose numbers grew with state support between Napoleon's efforts to re-establish authority in French society and the collapse of the July Monarchy a half century later, found no established equivalent in Britain.[56] Terms such as 'the most influential inhabitants' captured the sense that local social leaders were an unfixed, informal grouping resting on activity as well as position, a precise sense that the word 'gentleman' could no longer invoke. 'Gentleman' became essentially a term of social approval and moral approbation; gentlemanly character and a reasonably comfortable income were now what mattered. Phillips has claimed that the upper class had stopped using the term by the 1870s, finding it too heavy with moral overtones. He cites Lady Agnes Grove writing in 1907 that 'the male servers [in shops] are perhaps the only individuals about whom I use the word "gentleman".'[57] He exaggerates the rapidity of the decline, for the term remained precise in the setting of landed county elites. After the Liberal Party's split in the 1880s over Gladstone's Irish Home Rule bill, H. O. Nethercote, a Northamptonshire liberal, told Lord Spencer than 'in this whole county I believe that I am the only *Gentleman* who would have voted for the Second Reading!'[58]

The most coherent reconstruction of the idea of the gentleman came to express a new professional ideal that embraced both a moral character and public service. Here was the fundamentally middle-class notion of

[55] A good example of the lauding of urban social leaders and a discussion of how leadership was established can be found in B. G. Orchard's exhaustive *Liverpool's Legion of Honour* (Birkenhead, 1893).

[56] Nevertheless, the French 'notables' were expected to embody many of the characteristics identified in Britain with gentlemen: wealth, independence, and family networks.

[57] K. C. Phillips, *Language and Class in Victorian England* (Blackwell, Oxford, 1984), p. 5. Phillips provides a mass of quotations from Victorian novels and other literature, but unfortunately gives too little attention to assessing the value of such sources, which dominate his study.

[58] Quoted by J. Howarth, 'The Liberal revival in Northamptonshire, 1880–95: a case study in late nineteenth-century elections', *Historical Journal*, 12 (1969), p. 105; emphasis original.

the Christian gentleman, one shaped by the reform and expansion of the public schools, changing patterns of recruitment to state service, and the growth of professions with more coherent notions of ethics and service.[59] The bulk of the middle class, however, was less fastidious in its use of 'gentleman' than either Lady Agnes Grove or the proponents of a new professional ideal, and they weakened the term into yet another of those morally laden social descriptions that became so prominent in the middle of the Victorian period. Samuel Smiles called the final chapter of *Self-Help* (1859) 'Character – The True Gentleman', arguing that 'riches and rank have no necessary connexion with genuine gentlemanly qualities.'[60] Henry Knell, a wheelwright in the Royal Arsenal at Woolwich, agreed. 'By attention to the rules of good breeding . . .', he wrote in 1861, 'the poorest man will be entitled to the character of a gentleman.'[61]

'Lady' posed fewer problems, simply following class lines. Smiles captured it neatly, if unwittingly, when he reported in 1849 that 'institutions have been formed for the express purpose of educating young *women*. Some of them are very valuable institutions, one particularly at Huddersfield, where classes have been formed and conducted by young *ladies* of the middle classes belonging to the town.'[62] The simple terminological distinction was still in place at the end of the century, when the Home Office appointed the first Lady Inspectors of Factories, responsible for women workers. The trade union activist Clara James exploited the language to good effect when insisting to the Royal Commission on Labour that any female commissioners sent out to investigate industries such as her own confectionery trade 'must be working women, not ladies who do not understand the trade.'[63] Flora Thompson felt that rural schoolmistresses were in a particularly awkward social position, being 'neither lady nor woman'.[64] The dichotomy was one capable of adaptation to situations where social divisions remained only implicit. Female students at Owens College in Manchester were divided between

---

[59] On the role of the idea of the gentleman in professional ideology, see D. Duman, 'The creation and diffusion of a professional ideology in nineteenth-century England', *Sociological Review*, 27 (1979), pp. 113–38.

[60] S. Smiles, *Self-Help* (London, 1859), 1914 edn, p. 450.

[61] H. Knell, *Chips from the Block: an essay on social science* (London, 1861), p. 13.

[62] Select Committee on Public Libraries, *BPP*, 1849, vol. 17, p. 129; emphasis added.

[63] Royal Commission on Labour, *BPP*, 1892, vol. 35, Q. 8639.

[64] F. Thompson, *Lark Rise to Candleford*, World Classics edn (Oxford University Press, Oxford, 1971), p. 211.

those taking a single course, presumably for pleasure alone, who were known as 'ladies', and registered examination students, presumably needing the qualifications for career purposes, who were called 'women'.[65]

If moral terminology proliferated in mid- and late-Victorian Britain, so did describing people by occupation. An occupational title became a shorthand for a social group, as in S. J. Low's prediction of the relentless spread of suburbia. 'The clerk and the small trader', he wrote 'will move on to remote suburban villages, as the merchant and the stockbroker go further afield to the Sussex downs and the Hampshire commons; and cheap trains will whirl the artisan daily from Rickmansworth or Romford.'[66] The assumption that the name of an occupation – shoemaker, dock labourer, clerk, lawyer – stood for a great deal more than the simple description of a job has continued beyond the nineteenth century, allowing historians to assume that it carried with it a package of social meaning that is generally unspecified.[67] The development of the census after 1841 intensified this tendency to view the social structure through occupations and their titles, for the analytical occupational census tables, presented as if based on criteria emanating from the material being classified, were in fact the constructions of census-makers for whom occupational title was the key to understanding the structure of society.[68] The problems that a focus on occupation poses for historians of social mobility are immense, not least because most such investigations assume that change of occupational title up or down a hierarchy itself constitutes social mobility. The role of census classification in shaping social perceptions, as well as in responding to them, would warrant closer study. The French census distinguished between wage-workers, independent artisans, and employers from the 1830s, while the Prussian census as reformed by Dieterici in the following decade similarly began to sort out groups which had previously been undifferentiated. In Britain, however, it was not until 1891, and only after pressure from Charles Booth and others, that attempts were made to distinguish in the census between

[65] D. Rubinstein, *Before the Suffragettes: women's emancipation in the 1890s* (Harvester, Brighton, 1986), p. 195.

[66] S. J. Low, 'The rise of the suburbs', *Contemporary Review*, 60 (1891), p. 551.

[67] Alfred Marshall had commented in 1872 on this prevalent tendency to attach moral and social meanings to occupational titles: see *The Memorials of Alfred Marshall*, ed. A. C. Pigou (Macmillan, London, 1925), p. 103.

[68] On this issue, see A. Desrosières and L. Thévenot, 'Les mots et les chiffres: les nomenclatures socioprofessionnelles', *Economie et Statistiques*, 110 (1979), pp. 49–65.

employers, employees, and self-employed.[69] Higgs is correct to relate the changing system of occupational classification in the nineteenth-century census to shifting paradigms of social improvement and new demands for occupational statistics for government departments.[70] However, we know far too little about the social, as well as the ideological, origins of classification systems and the role of these systems in shaping social perceptions to understand the other forces involved.

An extension of the use of occupation saw types of labour taken to describe social and not just work-place divisions within the working class: 'skilled', 'unskilled', and around the turn of the century the less socially powerful term 'semi-skilled'. More common than these, however, was the use of 'artisan' and 'labourer' as the basic division within the working class. In much of Europe, the term 'artisan' or its equivalents continued to include the master craftsman working on his own or with hired labour. Indeed, there was no distinct notion of 'master artisan' in Britain, with terms such as 'little mesters' in Sheffield or 'little makers' in Birmingham identifying only the most marginal in specific trades. The weakness of the corporatist craft tradition in Britain helps to explain the absence of any standard term for such people; and only in Britain did 'artisan' refer exclusively to a skilled wage-earner, increasingly displacing the older 'tradesman' in referring to craft workers.[71] It was part of the process identified by Hobsbawm, by which 'artisan traditions and values in this country became proletarianized, as nowhere else.'[72] The term 'tradesman' in fact became polarized from the 1840s, continuing to mean a skilled wage-earner in working-class usage (see its survival in 'trades unions' long after these had ceased to be based on crafts alone), but a retailer for the middle- and upper classes. The term 'mechanic'

[69] In 1872 the French census had gone one step further and established the category of *chefs ouvriers* to cover the area of sub-contracting: A Desrosières and L. Thévenot, *Les categories socioprofessionelles* (Paris, 1988), p. 13.

[70] E. Higgs, 'The struggle for the occupational census, 1841–1911', in *Government and Expertise: specialists, administrators and professionals, 1860–1919*, ed. R. MacLeod (Cambridge University Press, Cambridge, 1988), pp. 73–86.

[71] The comparatively early decline of the craft guilds as effective organizers of craft production in Britain is the principal reason for the weakness of the corporatist craft tradition, though W. H. Sewell Jr has shown persuasively that in the French case the social milieu of corporatism could long survive the abolition of guilds themselves. See idem, *Work and Revolution in France: the language of labor from the Old Regime to 1848* (Cambridge University Press, Cambridge, 1980).

[72] E. J. Hobsbawm, *Worlds of Labour: further studies in the history of labour* (Weidenfeld, London, 1984), p. 254. His essay on 'Artisans or labour aristocrats', in ibid., pp. 252–72, provides a good discussion of some of these issues.

retained its essentially work-place connotation; but as 'artisan' became more widespread throughout society, its meaning blurred, as did so many terms in these decades. It came to mean the better paid, better organized, and better educated section of the working class, and carried assumptions concerned as much with lifestyle and morality as with roots in older craft ideals. The notion of artisanal skill always contained a dual element. On the one hand there was what might be called genuine skill, a technical ability not possessed by most other workers; on the other, we find the socially constructed dimensions of skill that relate to exclusiveness, custom, and the ability to control access to the occupation. As the later nineteenth century saw increasing emphasis on these socially constructed aspects of skill, so the concept of the artisan could more easily be extended to such well-paid but non-artisanal workers as engine-drivers, cotton-spinners, or boilermakers. This dichotomy was not simply imposed by outside observers. The *Bee-Hive*, the voice of trade union and radical working-class organizations in the 1860s, wrote that 'the working classes are divided into two sections, one comprising the skilled artisan and mechanic, and the other the labourer, the coster-monger, the men who find their daily living by means which they would find it hard to describe, although yet honest withal, and the roughs of all descriptions.'[73] The polarized terms could carry powerful messages. A Soho painter and decorator regretted the name given to the model housing blocks built by Peabody and others, on the grounds that 'the name frightens a labourer when he sees "Artisans' Dwellings", he says that will not suit me; he is afraid to go; there is a sort of intimidation upon them, they think it is too much above their position in life to live there.'[74]

The 'artisan class' thus became a fundamental nostrum of later nine-teenth-century social optimism among the propertied classes, an occupational designation whose moral colouring erected a division between 'artisan' and 'labourer' that dominated descriptions of the working class from the 1860s through to the end of the century. It was always more widespread than the term 'labour aristocrat', though the latter term was by no means as rare as some commentators suggest. It lost those pejorative connotations of the 1840s which led *Reynolds Political Instructor* to observe that 'the most intelligent and moral of the workmen are those associated in union. . . . By those who do not know you, you are called

[73] Quoted by Hobsbawm, *Worlds of Labour*, p. 230.
[74] John Field to the Select Committee on Artisans' and Labourers' Dwellings Improvement, *BPP* 1882, vol. 7, Q. 2360. Contemporary usage fluctuated between 'artisan' and 'artizan'.

aristocratic.'[75] By the end of the century, one call for the abolition of casual labour routinely noted that 'then the poor labourer might do what the aristocracy of labour does now – migrate to the suburbs.'[76] Far more common, however, were variations on the words of a leader of the Oddfellows Friendly Society – 'the intelligent, self-reliant, industrious artizans.'[77]

The simple dichotomy between artisan and labourer hardly fitted the complexity of the Victorian working class; but the power of its implicit moral distinction as well as of its simplicity ensured that it prevailed, even in more systematic analyses, such as those of Leone Levi (whose earnings survey simply requested that data be provided 'separating foremen, artisans and labourers'[78]), Charles Booth, and Seebohm Rowntree in his meticulous York inquiry, and in the evidence from a wide range of people, including the London Trades Council, to the Select Committee on Artisans' and Labourers' Dwellings Improvement in the early 1880s.[79] The way the division between artisan and labourer carried all before it shows the continuing power of the craft tradition to shape social classification, compelling social observation to be compressed into its idealized terminology. However imprecisely it was used, however laden with non-occupational meanings, it remains the one exception to the rule that older vocabularies of social description – whether estate language in Germany or corporate and then Republican languages in France – were markedly more important elsewhere in Europe than they were in Britain.

Mid-Victorian Britain was in these ways a society of linguistic eclecticism, one which proliferated competing and ill-defined terms of social description; but, although these did not disappear in the late nineteenth century, a variety of forces made a return to the public language of class more imperative. It entered everyday political discussion in a descriptive

---

[75] M. A. Shepherd, 'The origins and incidence of the term "labour aristocracy"', *Bulletin of the Society for the Study of Labour History*, 37 (1978), pp. 51–67.

[76] B. F. C. Costelloe, 'The housing problem', *Transactions of the Manchester Statistical Society* (1898–9), p. 49.

[77] Charles Hardwicke in Independent Order of Oddfellows (Manchester Unity), *Quarterly Report*, 1 Apr. 1863.

[78] L. Levi, *Wages and Earnings of the Working Classes* (London, 1885), p. 22.

[79] C. Booth, *The Life and Labour of the People in London*, 4th edn (17 vols, London, 1902–3); B. S. Rowntree, *Poverty: a study of town life* (London 1901), p. 259, Select Committee on Artisans' and Labourers' Dwellings Improvements, *BPP*, 1881, vol. 7; 1882, vol. 7.

sense, reinforced by such forces as the assertiveness of organized labour, arguments over electoral strategy with a mass franchise, and the early sociological surveys. Indeed, the growing use of the terminology of class in legislation at that time (such as the Housing of the Working Classes Act of 1890) opens up the issue of the role of the state in helping to shape a language of social description. Language has been too readily conceptualized as a cultural question, little connected with questions of the state and of law, and we know too little about such matters. Yet other European societies in the eighteenth and nineteenth centuries reveal explicit ways in which the state might shape or reinforce social terminologies: from the Prussian *Allgemeine Landrecht* of 1794, which both codified existing estates and defined other groups such as the intelligentsia and the professions; through the impact of voting laws, which in France helped to embed the concept of 'notables' and in German cities like Bremen adopted local terminology (merchants, *Kleine-gewerbetreibenden* or small tradesmen, university professors, those living off investments and so on) and then fixed them in law; to Bismarck's social legislation which, directed specifically at manual workers, established an effective legal distinction between workers and *angestellten*, or white-collar workers.

The role of the British state in influencing the language of social description was certainly weaker. On the whole, when governments in nineteenth-century Britain sought to define a social group to receive special rights, it did so by specifying amounts of property owned or occupied or by using the payment of a certain level of rates as a surrogate for these. This applied above all to the changing franchise and to rights of election for parliamentary and municipal elections. Such definitions were perhaps the only kind possible in the absence of differences in legal status, and we have already seen how the debates concerning the 1832 and 1867 franchise extensions sharpened certain public notions of social division.

There was some precision in such measures, but the fact remained that Britain did not attach social labels to those bearing distinct rights. As a result, when legislation developed which was directed at a specific social constituency, the terminology used was startlingly loose. The social constituency was variously named, but rarely defined. The terminology evolved unevenly, from Shaftesbury's success in obtaining a House of Lords standing order in 1853 which required railway demolition bills to be accompanied by a statement of how many members of the 'labouring classes' were to be displaced;[80] through a variety of housing Acts,

[80] *House of Lords Journals*, 85 (1853), p. 244.

from the Labouring Classes Lodging Houses Act of 1851 to the Housing of the Working Classes Act of 1890; and the Cheap Trains Act of 1883 which allowed the Board of Trade to intervene where 'sufficient train accommodation is not provided for workmen going to and from their work' at suitable fares.[81] As one reads the housing Bills and Acts of the second half of the century, one is struck by the sheer variety of terms used: 'labouring classes', 'artisans and labourers', 'mechanics and labourers', and other phrases, which led the Standing Committee on Law to complain in 1890 about the confusing vocabularies that had been used in previous legislation.[82] A single Act often moved between one term and another, even between short and long title in the case of the Artisans and Labourers Dwellings Improvement Act of 1875.[83] In the field of street improvement law, for example, the rehousing requirements in the provisional orders referred to 'persons of the working class that will be displaced by the scheme', whereas the schedule in the Confirmation Act referring to the identical measures spoke of 'persons of the artisan class'.

This terminological confusion was not only revealing in its failure to pinpoint the groups at which reforming effort was being directed; it was also significant in that many of these measures sought not to describe a general intention but to define a limited group which was to benefit. The Labouring Classes Dwelling Houses Act of 1866, for example, allowed the Public Works Loan Commissioners to make preferential loans for house building, where it was shown 'that the dwellings are suitable for the labouring classes' – but there was no definition of what the term meant.[84] The rehousing requirements of street improvement and railway bills were more serious, for the looseness of the vocabulary allowed improvement agencies and railway companies to exclude artisans from demolition statements that requested the numbers of 'the labouring classes' to be displaced (this was alleged to be the case, for example, with Metropolitan Board of Works improvements under an 1877 Act)[85] or to exclude labourers, and even tailors and shoemakers, on demolition

[81] Cheap Trains Act 1883, *BPP*, 1883, vol. 9, clause 3.

[82] *BPP*, 1890, vol. 5, p. 377.

[83] The long title was 'a bill for facilitating the improvement of the dwellings of the working classes in large towns', *BPP*, 1875, vol. 1, pp. 115ff.

[84] Labouring Classes Dwelling Houses Act 1866, *BPP*, 1866, vol. 3; and the Rules and Regulations governing these loans, ibid., vol. 60, p. 51.

[85] M. Stanley, 'West End improvements', *The Nineteenth Century*, 9 (1881), pp. 850–1. For an early example that involved only disclosure and not rehousing, see J. R. Kellett, *The Impact of Railways on Victorian Cities* (Routledge, London, 1969), pp. 327–8; and for demolition statements in general, see H. J. Dyos, 'Railways and the effect their building had on housing in Victorian London', *Journal of Transport History*, 2 (1955–6), pp. 11–21, 90–100.

statements where the standing order required the number of 'artisans' who would be removed (as with a railway bill to drive a line behind London's Oxford Street).[86] Here was legislation pretending to a precision of purpose, yet failing to define its social terms. When a railway bill in 1887 gave a full definition, one which was followed exactly in the recommendations of a select committee in 1902, it gave to the term 'labouring class' a breadth which included independent artisans and small traders:

> The expression 'labouring class' in this section includes mechanics, artisans, labourers and others working for wages; hawkers, costermongers, persons not working for wages but working at some trade or handicraft without employing others except members of their own family; and persons other than domestic servants whose income does not exceed an average of thirty shillings a week, and the families of any such persons residing with them.[87]

The social definitions contained within housing legislation, on which there is no room here to expand at length, confirm not only the imprecision of social terminology in Britain, where there was little precedent for the legal definition of social groups, and not only the ways in which those imprecisions could be manipulated, but also the gradual emergence of 'working classes' (albeit still undefined) in the language of housing legislation.

Class was becoming a routine element in social description by the end of the century, but still did not sweep all before it. Other terms of social dichotomy contined; thus the settlements that took graduates of the ancient universities into the slums of East London saw the division as between 'rich and poor'. 'Is there any increase of good will between rich and poor?', asked Canon Barnett in 1895.[88] Here we return to those mid-Victorian dichotomies and to the notions of the 'residuum' and the 'respectable' emerging in the 1880s; but 'the poor' was a complex term of remarkable durability in Victorian Britain, at times applied to most below the level of 'artisan', yet reappearing in an older assertive sense in an organization formed in Fakenham in 1870 to defend popular access

---

[86] As the vicar of St Bartholomew, Cripplegate, told the Royal Commission on the Housing of the Working Classes, 'I think the word "artisan" was not put in with any such meaning, but there it stands': *BPP*, 1884–85, vol. 30, Q. 10, 722–3.

[87] See Great Eastern Railways (General Powers) Act 1887, clause 29, subsection 1–3; *Local Acts*, 50 & 51 Victoria, vol. 4; and Joint Select Committee on Housing of the Working Classes, *BPP*, 1902, vol. 5, pp. 813–17. I have added the punctuation, which does not exist in the originals.

[88] *The Universities and the Social Problem: an account of the university settlements in East London*, ed. J. M. Knapp (London, 1895), pp. 65–6.

to common land, J. L. Flaxman's Association for the Defence of the Rights of the Poor.[89] On the whole, though, the language of 'class' increasingly dominated, and became a more accepted framework for social description The fact that Marxist ideas and politics played little part in contemporary usage, in contrast to France and Germany, must have eased the acceptability of class terminology among the middle and upper classes. State education may also have helped, especially the ostensibly meritocratic 1902 Education Act; for it encouraged a social ladder paradigm of society that made class less frightening. The social ladder returns us to a more comforting world of infinitely graded ranks which could virtually deny the existence of classes by stressing not only their blurring at the boundaries, but also the infinite variations within each class. It was an approach exemplified by Dicey's contribution to *Essays on Reform*: 'Classes no doubt exist, but they are not the distinct, clearly-marked, homogeneous kind which the class theory of representation requires.'[90]

The late-Victorian period brought new problems of vocabulary, with the expansion of a lower middle class of more numerous white-collar and minor professional employees on the one hand and more pressured shopkeepers and small producers on the other. A relatively incisive, if by no means unambiguous, terminology for these groups emerged elsewhere in Europe: *classe moyenne* in France, a narrowed-down *Mittelstand* in Germany, and in Belgium, using a term rejected in France as pejorative, *petite bourgeoisie*. The Belgian government even established a *Commission nationale de la petite bourgeoisie* at the turn of the century,[91] and the term carried strong ideological and political implications. In Britain neither the terms to be used nor the message they purported to carry developed with any such clarity, due not so much to the absence of these people as to their lack of an equivalent degree of both perceived and experienced social identity. The term 'lower middle class' was increasingly evident from the 1870s, signifying an attachment to the middle class as a whole. Only a minority stretched the term to include the best-paid skilled workers.[92] Notwithstanding the

---

[89] L. M. Springall, *Labouring Life in Norfolk Villages, 1834–1914* (Allen and Unwin, London, 1936), pp. 80–1.

[90] A. V. Dicey, 'The balance of classes', in *Essays on Reform*, p. 81.

[91] G. Kurgan-Van Hentenryk, 'A forgotten class: the petite bourgeoisie in Belgium, 1850–1914', in *Shopkeepers and Master Artisans in Nineteenth-Century Europe*, ed. G. Crossick and H.-G. Haupt (Methuen, London, 1984), p. 128.

[92] See, e.g., G. S. Layard, 'A lower-middle-class budget', *Cornhill Magazine*, 10 (1901), pp. 656–66; and the Report of the Taunton Commission which inquired into secondary education, *BPP*, 1867–68, vol. 28, pt 1. The Taunton Commission's attempt to stratify the middle class by the type of schooling

faith invested by liberal reformers in the notion of the 'intelligent artisan', it was rare to detach a manual group from the working class entirely. There was nothing new about this. France experienced the transition from an *ancien régime* social imagery, which had firmly detached craftsmen from unskilled wage-earners and identified them with commercial occupations as *gens de métier*, to the mid-nineteenth-century association of employed craftsmen as part of a larger manual working class; but no such transition was necessary in Britain, not even in imagery or vocabulary. The more fluid and linguistically diverse terminology of late-eighteenth-century Britain, lacking the formal conceptual framework of *ancien régime* France, was already setting the world of wage labour apart from other occupations.[93]

The term 'lower middle class' described the world of clerks and managers, shopkeepers and schoolteachers, which was perceived as the lower portion of a larger social group. Thus they were described by others. No clear terminology evolved among themselves, largely because no sense of distinct social or political identity developed that might have generated one. Around the turn of the century the retailer press displays an increasing sense that tradesmen were part of a larger middling group under pressure from both labour and capital, a feeling which grew as a response to social legislation, the fear of a stronger labour movement, and the growing rates crisis. They were designated 'the unconsidered class' by one writer in a shopkeeper journal and 'this great, despised, misunderstood middle class' of clerks, tradesmen, and minor professionals by a group aggrieved at education policy.[94] That sense of neglect and fear was the context for the emergence of L. P. Sydney's Middle Class Defence Organization in 1906. The title suggests the use of the term 'middle class' in a more continental European sense, to describe a supposedly distinct social group located between capital and labour, but the organization aroused little support, and even Sydney himself seems to have been unable to decide whether to call his constituency 'lower middle class' or simply 'middle class'.[95]

---

expected and the age at which full-time education ceased provides a fascinating attempt to wrestle with what became in the end circular definitions.

[93] On France, see Sewell, *Work and Revolution in France*.

[94] W. Wade, 'The great neglected', *The Tradesman and Shopkeeper*, 2 May 1903; S. Bullock *et al.*, 'The burden of the middle classes', *Fortnightly Review*, n.s., 80 (1906), p. 418.

[95] See Sydney's weak contribution, in comparison with contributions from elsewhere, to the 1911 meeting of the Association de Défense des Classes Moyennes, in *Les études fiscales et sociales: troisième congrès annuel (Nov 1910)* (Limoges, 1911), pp. 117–19. For the contrast between the political and social

Language, bound up with political opportunities and social identities, thus emphasizes the influence of metaphor and imagery in social relations. It is all the more surprising that historians of Victorian Britain have given so little attention to these matters, and that so many questions remain. Why, for example, do the categories of rural social description (landowner, farmer, labourer) seem so much sparser than the urban terminology on which this essay has focused? In Disraeli's *Coningsby*, Lord Henry's deeply traditionalist vision led him to draw up a petition of 'the nobility, clergy, gentry, yeomanry, and peasantry of the county', but 'could you believe it, they struck out *peasantry* as a word no longer used, and inserted *labourers*.'[96] Older terms could nevertheless survive. Small freeholding farmers in Westmorland at the end of the century were often still known as 'statesmen', while 'yeomenry' also persisted in various districts. John Bateman felt conscious that his use of 'yeomen' to describe holders of between 100 and 1,000 acres was no more than 'a makeshift title', employed only because 'no better name suggests itself.'[97] It was nevertheless the term used for the freeholders at Chagford, near Dartmoor, in 1882 when Harriet Stanton Batch witnessed their struggle against the Prince of Wales's attempts to enclose a section of moorland.[98] 'Peasantry' likewise lingered on, referring blandly to labourers and others who were peasants in no meaningful sense of the word, as in F. G. Heath's *Peasant Life in the West of England* (1880), though for George Sturt, in a perceptive yet nostalgic picture of his changing Surrey village, the term retained some of its real if idealized meaning as he used it to evoke a lost world of independence and vigour.[99] Whether we focus on the bald three categories which dominated discussion of rural life or these uses of more archaic terms, it is striking how little the class language of social description was used for village society.

A final question: what would happen if we could penetrate the every-day, rather than the public, language of Victorian Britain? We would

---

identity of shopkeepers in Britain and in other European countries, see G. Crossick, 'Shopkeepers and the state in Britain, 1870–1914', in *Shopkeepers and Master Artisans*, ed. Crossick and Haupt, pp. 239–69.

[96] B. Disraeli, *Coningsby or the New Generation* (London, 1844), pt 3, ch. 3.

[97] J. Bateman, *The Great Landowners of Great Britain and Ireland*, 4th edn (London 1883), repr. ed. D. Spring (Leicester University Press, Leicester, 1971), p. 527.

[98] Royal Commission on Agricultural Depression, *BPP*, 1894, vol. 16. 2, Q. 14,887–92; H. Stanton Batch, *Challenging Years* (New York, 1940), pp. 65–6.

[99] G. Bourne [George Sturt], *Change in the Village* (Duckworth, London, 1912), 1955 edn.

find not just as great and often contradictory a mixture of terminology within the framework described in this essay, but new levels of variation: between generations, between town and country, between regions. Regional (and national) differences could simply provide approximately equivalent terms in the specific dialect or language. Far more interesting, however, are the cases where the local terms are rooted in a quite different perception of the social system, as in late-nineteenth-century south Cardiganshire, where a distinct vocabulary expressed the intricate relationships of mutual dependency that maintained the supply of labour and services in an only partially monetarized agrarian system. Thus there were the *pobol tai bach* (people of the little houses), *y fedel* (literally the reapers, meaning the cottagers owing a labour debt to the farm), and farmers described by the number of horses or cows their holding could sustain or require, for that expressed their place in the structure of mutual dependency.[100]

The most serious gap in our knowledge reflects how little historians have explored the languages of social description for women and the extent to which this diverged from the terminologies explored in this essay. We have already seen the uses of the lady/woman distinction, but when was it that the word 'girl' came to be used to describe adult women, thus expressing not age but the dual meanings of both gender and class subordination? The strike of the 'match girls' at Bryant and May in 1888 is the most celebrated example, but the usage is even clearer in the title of the Hammersmith Sculling Club for Girls and Men, set up in 1896 and concerned only with *working* girls.[101] More significant was the way in which the dominant public language ascribed social labels to women largely on the basis of the occupation or position of the male (husband or father) to whom they were attached, and the labels followed male-centred perceptions of the social order. Yet a distinctive language developed which was rooted in gender and the assumptions that went with it. One clear case is the division between skilled and unskilled workers, for the former were by definition male, and women workers were by definition unskilled, almost regardless of the work-place situation. The respective fates of engine-drivers and milliners illustrates a point about which we need to know a good deal more. Indeed, identification by personal occupation was itself a highly gendered construct which assumed occupation to be in principle full-time, paid, and away

---

[100] D. Jenkins, 'Rural society inside out', in *A People and a Proletariat: essays in the history of Wales, 1780–1980*, ed. D. Smith (Pluto Press, London, 1980), pp. 114–26.
[101] Rubinstein, *Before the Suffragettes*, p. 219.

from the home.[102] It was consequently far less commonly used to describe women than men.[103]

A survey of usage in a society proliferating languages of social description can barely scratch the surface of a major and still largely neglected problem. This essay has argued that terminology was no ready reflection of a changing social world, but an active force defining that world, an intervention within it. The use of words – and of flags, ceremonies, modes of dress, and much else – points towards the complex verbal, but also non-verbal, ways in which people made sense of their experiences, gave them order and connections, and sought to influence them.[104] Words, seemingly the most explicit of statements, turn out to be the most deceptive. As one encounters such Victorian terms as 'class', 'people', and 'gentleman', one can feel sympathy for the French ethnologist who, seeking to pin down the historical meaning of 'bourgeois', was reminded of the children's theatrical story of Dame Gigogne, from under whose enormous skirts crowds of children poured.[105] Our problem is not just that the terms in use shift over time, but that they also shift their meanings and their implications within society at a given moment. What man would not be pleased to be thought a gentleman in mid-Victorian Britain? In Dickens's *Our Mutual Friend*, Jenny Wren talked to Lizzie Hexham about Mr Eugene Wrayburn:

> 'I wonder whether he's rich!'
> 'No, not rich.'
> 'Poor?'

[102] C. Hakim, 'Census reports as documentary evidence: the census commentaries, 1801–1951', *Sociological Review*, 28 (1980), pp. 561–2.

[103] Ellen Jordan has argued that the high proportion of women aged 15–19 who were without occupations according to the censuses between 1851 and 1891, as compared with men, is explained largely by structural unemployment: E. Jordan, 'Female unemployment in England and Wales, 1851–1911: an examination of the census figures for 15–19 year olds', *Social History*, 13 (1988), pp. 175–90. This may well be the case; but some of that differential will be explained by the assumption that young men, even if only intermittently in employment, had an 'occupation', while a young woman in a similar situation did not.

[104] Pickering, 'Class without words', is an interesting, if limited, attempt to explore the social meaning of Chartist symbols. For a powerful exploration of the language of the *sans-culottes* during the French Revolution and its location within the informal workshop conventions of *ancien régime* Paris, in which insult, honour, and personal transaction provided the basis for a *sans-culottes* political language and style, see M. Sonenscher, 'The *sans-culottes* of the Year II: rethinking the language of labour in pre-Revolutionary France', *Social History*, 9 (1984), pp. 301–28.

[105] B. LeWita, *Ni vue ni inconnue: approche ethnographique de la culture bourgeoise* (Paris, 1988), p. 30.

'I think so, for a gentleman.'

'Ah! To be sure! Yes, he's a gentleman. Not of our sort, is he?'

But Jenny Wren did not approve of Eugene Wrayburn, and from her lips the word 'gentleman' abounded with implied criticism. Gentlemen were to be neither admired nor trusted. Her own fantasies were clear: 'When He turns up, he shan't be a gentleman; I'll very soon send him packing, if he is.'[106]

---

[106] C. Dickens, *Our Mutual Friend* (London, 1865), Bk 2, ch. 11.

8

'To each a language of his own': language, culture, and society in colonial India

David Washbrook

At the turn of the nineteenth century, as the officials of the English East India Company first came to explore their recent South Asian conquests, they were but dimly aware of how differently from themselves their new subjects looked on the social relations of language.[1] Brought up in the Western classical tradition, in which the Greek concept of *logos* associated words with reason, Europeans were inclined to give spoken and written language a privileged position among systems of social communication.[2] Yet, for the society they encountered in South Asia, shared language represented but one, and a relatively minor, medium through which social information was conveyed. Dress, paint-markings, emblems, signs, and distinctive manners of bearing described identities and roles within complex social structures, without reference to commonalities of word.[3] Indeed, most South Asian social contexts contained

---

[1] For an introduction to the social history of early colonial India, see C. A. Bayly, *Indian Society and the Making of British India* (Cambridge University Press, Cambridge, 1988). There is no comparable single volume dealing simultaneously with social, economic, political, and cultural themes for the later colonial and independence periods, but some valuable regional studies are provided by Sugata Bose, *Agrarian Bengal: economy, social structure and politics, 1919–47* (Cambridge University Press, Cambridge, 1987), and C. J. Baker, *An Indian Rural Economy, 1885–1955: the Tamilnad countryside* (Clarendon Press, Oxford, 1984); and various aspects of the social process are also explored in the essays contained in Ranajit Guha (ed.), *Subaltern Studies* (6 vols, Oxford University Press, Delhi, 1981–9).

[2] See M. Foucault, *The Archaeology of Knowledge*, tr. A. M. Sheridan Smith (Pantheon Books, New York, 1972); also E. Said, *Orientalism* (Routledge, London, 1978), pp. 123–48.

[3] For a general introduction to the cultural dynamics of Indian society, see B. S. Cohn, *India: the social anthropology of a civilization* (Prentice-Hall, Englewood Cliffs, N. J., 1971).

congeries of peoples who could not, or would not, communicate through common language since they did not speak the same tongue. In Madras in the eighteenth century, for example, Telugu-, Tamil-, Persian-, Port-uguese-, Armenian-, Gujerati-, Marathi-, and Hindustani-speaking groups lived side by side (as in most cases they had done for hundreds of years) without developing a common lingua.[4]

This linguistic diversity frequently made Europeans wonder whether they were dealing with one society, or even one culture, in India or with a series of self-contained and separate para-communities. Yet unifying principles of cognition clearly existed, encompassing the variegations of speech and drawing them together within shared frameworks of meaning. Going back to the Prakrit tradition, dramatic works were constructed with the different characters speaking to a single audience in different languages, depending on their regional origins and social roles.[5] Equally, religious inscriptions, recording endowments or celebrating great events, were often carved into the same stone or copper-plate simultaneously in several different scripts.[6] Certainly, ideas and values were broadly shared. But their transmission owed little to uniformities of language, and society was accustomed to a multiplicity of 'tongues'.

The new colonial rulers of this era, inspired by the European Romantic movement and the philological 'science' to which it gave rise, were inclined to conceive language as a product of 'nature' and also as the fundamental defining parameter of a 'culture'.[7] Thus they sought to examine languages to 'discover' the basic principles of construction which demarcated one from another and provided clues to the 'essential' cultural genius of each. Variations of 'dialect' and idiomatic usage were recognized, of course; but, by definition, each language was taken to possess a 'standard', root form. Yet, to South Asian intellectuals (grammarians of the written and classical languages apart), the notion that language as it was spoken had to have a standard form or a territorial boundary or was an objectively definable artefact of nature must have sounded very

---

[4] Verbal communication took place largely through multiple translation, many South Asians being partially bi- or tri-lingual. See J. Gumperz, 'On the linguistic markers of bilingual communication', *Journal of Social Issues*, 23 (1967).

[5] L. Nitti-Dolci, *The Prakrita Grammarians* (Paris, 1938; Eng. tr. Delhi, 1972); also R. S. McGregor, *Hindi Literature of the Nineteenth and Early Twentieth Centuries* (Wiesbaden, 1974).

[6] See, e.g., B. Stein, *Peasant State and Society in Medieval South India* (Oxford University Press, Delhi, 1980), p. 132.

[7] For a discussion of European ideas about language and their impact on the definition of Indian languages, see B. S. Cohn, 'The command of language and the language of command', in *Subaltern Studies*, ed. Guha, vol. 4 (1985).

strange. It never seems to have elicited much intellectual curiosity before the nineteenth century, and there were no dictionaries or lexicographies of the spoken vernaculars prior to colonial times. Spoken language was simply what people spoke, and there were a whole series of reasons why members of the same society ought to speak it very differently, for they were understood, in a variety of Hindu cosmological theories, to be different kinds of being. In the first place, there was the influence of location: according to many sets of beliefs, soil and blood were closely intermixed, and people sprang from and were part of their natal villages.[8] From that viewpoint, each village might be expected to have its own 'tongue', as to some degree it did. One expert witness informed an 1880s British Commission that Hindustani dialect changed noticeably about every eight miles across the Gangenetic plain.[9]

Second, there was the question of social status and, particularly, of caste. To some degree, status was reflected in the different 'languages' which different groups possessed and whose exclusivity they jealously protected: Persian was widely associated (via the Mughal Empire) with state power; Sanskrit, the language of the gods, was reserved to Brahmins; in much of the Tamil south, Marathi was the mysterious language of administration, known only to dynasties of grasping revenue collectors, and Gujerati was a language of commerce and manufacture. This principle of role differentiation by tongue reached deep down into society through the functions of caste, and affected communities who, at least according to the British, were supposed to be speaking the same language. In Tamil, for example, the inflections engendered by caste status went beyond mere conventions of dialect to encompass differences in vocabulary and syntax. The Tamil spoken by Brahmins and that spoken by 'untouchables' even in the same village (if, indeed, untouchables were allowed into a Brahmin village) was variegated in the extreme.[10] And the principles of caste were dynamic, constantly throwing up new forms of social differentiation, which, in turn, were reflected in different forms of speech.[11]

[8] See E. V. Daniel, *Fluid Signs: on being a person the Tamil way* (University of California Press, Berkeley, 1984).

[9] *Indian Education Commission: report by the North-West Provinces and Oudh Provincial Committee* (Calcutta, 1884), pp. 195–211.

[10] A. K. Ramanujan, 'The structure of variation: a study in caste dialects', in *Structure and Change in Indian Society*, ed. M. Singer and B. S. Cohn (Aldine Publishing and University of Chicago, Chicago, 1968); M. Shanmugam Pillai, 'Caste isoglosses in kinship terms', *Anthropological Linguistics*, 7 (1965).

[11] The once widely held 'Orientalist' notion that the caste system held 'traditional' Indian society in stasis is no longer credible today. For discussions of

The pluralism of caste, like that of 'language', also made the British ponder whether India was one or many societies. But, once again, there were unifying principles and institutions enjoying broad recognition. Caste itself, in some form or other, was observed by almost all groups, as were common notions about the significance of kingship, kinship, and blood.[12] Also, festival traditions saw millions brought together to participate in mass rituals of worshipping the divine; rituals which, to the puzzlement of Protestant Englishmen, were frequently conducted in the 'dead' language of Sanskrit, which not only few of the participants understood but which most were forbidden, on pain of damnation, from ever aspiring to learn.

A third point over which colonial European and South Asian understandings of the social relations, and meanings, of language differed was the status of 'writing' and of 'print'. The ruling Europeans came from societies in which the written word had long established a cultural hegemony over the spoken and in which, through the printing press, literate elites sought to disseminate their ideas and to remould the beliefs of the populace at large.[13] In India, by contrast, literate elites were less concerned to convey their wisdom to 'the masses' and convert the latter into obedient models of themselves than to protect their own specialist skills and learning and to mark in every possible way their own distinction from the common herd. Written and spoken forms of language tended to exist at a considerable remove, with the former exercising a very limited influence over the latter.[14] Much scholarly writing took place in languages which were either 'dead' or so archaic and arcane as to be unintelligible in 'the street'. Indeed, much took place in deliberately coded scripts designed to be obscure to all but a limited group of

---

*

dynamism in pre-modern 'caste' society, see J. Silverberg (ed.), *Social Mobility in the Caste System in India* (Paris, 1968); also A. Appadurai, 'Kings, sects and temples in South India, 1350–1700 AD', *Indian Economic and Social History Review*, 14 (1977); K. I. Leonard, *Social History of an Indian Caste* (University of California Press, Berkeley, 1978).

[12] See L. Dumont, *Religion, Politics, and History in India: collected papers in Indian sociology* (Paris, 1970).

[13] L. Febvre and H.-J. Martin, *The Coming of the Book: the impact of printing, 1450–1800*, tr. D. Gerard (N.L.B., London, 1976); also B. Anderson, *Imagined Communities: reflections on the origin and spread of nationalism* (Verso, London, 1983).

[14] See, e.g., M. Shanmugam Pillai, 'Tamil – literary and colloquial', in 'Linguistic diversity in South Asia', ed. C. Ferguson and J. Gumperz, *International Journal of American Linguistics*, 26 (1960); and K. Zvelebil, 'Dialects of Tamil', *Archiv Orientalni*, 26 (1959) and 27 (1960).

cognoscenti.[15] The function of writing was more to transmit 'secrets' across distances of time and place to fellow experts in the arts or philosophy or sciences than to broadcast knowledge to the world.

Admittedly, at various times in Indian history, the exclusivity of writing had been challenged, particularly by popular devotional (*bhakti*) movements wishing to find a means of spreading their alternative spiritual messages and of giving their ideas a more permanent form. Periodically, manuscript traditions had appeared which 'wrote' versions of the spoken vernaculars.[16] But *bhakti*-ism was at a low ebb at the turn of the nineteenth century, following an epoch of intensified elite domination; and the general failure to overturn scholarly exclusivism in Indian culture may be judged from the latter's failure not merely to develop, but even to adopt, the printing press, long after knowledge of its basic technology was theoretically available. Printing came to South Asia only with the European conquest.

Between the officials of the East India Company and the millions of their South Asian subjects, there lay a wide, and to some degree insurmountable, gap in understanding of the nature of 'language', of 'society', and of the relationship between the two. This gap can, if one likes, be put down to irreducible differences in cultural rationality between the 'South Asian' and the 'European' minds.[17] Perhaps less problematically, however, it can be seen as the result of sharply differing social and cultural histories over the previous several centuries. Many European historians would now see the conventions about culture, social

---

[15] Scribal, trading, and other specialist caste groups tended to develop their own forms of script to protect the secrets of their knowledge. Amrit Rai has argued that Urdu court poetry developed as a deliberate attempt to take a Hindustani literature out of the hands of the vernacular multitude: A. Rai, *A House Divided* (Oxford University Press, Delhi, 1984).

[16] See ibid. for discussion of this in the context of Hindi/Hindustani literature. The literary forms or dialects of Marathi and Tamil were also subject to strong *bhakti* influences.

[17] As does Cohn, e.g., in 'Command of language'. Since Dumont's writings in the 1960s, as extrapolated by the Chicago school of McKim Marriott, Ronald Inden, and Stephen Barnett (among others) in the 1970s, anthropological studies of South Asia have been rent by debate over the need for an ethno-sociology of India, reflecting the supposedly unique principles of cultural rationality and cognition underlying its civilization. See L. Dumont, *Homo-Hierarchicus*, tr. M. Sainsbury (Weidenfeld, London, 1970); R. B. Inden and M. Marriott, 'Caste systems', in *Encyclopaedia Britannica*, 15th edn (Chicago, 1974); R. B. Inden and R. W. Nicholas, *Kinship in Bengali Culture* (University of Chicago Press, Chicago, 1976); and S. Barnett *et al.*, 'Hierarchy purified', *Journal of Asian Studies*, 35 (1976).

structure, and language held by elite Western Europeans at the end of
the eighteenth century as the products of their own recent past, a past
marked by 'revolutions' in the form of the state, in the relations of class
domination, in the spread of literacy, and in the rise of 'print capitalism'.[18] South Asian history, although by no means static, had not
developed along the same course, and its own traditions of the state,
of social dominance, and of human communication, with their many
implications for the social relations of language, now stood much further
apart from those of 'the West' than they had done a few centuries before.

Set against the increasingly centralized judicial and administrative
systems of the European state, with their demand for a unitary monopoly
of cultural authority, for example, the state systems of India were very
loosely articulated. Rulers sought more the recognition of a 'universal
dominion' over a broad range of corporate local groups enjoying a high
degree of autonomy than the establishment of an intrusive control. The
direct functions of the state seldom extended beyond the collection of
revenue and tribute; questions of justice and of right in local society
were largely left for local resolution.[19]

Equally loose by European standards was what might be termed the
structure of society. South Asian society was certainly hierarchic, but,
and crucially, there were (at least) two separate sources of authority for
hierarchy: one 'religious' and, in much of India, drawn from the Brahmanic spiritual tradition, the other 'secular', reflecting kingly and warrior
norms.[20] The two evaluated conduct quite differently, the 'purity/pol-
lution' considerations of classical Brahmanic thought being juxtaposed
to the celebration of power, violence, and bloodshed in the kingly
model. Although Louis Dumont has famously argued for the
'encompassment' of the kingly by the Brahmanic code, many historical

[18] Debates about the distinctive historical origins of Western 'modernity', of
course, go back to Weber, Marx, and beyond. For a reconsideration, see A.
Giddens, *Nation State and Violence* (Polity Press, London, 1986); and, on the
role of print, Anderson, *Imagined Communities*.

[19] For discussions on the nature of the state in India during the two centuries
immediately preceding colonial rule, see A. Wink, 'Sovereignty and universal
dominion in South Asia', *Indian Economic and Social History Review*, 21 (1984);
F. Perlin, 'The pre-colonial Indian state in history and epistemology', in *The
Study of the State*, ed. H. Classen and P. Skalnik (The Hague, 1981); and
Appadurai, 'Kings, sects and temples'.

[20] See Dumont, *Homo-Hierarchicus*. But some historians suggest that a third
model, based on a more egalitarian 'community' ideal, also influenced society:
see B. Stein, 'Politics, peasants and the deconstruction of feudalism in medieval
India', *Journal of Peasant Studies*, 12 (1985).

anthropologists would now doubt that to have been the case, at least (and paradoxically) before the colonial period itself and the reduction of the warrior function in society.[21] Rather, perhaps, the two existed in dynamic tension side by side, creating much room for dispute over questions of value and of role in schemes of hierarchy. No position in society possessed an indisputable status, and all groups seem to have existed in competition for precedence over those surrounding them.[22]

Indeed, competition and contention could be said to have been the real principles on which social order, tenuous as it was, was built. Would-be elite groups, be they kingly or Brahmanic, sought to define themselves by reference to their possession of skills and powers so specialized that it was difficult (though rarely impossible) for others to rival or emulate them. These groups then essayed to promote or perpetuate internal rivalries among the groups beneath them, in order to divert challenges to elite privileges. The Mughal Empire's manipulation of Rajput kingship followed this pattern, as did the much more ancient division of society into castes of the Left and Right Hand, above which stood Brahmins and dominant landholding clans, in the South.[23] India's new nineteenth-century colonial rulers did not invent the concept of *divide et impera* in South Asia.

Like the principles of hierarchy, those informing the formation of 'groups' were also flexible and, to a considerable degree, subject to contention, although there can be little doubt that South Asia was, ideologically, much more a society of corporate groups than of 'individuals'. *Bhakti*-ism introduced the concept of the individual standing in a direct relationship to his god; and certain scriptural sources inclined Brahmins to view themselves in a similar light.[24] However, as noted before, the *bhakti* tradition, although recurrent, failed to overturn institutionalized hierarchy; and the individualistic ethic of the Brahmin was not intended for general consumption.

But how, concretely, 'groups' were to be defined was always a prob-

[21] See N. Dirks, *The Hollow Crown: ethnohistory of an Indian kingdom* (Cambridge University Press, Cambridge, 1987).

[22] For an account of these contests in the context of the South Indian temple, see A. Appadurai and C. B. Appadurai, 'The South Indian Temple: authority, honour and redistribution', *Contributions to Indian Sociology*, n.s., 10 (1976).

[23] R. G. Fox, *Kin, Clan, Raja and Rule* (University of California Press, Berkeley, 1971); A. Appadurai, 'Right- and left-hand castes in South India', *Indian Economic and Social History Review*, 11 (1974).

[24] F. Hardy, 'Ideology and the cultural contexts of the Sri Vaishnava temple', *Indian Economic and Social History Review*, 14 (1977); R. G. Bhandarkar, *Vaishnavism, Saivism and Minor Religious Systems* (Strasbourg, 1913).

lematic issue, and has given rise to much debate in the contemporary academic literature. One of the most persuasive interpretations has been that of Ronald Inden and McKim Marriott, who have suggested a 'substantialist' undercurrent to much South Asian social thought.[25] Groups tended to define themselves in terms of their possession of a particular kind of bodily substance which made them genetically different, as it were, from the groups around them. In most North Indian 'tongues', the term *jati* (derived etymologically from the Sanskrit for birth or blood) was applied to the definition of group association. Moreover, each substantive group was considered to have a discrete 'code for conduct', reflective of its place in a scheme of hierarchy and informing its ethics and behaviour. Where the practical difficulty arose, however, was in putting borders around these 'substances' and marking with any clarity the boundaries between groups. Much Hindu cosmological thought reflected the notion of a continuum between the divine order, human society, and the domain of nature. Contact with the divine or with nature altered the substance of the human between them; and, as contact through sight, smell, sound, and touch was constant and dynamic, so substance was always given to change. If, at one level of theory, 'castes' consisted of people sharing a bodily substance, then caste membership was itself always in some degree of flux. Further, as the implications of hierarchy (of both kinds) affected the perception of substance, suggesting that substance might be improved by emulating the life-models provided by the sacred and the mighty, this flux was continuously in agitation.

South Asian cultural conventions with regard to language and linguistic usage are perhaps best understood against this background of loose, and contentious, state and social structures. On the one hand, there were many pressures pushing language towards the refining of ever more elaborate distinctions. People's language was regarded as part of their substance. As they sought to distinguish this substance from that of the groups surrounding them, so they were inclined to emphasize the differences in their style of speech (as of dress, appearance, dwelling house, food, and so on). Those distinctions were particularly important in underpinning claims to elite status and privilege. Brahmins, for example, were held worthy because of the proximity of their substance to the principles of the divine, a proximity which gave them mystical spritual powers. Part of their ability to maintain this mystique came from their unique possession of a language, Sanskrit, which provided

---

[25] Inden and Marriott, 'Caste systems'.

access to the wisdom and truths known only to the gods. Many other elite groups also held their privileges in relation to special forms of knowledge and power (in administration, military organization, agricultural economy, and trade) protected and manifested through distinctive languages and scripts.

But if these pressures were constantly pushing language towards diversity, there were others moving it back towards uniformity. The elements of hierarchical ideology in society guaranteed that 'inferior' groups would draw their own status models from their 'superiors' and seek to emulate them. This emulation involved, *inter alia*, attempts to copy the speech of superiors in order to join and share in their substance. Powerful families in village and local society often partially adopted the styles of their state-level superiors, just as non-Brahmin priests imitated Brahmanic styles in their ritual customs (sometimes even developing quasi-Sanskritic forms of liturgy). This provided some thread of linguistic continuity through society, although a thread with many knots in it. In Tamilnadu, for example, the courtly literary styles and Sanskrit rituals of the metropolis were linked through partial replication to the styles and rituals of local rural elite groups, whose own styles and rituals were then further linked to, and partially replicated by, lower-caste groups in the countryside.[26] But the knots were always at risk of being loosened, or even broken, as each upper stratum of privilege sought to maintain its distance from the one below it by adopting new or different cultural symbols and linguistic usages.

South Asian society was, then, multilingual (or, perhaps better, polyglot), as much by cultural design and social intention as by accident. From the European perspective, it represented a land of Babel brought to perpetual chaos by the sheer perversity of its natives. Yet there was a logic to its chaos, and there were conventions of understanding, which gave meaning and order to its diversity. Writing, for example, gained authority from the substance of the writer, quite apart from the rational import of his words. Similarly, the style and script which he (or she) used, the materials which were written upon, even the container in which the manuscript was kept, possessed significance for the reader and for illiterate audiences to whom manuscripts in an otherwise obscure

[26] See Stein, *Peasant State*, pp. 51–2, 240–3; also his 'Social mobility and medieval Hindu sects', in *Social Mobility*, ed. J. Silverberg. On the general question of syncretism and differentiation in Indian languages, see J. Gumperz, 'Some remarks on regional and social language differences in India', in *Introducing India in Liberal Education*, ed. M. Singer (University of Chicago Press, Chicago, 1957).

language might be read. Spoken language, too, signified very much more than 'words could say'. Position and status in the terrestrial world and the cosmos were conveyed by its sounds, with implications for speaker and listener alike. In a universe of constantly exchanging substances, the aural impact of a Sanskrit mantra, as the sight of a god, could raise and transform personal status, just as the sight or sound of an Untouchable could degrade it.[27] Language in Indian culture was both more as well as less crucial to social communication than *logos*.

The conceptual framework surrounding language, however, was so far removed from that of the nineteenth-century Europeans, who then took state power in India, that a fundamental cultural collision was inevitable. Dismissing South Asia's different traditions of the state, social structure, and language as 'backward', if indeed they even recognized the possibility of their existence, the new British rulers set out to 'civilize' Indian society and to bring it under the control of their own politico-economic and cultural norms. At one level, the colonial programme in India centred on introducing the institutional principles of 'modern' capitalist society. To this end, warrior forms of domination were displaced by those predicated on the possession of private rights of property; a 'modern' state, based on claims to a monopoly of both cultural authority and coercive force, was introduced; bureaucratic rationalities and instrumentalities were developed to consolidate elite command of society and defend 'social order'.[28] Language responded to these new imperatives, whose realization depended very much upon its transformation. For, as Gellner and others have seen, language plays a crucial role in the 'modernization' process, not merely as a facilitating mechanism but as a key instrument, itself promoting change through the transformation of cultural meaning and value.[29]

In the domain of language, the British rapidly set out to 'discover' the root forms and standard structures of the Indian vernacular languages, which their philological science told them existed as artefacts of nature. These would be used to provide training manuals to teach future generations of British administrators, to define languages of government and law, which would push the authority of the Queen Empress into

---

[27] On the transmission of 'substance' through sensual contact, see D. L. Eck, *Darsán: seeing the divine image in India* (Anima Books, New York, 1985).

[28] For an exploration of the principles behind the policies of colonial government, see the various essays of B. S. Cohn, *An Anthropologist among the Historians and Other Essays* (Oxford University Press, Delhi, 1988).

[29] E. Gellner, *Nations and Nationalism* (Blackwell, Oxford, 1983).

every village corner and to bring the word of the Gospels to the proverbially poor and benighted heathen.[30]

And, of course, in setting out to 'discover' something which science told them had to be there, the British succeeded in finding the root and standard forms of the vernaculars and in generating a huge defining literature of grammars, dictionaries, and lexicographies. The task was not without its difficulties, however; and some of its products, in retrospect, challenge the concept of 'scholarship'. Several authorities, following the European convention of giving greater weight to written over spoken forms, produced dictionaries, derived largely from literary sources, which reflected linguistic usages which hardly anybody supposedly speaking the language could understand. Many a young colonial-service wallah, arriving in his first district and eager to converse in the 'native tongue' he had just spent several years learning, was disconcerted by the discovery that the natives found him perfectly unintelligible. Other authorities, paying more attention to speech but finding the extent of variation virtually intractable to objective principles of categorization, settled matters either by deferring to the opinion of particular 'natives' whom they liked or else by following arbitrary procedures. There are some grounds for claiming that the Rev. C. P. Brown's first Telugu dictionary, for example, more or less invented the language to suit its author's idiosyncratic prejudices.[31] Occasionally, however, elements of self-doubt crept into the exercise, as when the first Linguistic Survey of India, conducted in the 1900s, shocked generations of British administrators by suggesting that the 'Hindustani' which those going to the Gangenetic plain had learned for decades as the language of the country was not truly one language at all but three.[32]

But self-doubt was a rare quality for British colonialists to betray, and, by one means or another, standard forms of the vernacular languages were 'discovered', disseminated, and, to a degree, absorbed into Indian society. Literacy based upon the vernaculars expanded, particularly from the later nineteenth century; an indigenous press and publishing industry grew; deepening bureaucratic regulation pushed 'government' languages further into society. Moreover, India was not short of *literati* and intellectuals impressed by the power and authority of the new rulers and eager to learn the mysteries behind their culture. By the early decades of the nineteenth century, Indian scholars themselves were actively

---

[30] For a discussion of British policies and practices with regard to Indian languages, see Cohn, 'Command of language'; also Gumperz, 'Some remarks'.
[31] Cohn, 'Command of language', pp. 315–17.
[32] *Linguistic Survey of India*, 9 (Calcutta, 1916), pp. 42–56.

engaged in the colonial project, and were advancing its influence over language, as all other aspects of culture.[33] In effect, if only to a degree, language in India started to become 'modernized', and, at least at one level, the sub-continent's social experience of language passed under the same rubric of change that had developed earliest in the West and was coming to affect most other parts of an increasingly Western-dominated world.

This 'modernization' manifested itself particularly in the way that the new concepts of language began to inform questions of social and political identity and to provide symbols of self-conscious ethnicity. As noted before, notions about the primacy of cultural nationalism were inherent in the 'scientific' approach to language taken by European elite culture in this age. And, as Benedict Anderson has argued, the appearance of a common 'print' language is likely to promote the 'imagination' of a common history and culture among those whose language it now purports to be.[34] The absorption of these notions by Indian intellectuals and their possession of the weaponry of print brought with it a reconceptualization of social and political space. Society in India was now conceived as based on underlying structures of culture, and even civilization, which had their origins in commonalities of language. Each linguistic group constituted a separate cultural community with, in the logic of nationalist theory, claims to the possession of its own 'territory' and, perhaps, even state.[35]

Moreover, as Paul Brass has argued, many of the conditions of 'social mobilization' which Karl Deutsch saw promoting linguistic ethnicity to a position of command over cultural identity in continental Europe also developed in the Indian case.[36] The social processes of 'modernization' undermined the pre-existing bases of elite authority, and created heightened tensions between elite groups. In response, such groups began to

[33] On the relationships between British scholars of India and early nineteenth-century Indian intellectuals in Bengal, see D. Kopf, *British Orientalism and the Bengal Renaissance: the dynamics of Indian modernization, 1778–1835* (University of California Press, Berkeley, 1969); on some of the wider implications for the Indian intelligentsia, see A. Nandy, *The Intimate Enemy: loss and recovery of self under colonialism* (Oxford University Press, Delhi, 1983).

[34] Anderson, *Imagined Communities*.

[35] For a theoretical exploration of structural change in the context of caste ideology, see S. Barnett, 'Approaches to change in caste ideology in South India', in *Essays on South India*, ed. B. Stein (Hawaii University Press, Honolulu, 1975).

[36] P. R. Brass, *Language, Religion and Politics in India* (Cambridge University Press, Cambridge, 1974).

search for new symbols, which could command loyalty (and thus preserve deference) among dislocated and disturbed mass constituencies.
The new cultural symbols of linguistic (as 'religious' and 'racial') ethnicity
supplied this function, and thus became built into the social politics of
modernity.

Yet, for Indian society, the ideology of modern linguistic ethnicity
has always represented something of a two-edged sword: promoting
new forms of cultural solidarity, but also sharpening social tensions and
conflicts. Pre-modern South Asian society, of course, had hardly been
conflict-free. Discrete clan, sectarian, and caste groups had fought one
another for millennia in a continuous struggle for political power. But
the objective of struggle had usually been to establish dominance over
a territorial space containing a pluralistic, multi-group, social order.
Now, however, the new ideology dictated that territorial space itself
must be culturally (or at least linguistically) homogeneous. Speakers of
other tongues were 'aliens' without legitimate rights, who could properly
be purged from the 'homelands' of majoritarian communities.[37]

This has brought an added, and savage, dimension to intra-group
relations of conflict. Over the course of this century, Hindi- and Urdu-,
Hindi- and Punjabi-, Tamil- and Hindi-, Tamil- and Telugu-, Telugu-
and Urdu-, Marathi- and Gujerati-, Marathi- and Tamil-, Bengali- and
Assamese-, and, most recently, Sindhi- and Urdu-, and Bengali- and
Gurkhi-speakers have murdered each other in considerable numbers for
possession of their own discrete cultural spaces. The modern ideology
of linguistic ethnicity offers Indian society a future of disintegrating and
brutalizing conflict.

Yet it may be a serious mistake simply to subsume India's recent social
experience of language under the general rubric of 'modernization'. For
a closer examination of its linguistic history reveals many distinctive
features not immediately explicable by, nor anticipated in, the model;
and, of course, Indian society, for all its problems, has not disintegrated.
In the first place, while standardization has taken place in most languages,
it has by no means brought written and spoken forms perfectly into
alignment; rather, as very noticeably in Tamil, two different standard
written and spoken forms have come into existence, while remaining
separate.[38] Moreover, social variations in speech-forms have continued

---

[37] For this development in the context of Tamil/Dravidian ideology, see M.
R. Barnett, *The Politics of Cultural Nationalism in South India* (Princeton
University Press, Princeton, 1976), pt 1.
[38] Shanmugam Pillai, 'Tamil – literary and colloquial'.

to exist, not as frozen relics of a caste past, but as dynamic creations of the present: word loans from other languages, including English, serve to act as novel contemporary markers.[39]

Second, the politics of language have generated social tensions not only between different linguistic communities but also within each one, over what the proper forms of its language are and who has the right to declare them. These internal divisions have been inclined to offset the political effects of the external divisions between different language groups, since none is entirely sure who its constituents are nor what constitutes the 'true' nature of their tongue. Such internal conflict was perhaps most overt in the case of 'Hindustani', where a battle developed during the nineteenth century between the proponents of the Sanskrit-derived 'Hindi' and the Persian-derived 'Urdu' literary forms for possession of 'it'.[40] But conflict has also recurred repeatedly in the processes constituting most of the vernaculars: between, for example, the proponents of a classical and a modern Telugu; and between those for a Sanskrit-literary, an Anglo-modern, and a Sen or pure version of Tamil.[41]

Yet, from the perspective of a modernization theory, what is even more peculiar about most of these debates is the degree to which many of the parties argued, and ultimately won, their cases not from most common usage, nor even most utilitarian formulation, but from antiquity of precedent and virtue of classical heritage. The nineteenth-century argument between Hindi and Urdu turned on the relative status to be accorded to elite Sanskrit as opposed to Persian 'letters'. Hindi's victory in the twentieth century represents a studied attempt to construct – or reconstruct – language in a way which would take it (and the mores of society) back to the Vedic Age.[42] In Tamil too, it has been the proponents of a Sen version, purified of the accretions of the last 2,000 years, who

[39] F. Southworth, 'Sociolinguistics research in South India', in Essays on South India, ed. Stein, pp. 197–200.

[40] Brass, Language, Religion and Politics; J. Lutt, Hindu-Nationalismus in Uttar Pradesh, 1867–1900 (Stuttgart, 1970); R. S. McGregor, 'Bengal and the development of Hindi', South Asian Review, 5 (1972); and F. C. R. Robinson, Separatism among Indian Muslims: the politics of the United Provinces' Muslims, 1860–1923 (Cambridge University Press, Cambridge, 1974).

[41] J. Leonard, 'Politics and social change in South India: a study of the Andhra movement', Journal of Commonwealth Political Studies, 5 (1967); E. F. Irschick, Politics and Social Conflict in South India; the non-Brahmin movement and Tamil separatism, 1916–29 (University of California Press, Berkeley, 1969), ch. 8.

[42] S. K. Chatterji, Indo-Aryan and Hindi (Ahmedabad, 1942); Lutt, Hindu-Nationalismus.

have proved themselves the most persuasive, and have succeeded in influencing both spoken and written language with a series of amazing circumlocutions and 'geralogisms', reverting usage towards the Sangam Age of *c*.300 AD and considerably before that.[43] It is not immediately obvious how a theory of 'modernization' can account for 'antiquity' becoming the test of 'authority' or for languages being shifted 'backwards' in time to recover their most ancient forms. This is particularly the case when, as in the instance of Sen Tamil, the 'regress' causes major problems for the functioning of modern communications systems and for the diffusion of scientific and technical learning.[44]

Third, in looking at the social, as opposed to the historical, direction in which linguistic usage has shifted, the Western 'modernization' conception that standardization would pass the norms of the elites to the masses is by no means borne out.[45] Early colonial rule strongly supported the authority of certain elite groups and, in its linguistic as well as its sociological programmes, anticipated that their cultural styles would enjoy a position of hegemony over the subsequent development of society. In the north, for example, the 'Mughlai' ruling elite of warriors, scribes, and courtiers once sheltered beneath the umbrella of Mughal imperial power was singled out for transmutation into a landlord-bureaucrat class, which was meant to provide the social base of the Indo-British state.[46] To facilitate this goal, Persian was retained as the language of British-Indian government until as late as 1837; and, even then, it was replaced only by 'Hindustani' in the Persianized Urdu script. In Bengal, where English played more of a role as the language of administration, official 'Bengali' was derived almost exclusively from the dialect of the *bhadralok*, the high-caste landlord-scribal gentry who underpinned colonial rule.[47] In the south, where the Raj rested on foundations of Brahmin collaboration, the first 'authorized' versions of Tamil showed a high degree of Sanskritic influence.[48]

But, with the singular exception of Bengali (which, in this matter as

---

[43] Irschick, *Politics and Social Conflict*, ch. 8.

[44] P. Spratt, *The DMK in Power* (Madras, 1969).

[45] For discussion and critique of elite and diffusionist models in social history, see E. P. Thompson, 'Happy families', *New Society*, 8 Sept. 1977, pp. 499–501; also R. Guha, 'On some aspects of the historiography of colonial India', in *Subaltern Studies*, ed. Guha, vol. 1 (1982).

[46] T. Metcalf, *Land, Landlords and the British Raj: northern India in the nineteenth century* (University of California Press, Berkeley, 1979).

[47] This was '*sadhu bhasa*' or 'decent speech'.

[48] So much so that some Orientalist authorities, such as H. H. Wilson, thought that it was derived from Sanskrit: see R. Caldwell, *A Comparative Grammar of the Dravidian or South Indian Family of Languages* (London, 1875).

in all others, was to go its own way), the new colonial elites never fully succeeded in establishing their authority over the development of the modern vernaculars. In most places, they encountered challenges from 'popular' forces, located in the middle ranks of society, for control of culture. Over time, it was these 'middling' groups whose voice became increasingly decisive. In the north, for example, the veneer of 'Mughlai' cultural authority, with its Persian-Urdu orientations, lay thin over a society whose demotic values came much more from sacred Hindu shrines located along the holy river Ganges, which ran through and dominated the region. The influence of a Sanskritic Brahmin priesthood was strong among merchant groups and peasant clans, who reacted to the notion that their culture and language should be unified around the symbols of Urdu-Persian (and, by implication, Islam) by generating a series of resistance movements. One of these movements was concerned to emphasize the virtues of a 'Hindustani' informed by Sanskrit and written in the Sanskrit-derived Devnagri script.[49] The struggle was long and bitter, and fed into the wider issues raised by partition. But eventually, 'Hindi' triumphed, and Urdu (together with many members of the Urdu-speaking elite) was cast out to become the language of a 'foreign' country in the newly formed Pakistan.[50]

The overthrow of 'Brahmin' and the rise of 'Sen' Tamil reflected a similar social process in the south. The British gave Brahmins, whose previous relationship with non-Brahmin peasant and merchant groups had been equivocal, an unquestioned position of authority over 'Indian' culture, which was sustained by the institutions of the colonial state and law.[51] Brahmanic and Sanskritic dialect was supposed to 'take command' of the standardization of Tamil. But the aspiration soon encountered fierce resistance from below, and, ultimately, was turned back by a popular movement seeking to purge Tamil of what was now seen to be the 'alien' influence of Sanskrit and to restore the language to 'the people'.[52]

---

[49] Robinson, *Separatism among Indian Muslims*, ch. 2; C. A. Bayly, *The Local Roots of Indian Politics: Allahabad, 1880–1920* (Clarendon Press, Oxford, 1974), chs 5–6.

[50] Brass, *Language, Religion and Politics*.

[51] B. Stein, 'Integration of the agrarian system of South India', in *Land Control and Social Structure in Indian History*, ed. R. E. Frykenberg (University of Wisconsin Press, Madison, 1969); A. Appadurai, *Worship and Conflict under Colonial Rule: a South Indian case* (Cambridge University Press, Cambridge, 1981); Dirks, *Hollow Crown*.

[52] Irschick, *Politics and Social Conflict*, ch. 8; Barnett, *Politics of Cultural Nationalism*, pt 1.

The development of Gujerati and of Marathi too progressed along similar lines, although the relationship between elite and middling groups was rather different. Here, there was an attempt less to dismiss elite styles than to take them over from below and 'vulgarize' them. In early colonial Gujerat, the term *Patidar* referred to a revenue- or rent-receiving notable, whose quasi-aristocratic style (including linguistic style) was highly differentiated from that of the *kunbi* peasantry. From the late nineteenth century, however, the upper *kunbi* stratum began to adopt *Patidar* symbols and to seek incorporation into *Patidar* 'blood' through intermarriage. With widening vernacular literacy, *Patidar* usages and symbols percolated into, and became inextricably conflated with, peasant language and culture. The original *Patidar* families appear to have disapproved of these developments strongly, but ultimately were unable to resist them. Much against their will, a corrupted *Patidari* style has become the culture of the massive petty-farmer stratum of Gujerat, and lord/peasant distinctions have largely been lost.[53] In adjacent Maharashtra, much the same seems to have happened to the once crucial *Maratha/kunbi* status line. Pressure from below also fused together *Maratha*-princely and *kunbi*-peasant usage to constitute the bases of the contemporary Marathi standard vernacular.[54]

Theories of 'modernization' tend to be very elite-centred, with processes of social and cultural change conceived as percolating downwards through society. It is not at all clear how such theories can comprehend an Indian social history – of language and much else – in which 'modern' elites have always faced strong challenges and in which peasants and middling groups possess the major share of authority over culture and society.

In a fourth way, too, the social politics of language in India do not easily fit the anticipations of modernization. Very often the rationale of such politics seems sharply at odds with the cultural logic of modernity. Given the importance of language to the relations of the modern state, for example, it might be supposed that conflicts between language groups

[53] D. F. Pocock, *Kanbi and Patidar: a study of the Patidar community of Gujarat* (Clarendon Press, Oxford, 1972); C. Bates, 'The nature of social change in Gujarat', *Modern Asian Studies*, 15 (1981); D. Hardiman, *Peasant Nationalists of Gujarat* (Oxford University Press, Delhi, 1981); and J. Breman, *Of Peasants, Migrants and Paupers: rural labour circulation and capitalist production in West India* (Oxford University Press, Delhi, 1985).

[54] R. O'Hanlon, 'Maratha history as polemic', *Modern Asian Studies*, 17 (1983); and idem, *Caste, Conflict and Ideology: Mahatma Jotirao Phule and low caste protest in nineteenth-century Western India* (Cambridge University Press, Cambridge, 1985).

would centre on differential access to state power. Such types of conflict have taken place, of course, and continue to do so. But there are many conflicts which are difficult to reduce to propositions about state power, and appear to have more to do with issues of symbolic status. Why, for example, should Tamil nationalists be desperately concerned to 'Tamilize' the liturgy of Hinduism in the context of what is now officially a 'secular' state?[55] Why should Sen Tamil purists also resist Anglicization, even of the language of science and technology, long after the withdrawal of the British has taken the English out of contention for state power and when this resistance creates severe problems of development and of career opportunity?[56]

Equally, if the ideology of modernity associates linguistic-cultural 'communality' with the legitimate bases of the state, why should so many language groups in India insist on the recognition of their own 'autonomy' (whatever that is precisely) and yet not seriously challenge the framework of a pluralistic modern Indian state? The special issues raised by Pakistan (and, more recently, 'Khalistan') apart, the constant feuding over possession of territorial space between different language groups has only very rarely led to any of them demanding 'partition' and questioning the existence of an overarching unitary 'Indian' state containing them all. Even the Tamil movement, which briefly flirted with separatism in the 1940s and 1950s, has long since abandoned this goal. It merely insists that Tamil be the language of the state in its domain, and resists the attempts of the central government to promote a national 'Hindi-ization'.[57] Other regional language movements, although less vociferously and violently, take much the same stance, and have effectively prevented Hindi-ization from reaching far into their domains. The question which this poses is what vision and understanding of 'the state' actually informs these 'regionalist' vernacular ethnicities? The implication is that 'India' should possess no fully authorized national language, but operate on the basis of multilinguality and the recognition of 'autonomy' for each of its many languages. Yet can such a state meaningfully be described as 'modern', either in its techniques of communication and cultural 'symbolization' or in its ideological self-conception?

To respond to these questions, it is necessary to take account of a number of specific historical features which divorce India's social experience from

[55] Barnett, *Politics of Cultural Nationalism*, ch. 9.
[56] Ibid., ch. 10.
[57] Ibid., chs 4–6.

that assumed by the theory of modernization and, indeed, to raise serious doubts about the construction and utility of that theory itself. In particular, the theory may overlook some central contradictions in the processes constituting state and legal systems in the modern world, which extrapolate the social logic of capitalism and relate new principles of rationality to old. These contradictions are brought out particularly strongly by the 'colonial' context of Indian history.

In the first place, the curious intellectual search to locate the most ancient 'roots' of the vernaculars and to base contemporary usage upon them can be seen as inspired by the concepts of 'right' and 'identity' given in the ideology and institutions of the modern state itself, at least as this form of the state came to India via British rule. One of the most important means by which the British sought to 'civilize' India and bring it into the 'bourgeois' nineteenth century was through the creation of private rights of property sustained by a uniform system of laws. But for the British, law was never simply the product of voluntaristic legislation: it had a quasi-mystical status derived from the tradition of common law. In this tradition, in which the function of the courts was not to create but to 'discover' law, rights and privileges were validated by reference to a prehistorical and changeless conception of the past. 'Customary rights' had to be shown as held continuously 'from time immemorial'; to reveal either a precise date or act of origination or the influence of 'lapse' or 'change' was to invalidate them. Equally, in arbitrating the disputes of claimants, whose rights were based on documents and charters, precedence was conventionally given to antiquity. What was oldest was most 'authentic' and possessed most 'right'.[58]

Of course, in nineteenth-century Britain itself the authority of the common law could be overridden by parliamentary statute and by judicial notions of 'equity' which allowed the needs of the present to take precedence over the dictates of the past. But the regulation of common law held unless or until it was so modified. Thus it provided the base of the ideology of the law, a base which was carried over into the colonies. At one level, the British legal 'revolution' in India consisted mainly of 'discovering', writing down, and fixing in perpetuity 'the laws and customs of the Hindoos and Musselmen' by reference to their most

[58] For a discussion of this ideology, see J. G. A. Pocock, *The Ancient Constitution and the Feudal Law: a study of English historical thought in the seventeenth century* (Cambridge University Press, Cambridge, 1957); and, for its continuing influence into the nineteenth century, see J. Burrow, *A Liberal Descent: Victorian historians and the English past* (Cambridge University Press, Cambridge, 1981).

ancient precedents and least changing forms.[59] Moreover, these laws and customs, once established, were far less frequently 'modified' by statute and equity than in the British case. For the ultimate legitimacy of statutory law depends upon the existence of representative institutions, of which colonial India had few; and British judges were constantly reminded that their own notions of equity might not be those of their morally perverse 'Oriental' subjects. The Raj exercised extreme caution in 'interfering' with the customs and institutions of 'native' society, which its courts defined by reference to ancient texts and practices 'from time immemorial' and proposed to freeze for all eternity.

Nor was it only the ideology of the Anglo-Indian law which rested on this time-collapse: it was also that of the British-Indian state itself. As in Britain, where the state validated itself by reference to the succession of kings and to charters provided by the Anglo-Saxon witan, Magna Carta and '1688', so in colonial India, the state sought its legitimacy in terms of 'inheritances' from the Mughal and many previous imperial traditions and from the concept of a pre-Islamic 'Hindu golden age', which its defence of Hindu tradition was intended to restore.[60] What all this meant for the conception of 'right' received by Indian society from its 'modern' colonial masters was that 'authenticity' and 'legitimacy' were seen to derive almost exclusively from direct connection with the remotest history. Rights and privileges in the present and future were determined by the status of the past.

Indian society learned its lesson well, and still learns it – for the legal and constitutional systems of the British were carried over into independent India after 1947, and continue to provide the foundations of the state. But the learning process was promoted not only by conscious imitation. Perhaps more deeply, it was advanced as the unconscious product of opposition. Certain elements in Indian society had always disputed the legitimacy of the Raj, and, given the character of colonial ideology, this legitimacy was most vulnerable at the point of its interpretation of history and 'tradition'. If the past could be shown to be other than the British conceived it, then their warranty to rule became suspect. By the late nineteenth century, as opposition grew, so reinterpreting the

---

[59] J. Derrett, *Religion, Law and the State in India* (Faber, London, 1968).

[60] For Britain, see D. Sayer and P. Corrigan, *The Great Arch: English state formation as cultural revolution* (Blackwell, Oxford, 1985); for India, B. S. Cohn, 'Representing authority in Victorian India', in *The Invention of Tradition*, ed. E. Hobsbawm and T. Ranger (Cambridge University Press, Cambridge, 1983), pp. 165–209.

past in order to 'un-British' a future India became a major intellectual project.[61]

Moreover, as the Indian intelligentsia started to think beyond merely displacing the British and towards constructing a national social order to replace them, so the significance of the past to the future gained an added dimension. The Romantic strand in European nationalist thought suggested that identity was primordial and inherently unchanging, to be located in its purest form in the most distant history of 'the *Volk*'. The future of a 'true' Indian society must needs be built by returning to its most ancient roots. Given South Asia's pluralistic cultural past, of course, just what those roots were remained open to wide dispute: from high-caste notions of *Rajya Dharm* and rule according to Brahmanic norms to anti-Brahmin notions of a pre-Aryan egalitarian community to Mahatma Gandhi's idiosyncratic formulation of a simple, harmonious 'village community' extant from time immemorial.[62] But all eyes looked to a distant past condition before the 'distortions' created by latter-day history had 'corrupted' Indic civilization to find clues to India's national identity. Ironically, in seeking to overcome its subjection to British rule and European cultural hegemony, Indian society drank its largest draft of Western ideological medicine.

The paradoxes of 'modernity' may also be seen to account for the failure of the colonial elites to stamp their authority on the development of language and culture and to explain the rise of 'middling' and peasant groups to positions of hegemony. The tension here was between the universalizing imperatives of modern culture and the 'peripheralizing' tendencies of the modern world economy. Harnessed to a Western-centred international economy, India was gradually converted from one of the world's leading manufacturing economies into an agricultural satellite.[63] In those circumstances no real socio-economic base emerged

[61] See P. Chatterjee, *Nationalist Thought and the Colonial World: a derivative discourse* (Zed, London, 1986); L. Gordon, *Bengal: the nationalist movement, 1876–1940* (Columbia University Press, New York, 1976); and O'Hanlon, 'Maratha history'.

[62] Chatterjee, *Nationalist Thought*; R. I. Cashman, *The Myth of the 'Lokamanya': Tilak and mass politics in Maharashtra* (University of California Press, Berkeley, 1975); Gordon, *Bengal*; L. L. and S. H. Rudolph, *The Modernity of Tradition: political development in India* (University of Chicago Press, Chicago, 1967), pt 2.

[63] The debate about 'de-industrialization' and 'underdevelopment' remains fierce; but for views on the importance of the period from 1830 to 1850 in altering the structure of the Indian economy, see Bayly, *Indian Society*; and

upon which an authoritative metropolitan bourgeoisie could be built. Only in one region, perhaps, did such a structure start to develop, albeit at second hand: this region was Bengal, where Calcutta, the capital of British commerce and (until 1911) government, overshadowed most of eastern India. The power concentrated there was most obviously 'British', but the British themselves were little concerned to use it to influence Indian culture. Rather, it was captured by the upper-caste Bengali *bhadralok*, the Raj's chief collaborators throughout the nineteenth century, and was utilized by them to establish dominance over the Bengali-speaking hinterland, and, for some time, considerably beyond.[64] But Bengal was very exceptional, and elsewhere in India, colonial elite groups represented a thin and dispersed social stratum whose authority was precarious at best.

Their class base lay in structures of rentier landlordism and state service erected by the Raj in its earliest days. From the later nineteenth century, however, these structures were starting to be undermined by the growth of commercial agriculture, which saw a greater share of profits passing to a *petite bourgeoisie* consisting of larger peasant producers and merchant capitalists.[65] Changing distribution of wealth brought with it demands for a change in the distribution of social power. 'Middling' peasant and merchant groups sponsored attacks 'from below' which have already been noted, on the status of the Mughlai elite's Urdu and on the South Indian Brahmin elite's Sanskritized Tamil. Class antagonisms sharpened the edges of cultural and ethnic conflict; the demand for Hindi was closely related to demands for the abolition of landlord rights and for the banning of cow slaughter (which Muslims had ritualized at *Bakr Id* as a way of expressing their erstwhile contempt for Hindu sensibility).[66] The demand for Sen Tamil was similarly part

---

S. Guha, *The Agricultural Economy of the Bombay Deccan, 1818–1941* (Oxford University Press, Delhi, 1985).

[64] J. H. Broomfield, *Elite Conflict in a Plural Society: twentieth-century Bengal* (University of California Press, Berkeley, 1969); S. Sinha and R. Bhattacharya, 'Bhadralok and Chotolok in a rural area of West Bengal', *Sociological Bulletin*, 18 (1969).

[65] Robinson, *Separatism among Indian Muslims*, ch. 2; Bose, *Agrarian Bengal*, chs 3–4; Baker, *Indian Rural Economy*, chs 3–4.

[66] S. Freitag, 'Sacred symbols as mobilizing ideology', and A. Yang, 'Sacred symbol and sacred space in rural India', *Comparative Studies in History and Society*, 22 (1980); J. R. McLane, *Indian Nationalism and the Early Congress* (Princeton University Press, Princeton, 1976), chs 9–11; G. Pandey, *Ascendancy of the Congress in Uttar Pradesh, 1926–34: a study in imperfect mobilization* (Oxford University Press, Delhi, 1979), ch. 5.

of a complex set of demands involving the expulsion of Brahmins from the south and the redistribution of wealth through the provision of 'fair shares' for all.[67] Ultimately, these demands proved politically irresistible; and the waning power of the colonial elites has made way for a 'populist' revolution in cultural style, which has informed Indian society (and language) through to the later twentieth century.[68]

Yet differences in historical experience did not derive only from inherent contradictions in modern Western imperialism. They also came from the specific character of South Asian social and cultural tradition. As noted above, many aspects of the sociology and politics of language in India are difficult to accommodate within the paradigms of language-standardization and modern ethnicity. On the one hand, written and spoken forms refuse to unite, and 'non-standard' variants are constantly being created. On the other, the notion that Indian national identity requires a single national language is strongly resisted (in all regions but the Hindi-speaking north) in a way which would seem to divorce the concept of state legitimacy from that of culturo-linguistic 'communality'. But, if these idiosyncracies create problems for the logic of modernity, they scarcely do so for that of Indian history. For they seem to replicate, around the 'modern' issue of language, the structure of relations, which strongly characterized pre-colonial South Asian society.

Written language had a special status, separating it from the domain of speech; and language differentiation was a tool of social differentiation. Further, the concept of the state was of an emperorship of 'universal dominion', loosely incorporating a series of quasi-autonomous 'groups'. The key political concern for most of society was to secure discrete group position within this pluralistic order, not to challenge emperorship or to separate territorially into a series of self-contained group-isolates. Position within the order, and indeed group definition itself, was achieved through status competition for 'honour'. The social politics of language in 'modern' India seem to reflect this anterior logic in a very precise way.

But can this replication mean, therefore, that the impact of modern Western ideology on Indian society, for all the long and intimate relationship provided by colonialism, has been essentially superficial, that Indian society has 'carried on regardless' of the nineteenth and twentieth centuries? The difficulty of accepting this position is that language itself does

[67] See D. Washbrook, 'Caste, class and dominance in modern Tamilnadu', in *Social Dominance and State Power in Modern India*, ed. F. R. Frankel and M. Rao (Oxford University Press, Delhi, 1989).
[68] For discussions of this populist style in various regions, see ibid.

not appear to have been a critical issue of identity in Indian society or a self-conscious symbol of group ethnicity before the nineteenth century. Modernity has changed Indian society, by inserting the concept of linguistic ethnicity into its relations. But the change has not followed the cultural logic of modernity itself. Rather, it has been led in a distinctively Indian direction, informed by the logic of South Asia's pre-modern social relations.

But how is this nexus between present and past to be comprehended? The theory of modernization implies a sharp discontinuity between 'tradition' and 'modernity', with the latter displacing the former. Yet recent Indian history suggests continuity and a process of dynamic interaction between the two, an interaction whose composite product bears traces of both but is strictly explicable in terms of neither.[69] Clearly, a full exploration of these problems lies beyond the scope of this essay. But two relevant points for the history of language may be worth noting. First, the rise of the *petite bourgeoisie* brought to positions of authority over the development of Indian culture groups who were much less exposed to Western ideas and institutions than the colonial elites and who, even today, are only partially literate. Such groups also possessed social relations which were still deeply embedded in the structures of caste, clan, and sect. As the new ideology of language impacted upon them, it is perhaps not surprising that they should 'translate' it into political and cultural idioms with which they were familiar and which, in other regards, were still highly relevant to the circumstances of their lives.[70]

Second, this 'translation' was facilitated by the highly flexible nature of Hindu categories of identity. As noted above, conceptions of identity were related to notions about shared 'substance' and blood (*jati*). But reference to the underlying continuum between divinity, humanity, and nature made it possible to define this substance in a wide variety of different ways and to keep identity in constant flux. Many historians and anthropologists would argue that what was most relevant to identity at any one time was power, and that society reshaped its relations, varying identities between clan, sect, and caste, depending on the nature

[69] This problem was first raised, but not resolved, in L. and S. Rudolph, *Modernity of Tradition*. See also R. Fox, 'The avatars of Indian research', *Comparative Studies in Society and History*, 13 (1971).
[70] See Washbrook, 'Caste, class and dominance'.

of the power structure imposed upon it.[71] The colonial modern state had imposed a distinctive structure of power relations, which stressed the significance of language. Society responded by restructuring its own relations to make language a central category of group (*jati*) identity. Tamil speakers, for example, who a few years before would have been highly sensitive to the differences of substance among them occasioned by caste, began in the 1930s to enthuse about 'the blood of the Tamils', which supposedly ran through their veins and united them all into a single community.[72] But, critically, the response was framed in the terms of the older cultural logic. India became a society of language *jatis*, much as it had previously been one of caste *jatis*, competing for honour and status within a continuing multi-*jati* social order. The novel principle of linguistic identity was accepted, but only in a way which fitted into a pre-existing cognitive structure, which dispersed the principle's 'revolutionary' implications. Indian society changed – in order to remain the same.

In effect, the supreme flexibility of Indian social logic defeated the wider purposes of the colonial-modern ideology of language, not by outright resistance but by epistemological subversion. Indeed, that would seem to have been the fate not only of the ideology of language but of virtually all the ideas and artefacts of the 'modern' era. Indian society has accommodated, and then subverted to its own predilections, the entire gamut of Western invention – from Marxism to democracy to the internal combustion engine. By so doing, it has plotted its own idiosyncratic course in the context of an increasingly uniform world, and has repeatedly exposed the piety and the contradiction of that perspective on modern history which would speak of the latter simply as 'the triumph of the West'.[73]

---

[71] See R. B. Inden, *Marriage and Rank in Bengali Culture: a history of caste and clan in middle-period Bengal* (University of California Press, Berkeley, 1976); Dirks, *Hollow Crown.*

[72] Barnett, *Politics of Cultural Nationalism*, ch. 7.

[73] As in J. H. Roberts, *The Triumph of the West* (BBC, London, 1988).

9

The language of representation: towards a Muslim political order in nineteenth-century India

Farzana Shaikh

Few ideas were as widely or as loosely deployed in the political discourse of nineteenth-century colonial India as the idea of representation. For the historian more familiar with the changes that accompanied the rise of representative government in Europe and the United States, this poses special problems. For while the great debates about political representation that characterized nineteenth-century European history were also in some sense statements about democracy and liberty, these issues were singularly absent in the discourse on Indian representation. Yet, it is by probing the language of representation, its richness and its variety, that some understanding may be obtained of how nineteenth-century Indians conceived society, politics, and the ends of human organization.

Nowhere can the relationship between language and the sociopolitical order be more closely established than in the case of the class of well-born Indian Muslims, otherwise known as the *ashraf*.[1] What they did and how they did it depended ultimately upon how they saw themselves

---

[1] On the Muslim *ashraf*, see Imtiaz Ahmad, 'The Ashraf-Ajlaf distinction in Muslim social structure in India', *Indian Economic and Social History Review*, 3 (1966), pp. 268–78. For a superb discussion of the social and cultural milieu of the north Indian Muslim *ashraf*, see David Lelyveld, *Aligarh's First Generation: Muslim solidarity in British India* (Princeton University Press, Princeton, 1978), ch. 2. See also Rafiuddin Ahmed, *The Bengal Muslims, 1871–1906: a quest for identity* (Oxford University Press, Delhi, 1981), pp. 7–27. For another, more general attempt to probe the 'language of politics' in the context of modern India, see W. H. Morris-Jones, 'Politics and society', in idem, *The Government and Politics of India* (Hutchinson, London, 1967), pp. 52–61.

and the world they lived in. The vocabulary of representation served these Muslims as a vehicle to convey some of their most cherished ideas about the organization of society, the nature of political consensus, and the distribution of power. These ideas helped shape their political actions, which, in turn, were decisively to affect the course of modern Indian history. What, then, were the elements that defined and lent substance to this language of representation, and what did it express about the way in which these Indian Muslims apprehended the society in which they lived?

There were at least four principal considerations that impinged upon, and contributed substantially to, the evolution of an Indo-Muslim language of representation in the mid-nineteenth century. The first, and perhaps most obvious, were derived from the immediate political concerns of the class of Indian Muslims drawn variously from the service and landed gentry of the North-Western provinces and Bengal.[2] The second was the convergence of a recognizable Indo-Muslim language of representation with prevailing British official ideas of representation.[3] The third derived from a Mughal political culture closely associated with Muslim domination in India in the sixteenth and seventeenth centuries.[4] The fourth, and possibly the most important, came from the assumptions of a political tradition grounded in Islamic principles.[5]

For Muslims like the urban *ashraf*, the question of Muslim representation in high office assumed a much greater degree of urgency than it did for others such as the *ulama* or body of religious scholars, who were more preoccupied with the task of religious reform. Yet, however

[2] Some of the best analyses of these concerns are to be found in Paul Brass, *Language, Religion and Politics in India* (Cambridge University Press, Cambridge, 1974); Peter Hardy, *The Muslims of British India* (Cambridge University Press, Cambridge, 1972); and F. C. R. Robinson, *Separatism among Indian Muslims: the politics of the United Provinces' Muslims, 1860–1923* (Cambridge University Press, Cambridge, 1974).

[3] Farzana Shaikh, *Community and Consensus in Islam: Muslim representation in colonial India, 1860–1947* (Cambridge University Press, Cambridge, 1989), pp. 89–93.

[4] The cultural values that shaped the outlook of the Mughal ruling classes are discussed in some detail in Marshall Hodgson, *The Venture of Islam: conscience and history in a world civilization* (University of Chicago Press, Chicago, 1974), vol. 3, pp. 60–86. See also Lelyveld, *Aligarh's First Generation*, pp. 20–34.

[5] The relationship of Islamic values to the conduct of Muslim politics is cogently discussed in Francis Robinson, 'Islam and Muslim separatism', in *Political Identity in South Asia*, ed. David Taylor and Malcolm Yapp (School of Oriental and African Studies, London, 1979), pp. 78–112. See also Shaikh, *Community and Consensus*.

concerned they were with the political survival of their class, which many deemed to be synonymous with their community, few, if any, among these Muslims believed that the concept of political representation had anything at all to do with either popular support or a notion of political mandate. What they believed it to entail was the espousal of a loyalist credo which regarded representation as the consequence of British official recognition. To aspire to representation was seen, therefore, as effectively to seek and to obtain recognition; to be thus recognized was to be able to demonstrate a measure of political support for a continued British presence in India. Indeed, for many among these Muslims, the language of representation was steadily to become coterminous with the language of political loyalism.[6]

The idea of representation favoured by these well-placed Muslim gentlemen was not, however, shaped only by the exigencies of political survival. As important to the emergence of an Indo-Muslim language of representation was its convergence with prevailing British official ideas of representation. These stemmed as much from the imperatives of sustaining a more durable British presence in India as from a mode, common to officials and non-officials alike, of explaining Indian society in terms of its diversity of creeds, castes, and classes.[7] Its effect was radically to restrict both the sense and the scope of representation as a substantive activity involving a measure of creative political action. Instead, representation came to signify no more than a descriptive activity whose purpose was to reflect, and in so doing sustain, divisions in an already divided society.[8] Within the parameters of official discourse, to be 'representative' was to be able to establish a likeness; it was to 'stand for', rather than to 'act for', one or other section of society. The question confronting Indian Muslims, then, was how best to adapt and adjust to a language designed and defined by officials, in order to sustain their claims to representation.

There were two additional elements, more difficult to establish but no less significant, that also helped to crystallize a distinctive Indo-Muslim language of representation. The norms of a Mughal political

---

[6] Lelyveld, *Aligarh's First Generation*, pp. 302–20; Ram Gopal, *Indian Muslims: a political history, 1859–1947* (Book Traders, Lahore, 1976), pp. 44–52; and S. R. Mehrotra, *The Emergence of the Indian National Congress* (Barnes and Noble, New York, 1971), pp. 212–21.

[7] Anil Seal, 'Imperialism and nationalism in India', *Modern Asian Studies*, 15, (1981), pp. 415–54.

[8] The notion of 'descriptive representation' is pursued more thoroughly in Hanna F. Pitkin, *The Concept of Representation* (University of California Press, Berkeley, 1972), ch. 4.

culture encouraged the belief, common among *sharif* Muslims, that wealth, ancestry, and social status were prerequisites of leadership; while the assumptions of an Islamic tradition helped sustain the implicit claim that being Muslim entailed a special relationship to the political order. Each contributed to a specific, though by no means mutually exclusive, understanding of representation. For those attached to the repertory of Mughal values, to be 'representative' was to suggest membership of a cosmopolitan ruling class whose men of influence had served as inter-mediaries between rulers and subjects. For others, more given to the terms of an 'Islamically-supplied' discourse, to be 'representative' was to assume charge of a superior moral ethic whose sources lay in divine revelation.

The quest for survival

The years that followed the outbreak of the Indian Mutiny of 1857 constituted a period of long, and sometimes painful, introspection for Indian Muslims. The firm, and often brutal, suppression of India's first 'war of independence' and the formal consolidation of British power after 1858[9] left few with any illusions about the restoration of Muslim political hegemony. Yet, what is surely noteworthy about this period is that despair was not more widespread. Indeed, there was good evidence to suggest that Indian Muslims, prompted by their community's political and cultural decline, were determined to seek new modes of accommo-dating British rule in India. Some, like the *ulama*, encouraged, through the revival of the *madrasas*, or religious seminaries, the cultivation of the moral qualities of the individual, in the belief that therein lay the strength, political or otherwise, of the community.[10] For them there was, at least for the time being, little or no interest in the organization of the state or in collective political action. Others, like the class of Muslims drawn predominantly from the professions and the service and landed gentry, believed that the regeneration of Muslim social and political life depended upon a commitment to Western education. For them, the pre-eminence of their community was to be ensured not so much by the defence of Islam as a cultural ideal, but by the participation

[9] Thomas R. Metcalf, *The Aftermath of the Revolt* (Princeton University Press, Princeton, 1965).
[10] Barbara D. Metcalf, *Islamic Revival in British India: Deoband, 1860–1900* (Princeton University Press, Princeton, 1982).

of Indian Muslims in the newly established hierarchy of power.[11] Both groups symbolized the beginning of a series of bold initiatives which stressed the need to restore Muslim self-esteem.

Not surprisingly, despite their seemingly different concerns, these groups shared a common vision. This presupposed, above all, that the temporal destiny of Islam in India and elsewhere was bound inextricably to power. Although few believed that such power could any longer be 'Islamically' wielded, many held tenaciously to the view that it ought at least to be wielded by Muslims. It was not unusual, therefore, for some sections of the *ulama*, who were otherwise committed to the restoration of an Islamic order in India, to argue that Muslim participation in the colonial administration should be encouraged or that 'more of these jobs should be in Muslim hands.'[12] In turn, members of the lay elite actively associated with the revival of 'Muslim politics' were deeply cognizant of the *ulama's* concern to ensure that such politics should rest upon a measure of religious and educational reform.[13] Yet, what finally bound together these otherwise disparate groups, for whom the political and cultural hegemony of their community had not, until then, been in question, was the survival of Indian Muslims, whether as a body of believers or as a distinct sub-culture.

None were as conscious of its political implications as the class of Muslim *ashraf* raised in and around the great urban centres of the North-

[11] Lelyveld, *Aligarh's First Generation*. Comparing the orientations of the reformist *ulama* with those of students from the modernist establishment, the M. A. O. College, founded in Aligarh by Sayyid Ahmad Khan, Metcalf observes: 'The *ulama* . . . tended, in these early decades, to avoid political issues, whereas the Aligarh people sought out a place for themselves in the councils of the rulers': ibid., p. 335. For some general introductions to the history of modern India, see among others Hafeez Malik, *Moslem Nationalism in India and Pakistan* (Public Affairs Press, Washington, 1963); S. Gopal, *British Policy in India, 1858–1905* (Cambridge University Press, Cambridge, 1965); Anil Seal, *The Emergence of Indian Nationalism* (Cambridge University Press, Cambridge, 1971); John Gallagher *et al.* (eds), *Locality, Province and Nation: essays on Indian politics, 1870–1947* (Cambridge University Press, Cambridge, 1973); and Mushirul Hasan, *Nationalism and Communal Politics in India, 1916–28* (Manohar, Delhi, 1979).

[12] Metcalf, *Islamic Revival in British India*, p. 253; see also pp. 335–47. For another fine discussion of how rural-based religious preachers propagated the political interests of a sophisticated urban elite in the late nineteenth century, see Ahmed, *The Bengal Muslims*.

[13] Nowhere is this more clearly underlined than in Lelyveld, *Aligarh's First Generation*.

Western provinces and Bengal. [14] This is not to suggest that these Muslims were a class in the sense of being homogeneous or, indeed, that they were in any sense characteristic of Indian Muslims as a whole. While Indo-Muslim society has rarely conformed to ritual notions of pollution and purity more familiar to the Hindu caste system, hierarchical divisions are not unknown. Of these, the commonest are those between the *ashraf*, or well-born who claim foreign descent, and the *ajlaf*, or low-born, often descended from local converts to Islam. Among *sharif* Muslims, there are yet other significant differences of status between those who, like Sayyids, claim pre-eminence on grounds of descent from the line of the prophet Muhammad and others like Mughals, Pathans, and Shaikhs. [15]

It is worth bearing in mind, however, that while these distinctions among the *sharif* classes remained intact in the nineteenth century and sometimes contributed to differences in approach, many were inclined to espouse a common political ethos. It was not unusual, therefore, for the staunchly Sayyid Sayyid Ahmad Khan to share with the somewhat less distinguished Nawab Abdul Latif the view that official perceptions of Indian Muslims as fomenters of the great Mutiny of 1857 had contributed much to their community's embattled status. More important, they believed that it had encouraged the unwarranted suspicion that they and their fellow Muslims were disloyal and, as such, unworthy of representation. Not surprisingly, many were persuaded that the representation of their class and, by extension, of Muslims as a whole depended in the first instance upon obtaining recognition as loyal allies of the British Raj. Concerned as they were, most immediately, with the issue of official recognition as the basis of representation, few, if any, were inclined to presume that representation could entail claims to broader-based political support. On the other hand, what was fostered was an understanding of representation as a consequence of official recognition, the conferment of which was deemed to depend squarely upon the espousal of a loyalist credo.

One of those who did much to nurture this view of representation was the influential Muslim reformer Sayyid Ahmad Khan. Born into an illustrious family with a long history of distinguished service under both the Mughals and the East India Company, he is widely credited with the success of weaning large numbers of Muslims away from political

---

[14] See Robinson, *Separatism among Indian Muslims*, pp. 10–83; and Ahmed, *The Bengal Muslims*, pp. 1–27.

[15] Imtiaz Ahmad (ed.), *Caste and Social Stratification among the Muslims* (Manohar, Delhi, 1973).

opposition to British rule.[16] In his celebrated *Essay on the Causes of the Indian Revolt*, published in 1858, Sayyid Ahmad undertook not only to restore the political credibility and dependability of the class of Muslim *ashraf* to which he belonged, but also to call for fresh initiatives in the application of official policy on Indian representation.[17] He argued that the Indian Mutiny was due not so much, if at all, to Muslim treachery, as to the limitations of existing official policy. The latter, he believed, stemmed from Britain's suppression of its Indian subjects and from the absence of 'communication' between the government and its people. The basis of good government, he claimed, depended upon the presence of 'intermediaries' willing and able to furnish executive authority with information concerning the people's 'habits and customs'. This, he suggested, demanded a much greater commitment to Indian participation than had hitherto been displayed by British officials, as well as the creation of formal consultative councils charged with the responsibility of advising government.

Although Sayyid Ahmad's elaborate blueprint for good government served as the basis for a powerful moral indictment of rule by *diktat*, it also underlined the essentially conservative purpose of representation as a means of endorsing, not endangering, British rule in India. For what was inherent in this understanding of representation was not the germ of some vision of Indian self-government, but rather the co-optation of recognized Indian notables who would act as sounding-boards in the service of government.[18]

Sayyid Ahmad's terms for a working relationship between Britain and its Indian subjects shaped the emerging Indo-Muslim understanding of political representation. Two important Muslim organizations of the time, namely, the Mahommedan Literary Society and the National Mahommedan Association, exemplified the elements of the new discourse. Both were Bengal-based organizations dominated by Muslims drawn from among government employees, lawyers, and resident nobility. Both were controlled by men who had close links with government and who were, as a consequence, better placed than most to grasp the rules

[16] Altaf Husain Hali, *Hayat-i-Jawed* (in Urdu) (Ishrat Publishing House, Lahore, 1965), pp. 39–55. See also Hafeez Malik, *Sir Sayyid Ahmad Khan and Muslim Modernization in India and Pakistan* (Columbia University Press, New York, 1980).

[17] Sayyid Ahmad Khan, *Asbab-i-baghawat-i-Hind* (in Urdu) (Munshi Fazluddin, Lahore, n.d.), esp. pp. 11–15, 27–30, 31–42.

[18] G. F. I. Graham, *The Life and Work of Syed Ahmad Khan, K.C.S.I.* (Hodder and Stoughton, London, 1909), pp. 26–36.

of official patronage. Their predominantly *sharif* membership neither possessed nor sought a mass following. What they did aspire to, however, was the protection of their privileged status by obtaining official recognition as intermediaries between the government and their own community.[19] This is not to say that these Muslims were prompted solely by motives of self-interest or the interests of their class. On the contrary, many believed that their privileged status bestowed on them the responsibility not only of protecting their community as a whole, but also of undertaking the amelioration of those classes less fortunate than their own.[20] What is relevant here, however, is not to raise questions about the true intent of *sharif* Muslim politics, but to show how such politics helped promote and sustain prevailing Indo-Muslim notions of representation as essentially the consequence of official recognition.

The inclusion of large numbers of Muslims drawn from the Calcutta establishment in the organization of the Literary Society helped transform a gentlemen's *conversazione* club into a powerful pressure group.[21] Its founder, Nawab Abdul Latif, whose service in government was the source of some personal pride, was a tireless advocate of British rule. By the mid-1870s, his loyalism ensured that the Society was regularly consulted by officials on all matters affecting Indian Muslims in areas of social and educational policy.[22] Latif's personal standing in official circles led him, in later years, to assume for himself the distinction of being the first 'true' representative of Indian Muslims.[23]

Latif's Society was not alone in vying for government recognition and representation. As important were the activities of a group of younger Muslim notables who belonged to Sayyid Amir Ali's National Mahommedan Association.[24] Although its brand of loyalism has been seen to be more 'conscientious' than that professed by the Literary Society,[25] there is little to suggest that it did not share established notions of

[19] Ahmed, *The Bengal Muslims*, p. 116.
[20] Muhammad Yusuf Abbasi, *Muslim Politics and Leadership in South Asia, 1876–92* (Institute of Islamic History, Culture and Civilization, Islamabad, 1981).
[21] Mehrotra, *Emergence of the Indian National Congress*, pp. 215–17.
[22] Ahmed, *The Bengal Muslims*, pp. 51–2. See also Seal, *Emergence of Indian Nationalism*, p. 310.
[23] Nawab Abdool Luteef Khan, *A Short Account of my Public Life* (Calcutta, 1885).
[24] Leonard Gordon, *Bengal: the nationalist movement, 1876–1940* (Columbia University Press, New York, 1974), pp. 60–74.
[25] Ibid., p. 66.

representation.[26] Like the Literary Society, members of the Association prepared memorials and petitioned the government to introduce measures that would protect Muslim interests in education and government service. Above all, they too sought to render advice to officials and, whenever possible, to do so as the representatives of the Muslims of India.

Like the Literary Society, the Mahommedan Association was little inclined to equate representation with any form of popular mandate. Amir Ali condemned the fledgling demands for Indian self-government, and denounced the 'obsession with democracy' common among some Western-educated Indians like Romesh Chunder Dutt and Surendrenath Banerjea.[27] Like Sayyid Ahmad Khan, with whom he was sometimes at odds, he shared the premise that the object of Muslim participation and of representation was to strengthen and preserve British supremacy in India. Both were persuaded that the representation of their class could best be secured by acting as adjuncts of government rather than as spokesmen for Muslim popular opinion. This may well have reflected sound political judgement on their part. For while both men were keen to consolidate a sense of Muslim identity in India, it is far from clear that either could, at the time, have readily presumed the existence of a recognizable Muslim consensus distinct from, and exclusive of, a broader Indian consensus.

Indian Muslims, officialdom, and the ideology of representation

The hold of so restricted a view of representation cannot be fully explained, however, without some attention to the considerations that governed official discourse on representation. Of these, the effects of the Indian Mutiny of 1857 cannot be over-emphasized. It forced officials to re-appraise the value of Indian participation, and led many to regard Indian discontent as the consequence of the exclusion of 'Native chiefs' from 'the management of affairs in their country'.[28] This in turn led to the view that the recurrence of events such as those of 1857 could effectively be forestalled by allowing more Indians to participate in law-

[26] Ahmed, *The Bengal Muslims*, p. 164.

[27] Amir Ali, 'Memoirs', in *Ameer Ali: his life and work*, ed. K. K. Aziz (Publishers United, Lahore, 1968), pt 2, p. 566.

[28] Sir Charles Wood's speech to the House of Commons, 6 June 1861, *Hansard's Parliamentary Debates* (Commons, 1861), vol. 163, col. 653.

making bodies. Although few believed that Indian participation could extend much beyond an advisory role, let alone towards self-government, many were persuaded of the merits of limited reform.[29]

The Councils Act of 1861 recognized this, and was designed precisely to remove some of the limitations of the existing system of government. It envisaged the creation of consultative bodies modelled along the lines of traditional Indian institutions like the *durbar*, or public audience, the merits of which were seen to lie in their limited role as 'channel[s] from which the ruler learns how his measures are likely to affect his subjects.'[30] These consultative bodies were meant, therefore, to introduce a 'native element' rather than to establish some measure of political accountability, with a view to correcting 'our diminished opportunities of learning through indirect channels what the natives think of our measures.'[31]

It is clear that while officials recognized the need for some Indian participation through institutional means, few were willing to concede that such participation implied the representation of a wider Indian consensus. Indeed, a 'Western-style' representative body, maintained Sir Charles Wood, was 'impossible' where 'you cannot possibly assemble at any one place . . . persons who shall be the real representatives of the Native population of that empire.'[32] Wood's categorical assertion was a reflection not only of much contemporary British thinking, both official and non-official, on the nature of Indian society, but also of existing trends in official policy. Although some, like the liberal viceroy Lord Ripon, viewed Indian representation as a creative process designed to prepare Indians for self-government, few were willing to concede that representation had anything at all to do with the business of government.[33]

Part of the difficulty in envisaging the precise nature of Indian government stemmed from a tendency to regard Indian society as a world radically divided by class, creed, and caste. To the extent that government required a degree of consensus, Indians were believed by officials not

[29] Gopal, *British Policy in India.*
[30] See Sir Bartle Frere's Official Minute of 16 Mar. 1860, quoted in 'Indian constitutional reforms', *British Parliamentary Papers* (1918), Cmd 9109, para. 60.
[31] Ibid. See also Cecil Cross, *The Development of Self-Government in India, 1858–1914* (University of Chicago Press, Chicago, 1922), pp. 31–48.
[32] Wood's speech to the House of Commons, 6 June 1861, col. 640.
[33] See among others S. Gopal, *The Viceroyalty of Lord Ripon, 1880–84* (Oxford University Press, London, 1953); R. J. Moore, *Liberalism and Indian Politics, 1872–1922* (Edward Arnold, London, 1966); and Seal, *Emergence of Indian Nationalism,* esp. pp. 147–57.

yet to be 'fit' for self-government.[34] Indian representation, however, was given much serious consideration, although Ripon and his successors, Dufferin and Lansdowne, were persuaded that even such representation could not proceed without the recognition of the diverse 'interests' which sustained Indian society.

The notion that political society in India was essentially an extension of civil society exercised a decisive influence on the way in which the idea of representation was understood and employed by officials.[35] The pre-occupation with India's heterogeneous civil society led many to interpret representation as the representation of an established order of distinct, and sometimes warring, social groups. For what was believed, at heart, to constitute Indian society were not Indians, let alone individual Indians, but groups of 'Kayasths', 'Muslims', 'peasants', 'landlords', to name but a few, each with its exclusive 'interest'.[36] Some scholars have explained this emphasis on groups and 'interests' as part of an attempt by British officials to comprehend a society which they regarded as both complex and fundamentally alien. They suggest that by classifying and categorizing Indian society, officials hoped ultimately to render it more accessible. However, because official constructs bore little relation to the 'structural reality' of society, the practical consequences for Indian representation were enormous.[37] In the words of one historian, it meant

[34] This argument was substantially bolstered by influential treatises like those of John Stuart Mill, who had underlined the importance of 'a united public opinion' as a necessary condition for 'the working of representative government': J. S. Mill, *Considerations on Representative Government* (1861; repr. Henry Regnery, Chicago, 1962), p. 307. John Stuart Mill's ideas about the relationship between India's inherent social diversity and its fitness for modern political institutions have been seen to derive in part from a line of Utilitarian thinking commonly associated with Jeremy Bentham and James Mill. See T. G. P. Spear, 'British historical writing in the era of the nationalist movement', in *Historians of India, Pakistan and Ceylon*, ed. C. H. Philips (Allen and Unwin, London, 1961), pp. 404–15.

[35] Lucy Carroll, 'Colonial perceptions of Indian society and the emergence of caste(s) associations', *Journal of Asian Studies*, 37 (1978), pp. 233–49.

[36] See the Report on the subject of provincial councils by Chesney, Aitchison, and Westland, 1888, and the Summary of Conclusions, enclosures no. 1 and no. 2; and Dufferin to Cross, 20 Oct. 1888, India Office Library Dufferin Papers, MSS Eur. F. 130/11b.

[37] Bernard Cohn, 'The census, social structure and objectification in South Asia', *Second European Conference on Modern South Asia* (Elsinore, Denmark, June 1980); Hardy, *Muslims of British India*, pp. 116–25; Robinson, *Separatism among Indian Muslims*, pp. 99–100; David Washbrook, 'The development of caste organisations in South India, 1880–1925', in *South India: political insti-*

that 'those seeking patronage or protesting proscription had to speak in the name of a bureaucratically recognized category.'[38] While much was made of Indian representation, therefore, few officials believed in the reality of an Indian 'interest' that could justifiably be represented.[39] For to have acknowledged such an 'interest' would have been also to acknowledge the potential for an Indian political consensus and, possibly, a demand for Indian self-government.

The idea that social groups possessed 'interests' that were mutually exclusive encouraged the view that their representation could be best obtained when their representatives could be shown to 'stand for' them. To be judged 'representative' was, therefore, to be able to establish a likeness with the social group on whose behalf the representative claimed to speak. Representation itself became a medium of description, a measure of accurate resemblance or correspondence with little or no relation to its understanding as a substantive political activity. Its most important function was to yield information about 'the various divisions in the electorate'[40] and to recognize the range and diversity of existing 'interests'. It was this idea of representation that subsequently came to shape official thinking behind the Councils Act of 1892, which unequivocally endorsed the representation of 'classes and types' against 'areas and numbers'.[41]

To suggest that officials regarded representation as a descriptive, rather than a substantive, activity is not, however, to suggest that they deemed Indian representation to be merely symbolic. On the contrary, many were known to be deeply sympathetic, particularly after 1857, to the idea that Indian representation should entail a degree of 'activity', even if some were determined to ensure that such activity did not presuppose claims to act for or on behalf of others. What, then, did this 'activity' entail, and how did Indian Muslims, in particular, interpret the scope of such 'activity'?

---

tutions and political change, ed. C. J. Baker and D. Washbrook (Macmillan, Delhi, 1975), pp. 150–203.

[38] Carroll, 'Colonial perceptions of Indian society', p. 249.

[39] In one typical statement of its kind, Lord Dufferin assured his colleagues in London that the reform of Indian councils would proceed on the assumption that 'there were other communities and interests' besides those professed by 'nimble-witted students from Bengal': see Dufferin to Kimberley, 21 Mar. 1886, Dufferin Papers, MSS Eur. F. 130/5.

[40] Pitkin, *Concept of Representation*, p. 61.

[41] *Proceedings of the Legislative Council of the Governor-General of India*, 32 (1893); quoted in Cross, *Development of Self-Government*, p. 161.

Few historians today could fail to remark on the number of well-placed, predominantly urban Muslims who readily espoused official ideas about the nature of Indian society and representation. Like their colonial masters, these Muslims tended also to preface their political statements with ritual observations on Indian social heterogeneity. Categories of race and religion were indiscriminately superimposed on complex social and political phenomena, while group conflict was accepted as the dominant mode of interaction. Indeed, one of the most powerful arguments used by Indian Muslims opposed to the extension of Western representation was the claim that such representation ignored the inherent constraints of a racially and religiously divided society like India.

Sayyid Ahmad Khan spoke of the prospects of 'the dominancy of race over race, religion over religion', and urged Ripon to reconsider his proposals for the reform of local councils.[42] Amir Ali pointed to the political salience of social and religious divisions, and argued that Western education had done little to generate the conditions necessary for Western representative institutions.[43] Others, like Sayyid Husain Bilgrami, one of a small group of Western-educated Muslims associated with Sayyid Ahmad Khan, also stressed their opposition to Western representation on the grounds that it failed to take into account the hostility between India's 'races, castes and classes'.[44] These views were more widely disseminated through influential Muslim organizations like the Mahommedan Literary Society,[45] and Aligarh College's Union Club, whose members concurred that 'the complicated nature of the ethnological and religious differences' in India precluded any meaningful application of the practices of Western representation.[46]

At the heart of these observations lay the assumption that communities, based on race, religion, and language, and not individuals constituted the fundamental units of society. These communities and the loyalties they generated determined the way in which individuals acted politically. Indeed, men's political actions were deemed to be extensions

[42] Sayyid Ahmad's speech on the Central Provinces' Local Self-Government bill, 12 Jan. 1883, in *Writings and Speeches of Sir Syed Ahmad Khan*, ed. Shan Mohammad (Nachiketa Publications, Bombay, 1972), p. 156.

[43] Amir Ali to H. W. Primrose (private secretary to the viceroy), 10, 12 Mar. and 12 Apr. 1884, Ripon Papers, B. P. 7/6, nos 104a, 107a, and 158a; cited in Mehrotra, *Emergence of the Indian National Congress*, p. 219.

[44] *Aligarh Institute Gazette*, 6 Oct. 1888.

[45] S. Chakravarty, 'The evolution of representative government in India, 1884–1909' (unpublished Ph.D. thesis, University of London, 1954), pp. 141–2.

[46] *Aligarh Institute Gazette*, 24 Jan. 1888.

of their communal loyalties and obligations. Western elective representation, with its stress upon individual judgement, argued Sayyid Ahmad,
would constitute a travesty where men's political interests were always
dictated by their religious affiliations.[47]

The debate on Indian representation raises vital questions for the
historian concerned with interpreting social and political structures from
belief systems. It has been argued, for example, that the language of
'community', of 'interest', and indeed of 'representation' in nineteenth-
century India tells us more about perceptions of Indian society and the
imperatives of colonial policy than it does about the existing social and
political order. Thus, it is claimed, what can be established is that the
predominant image of Indian society was one that stressed its diversity,
not its unity, and that Indians were encouraged 'to voice the interests
of others' in a language that was consistent with this image.[48] As Peter
Hardy and some others have convincingly shown, the emergence of
Muslim 'communalism' and, indeed, the exploitation of 'community'
by other Indians suggests more about official constructs of a Muslim
'community' than about the actual organization of an otherwise highly
diverse Indo-Muslim society.[49] While the force of these arguments cannot be discounted, and indeed poses crucial questions for the historian
concerned to understand past societies through a study of their conceptual apparatus, they are far from complete historical explanations. What
is lacking is any insight into the sources which shaped the moral vision
and sometimes constrained the political choices of these societies. It is
here that the study of language, of ideas, and of belief systems can
enrich historical analysis by probing the idioms and the assumptions that
governed the world-view of past societies and contributed to their distinct social and political evolution.

It might reasonably be argued, therefore, that while British and Indo-
Muslim conceptions of Indian society cannot be deemed to be accurate
descriptions of this society, their convergence in the late nineteenth
century can provide some insight into the parameters which defined the
Indo-Muslim understanding of representation. Sayyid Ahmad's blueprint
for Indian representation is a notable instance of how Indian Muslims
apprehended the limits imposed by official notions of representation and
of how they sought to manoeuvre within those limits. For him, the

---

[47] Sayyid Ahmad, in *Writings and Speeches*, ed. Shan Mohammad, p. 157.
[48] Anil Seal, 'Imperialism and nationalism in India', *Modern Asian Studies*, 7,
3 (1973), p. 338.
[49] Hardy, *Muslims of British India*, p. 116–18; Robinson, *Separatism among
Indian Muslims*, pp. 98–105, 345–54.

'activity' of representation was conceived primarily as one of yielding information to executive authority. His 'intermediaries' were sources of communication, not makers of consensus. The underlying premise, fostered and encouraged by officials, was that representation was one thing, and governing quite another.

The hold of a descriptive, rather than a substantive, notion of representation led also to the idea that what finally determined a representative's claims were his attributes, not his 'activity'. Thus, those who claimed to speak on behalf of Indian Muslims had first to establish their 'Muslimness'. Men like Nawab Abdul Latif Khan and Sayyid Amir Ali who professed these claims reflected the pervasive influence of this understanding of representation. Each, through his respective association, sought to represent Muslims not so much by claiming to act for them, but by demonstrating that they stood for them, or at least those of them that counted. What was crucial in their competing claims to representation was the assertion that they were more typical examples of the constituency at large – that is to say, of Indian Muslims. By the 1890s Sayyid Ahmad himself was at the forefront of a campaign which called for Muslim representation to be obtained by Muslims elected from exclusively Muslim electorates.[50]

In the final analysis, of course, it mattered little whether the Nawabs and the Sayyids were prototypes of Indian Muslims as a whole. For many were shrewd enough to realize that the true test of representation in the 1870s and 1880s had less to do with professing to be communal stereotypes than with the grace of official recognition from Britain.

Not all *sharif* Muslims endorsed this official 'ideology of representation'. Some, like the small group of 'nationalist' Muslims led by the eminent Bombay lawyer Badruddin Tyabji, preferred to throw their lot with the Indian National Congress and work for Indian representation as the first step towards Indian self-government. They believed that although differences of religion, caste, and class among Indians were indisputable, their causal influence upon the validity or otherwise of Western representation had not yet been established conclusively. They argued that, however real the 'peculiar social, moral and educational and even political difficulties' that confronted Indian Muslims, they shared

[50] Rafiq Zakaria, *Rise of Muslims in Indian Politics: an analysis of developments from 1885 to 1906* (Somaiya Publications, Bombay, 1970), p. 131; and M. S. Jain, *The Aligarh Movement: its origin and development, 1858–1906* (Sri Ram Mehra, Agra, 1965), pp. 128–9.

with 'the whole of India' some 'general questions' which affected them as Indians.[51]

The position adopted by Tyabji and his group of 'nationalist' Muslims was, however, deeply problematic. The close collaboration between colonial officials and influential Muslims like Sayyid Ahmad Khan and Sayyid Amir Ali helped sustain a view of Indian society and of the nature of political representation that made alternative claims appear to be untenable. These claims were all the more vulnerable when seen against the background of traditional Mughal and Muslim assumptions whose hold among Indian Muslims was far from eroded.

Mughal culture and the language of representation

It has been suggested that the political thinking of Muslims like Sayyid Ahmad Khan owed more than is commonly acknowledged to 'a theory of universal empire that had its origins in the Mughal concept of society.'[52] Indeed, the idea of representation as a mode of consultation between rulers and ruled which required the mediation of notables is seen to constitute the very essence of a Mughal view of good government.[53]

That Sayyid Ahmad was deeply immersed in, and committed to, the values of Mughal culture cannot be disputed. Contemporaries and biographers alike have testified to his lasting pride in his Mughal heritage.[54] It was a heritage that imparted to him not only the norms of *sharif* culture in social manners and styles of dress, but also the rules governing political power and authority. These assumed that the basis of strong government lay in the ruler's ability to establish 'ritual ties of loyalty . . . with strategically significant lineage groups'.[55] While in practice this led to the consolidation of a cosmopolitan ruling class that justified Mughal rule by providing links between the imperial government and society at large, it also contributed to a moral climate which stressed the importance of ancestry, wealth, and social status as determinants of a group's claim to power.

Sayyid Ahmad was acutely aware, of course, that the days of Mughal

[51] Tyabji's presidential address to the third annual session of the Indian National Congress, Dec. 1887; quoted in Seal, *Emergence of Indian Nationalism*, pp. 332–3.

[52] Lelyveld, *Aligarh's First Generation*, p. 344.

[53] Metcalf, *Islamic Revival in British India*, p. 319.

[54] Hali, *Hayat-i-Jawed*, pp. 65–72; and Malik, *Sir Sayyid Ahmad Khan*, pp. 59–61.

[55] Lelyveld, *Aligarh's First Generation*, p. 23.

supremacy were gone for ever. It is far from certain, however, whether he also believed that the basis of Mughal political legitimacy as he knew it was thereby irretrievably lost.[56] To pursue the investigation along these lines is to attempt to grasp more fully the spirit of Sayyid Ahmad's recommendations for change in the direction of British official policy in India. For his was not some clarion call for 'democratic' government, but an appeal for good government. This, in his view, depended primarily upon restoring to men of influence their erstwhile role as intermediaries whose privileged access to ruling power might enable them to convey the true intent of India's rulers.

Others, like Nawab Abdul Latif and Sayyid Amir Ali, whose links with Mughal culture were perhaps more tenuous than those of Sayyid Ahmad, also espoused the ethos of Mughal *sharif* culture. This led them to stress their participation in the culture of a cosmopolitan ruling class, dominated by Muslims of superior foreign descent, whose members had served as links between Mughal rulers and their subjects. Both men 'regarded themselves as custodians of Mughal culture and guarded it as their most precious possession.'[57] Both were fundamentally persuaded that the ancestry of their class, its wealth, and its social status qualified its members to assume the role of 'natural leaders'.

Some of these assumptions of Mughal political culture were most tellingly expressed in the demand, later known as 'weightage', which sought for Indian Muslims representation in excess of their actual numerical proportion. The rationale for such representation, which first emerged as part of a more general body of objections against the application of numerical criteria as the sole basis of representation, stemmed from the notion of the historical and political importance of Muslims in India. What such 'importance' implied in more concrete terms can best be understood in the light of Mughal political culture.

Here the importance of ancestry and class as determinants of political power was crucial. In a letter to his friend and biographer Altaf Husain Hali, Sayyid Ahmad wrote: 'I am a Muslim, an inhabitant of India and descended from the Arabs.'[58] Later, in 1887, in a stringent denunciation of the government's liberal experiment in India, he revealed the essence of his Mughal heritage. 'Would our aristocracy like,' he demanded:

---

[56] Lelyveld argues that Sayyid Ahmad regarded the consolidation of British power as no more than a change of hands: 'the sultanate now belonged to Queen Victoria': ibid., p. 344.

[57] Ahmed, *The Bengal Muslims*, p. 14.

[58] Hali, *Hayat-i-Jawed*, p. 562.

that men of low caste or insignificant origin, though he be a BA or MA, and have the requisite ability, should be in a position among them and have power in making laws that affect their lives and property? Never! . . . Our nation is of the blood of those who made not only Arabia, but Asia and Europe tremble. It is our nation which conquered with its sword the whole of India'.[59]

Similar sentiments, differently expressed, prevailed also in the spoken and written discourse of other Muslims. In the autumn of 1888, Nawab Imad-ad-daulah, secretary to the Nizam of Hyderabad, expressed the fear that the introduction of Western representation to India would result in the 'election of BA's and MA's from ordinary families . . . hardly the sort of men [one] would care to hob-nob with.'[60] In essays by Sayyid Amir Ali, much also was made of Muslims as 'a nation . . . with great traditions',[61] a 'paramount race' descended from the Turko-Afghan aristocracies and in rare instances 'from the higher Hindoo castes like the Rajpoots'.[62] Everywhere there was, as Leonard Gordon observes, a marked 'identification with the just and the powerful'.[63] Everywhere there was a profound sense that Muslims, as members of a ruling race, deserved more than the vagaries of Western representation could assure them.

Whilst this repertory of Mughal assumptions was quite evidently a part of the Indo-Muslim vision of a just political order, there are some important caveats to be borne in mind. Firstly, Muslim concerns about the inclusion of ancestry and social status as additional bases for representation reflected the genuine fears of a minority whose claims to political recognition were steadily being questioned by new ideas of how power and prestige were to be distributed. Secondly, although Sayyid Ahmad and Sayyid Amir Ali were well aware that not all Indian Muslims were descended from foreign ruling races, their stress upon a distinct Muslim ancestry provided the basis of a political solidarity that was effectively to resist the comprehensive extension of Western representation.[64]

---

[59] Sayyid Ahmad, in *Writings and Speeches*, ed. Shan Mohammad, pp. 204, 213.
[60] *Aligarh Institute Gazette*, 11 Sept. 1888.
[61] Ali, 'Memoirs', pt 2, p. 71.
[62] Ibid., p. 49.
[63] Gordon, *Bengal*, p. 70.
[64] The reference here is to the campaign for separate Muslim electorates which dominated the years from 1906 to 1909. This demand, which postulated a cohesive Muslim community, rejected the application of majority rule, and insisted that the choice of Muslim representatives should rest with exclusively

Finally, to the extent that Mughal assumptions sustained the notion of a distinct Muslim sub-culture, a *qawm*, it helped also to reinforce the idea of Muslims as a community, an *umma*, whose acceptance of God's final and most perfect revelation to man entitled its members to seek its vindication in political power.

Muslim tradition and the language of representation

This leads to the final, and perhaps most important, consideration that impinged directly upon Indo-Muslim notions of representation and, more generally, upon Muslim ideas of the existing social and political order. This pertained to the body of assumptions derived from an Islamic political tradition which was concerned, among other things, with questions of political responsibility and the idea of representation as a trust.

Implicit in Indo-Muslim discourse in the nineteenth century was an understanding of representation that had been both familiar to, and characteristic of, classical Islamic thinking. This is not to say that Indian Muslims like Sayyid Ahmad Khan and Sayyid Amir Ali consciously invoked such thinking in their approach to political representation. It is to say, however, that as Muslims they tended to draw from their faith not only a set of religious prescriptions, but the elements of a code of political practice. That, in turn, led them to rely on a historic tradition of political realism which, while being wholly cognizant of the modalities of power, was firmly grounded in the ethical teachings of Islam.

Its earliest manifestations appeared in the brand of utilitarian morality favoured by the twelfth-century Iraqi jurist Ibn al-Tiqtaqa, who sought to combine the ethical and religious duties of the ruler with the exigencies of stable rule.[65] He believed that, while just government could be obtained without strict conformity to the letter of the *Shari'a*, or body of Islamic law, political stability depended upon the ruler's ability to

---

Muslim constituencies. Although the measure was deemed by many Indians to cut at the heart of an evolving national political consensus, its acceptance as part of the Indian Councils Act of 1909 was justified on the grounds that it offered real protection to Muslim interests in India. See M. N. Das, *India under Morly and Minto: politics behind revolution, repression, and reform* (Allen and Unwin, London, 1964); S. R. Wasti, *Lord Minto and the Indian Nationalist Movement* (Clarendon Press, Oxford, 1964); and Matiur Rahman, *From Consultation to Confrontation: a study of the Muslim League in British Indian politics, 1906–12* (Luzac, London, 1970).

[65] E. I. J. Rosenthal, *Political Thought in Medieval Islam* (Cambridge University Press, Cambridge, 1958), pp. 62–7.

forge alliances, based on consultation, with men of influence. Wealth and social status determined influence; and al-Tiqtaqa was persuaded that only a careful handling of the classes that enjoyed these assets could ensure a ruler's stay in power.[66]

The spirit of al-Tiqtaqa's counsels was widely shared by medieval Indo-Muslim jurists and men of letters in the service of absolute Muslim rulers. But while al-Tiqtaqa was concerned to secure a just government that rested on stable foundations, medieval jurists were confronted with the problem of how best to ensure that absolute rule was contained within the parameters of just government. While it was common, therefore, for medieval Muslim historians to glorify absolute monarchical rule, many did so by drawing the ruler's attention to the importance of the Islamic practice of *shura*, or consultation, with men of influence and religious standing as the essential condition of a just Muslim polity.[67]

The same point might also be made, in all fairness, of those like Sayyid Ahmad Khan and Amir Ali whose commitment to British rule in India did not exclude the standards of moral conduct which they, as Muslims, had come to expect of their political masters. Sayyid Ahmad's moral strictures on the declining code of political justice and responsibility under the British East India Company, which lay at the heart of his *Essay* on the Indian Mutiny, would not have been unfamiliar to his medieval forebears. Nor, indeed, would his appeal for greater consultation between rulers and subjects as the basis of good government have appeared inconsistent with Muslim political principles.

Like Sayyid Ahmad, Amir Ali also stressed the value of mutual political consultation as an essential feature of a just constitution.[68] For him, the constitutional checks on executive authority were best embodied in the classical Muslim concept of *ijma*, or consensus. The power to formulate or represent this consensus, he believed, ought to rest with a lay elite whose authority stemmed not from a popular mandate but from its social standing, its capacity for learning, and its intellectual training.[69]

It would be naïve to suppose that either Sayyid Ahmad or, for that matter, Amir Ali hoped to render British rule more accountable to

---

[66] Ibid., p. 66.

[67] K. A. Nizami, *Some Aspects of Religion and Politics in India during the Thirteenth Century* (Asia Publishing House, Bombay, 1961), p. 111. See also S. A. A. Rizvi, *A History of Sufism in India: from sixteenth century to modern century* (Munshilal Manoharlal, Delhi, 1983), vol. 2, pp. 348–89.

[68] Syed Ameer Ali, *The Spirit of Islam: a history of the evolution and ideals of Islam* (1922; repr. Christopher's, London, 1961), pp. 278–9.

[69] Ibid., p. 251.

Indians by invoking Muslim notions of *shura* and *ijma*. At the same
time, it would not be unreasonable to assume that their expectations of
good government and of the purpose of representation as they understood it were governed by a tradition that they, as Muslims, held to be
authoritative.

This tradition also shaped the thrust of the arguments they brought
to bear against the extension of Western representation to India. For
they rested upon two important assumptions that were common to
Muslim political thinking, both in India and elsewhere. The first was
the notion that the communal group, whether as a religious fellowship
or as a sub-culture, was the basic unit of society, and its solidarity the
individual's primary concern. The second derived from the premise that
religious loyalty constituted the only authentic basis of political loyalty.
The institution of the Muslim Caliphate typifies most fully the essence
of this premise.[70] Here, representation was nothing if not a pledge, a
political trust undertaken on behalf of God and the *ummat al-Muslimin*,
or the community of Muslims. To have sought to delegate this pledge
to non-Muslims was both inadmissible and a contradiction in terms.

The idea that communities, not individuals, determined the course of
political action led substantial numbers of Indian Muslims in the nineteenth century to resist the theory and practice of Western representation. Many deplored a system which held that individual conduct bore
little or no relation to either creed or caste and which asserted that men
were not ultimately bound by the constraints of communal loyalty. They
argued that the power of religion to shape men's political impulses
would substantially erode the chances of securing the representation of
minorities like the Indian Muslims. As Sayyid Ahmad put it, where
'Hindus will have four times as many [votes] because their population
is four times as numerous,' the adoption of a 'system of election pure
and simple' would be wholly unsound.[71] Others, like the editor of the
Mahomedan Observer, asserted that to the extent that individuals acted
always in defence of the interests of their communal group, Hindus
would look 'primarily, but naturally' to the interests of their own
'bulk'.[72] The campaign for separate Muslim electorates, which first
emerged in the 1890s, testified to the strength of Muslim feeling on the

---

[70] H. A. R. Gibb, 'Some considerations on the Sunni theory of the Caliphate',
Archives d'histoire du droit Oriental, 3 (1948), pp. 401–10.
[71] Sayyid Ahmad, in *Writings and Speeches*, ed. Shan Mohammad, p. 210.
[72] *Mahomedan Observer*, 1 Jan. 1887; quoted in Seal, *Emergence of Indian
Nationalism*, p. 315.

question of the relationship of the individual to his communal group.[73] Although the campaign cannot be dissociated from the 'politics' of Muslim representation, it must be seen in the context of a wider religious tradition which regarded political conduct as the extension of men's religious fellowship.

The issue of separate Muslim electorates also raised questions about the second of the two assumptions discussed above: namely, the notion of representation as a pledge or trust. For what Muslims who favoured separate electorates found objectionable in the organization of territorial constituencies was not only that such constituencies would be dominated by Hindus, but that non-Muslims could legitimately claim to represent a Muslim consensus. In 1883, Muhammad Yusuf Ali, a member of the Bengal Legislative Assembly, called upon the government to institute separate Muslim electorates on the grounds that territorial constituencies would permit elected Hindus to act on behalf of Muslims, a condition, he declared, which most Muslims would deem fundamentally unacceptable.[74]

It remains to sum up what might be broadly described as the ingredients of the emerging Indo-Muslim language of representation in the late nineteenth century. As the discussion above shows, this language owed much, though by no means everything, to political assumptions grounded in a religious tradition. These assumptions led Muslims to believe that the communal orientations of their faith could not be reconciled with the theory and practice of individual representation. Nor could a Muslim consensus be legitimately subjected to representation by

[73] Here it is worth noting that the 'language of representation' employed by Indian Muslims was predicated primarily upon notions of male representation. This is hardly surprising. For not only were issues of female suffrage unknown in the late nineteenth century, but to the extent that women were deemed to have a voice, it was firmly and unreservedly confined within the family. Although issues like female education were beginning to command attention at this time, their discussion did not so much envisage the representation of larger numbers of women in public life as seek to reinforce their status as managers of the household and the focus of family life. See Gail Minault, 'Hali's *Majalis Un-Nissa*: purdah and woman power in nineteenth-century India', in *Islamic Society and Culture: essays in honour of Professor Aziz Ahmad*, ed. Milton Israel and N. K. Wagle (Manohar, Delhi, 1983), pp. 39–50; Barbara D. Metcalf, 'The making of a Muslim lady: Maulana Thanawi's *Bihishti Zewar*', in ibid., pp. 17–38; and Hanna Papanck, 'Purdah: separate worlds and symbolic shelter', *Comparative Studies in Society and History*, 15 (1973), pp. 289–325.

[74] Cited in B. B. Majumdar, *History of Indian Social Ideas: from Ram Mohun to Dayananda* (Bookland Private, Calcutta, 1967), pp. 242–3.

non-Muslims. For those whose faith had led them to presuppose that power was the consequence of superior moral attributes, rather than of numerical clout, the question of democratic elections was deeply problematic.

There were other concerns that impinged directly upon Indo-Muslim discourse on representation. Here, the influence of official perceptions of Indian society and political reality was of singular importance. Indian Muslims took readily to official modes of explaining Indian society, and endorsed the sociological apparatus with which British officials approached the question of Indian representation. Indo-Muslim ideas of representation were also sustained by complex social and cultural Mughal norms which stressed the importance of wealth and social status as prerequisites of political participation. These, in turn, were to lend substance to the notion that being Muslim was synonymous with being an essential part of the ruling classes.[75]

[75] For some perspectives on the antecedents of Indo-Muslim nationalism and the partition of India, see variously C. H. Philips and M. D. Wainwright (eds), *The Partition of India: policies and perspectives, 1935–47* (Allen and Unwin, London, 1970); R. J. Moore, *The Crisis of Indian Unity, 1917–40* (Clarendon Press, Oxford, 1974); David Page, *Prelude to Partition: the Indian Muslims and the imperial system of control, 1920–32* (Oxford University Press, Delhi, 1982); Ayesha Jalal, *The Sole Spokesman: Jinnah, the Muslim League and the demand for Pakistan* (Cambridge University Press, Cambridge, 1985); and Shaikh, *Community and Consensus.*

10

Chinese views of social classification

Philip A. Kuhn

What is the cultural background of contemporary Chinese ideas about social classification? As China modernizes, new social groups will emerge, along with new relationships among existing groups. Such reorganization will not, however, constitute an 'objective' system of social differences which need only be perceived in order to be appropriately codified. Factors such as hierarchy, division of labour, and social mobility will be mental constructions even while becoming social realities: they will (as a system) constitute one among many possible patterns of perceiving the Chinese social world. Although we can readily concede that patterns of perception do not emerge in any simple one-to-one manner from earlier patterns, we can assume as a working principle that earlier patterns do *limit* the range of mental instruments by which people classify the elements of their social environment. So it is reasonable in any study of class and stratification in contemporary China to pay careful attention to the values and meanings that Chinese were carrying with them as their nation entered the modern age.

What I am seeking here is a complex of views, all current in late imperial times, but often inherited from earlier periods, which will illuminate some of the special features of Chinese ideas about social class since 1949. It will be important to examine not only the range of attitudes, but also the mechanisms by which those attitudes conditioned acceptance of Western social theory.

For these purposes, I shall be particularly interested in how Chinese dealt theoretically with social hierarchy: how the *causes* of human

This essay was first published in J. L. Watson (ed.), *Class and Social Structure in Post-Revolution China* (Cambridge University Press, Cambridge, 1984).

inequality were understood. We should know, for example, whether they are of cosmological origin, fitting some kind of supra-social, supra-historical pattern; or may they originate in some societal process, such as the division of labour? Perhaps they are man-made, perhaps related to inherent qualities of persons, or perhaps purely random? We should also inquire how Chinese viewed the *justness* of the inequality: did it accord with people's deserts? Was there inevitably to be social inequality and therefore no desire to change the system (as distinct from bettering the status of oneself or one's social group)? In addition to the general problem of hierarchy, our concern with the background of twentieth-century notions of social class prompts me to examine Chinese ideas about social *groups* which stand in hierarchical status relationship. Whether or not social groups were seen as constituting 'classes' (in the sense that Marx saw them), defined by their relations in a system of production, it will be important to define the total system in which such groups were seen to operate.

First, however, consider how the term 'class' in its modern sense entered the Chinese world. The word *jieji*, which is now used routinely to translate 'social class', is a very old ideographic compound. Like many other social terms, it was taken over and given new meaning by the Japanese around the turn of the twentieth century, and then reintroduced into China.

Originally, the ideograph *jie* seems to mean steps, like rungs on a ladder; and *ji* is the order of threads in a fabric. The term thus connotes hierarchical degrees on a continuum, rather than groups of people. In late antiquity, it seems to have meant a system of social ranks in a fixed order of aristocratic distinction, which was linked to a routinized system of political preferment. In the Wu Kingdom (third century AD), the Prince of Lu, named Ba, was accorded such favour by the monarch that his status became virtually equal to that of the heir apparent. As the story goes, the minister Gu Tan protested that rulers must make clear distinctions 'between the sons of principal and secondary wives', and must 'differentiate between the ceremonies accorded the noble and the mean, cause the statuses of high and low to be distinguished, and the degrees of rank [*jieji*] to be distantly separated.'[1] The point here is that *jieji* does not refer to groups of persons but to ranks on a scale. Gu

---

[1] *Sanguozhi, Wushu*, in *Ershisi shi jiaotianben* (*The twenty-four dynastic histories*) (Beijing), p. 1230. See also the excellent treatment of classical ideas on stratification by Ch'ü T'ung-tsu, 'Chinese class structure and its ideology', in *Chinese Thought and Institutions*, ed. John K. Fairbank (University of Chicago Press, Chicago, 1957), pp. 235–50.

meant that a clear distinction among the privileges pertaining to the various degrees of rank would make relations among aristocrats harmonious by giving fewer occasions for envy. Here are reflected the norms of an aristocratic society, in which *jieji* referred to social and political rank within an accepted hierarchy of status distinctions.

The image of *jieji* as fixed degrees on a continuum is reinforced by a sixth-century usage, in which an aristocratic family is described as gaining 'a single step or a half-grade' (*yijie banji*) in its political rank over several generations.[2] By late imperial times, the meaning of *ji* had shifted entirely away from inherited aristocratic status and was associated with the eighteen-rank system of bureaucratic distinctions: *dengji*, in which *deng* was the major division and *ji* the minor. *Ji* was thus linked to the highly formalized status ladder of official rank.

The idea of *jieji* as 'rungs on a ladder' was still current when Liang Qichao (one of China's pioneer students of Western thought) first used the term in 1899, shortly after he fled to Japan and was exposed to Japanese interpretations of European social thought. Liang was gamely trying to work the theory of the 'three ages' (which he owed to his mentor, Kang Youwei) into his new information as he laboured to deal with the distribution of social and economic power (*qiangquan*). Each age, he proposed, displayed a characteristic set of power relations among social groups. In the first age (chaos), power is very limited, because the differences in power between ruler and ruled and between men and women are very slight. In the second stage (approaching peace), the power of ruler over ruled increases. At the same time, the ruled begin to resist. By the third stage (great peace), everyone has power; and hence there is equality. (This equality is different from that of the primitive first age, when *nobody* had much power.) Is Europe now in the final stage of power development? Not yet, thought Liang, because the differentials (*jieji*) between capitalists and workers and between men and women have not yet been eliminated. Such differentials are seen by Liang as an obstacle to the full development of a society's power. Here *jieji* certainly does not refer to classes (although Liang presumably had access to such usage in Japanese writings), but rather to the gradient that separates social groups: still social distance, not social groups.[3]

---

[2] Zhou Fagao (ed.), *Yenshi jiaxun huizhu* (*The household instructions of Yen Zhitui with collected commentaries*) (Taipei, 1960), p. 33. The passage is referring derisively to high-official *literati* families who abandon scholarly ambition as soon as they achieve a slight advancement in rank.

[3] Liang Qichao, 'Lun qiangquan' ('On power'), in *Yinbingshi quanji, zawen*, p. 32.

In this connection, Raymond Williams points out that in England throughout the early nineteenth century 'rank', 'order', and 'degree' were more commonly used than 'class' to describe hierarchically ordered social groups. 'All the older words, with their essential metaphors of standing, stepping, and arranging in rows, belong to a society in which position was determined by birth.'[4] In the Chinese case, these 'step' and 'arrangement' metaphors grew out of a society in which social position, while linked by distant association to feudal and aristocratic antecedents, was heavily laden with concepts of bureaucratic status.

In Japan, the use of *jieji* (in Japanese *kaikyū*) to mean 'class' as a social group was current by the first decade of the twentieth century. For example, Tazoe Tetsuji's *History of Modern Socialism* (*Kinsei shakai-shugi shi*) of 1907 uses the term in the Marxist manner for a social group defined by a system of production relations. 'The organization of production in certain periods' gives rise to 'two totally opposed social classes (*shakaiteki kaikyū*). Although this is seen as a worldwide phenomenon, applicable to East Asia as well as to the West, the foreign and exotic character of the terminology is emphasized by the use of syllabic *furigana* next to the ideographs: instead of *shakaiteki kaikyū*, the author instructs us to read *sōshiaru kurasu*.[5]

In view of the wide accessibility of Marxist literature by the 1920s, it is astonishing how much trouble the young Mao Zedong had in deciding how to apply the term *jieji* to the Chinese scene. His early work 'The Great Union of the Popular Masses' (1919) uses the term not at all. Instead, we have an unsystematic array of social elites (aristocrats, capitalists, and 'powerful figures') mixed with occupational and special-interest groups (farmers, students, policemen, and primary-school teachers). These groups are arranged according to no general theory of social order.[6]

Probably Mao's first use of the term *jieji* in print occurs in his 1921 piece 'Founding Proclamation of the Hunan Self-Study University'. Here

[4] Raymond Williams, *Keywords: a vocabulary of culture and society* (Fontana, London, 1976), p. 52.

[5] Tazoe Tetsuji, in a 1955 Tokyo edition, ed. Kishimoto Eitarō, *Katayama Sen, Tazoe Tetsuji shū*, p. 214. An earlier work that may have used the term similarly is Fukui Junzō, *Kinsei no shakaishugi* (1909), which was translated into Chinese in 1903; but I have not been able to find a copy of this work. See Martin Bernal, *Chinese Socialism to 1907* (Cornell University Press, Ithaca, 1976), pp. 94–5. It may have been through Fukui's work that the Marxist use of 'class' first became available to Chinese readers.

[6] Takeuchi Minoru (ed.), *Mō Takutō shū* (*Collected Writings of Mao Zedong*) (Tokyo, 1972), vol. 1, pp. 57–69.

we find that *jieji* are indeed social groups arranged hierarchically: the 'intellectual class' (*zhishi jieji*) and the 'commoner class' (*pingmin jieji*). Here is a systematic analysis which at least covers the entire social ground. The categories, however, are wholly traditional, and in fact correspond to the old Confucian dichotomy between those who labour with their minds and those who labour with their hands.[7]

So by the third decade of this century, Chinese thinkers were still having trouble relating the Western concept of class to their own sense of social organization. What that sense comprised, I suggest, appears in pre-modern sources along four axes of social differentiation.

Occupational status

The division of Chinese society into four large occupational status groups dates from the earliest period of Chinese thought. It occurs in the *Book of Documents* and other classical texts in the expression *simin*, or the four occupational groups among the people (scholars, agriculturalists, artisans, and merchants). Only a few remarks need be made here about this well-known system of social differentiation. First, it comes closest of any Chinese idea to the 'estates' idea of the West. The system says nothing about economic gradations within each group. Agriculturalists (*nong*), for example, would include both rich landowners and poor tenants. And there is a strong feeling of naturalness and universality about the system: it is thought to cover the entirety of the natural and necessary human occupations. Thus it forms a complete and interrelated system. It is generally assumed to imply hierarchy, though the actual principles on which that hierarchy is constructed are worth careful examination. By what rationale, for example, are agriculturalists thought superior to merchants? The superiority lies not in gradations of purity or virtue, but is founded on economic priorities, in which agriculture is considered a 'root' occupation (*benye*) from the standpoint of the state's fiscal interests, while trade is considered the subsidiary 'branch' (*moye*).

Unquestionably, there existed a hierarchy of value among these four estates. Just how strong such a sense was, however, or how firm the conceptual separation, is not so obvious. In late imperial times it did not involve prohibitions against intermarriage. Nor was it the basis for prohibitions against commensality (as in the case of Indian castes). In

---

[7] Ibid., p. 83. Later in the piece, the term 'proletariat', or 'propertyless class', occurs once; but it is in quotes (being an exotic foreign term) and in context simply means poor people.

fact, a curious and striking fact about this system is that, from very early times, it was used of 'subjects' in the aggregate: of all people except the ruling stratum. This meaning of *simin* persisted throughout late imperial times, when it was used simply to mean 'ordinary subjects', as distinct from pariah groups.[8]

In short, it seems likely that, although the conception of four estates did involve a sense of hierarchy, its aggregate sense of 'ordinary subjects' was the dominant one in late imperial times. And this fits closely with an equally pervasive scheme of classification: namely, that between the ruling stratum and nearly everyone else.

Rulers and ruled

In 1974 a young scientist in Manchuria told me, with a perfectly straight face, that a 'cadre' was 'one who works with his brain as distinct from one who works with his hands.' Though this man was not particularly old-fashioned in other respects, he was certainly hewing to an old and respected conceptual division of society, which goes back at least to the *Mencius*. Now when this axis of differentiation is placed next to the 'four estates' axis just discussed, the anomaly is that the estate of 'scholars' (*shi*) overlaps with the stratum of rulers: those who do brainwork. Whether the *shi* are to be considered 'ordinary subjects' or part of the ruling elite is central to the debate over the nature of the lowest stratum of the late imperial gentry, and was probably an ambiguity in Mencius's day as well. The implication that *simin* means *all* subjects (that is, those who were neither officials nor candidate-officials), including the scholars or top-most estate, lends support to Ho Ping-ti's assertion that scholars who lacked qualification to serve in the state bureaucracy were considered the top rank of the commoners.

For our purposes, the importance of the rulers-ruled axis is the levelling effect it has on social distinctions within the scheme of estates. The equation of *simin* with 'ruled stratum' minimizes status distinctions among them by comparison with the overriding importance of the rulers-ruled axis. The rulers-ruled division, like that of the four estates, is systematic and universal in its application, covering the entire symbolic ground and leaving nobody out. Thus it takes on the appearance of a

[8] For example, see the memorial of Ge'ertai to the Yongzheng emperor (1723) concerning a certain pariah group in Zhejiang: 'They cannot occupy professions proper to ordinary subjects [*simin*]; they cannot register in the same registers in which ordinary subjects are inscribed': *Yongzheng zhupi yuzhi*, Ge'ertai, 1b.

natural system, one built into the very nature of human society, to be legislated neither into existence nor out of it.

Free and unfree

Unlike the two systems just discussed, this one was by no means considered universal or built into the natural order. It consisted of two sub-categories: hereditary service groups and pariah groups (including slaves). Although these groups have very different historical origins, the rationale for their existence was similar, in that they were both considered man-made. By hereditary service groups, I refer to the special categories of families liable for certain types of service to the state: for example, those recorded in the vast military registers (*junji*) of Ming and Qing times, which were designed to ensure the maintenance of a self-supporting and self-perpetuating standing army. This system was reinforced in Qing times by ethnicity, with the various 'banner' garrisons registered separately from the Han population. In the economic system of the late empires, hereditary service tended to lose its efficiency and to be replaced by hired service (nowhere was this more obvious than in the military sector).

Slave and pariah groups, like the hereditary service groups, were considered to have been essentially man-made rather than naturally occurring. Though the more familiar phenomenon in other societies is to see such invidious social distinctions as part of the natural order, the Chinese seemed inclined to establish and maintain a causal nexus between a person's unfree status and some past circumstance which could reasonably account for it.

The work of Niida Noboru has indicated a great variety of unfree conditions in China, from ancient times onwards. There were outright slaves (*nuli*), who were considered half men and half things and who could be bought and sold; their status was traced to human actions, including capture in warfare or penal servitude. There were indentured retainers, who were called *buqu* in medieval times, but took many institutional forms thereafter. This was an intermediate status of servitude traceable to a procedure of commendation like that connected with early Western feudalism. Such semi-servile status extended also to tenants who, by virtue of some act of renunciation of freedom, owed certain hereditary services to landlords. Certain pariah groups descended from people who had suffered some sort of state punishment (as criminals or war captives) were attached as specialized practitioners of socially despised occupations (for example, entertainers) and were not allowed to intermarry with other strata. Here was a wide range of servility and dependency, all traceable to man-made causes and not to the order of nature (not, for example, to be compared with an axis organized around purity and impurity).[9]

Certain attitudes toward free and unfree status can be illustrated by an edict from the Yongzheng emperor dated 1727:

> **Edict to the Grand Secretariat**: We take the improvement of customs and mores as a central concern. Those who have [bad] customs and mores which are long transmitted, and have not been able to shake them off, ought all be given a route toward self-renewal [*zixin*]. Such was the case with the 'entertainer households' [*yuehu*] of Shanxi and the 'lazy people' [*duohu*] of Zhejiang, all of whom have had their mean status expunged and been reclassified as 'good subjects'. This was in order to encourage honesty and a sense of shame, and to extend the transformation of values.
>
> Now we have learned that in Huizhou prefecture, Anhui, there are 'servitors' [*bandang*] and in Ningguo prefecture there are 'hereditary servants' [*shipu*]. These are called, locally, 'mean people' [*ximin*]. Their status is even worse than that of the 'entertainer households' and 'lazy people'. For example, there may be two surname groups whose tax classifications are equivalent, but one surname group may be the servitors and hereditary servants of the other. When those of the first surname have weddings or funerals, those of the second must present themselves for service. If they do not comply in any small particular, they may be flogged. Inquiring as to when these servile obligations began, the matter is obscure and impossible to determine. It is not that there is really any division between superior and inferior. It is absolutely nothing more than an evil custom being long perpetuated. This matter came to our attention by hearsay. Now if there really is such a situation, we considered that they ought to be emancipated to be good subjects [*liangmin*]. Thereby may they energetically raise themselves up and avoid having this vile status for their whole lives and passing it on to their descendants.[10]

The emperor then approved a recommendation by the Anhui governor which distinguished between servile dependents bound by a written contract and those who were not. The latter were to be freed unconditionally.[11]

---

[9] Niida Noboru, *Chūgoku hōsei shi* (Tokyo, 1963), pp. 123–42.

[10] *Daqing lichao shilu*, Yongzheng, 56: 27–28b. The memorial which started all this was apparently by the censor Nianxi, dated Yongzheng, 1:3 (1723), *Yongzheng zhupi yuzhi*.

[11] Nevertheless, the agnatic descendants of indentured servants who had redeemed their freedom would still be held to observe 'the distinction between masters and servants' if they had been born in the master's household. The

What mattered to the emperor was the status of the people in question from the standpoint of the state fisc. True, servile status was correlated in some way with moral taint. Nevertheless, this was not taint in the bone and marrow, but could be expunged once the objective conditions of social inferiority were removed by law. In other words, the juridical context, which was man-made, was what made self-renewal possible. This was certainly distinguishable from any concept of caste hierarchy, in that the social impurity was a secondary characteristic. Notice the importance of contracts of indenture – whether voluntary or not – as reasonable causes to which one could ascribe social inferiority. What man could make, man could unmake as well.

Rich and poor

Of our four axes of social differentiation, this is the most difficult to deal with in the Chinese case. That is because it is not entirely clear whether it really represents an axis in the Chinese scheme of classification. Is there a 'culture of poverty' in Chinese thinking? There seems to be considerable evidence to the contrary. Some questions may clarify the point. First, what do wealth and poverty mean in terms of other systems of status differentiation? Second, what do they mean in terms of innate human qualities? Third, what are the causes of wealth and poverty with respect to particular families or groups? Here I should like to adduce some rather conventional material from stories and informal writings in which wealth and poverty play a part. Although some of these date from medieval times, all were available to readers of the late empires, and were read and reprinted. The twelfth-century writer Hong Mai observed:

> When I was young, I read a passage by someone of an earlier generation as follows: 'when a rich person has a son, she does not nurse him herself but has someone put aside her own son and nurse him. When a poor person has a son, she may not nurse him herself but must put him aside in order to nurse someone else's son. A rich person travels leisurely and has people carry him by sedan chair. A poor person not only may not travel on his own but must even carry someone else.' These things exist because they have persisted customarily for a long time without being looked into. These examples may be extended to many things in the world

---

Jiangnan gentry were not about to put up with the loss of their servants quite so easily.

which have so persisted, and which nobody thinks of as unusual. How tragic![12]

Several important attitudes toward the wealth-poverty axis are embedded here: poverty and wealth in themselves are not indicia of injustice. Differences in wealth are not wrong in themselves; rather, it is the way people treat one another in such a situation. Furthermore, the way the rich treat the poor is one cultural trait among many possible ones. Rather than a natural outgrowth of the disparity in wealth, wet-nursing and palanquins are practices which might be 'looked into', and perhaps ameliorated. As to the nature of the exploitation discussed in this passage, it obviously has nothing to do with the system of economic production, but rather concerns basic human desiderata: nursing babies and moving about. The attitude about the universality of human needs suggests a society in which wealth and poverty are exchanged comparatively freely. Certainly there is no natural difference among men which can be said to result from their economic position.

Qian Yong (1759–1844) likened economic fortune to seasonal changes:

> Wealth and high status are like flowers. They wither in less than a day. Poverty and low status are like grass: they remain green through winter and summer. But when frost and snow ensue, flowers and grass all wither, and when spring breezes suddenly arrive, flowers and grass flourish. Wealth, high status; poverty, low status; being born and being extinguished; rising and declining: this is a principle of heaven and earth.[13]

Here the alternation of wealth and poverty is metaphorically linked to time, rather than to some other universal phenomenon such as *karma*, division of labour, virtue, or human effort. They are changeable, but not changeable arbitrarily. Rather, they replace one another with the regularity of the seasons. The natural condition of man seems to be poverty (persisting, like grass, over a long period); whereas wealth is a more exotic quality, and hence more fragile. Extremely hostile conditions, however, will victimize both the rich and the poor household, and good conditions will permit both to revive and continue their modes of life. Here is a society with a broad, poor base and a very narrow elite at the top, with the elite far more vulnerable to the winds of the season. Finally, differences between wealth and poverty have nothing to do with inherent human characteristics, and there is no natural disparity in virtue between rich and poor. In another passage, Qian deals with the relationship between wealth and social roles:

[12] Hong Mai, *Rongchai suibi, xia*, 864 (repr. Shanghai, 1978).
[13] Qian Yong, *Meixi conghua* (Shanghai, 1936), *shang*, p. 111.

Merchants regard wealth as proper; for with wealth, profits and interest will be increasingly generated. Buddhist and Taoist clerics regard poverty as proper; for with poverty, desires and evil conduct will seldom come. The scholar regards as proper a condition of neither wealth nor poverty. Without wealth, there is nothing to agitate the spirit. Without poverty, he can concentrate his mind on study.[14]

Here, wealth and poverty take on a free-floating quality not inherent to social role, but somehow furthering its appropriate vocation. Economic status has an instrumental benefit: instead of being determined by social role, it is desired in order more effectively to fill a social role.

Indeed, social role may be virtually without any necessary connection to a particular economic status, as Qian goes on to relate:

In the *Hongfan* chapter of the *Book of Documents*, among the five blessings, wealth is listed as number two [in descending rank order]. I, however, believe wealth to be an extremely miserable matter and a source of ill feeling. There are those who are wealthy and of high status. There are those who are wealthy and of mean status; those who work the fields and are wealthy, those who work as merchants and are wealthy. Their kinds of wealth are dissimilar, and their sufferings are of multifarious kinds. How can wealth simply be termed a blessing?[15]

Here the connection between wealth and status is so loose as to be virtually non-existent. Anyone can get rich, whatever his social role, so that wealth is neither a determinant nor a necessary result of one's place in the world. The wealth-poverty axis is poorly correlated with other social divisions.

Finally, an amusing medieval story offers some revealing views about the relation between wealth and social position:

In the *Collected Song Ephemera* [*Songbai leichao*] there is a story called 'The eight cyclical characters[16] of Duke Wenlu'. In Loyang lived an old man who shared the eight characters with Duke Wenlu. But their attainments in life were different. Once a fortune-teller was asked to predict the old man's fate. He said that, indeed, although the gulf between him and the Duke was like the division between North and South or between water and land, yet in a certain month in the following year he would rest and rise with the Duke, eat and drink with him, and share equally with him; but that this situation would not last beyond the ninth month.

[14] Ibid., p. 114.
[15] Ibid., p. 109.
[16] 'Eight cyclical characters' (*bazi*) refer to the notations of the year, month, day, and hour of birth. Those sharing the eight characters are supposed to be linked by fortune in some way, presumably astrologically.

The next year, the Duke entered Loyang and desired to meet with an old-timer to chat about past events. Someone recommended the old man to him. As soon as the Duke met him, he was delighted. He caused the old man to accompany him wherever he went. Whenever there was an official banquet, or a visit to relations or friends, he took him along. When the Duke sat on the right, he would seat the oldster on his left, and vice versa. After the ninth month, the Duke left Loyang, and the old man went his separate way.[17]

Here is a suggestion that beyond the world of human arrangements (in which are vast differences of social position) is a realm of cosmological truth which links men according to some prior system of affinities and which breaks through the world of appearances from time to time. When it does, human connections can transcend the accidents of station. Clearly, socializing between high and low is a remarkable thing, otherwise there would be no story. Yet, even though unusual, such closeness is not seen as defiling to the person of high status. The connection with the old man rather reflects credit on the Duke. That such a connection could be achieved may also have something to do with old age, when presumably status differences begin to lose their sharp outlines in the twilight of life. The story would hardly have the same appeal or plausibility if both men had been young. Finally, the appeal of the story seems to depend on the idea that, however steep a status gradient, it can be bridged by shared human characteristics. One pictures a rather jolly time between the two protagonists, despite the vast difference in their rank.

Trying to distil from these materials a set of principles that we can say constitute 'the Chinese view' of social stratification is surely risky, if for no other reason than that we have yet to describe such a unified Chinese view about *any* social question. But at least one can say that the foregoing material is not in serious conflict with the following conclusions:

Firstly and historically, Chinese views about social hierarchy have been closely related to the hierarchy of state office. Furthermore, only in the twentieth century has hierarchy been (however awkwardly) seen in terms of human groups rather than points on a scale.

Secondly, occupational status hierarchy has had a place in Chinese social theory, but it has been largely overshadowed by a political distinction dividing the state sector from all others.

Thirdly, status distinctions which denote the natural and hereditary

---

[17] Liang Shaoren, *Qiuyu'an suibi* (Shanghai, n.d.; Jinbushuju edn), 1:26b.

inferiority of certain groups have existed, but have been subject to rationalization in the search for some human act which caused them, and it has been thought necessary that servile status be documented by some legal instrument.

Fourthly, distinctions of wealth have been only loosely linked to other human characteristics and other systems of social differentiation. Moreover, a powerful fatalism underlay the view of how wealth was acquired. Beneath distinctions of wealth was seen to persist a set of universal human characteristics.

If these can be said to sum up the cultural background from which twentieth-century Chinese have viewed the question of class and hierarchy, we should guess that Chinese social theory would be somewhat uncomfortable with ideas of hereditary and immutable class status. We would further expect the political order to play a dominant role in defining any new system of classification that emerges.

In fact, the current Chinese system of social classification suggests just such an orientation. There are actually two systems in force: that of 'social role' (*chengfen*) and that of 'social origin' (*chushen*). Social role is defined in the official dictionary published in 1973 by the Chinese Academy of Social Sciences as 'a person's most important background or occupational status before entering upon revolutionary work [*geming gungzuo*] – that is, before being assigned to a job. For instance, one's official 'social role' might be worker or student. The important thing is that 'social role' can change. It is not ascribed by accident of birth, and may be different from that of other family members.

'Social origin', by contrast, designates (in the same dictionary) 'A person's status as determined by his early experience or his family's economic circumstances.'[18] Social origin is the designation by which most persons were formally categorized during the early 1950s (for instance, 'textile worker' or 'landlord'). It corresponds closely to 'class background', and ordinarily does not change as one's social activities or consciousness change.

The relative importance of 'social origin' seems to be in decline, as China's leadership moves toward a less conflictual view of internal social relations. Though there are doubtless current policy reasons for this tendency, a more profound reason may perhaps be sought in layers of Chinese consciousness about social classification which lie far back in history. So basic a component of man's social awareness does not change quickly or easily.

[18] *Xiandai Hanyu Cidian* (Beijing, 1973), pp. 122, 141.

11
Languages of power in the United States

Daniel T. Rodgers and Sean Wilentz

'*We, the People*'. From the moment the Philadelphia delegates placed the words at the head of the new federal Constitution, the phrase compacted in itself both irony and ambiguity. Irony first, for though the Constitution was to run the gauntlet of a series of generally elected ratifying conventions before coming into force, it was hardly the work of the revolutionary *populus* itself. Meeting in closely contrived isolation from the egalitarian political forces unleashed by the Revolution, few of the delegates had ventured a good word for what Edmund Randolph had branded 'the fury of democracy'.[1]

Still less could the phrase 'We, the People' hide its massive ambiguity. In the ratifying debates, the friends of the Constitution insisted on the principle of the people's sovereignty. Power in the new Constitutional order derived not from any classical balance of the powers of the separate social orders, but from the people considered as a single, undifferentiated whole. 'The People are the King', Gouverneur Morris had declared in the convention itself.[2] But who the people were, the Constitution left deliberately and almost wholly undefined. Not *all* of the people, certainly, for the exclusion of certain groups – all women, all slaves, all Indians – the convention took for granted. All those Americans whose entanglement in dependent relations seemed to the delegates to preclude political independence provoked concern. On those grounds, some delegates wanted to exclude poor white men, even though trying to do so would almost certainly have doomed all chances for ratification. Instead,

---

[1] Max Farrand (ed.), *The Records of the Federal Convention of 1787* (Yale University Press, New Haven, 1911), vol. 1, p. 59.

[2] Ibid., vol. 2, p. 69.

they side-stepped all these issues and took refuge in an abstraction: 'the people'.

By elevating popular sovereignty to a nationalist creed, the Constitution helped to solidify a new language of politics, powerful enough to be mistaken by many later observers as the only language of power natural to the new nation. Over age-old talk of inequality, the framers presumed to lay a new language of the undifferentiated and sovereign people – unifying, where older vernaculars of rank and hierarchy were divisive; abstract and egalitarian, where the others prickled with the pride and resentments of everyday social experience. Call these rival families of languages, for short, languages of dominance and languages of common right. Consciousness of inequality, hierarchy, or class framed the first; assertions of common political and legal status framed the second. They constituted distinct and powerful linguistic resources in post-Revolutionary America – always at odds and yet (as we shall see) always historically entangled.

The rivalry in this clash of tongues was not lost on the Constitution's contemporaries. In the ratifying conventions of 1787–8, the antifederalists tore into the new Constitution with a language redolent of social division. How could a Congress one-sixth the size of the House of Commons be said to be an organ of 'the people' in all their diversity or 'possess the same interests, feelings, opinions, and views the people themselves would were they all assembled?' In so centralized a government, 'the *better sort*, the *well born*, etc.' would so entrench themselves as to 'be in practice a *permanent* ARISTOCRACY.' This was a government for 'the great, the wealthy, the well born'. As for the rest (in the words of a Massachusetts antifederalist), the managers of this Constitution will 'swallow all us little folks like the great *Leviathan*.'[3]

The federalists' response was to draw as thick a verbal veil across such social differences as possible. There was no aristocratic branch in the new government, they insisted; no special role for rank or property, no formal class privilege, no power that did not come, by one path or another, from the people – 'one great and equal body of citizens', in Charles Pinckney's words.[4] The claims obscured the reality – so much

[3] Cecelia M. Kenyon (ed.), *The Antifederalists* (Bobbs-Merrill, Indianapolis, 1966), pp. 209, 12–13, *1*; Jonathan Elliot (ed.), *The Debates in the Several State Conventions on the Adoption of the Federal Constitution* (4 vols, Washington, 1836; rep. Salem, N. H., 1987), vol. 3, p. 266.

[4] Gordon S. Wood, *The Creation of the American Republic, 1776–87* (University of N. Carolina Press, Chapel Hill, 1969), p. 555; Edmund S.

so that, ever since, historians have misconstrued the federalist victory as a crucial step in insulating politics and the law from talk of social inequality. Indeed, the language of common political status was never entirely to lose this handy obscurity, its intermittent capacity to swamp consciousness of inequality in patriotism's call to arms, the fictions of legal right, or myths of consensus.

Yet power in this relation has not flowed in simple channels. If in the United States the terms of common right which swept through politics were often employed to dampen the legitimacy of claims constructed in metaphors of sharp social division, they also proved to be a powerful democratic resource. The very abstraction and ambiguity in which the terms of popular rights were pitched gave egalitarian political movements a purchase far different from that which they possessed in the United States' closest linguistic cousin, England. Both languages of common right and languages of dominance were languages of power and conse- quence – just as both were ultimately *about* power.

Any inquiry into language invites the illusion of having blundered into the labyrinthine cross-references of a dictionary. Vocabularies of social description overlay vocabularies of gender and family relations in patterns historians have only begun to unearth. Everywhere verbal invention and variation have ruled, not only in the narrow segment of public talk preserved in print, but still more in the spoken languages which remain hidden or obscure to the historian. Like all social vocabu- laries, the terms of social description were open to appropriation and reappropriation to divergent uses and a multitude of users. But random variation no more governs words than social experience. The languages of dominance and common right in the United States developed within the shifting contours of society and politics themselves. It was within that history, by necessity, that their relationship unfolded.

Languages of dominance were older in the revolutionary period than the language of common political right. From the start, seventeenth-century passenger lists had grouped the emigrants according to Old World social hierarchies, in a search for a familiar, vertical ordering that only intensified in the earliest, disease-decimated settlements. From the New Englanders' plain, but insistent, distinction between masters and servants to the much more elaborate hierarchical ordering of the first Virginia passenger manifests, there was no missing the imported language of

---

Morgan, *Inventing the People: the rise of popular sovereignty in England and America* (Norton, New York, 1988).

rank. Profoundly as New World experience was to reconstitute these categories, the terms of class and station endured.

Those that came to dominate the printed page in the eighteenth and nineteenth centuries represent only the tip of an immensely larger structure; they offer a view from the top or (at best) the middle down. By the eve of the Revolution it was nonetheless clear that considerable fractioning had taken place. The white Southern slave-holding elite commonly talked in terms of a four-tier conception of society: 'gentlemen' at the top; 'common planters' next (from modestly successful slaveholders to 'the poor Planters who have but one Bed', as Robert Beverley put it); white 'servants' below them in temporary unfreedom; and at the bottom 'Negroes', so rarely free that the slave relation was on most occasions subsumed in the language of race.[5] In New England the term 'esquire' cut a simpler line between elites and common folk, just as 'servant' set off common folk from the bottom.[6] Occupational categories formed another potential grid, most fully elaborated in the infant seaboard cities of the middle colonies and their surrounding hinterlands: men were 'Farmers, Artificers, or Men in Trade', Benjamin Franklin wrote in 1756; 'masters', 'merchants', 'mechanics', 'laborers'.[7]

Where eighteenth-century elites needed a more uniform lexicon, they converged on a tripartite, English-derived language of 'sorts'. At the Constitutional convention, the delegates talked freely of the 'rich' (or 'better sort'), the 'middling sort', and the 'poor' (or 'lower sort').[8] Suppression of the slavery question led them to veil a fourth no less critically important term, 'Negro slaves'. Add that in, and one has a good approximation of the dominant language of social division in eighteenth-century America.

The Revolution struck its sharpest blow at the first term in this social vocabulary. Few Americans anticipated that the mobilization of popular resistance would ultimately undercut the idea of a non-hereditary 'natural aristocracy' of wealth, family ties, and gentle manners. Most of the drafters of the first state constitutions took for granted the need to establish an analogue to the aristocratic element in the British

---

[5] Rhys Isaac, *The Transformation of Virginia, 1740–90* (University of N. Carolina Press, Chapel Hill, 1982), p. 71; idem, 'Communication', *William and Mary Quarterly*, 3rd ser., 31 (1974), p. 530.

[6] Jackson T. Main, *The Social Structure of Revolutionary America* (Princeton University Press, Princeton, 1965), pp. 215–20.

[7] Ralph L. Ketcham (ed.), *The Political Thought of Benjamin Franklin* (Bobbs-Merrill, Indianapolis, 1965), p. 134.

[8] Main, *Social Structure*, pp. 232–4.

constitution – a 'Senatorial part' based on special qualifications of wealth or virtue – in order to reflect the classic Aristotelian balance between the qualities of aristocracy, monarchy, and democracy. By 1787, however, the democratizing effects of the revolutionary mobilization were rapidly emptying the term 'aristocracy' of positive weight. To be sure, Gouverneur Morris, among others, defended the word 'aristocracy' at the Philadelphia convention: 'his creed was that there never was, nor ever will be a civilized Society without an Aristocracy.' But in the face of the antifederalists' employment of the term 'aristocracy' as a vehement term of abuse, the federalists quickly shed it from their vocabulary.[9]

This assault on one of the linguistic fulcrums of European conservatism did not homogenize social imagery or inhibit popular linguistic resources for the 'few', the 'rich', 'the monied men', the 'nabobs', or (in time) the cotton mill 'lords', the money 'kings', and 'plutocrats'. 'Gentleman' continued to be a term of weight, and of particular weight in the slave-holding South. Still the federalists' insistence that the only political actors in the polity were the 'people' cut off a certain amount of self-referential linguistic legitimacy among the elites, a constraint which did not always go down easily among the well-to-do, as Aléxis de Tocqueville would discover in the 1830s.

On the American as on the English side of the Atlantic, however, the more far-reaching influence on the vocabulary of social division was the onward course of merchant and industrial capitalism. On the boundary between the 'middling class' and the 'poor', urban mechanics and rural yeomen began to build new categories: the 'working classes', 'the producing classes', the ranks of 'labor'. As early as the 1790s, bitter conflict over Alexander Hamilton's finance programme had led dissenting writers to challenge the privileges of money with the counter-claims of labour. One such partisan, the Massachusetts farmer William Manning, called in 1798 for the creation of a national Labouring Society, open only to those who followed hard labour for a living. In 1827, the Philadelphia artisan radical William Heighton issued a summons to political action addressed to 'the Members of Trade Societies and to the Working Classes Generally'. The short-lived Working Men's movements and general trades' unions of the 1820s and 1830s, combining old and new usages, depicted themselves as spokesmen for the 'producers' against a

---

[9] Farrand, *Records of the Federal Convention*, vol. 1, p. 545; Wood, *Creation of the American Republic*.

resurgent 'mushroom aristocracy' of bankers, employers, and corrupt politicians.[10]

Over the next fifty years, the rise of an industrial work-force brought with it a profusion of social vocabularies suited to every political persuasion; most often, organized workers distinguished between honest 'producers' (or 'labor') and parasitic 'non-producers' (or 'capitalists'). In 1878, when the largest of all nineteenth-century American labour movements, the Knights of Labor, adopted a national constitution, the group claimed to represent the 'toiling masses' and the 'producing masses' against 'capital' and the 'aggression of aggregated wealth'.[11] The language of middling circumstances, to be sure, retained a certain degree of attraction for American workers. In the mid-1880s, a New York City machinist told an investigating committee that ten years earlier he had 'considered himself a mechanic, and felt he belonged to the middle-class; but to-day he recognizes the fact that he is simply the same as any other ordinary laborer, no more and no less.'[12] Still, the stronger pull was towards the language of labour, reinforced by both the pain of exploitation and fierce reserves of pride.

The result was a language rooted not in adjectives (like 'middling') but verbs and action: work, toil, production. It was this that made appeal to 'the wealth-producing classes' (to 'the ever-present contest of the wealth-producers to conquer their rights from the wealth-absorbers,' as the American Federation of Labor's Executive Council put it in the railway strike of 1894) a powerful engine of labour mobilization well into the twentieth century.[13] The transition from a vocabulary of social rank to a language of labour entailed not simply a reformulation of categories, but reformulation of the linguistic base itself, from condition to production and relations.

[10] Samuel Eliot Morison (ed.), 'William Manning's *The Key of Liberty*', *William and Mary Quarterly*, 3rd ser., 13 (1956), pp. 202–54; [William Heighton], *An Address to the Members of Trade Societies, and to the Working Classes Generally* . . . by a Fellow Laborer (Philadelphia, 1827); Bruce Laurie, *Artisans into Workers: labor in nineteenth-century America* (Hill and Wang, New York, 1989), ch. 2; Sean Wilentz, *Chants Democratic: New York City and the rise of the American working class, 1788–1850* (Oxford University Press, New York, 1984).

[11] Quoted in Laurie, *Artisans into Workers*, p. 150.

[12] U.S. Senate, Committee on Education and Labor, *Report upon the Relations between Labor and Capital* (Washington, D.C., 1885), vol. 1, p. 757.

[13] John Swinton, *Striking for Life: labor's side of the labor question* (1894; Greenwood Press, Westport, Ct., 1970), p. 311.

As a language of working-class identity took shape, the term 'middle class' devolved on a narrower group than the 'middling sort' had embraced in the eighteenth century. The transition from 'middling classes' to 'middle class', begun in the 1850s, was still uncertain enough at the time of the Civil War for editors employing the new term to apologize for writing 'after the fashion of the day'. By the end of the century, however, the new term was firmly implanted in general speech.[14] Just as wage-earners were sometimes reluctant to abandon the language of the middle ground, so manufacturers resisted abandonment of the language of labour to their employees. 'Manufacturer', 'industrialist', and (in time) 'businessman' vied with 'merchant', 'entrepreneur', and 'capitalist' – a vocabulary of production set against a vocabulary of trade and money. The term 'middle class', however, proved elastic enough to cover both. Here too the language of condition, of a *via media* between the extremes of opulence and destitution, was replaced by one rooted in new forms of action: thrift, restraint, deferral of gratifications, civility, commercial ambition, and acuity.

There was, of course, a huge exception to these general developments: the social vocabulary of the South. Never completely isolated from the northern revolutions in social relations and production, antebellum Southerners knew something of the terminology of labour and capital. But as slavery shaped the entire structure of Southern power, stunting capitalist development, so Southerners drew maps of their own social order that differed fundamentally from those of Northerners. At the top of Southern society, the language of vertical ranking persisted as a way to distinguish 'gentlemen' and 'ladies' from common white folk and all whites from 'Negroes'. The master-slave connection provoked a more ambivalent linguistic response. When they tried to describe not the South in general but their own plantations, Southern planters turned to images of household and family. Slaves (according to these conventions) were at once a troublesome class – depraved, brutish, potentially savage – but also childlike, requiring paternal care and Christian protection. Slavery was supposedly but an enlargement of the reciprocal mutualist dependencies natural to any household, governing what (at their most wishful) masters spoke of as 'our family, black and white'.[15]

[14] David Montgomery, *Beyond Equality: labor and the radical Republicans, 1862–72* (Knopf, New York, 1967), p. 14; Stuart M. Blumin, 'The hypothesis of middle-class formation in nineteenth-century America', *American Historical Review*, 90 (1985), pp. 309–12; John S. Gilkeson, Jr, *Middle-Class Providence, 1820–1940* (Princeton University Press, Princeton, 1986), ch. 2.
[15] Eugene D. Genovese, *Roll, Jordan, Roll: the world the slaves made* (Knopf, New York, 1974); Elizabeth Fox-Genovese, *Within the Plantation Household:*

Other Southerners talked differently. The poorer, non-slave-holding farmers of the back country had little use for the romanticized deferential imagery of planter paternalism, at least with regard to white society. Depicting themselves as the bone-and-sinew of Southern society, 'the republican yeomanry', non-slave-holders spoke the democratic language of the producing classes with all the fluency of Northern workers. At the same time, however, yeomen did not challenge the basic legitimacy of slavery, sharing with the planters the bond of a common white supremacy.[16]

The slaves, meanwhile, had their own conceptions of class, though they are sometimes difficult to perceive through the veiled, highly ritualized conventions that, perforce, deflected the slaves' remarks outside their own quarters. At one level, slaves spoke of 'good' whites and 'bad', as if to demarcate those who lived up to the prescribed tenets of the paternalist code from those who did not. At a deeper level, however, slaves fostered a broad sense of themselves as a people and an exploited class: 'We peal de meat / Dey gib us de skin / And dat's de way / Dey takes us in,' ran an old slave song.[17]

In the aftermath of emancipation, the most wrenching change in the history of nineteenth-century labour relations, the freed slaves, poor whites, and former slave-holders experimented with new words to master their new situation. For one group of ex-slaves, for example, it was obvious (as they wrote in a petition) that, though free, they belonged to 'the Working Class of People'.[18] Among re-emergent elites, however, linguistic conventions of vertical, hierarchical ordering survived with redoubled force (even as promoters and parvenus began boasting of the rise of a 'new South'). As late as the 1920s, when sociologists Allison Davis, Burleigh Gardner, and Mary Gardner descended on Natchez, Mississippi, they found precious little trace of the term 'middle class'. Some Southerners, especially blacks, had a word for it: 'Strainers', they called them, white urban Southerners aching to colonize a space between 'quality' and 'common' folks. But linguistically and socially that space was narrow in the rural and small-town South. The dominant language

---

black and white women of the Old South (University of N. Carolina Press, Chapel Hill, 1988).

[16] Steven Hahn, *The Roots of Southern Populism: yeoman farmers and the transformation of the Georgia Upcountry, 1850–90* (Oxford University Press, New York, 1983).

[17] John W. Blassingame, *The Slave Community: plantation life in the antebellum South* (Oxford University Press, New York, 1972), p. 51.

[18] Quoted in Edward Magdol, *A Right to the Land: essays on the freedmen's community* (Greenwood Press, Westport, Ct, 1977), p. 273.

of Southern class relations, simplified slightly by emancipation, was tripartite. 'Gentlemen' (or, in time, 'society folk') occupied the top layer. Next came the 'poor folk', 'poor whites', 'crackers', 'lint-heads', 'sandhillers', 'rednecks', 'white trash' – the terms, in ascending order of contempt, were as current in Huey Long's South of the 1930s as they had been in Jefferson Davis's before the Civil War. At the bottom, as always, were the 'Negroes' or, in plainest white Southern talk, 'niggers'.[19]

Or so it seemed to outsiders. Behind the scenes of black society, there were innumerable subtle distinctions which at once complicated and softened the harsh classifications familiar to whites. In Chicago's South Side ghetto in the late 1930s, St Clair Drake and Horace Cayton caught the taxonomy which set the 'respectables', a stuck-up 'dictie' black middle class, against the poor, 'low-class' majority. In Natchez, too, there were 'better class' and 'common' blacks. Still, in an important sense, this was a secret inner language, disguised from white outsiders and still more urgently repressed by white Southerners in the interests of shoring up a dichotomous vocabulary of race – all the more so as sharecropping caught poor black and white farmers in the same economic snare. Strictly maintained terms of address ('boss' and 'boy', 'mistah' and 'nigger'), a stubborn denial of the term 'mister' to the black middle class (even to the extent, in the black society pages of some white Southern newspapers, of resorting to *mesdames* and *monsieurs*): these were the linguistic rituals of critically important power.[20]

These distinctive Southern languages of dominance survived at least until the Second World War, companion to the enduring kingdom of cotton, tobacco, agricultural exploitation, and racism. In the industrial regions of the North, by contrast, the language of 'labor' and 'capital', 'working class' and 'middle class', began to fracture in increasingly complex ways amid the massive immigration waves between 1880 and 1920 and the beginnings of Southern black migration to northern cities. An extraordinary profusion of pseudo-scientific racial categories – slav, teuton, hunkie, dago – was spread lavishly and none too carefully over

---

[19] Allison Davis, Burleigh B. Gardner, and Mary R. Gardner, *Deep South: a social anthropological study of caste and class* (University of Chicago Press, Chicago, 1941); John Dollard, *Caste and Class in a Southern Town* (Yale University Press, New Haven, 1937).

[20] St Clair Drake and Horace R. Cayton, *Black Metropolis: a study of negro life in a northern city* (Harcourt Brace, New York, 1945), pt 3; Arthur F. Raper and Ira de A. Reid, *Sharecroppers All* (University of N. Carolina Press, Chapel Hill, 1941), p. 80.

the new immigrant groups, both in common and in academic speech. Erosion of the older, simpler vocabulary proceeded most rapidly among the middle class, though labour's spokesmen were themselves not immune to the pressures which fuelled the new taxonomies of race. The great social investigations of the turn of the century reflected the new linguistic complexity. Charles Booth had surveyed working-class London with a powerfully simple grid of essentially economic categories, half of them above, half below the 'poverty line'. The summary volume of the major American analogue to Booth's London work, the Russell Sage Foundation's Pittsburgh survey of 1907, set vertical imagery aside altogether for a series of 'racial studies'.[21]

By the 1920s, with free immigration at an end, this fracturing had begun to call forth strenuous efforts at sociological reclassification and simplification. Robert and Helen Lynd, deliberately picking a small midwestern manufacturing city (Muncie, Indiana) with few blacks or immigrants to confuse the picture, essayed a simple two-fold description in 1928: business class on top, working class on the bottom. At another pole was the classificatory scheme adopted (on English models) by the Census Bureau, in an attempt to recast the terms of inequality in a metaphor of a carefully graded school of ascending skill levels: unskilled workers; semi-skilled workers; skilled workers and foremen; clerical workers; proprietors, managers, and officials; and professionals. Most influential of all in sociological circles was W. Lloyd Warner's heroic effort to sort the self-referential status assumptions of the population of Newburyport, Massachusetts, in the 1930s into six distinct and (so he thought) generally recognized strata from upper-upper class to lower-lower class.[22]

In common speech, however, simpler patterns prevailed. One of those, heralded with much academic acclaim at the end of the Depression, was a putative convergence on the label 'middle class'. Much of this discussion was set off by a *Fortune Magazine* survey of 1940, which seemed to demonstrate that 'middle class' had virtually swallowed all other referents. Asked to pick between upper class, middle class, or lower class, 80 per cent of those the magazine surveyed took the middle category.

---

[21] Charles Booth, *Life and Labour of the People in London*, vol. 1 (London, 1892); Paul U. Kellogg (ed.), *Wage-Earning Pittsburgh* (New York, 1914).
[22] Robert S. and Helen M. Lynd, *Middletown: a study in contemporary American culture* (Harcourt Brace, New York, 1929); Arthur Marwick, *Class: image and reality in Britain, France and the USA since 1930* (Oxford University Press, New York, 1980), p. 61; W. Lloyd Warner, *The Social Life of a Modern Community* (Yale University Press, New Haven, 1941).

To the editors the poll seemed proof of a post-Depression *embour-geoisement*: 'a rejection of the idea that classes, proletarian or plutocratic, exist among us; a sweeping confidence that for the individual the present is better than the past, that the future will be better than the present.'[23] But the *Fortune* survey data turned out to be the artifice of a mismatch between embedded patterns of speech and the peculiar dialect of the social scientists. When in the mid-1940s the category of 'working class' was added to the choice, 51 per cent of the Americans polled took it. (In 1975, 46 per cent still did, *vis-à-vis* 49 per cent who identified themselves as middle class.) That still left anomalies at both the bottom and the top, where only tiny fractions of the population (1–3 per cent in the polls made since 1945) identify themselves as either 'upper' or 'lower' class. Change the bottom category to 'poor', however, and the sudden rise in takers (up to 28 per cent of black Americans in a poll in 1975) suggests a term with powerful social resonance.[24]

Cutting across this explicit language of 'class', ethnic and racial talk persists, as a resource both of vilification and of pride. But a four-class system is no less deeply entrenched in popular speech: an upper class of some sort, a middle class, a working class, and the poor. After the collapse of the Southern staple economy and the post-war challenge to its racial order, even the distinctive vernacular of the South seems to have been absorbed into these terms. Polled in this way, at any rate, only 2 per cent of contemporary Americans do not understand the question or deny its premises.[25]

To a great extent the historic development of languages of dominance in America paralleled contemporary trends in England, linked as the two nations were by common language and economic processes. In politics and the law, on the other hand, the outcome seems unmistakably different. The terms of class and social rank which ran so hard through common talk in the United States seemed to have failed almost entirely to penetrate these adjacent arenas of discussion.

In politics, numerous parties have borne the name labour, but they

---

[23] 'The Fortune Survey: XXVII', *Fortune*, 21 (Feb. 1940), pp. 14, 20.

[24] E. M. Schreiber and G. T. Nygreen, 'Subjective social class in America, 1945–68', *Social Forces*, 48 (1970), pp. 348–56; Leonard Beeghley, *Social Stratification in America: a critical analysis of theory and research* (Goodyear, Santa Monica, Calif., 1978), p. 113; Mary R. Jackman and Robert W. Jackman, *Class Awareness in the United States* (University of California Press, Berkeley, 1983).

[25] Ibid., p. 18.

have been usually locally based, and always short-lived: the Working Men's parties of the 1820s, the California Workingmen's party of the late 1870s, the Greenback-Labor and United Labor parties of the Gilded Age, the Minnesota Farmer-Labor alliance, and the American Labor Party of the 1930s. The language of the law, where, from the middle of the nineteenth century onwards, courts and constitutional lawyers kept up an extraordinary counter-assault on 'class' legislation which would either favour or name a class distinct from the people as a whole, was still more impregnable. In Britain, a critical, formal breach of this sort came with the Housing of the Working Classes Act of 1885. By contrast, none of the crucial ingredients of the New Deal – 'public' housing, 'social' security, the 'labor relations' Act which was to be the organized workers' Magna Carta, 'farm' security, 'emergency' relief, or aid to 'dependent families' – breathed more than a hint of the terms of class.[26]

But the commonplace conclusion that in the United States the language and resentments of class have been of negligible effect in politics misses the mark. Precisely because the nation was promulgated in political terms – as the political empowerment of the people – controversies, which elsewhere found social forms of expression, were pulled with terrific force in the United States into the terms of democratic politics. Not the least of these categories was the 'people'. The boundaries of that term, the practical power with which it should be invested, the rights of the 'people', and, not the least, the right (by nature) to be included fully in the 'people': these were to be a pivot of American politics from the Revolution through the Civil Rights movement of the 1960s. By itself the Constitution's acknowledgement of the people's sovereignty by no means ensured a gradual extension of the classes of those who could claim membership in the 'people'; it ensured only that the issue, and related matters of democracy and dependence, would never be out of the eye of controversy.

Suffrage and representation were among the crucial markers in these contests; in clashes over them – and the broader definitions of democracy and popular rights – social claims and the terms of politics converged with particular force. Here Americans not only fixed a key social category in law, but struggled over its congruence with the terms of inequality they knew so well. In England in the 1830s and 1840s, the language of Chartism had resounded with similar talk, in which the political and economic threads were wound around each other beyond

[26] Marwick, *Class*, pp. 62–76.

any simple untangling.[27] In the United States, in this sense, the Chartist 'moment' was a permanent condition.

These battles over the constituent terms of politics began with the Revolution. By any standard, the winning of American independence was an epochal event, sweeping away an established imperial ruling order, breaking up the old connection between rulers and subjects, and establishing the first successful modern republic. That the new nation would be a republic few patriots doubted. Well before the British surrender at Yorktown, however, Americans began struggling over what the republic would look like, and how popular sovereignty would be defined and exercised. Different groups of radicals and plebeians seized upon the doctrines of natural rights to demand broad-based suffrage, curtailment of 'balanced' government, and the elimination of all vestiges of exclusive political privilege. Their greatest spokesman was Thomas Paine, in whose immensely popular tracts ideas about democracy (if not quite yet the word itself) ceased to have their traditional pejorative implications.[28] Inspired by Paine's *Common Sense*, some American republicans sought to win the closest practical thing to a direct democracy as was humanly possible, insistent, in the words of Paine's Pennsylvania associate Thomas Young, that the 'people at large [are] the true proprietors of governmental power.'[29]

Conservative and patrician patriots viewed such talk with an anxiety that turned into alarm once the democrats began to help shape the new revolutionary state governments. In the traditional conservative view, some sort of balanced government was essential, lest tyranny and anarchy be loosed upon the world. Their political language slipped easily into the vocabulary and cadences of the classical civic humanist tradition. For a republic to survive, they believed, its framers had to ensure that virtuous men would be left to deliberate selflessly in pursuit of the common weal; to that end, checks had to be instituted on all forms of power, to prevent corrupt, selfish individuals or groups from legislating their own private interests or passions. Above all, they beheld government as a realm fit only for independent men, free from the kind of economic and political leverage that could compromise or destroy their

---

[27] See esp. G. Stedman Jones, *Languages of Class: studies in English working class history, 1832–1982* (Cambridge University Press, Cambridge, 1983).

[28] For traditional views, see C. Hill, 'The many-headed monster', in his *Change and Continuity in Seventeenth-Century England* (Weidenfeld, London, 1974), pp. 181–204.

[29] Quoted in Eric Foner, *Tom Paine and Revolutionary America* (Oxford University Press, New York, 1976), p. 134.

attachment to the public good. The idea was as old as Aristotle (although conservative Americans were just as likely to cite the authority of William Blackstone): dependent persons of mean circumstances literally had no political will of their own, and could be easily manipulated by 'a great, an artful, or a wealthy man'. With these principles engraved on their political souls, conservative republicans recoiled at how much power the lower and middling sort seemed to have won, especially in the state legislatures – 'men whom Wisdom would have left in obscurity', one critic sneered.[30]

By the late 1780s, conservative republicans had had considerable success in containing the democratizing movements; in some respects, the federal Constitution was their crowning achievement. Yet not only did the democrats hedge in the power of the new national government by attaching a Bill of Rights to the Constitution, the Constitution itself, by leaving undisturbed the state governments, rejecting the conventional idea of a balanced government of the separate social orders, and bowing to the principles of representative popular sovereignty, narrowed the possibility that some new privileged class would assume national power uncontested. To some of the most democratic of minds, including those of Paine and Thomas Jefferson, the Constitution was an absolute necessity, in order to keep what had been a loose confederation of states from falling victim to internal dissension and dismemberment by hostile nations. And when, in the 1790s, Federalist policies did seem to augur the consolidated rule of monied men, a national opposition arose under Jefferson to sweep the Federalists out of national office, all within the limits of the Constitution.[31]

The market revolution that stimulated capitalist development in the North and the revival and spread of plantation slavery in the South helped to seal the doom of what remained of eighteenth-century deferential patrician politics. With the rapid proliferation of commercial networks, there emerged a new class of ambitious and articulate men, with little or no attachment to the established gentry regime. Merchants, manufacturers, lawyers, commercial farmers, *arriviste* slave-holders, all chafed at the old political presumptions – the distrust of factionalism and parties, the stress on order and balance, the notion that only those

[30] William Blackstone, *Commentaries on the Laws of England* (4 vols, London, 1765), vol. 1, p. 171; and John Jay to Alexander Hamilton, 8 May 1778, quoted in Wood, *Creation of the American Republic*, p. 477.
[31] John R. Nelson, *Liberty and Property: political economy and policymaking in the new nation, 1789–1812* (Johns Hopkins University Press, Baltimore, 1987); Foner, *Tom Paine*, pp. 204–5.

with a landed stake-in-society should exercise full political rights. Armed with a conception of all free men as autonomous moral agents, these new arrivals entered politics in the opening decades of the nineteenth century, determined to reform the basic structure of American political participation by widening the suffrage and by building frankly partisan, democratic, and permanent political parties.[32]

Pressure for democratic change also came from outside the halls of power. For some Americans – petty planters, upstart local bankers, aspiring commercial farmers – the fruits of the market revolution did not extend quickly or evenly enough. For many more – displaced artisans and wage-earners, debtors without power or influence, yeoman farmers unable or unwilling to adjust to the new market's rules – the onrushing shapes of commercial growth looked ominous. In either case, the best cure for the nation's ills seemed to be more democracy, eliminating inherited or newly accumulated privileges from economic and political life and removing the hands of private interests from the levers of public power. A succession of popular movements arose towards that end in the early nineteenth century, in campaigns for everything from debtor relief to disbandment of the allegedly malevolent and 'aristocratic' Masonic lodges.[33]

By tapping into these reserves of popular anxiety and aspiration, the new politicos forged their political followings, welding the injuries and apprehensions of domination to the continuing battle over the terms of popular sovereignty. No issues of public policy struck the combined themes of democracy and class more surely than those connected with currency and banking, the motors of the market revolution. In his various pronouncements about his war against the Bank of the United States, President Andrew Jackson tied his cause to that of 'the real people', 'the humble members of society – the farmers, mechanics, and laborers', as opposed to 'the rich and powerful [who] too often bend the acts of government to their selfish purposes.' Other spokesmen were even sharper: popular government, according to one Georgia Democrat, depended on uprooting the political power of bankers, 'a class of people

[32] Richard Hofstadter, *The Idea of a Party System: the rise of legitimate opposition in the United States, 1780–1840* (University of California Press, Berkeley, 1969); Morgan, *Inventing the People*, Epilogue.

[33] Arthur Schlesinger, Jr, *The Age of Jackson* (Little Brown, Boston, 1945); John Ashworth, *'Agrarians' and 'Aristocrats': party political ideology in the United States, 1837–46* (Royal Historical Society, London, 1983); Paul Goodman, *Towards a Christian Republic: antimasonry and the great transition in New England, 1826–36* (Oxford University Press, New York, 1988).

who have built fine carriages, which they have made out of the labor
and industry of the working classes.'[34]

A full-scale revival of natural-rights claims and the prerogatives of
'His Majesty, the People' accompanied these events. 'We believe, then,
in the principle of *democratic republicanism* in its strongest and purest
sense,' the editor John O'Sullivan declared in 1838 (in his aptly named
Democratic Review). 'We have an abiding confidence in the virtue,
intelligence, and full capacity for self-government, of the great mass of
our people.'[35] Behind these words (among other things) lay a determination to sever voting rights and representation entirely from the remnants of the old 'stake-in-society' principle, a crusade which, by the
1850s, had established universal white manhood suffrage virtually everywhere, in fact if not in name. In some places, to be sure, partrician
conservatism died hard: in the early 1830s, spokesmen like Philip Nico-
laus of Virginia could still defend the freehold suffrage on the premise
that only those with 'a lasting ownership of the soil of the country'
enjoyed sufficient independence to be entrusted with the franchise. Ten
years later, however, such talk was largely limited to private grumbling,
as even stiff-necked conservative politicians rushed to court the sovereign
people.[36]

Heady as it was, however, the democratization of political life and
language had its darker side. If, by the 1830s, rich white and poor white
men spoke of each other as political equals, independent persons with
the same natural rights, the social transformation of the new country
made other Americans seem all the more dependent. Neither the Northern bourgeois 'cult of domesticity' nor the very different experiences of
Southern ladyhood did anything to relieve women's legal, economic,
and political subservience to men. Blacks, long held by whites as dependent by nature, seemed even more so with the rise of the cotton kingdom.
Nor were all white men above suspicion. Growing numbers of American
paupers, the hard-luck cases of the market revolution, were dependent
on town and city authorities for their daily bread; to some native-born

[34] James Richardson (ed.), *A Compilation of the Messages and Papers of the
Presidents*, 2nd edn (Washington, D.C., 1910), vol. 2, pp. 1153–4; Marvin
Meyers, *The Jacksonian Persuasion: politics and belief* (Stanford University Press,
Stanford, 1957), ch. 2; Warren Colquitt, quoted in Ashworth, *'Agrarians' and
'Aristocrats'*, p. 90.
[35] [John L. O'Sullivan], 'Introduction', *United States Magazine and Democratic Review*, 1 (Oct. 1838), pp. 1–15.
[36] Quoted in Merrill D. Peterson (ed.), *Democracy, Liberty, and Property:
the state constitutional conventions of the 1820s* (Bobbs-Merrill, Indianapolis,
1966), p. 389.

Protestants, the Catholic immigrants who had begun to fill the bottom rungs of the emerging working class seemed to be the mental and spiritual bondsmen of the Vatican.

Not surprisingly, then, at the very moment that state legislatures and constitutional conventions widened suffrage laws for white men, they often disenfranchised free blacks and paupers, rejected women's suffrage, and in some cases stiffened naturalization requirements. Having broken through the classical equation of property-owning and political autonomy, some of the newly enfranchised (along with those already enfranchised) bore down all the harder on those whose legal and natural submission appeared all the greater – 'peculiar people', as one New York official said of blacks in 1821, incapable of voting 'with any sort of discretion, prudence, or independence.'[37]

Except for one huge social fact, the situation might have stayed that way for a long time, with rival politicians appealing vigorously for white men's votes in a language steeped in the vocabulary of popular rights. The disagreeable fact, of course, was the extension of slavery into the western territories. In the early 1840s, there was no way to predict just how severe the political crisis over the extension of slavery would become, or how it would upset the notions of popular sovereignty hammered out over the previous four decades. Even as the crisis deepened, there were few clues that it would eventually crush the slaveholders' regime; certainly, there was nothing in the Republican Party platform of 1860 to encourage slaves or the nation's disenfranchised free blacks to believe that Lincoln's election would admit them to the polity. But Lincoln's election *was* enough to trigger Southern secession and the Civil War, and after the Union victory and ratification of the Thirteenth Amendment in 1865, the entire matter of democracy and dependence cracked open again. The old question returned in a new form: did 'the people' include the ex-slaves?

The battle over the reconstitution of the republic's key social category was complicated by the claims of yet another group, woman suffragists. Born of the reforming passions surrounding northern abolitionism, an articulate (if small) women's rights movement had begun demanding the vote as early as the 1840s. Although buoyed up in certain places by perfectionist religious notions of women's equality, the movement largely adapted the existing language of natural rights to its own cause. The famous Seneca Falls convention of 1848 began its manifesto simply by adding two words to Jefferson's opening to the Declaration of

[37] John Z. Ross; quoted in ibid., p. 215.

Independence, announcing as self-evident truth 'that all men and women are created equal.'[38] After the Civil War, suffragists pressed this argument again, only to be spurned by those who asserted that the hour belonged to the Negro. Torn by recurring ideological and factional disputes, checked by the vast presumptions of male supremacy, the cause of women's suffrage faced a rocky road over the rest of the nineteenth century.[39]

For the freedmen and their allies, on the other hand, the impressive political gains made after Appomattox only proved a prelude to a long and bitter defeat. Aided by the Freedmen's Bureau and the presence of federal troops, Southern blacks managed to secure the vote and beat back the planters' attempts to reimpose their unchallenged political rule. Into the early 1870s, black voters elected national representatives and (more important) local officials throughout the old Confederacy. The Fifteenth Amendment, ratified in 1870, confirmed – or so it seemed – the revolution in social relations triggered by the Civil War. But revolutions in American politics sometimes move backwards. A generation of Northern reformers, once energized by the prospect of emancipation, felt the pull of other causes and less optimistic ideologies. Temporarily disarranged by the war, old alliances between Northern and Southern elites revived, and in 1877 sealed the end of Reconstruction. Abandoned by the North, Southern blacks were powerless after 1877 to halt the tide of reaction that would leave them trapped in chronic poverty, segregation, and disfranchisement.[40]

With the collapse of Northern commitment to the political reconstruction of the South, with a flood-tide of immigration in full spate, and with conflicts between labour and capital at unprecedented intensity, new and harsher social vocabularies – social Darwinism, racialism, and the cult of success – began to crowd out the language of democratization and equal rights among Northern and Southern elites alike. A conspicuous sign was much more open talk of the 'mistake' of universal white male suffrage. The elite reviews looked enviously towards European schemes of educational tests, plural voting, and proportional represen-

---

[38] Elizabeth Cady Stanton, Susan B. Anthony, and Matilda Joslyn Gage, *The History of Woman Suffrage* (6 vols, Rochester, N.Y., 1881), vol. 1, p. 67.
[39] Ellen Carol DuBois, *Feminism and Suffrage: the emergence of an independent women's movement in America, 1848–69* (Cornell University Press, Ithaca, 1978).
[40] Eric Foner, *Reconstruction: America's unfinished revolution, 1863–77* (Harper and Row, New York, 1988); C. Vann Woodward, *Origins of the New South, 1877–1913* (Louisiana State University Press, Baton Rouge, 1951).

tation. In Northern cities, where immigrants and old elites vied for political dominance, conservatives brushed the discredit off the old 'stake-in-society' argument to defend special voting rights for property-owners – at least where city taxes were at stake. Late-nineteenth-century political scientists, for their part, worked hard to scotch every claim of natural right to the suffrage; the vote, to the contrary, was a 'privilege', granted by the polity on its own terms, to those – and those alone – it judged able to use it safely.[41]

In the urban North, where the reaction against universal male suffrage, bolstered though it was by a recrudescence of racialist thinking, was no match for the immigrant majorities, the result was a complicated set of compromises. Educational tests, voter registration laws, the replacement of urban ward representatives by smaller, notable-dominated city coun-cils, all worked to squeeze significant numbers of the urban immigrant poor out of the ranks of voters – though in practice the line was drawn not (as some would have preferred) between the propertied and the propertyless but between the stable and the most transient segments of a highly mobile working class. Still, the counter-attack on the terms of antebellum democracy had important consequences, not least for the woman suffrage movement. Only by compromising claims of women's equal right, by reconstructing the argument for female suffrage in terms of women's special fitness for the 'duty' of voting, did suffrage reformers early in the twentieth century finally convince male electorates to extend the mantle of the 'people' to women.[42]

In the South, the late-nineteenth-century anti-democratic reaction was bolder and more far-reaching. A certain amount of black voting had survived the end of Reconstruction, albeit in sharply diminished quan-tity. Between 1890 and 1902, however, white majorities, no longer content merely with tactics of intimidation, rushed to put in place constitutional and statutory devices which now effectively put an end to black voting in the South. The same devices, literacy tests and poll taxes, swept thousands of poor Southern whites into the ranks of the disfranchised. Deeply shaken by the Populist upheaval and by the deter-

---

[41] Daniel T. Rodgers, *Contested Truths: keywords in American politics since independence* (Basic Books, New York, 1987), ch. 5.

[42] Walter Dean Burnham, *Critical Elections and the Mainsprings of American Politics* (Norton, New York, 1970), chs 3–4; Michael H. Ebner and Eugene M. Tobin (eds), *The Age of Urban Reform: new perspectives on the Progressive Era* (Kennikat Press, Port Washington and London, 1977); Aileen S. Kraditor, *The Ideas of the Woman Suffrage Movement, 1890–1920* (Columbia University Press, New York, 1965).

mination of the wool hats, poor whites, and yeomen to restore the government to the 'people', propertied white Southerners found little to mourn. In both these ways, by the turn of the century, the struggle over the meaning of 'the people' had returned in the South in many respects to where it had been before the upheavals of the Civil War; and white, propertied Southerners had managed to reinstate something close to the terms of domination as the formal terms of Southern politics.[43]

Reaction, however, is neither the whole story nor the end of it. The Populists, though eventually routed, built an impressive democratic political culture that, despite its tinge of provincial prejudices, reformulated natural-rights talk into a many-sided attack on bankers, railroads, and the rest of the 'money interest'. Labour movements likewise described their challenges to 'capital' pre-eminently as a vindication of democracy and of the egalitarian principles of the American Revolution. Although far more ambivalent than the Populists about the uses of state power, the Knights of Labor did propose 'to exercise the right of suffrage' as part of its 'revolutionary' effort 'to establish a new and true standard of individual and national greatness'. In the mid-1880s, a string of labour insurgency campaigns brought this working-class republican language squarely into electoral politics. More generally, in their strikes and other protests, local and national labour leaders adapted the old democratic republican vocabulary to their rapidly changing, increasingly difficult circumstances, portraying 'labor in this Republic, and in the European monarchies' as 'the slave of capitalism'. Both this language and that of the Populists would remain powerful weapons for workers' and farmers' movements – including the early Socialist Party – through the era of the First World War.[44]

The first half of the twentieth century, meanwhile, brought a fitful enlargement of the boundaries of formal political rights. The First World War witnessed the completion of women's suffrage, in an atmosphere of war mobilization and strenuous appeal to patriotic duty. Twenty years later, a still more urgent series of crises – the Great Depression,

[43] J. Morgan Kousser, *The Shaping of Southern Politics: suffrage restriction and the establishment of the one-party South, 1880–1910* (Yale University Press, New Haven, 1974).

[44] Lawrence Goodwyn, *Democratic Promise: the populist movement in America* (Oxford University Press, New York, 1976); Leon Fink, 'The uses of political power: toward a theory of the labor movement in the era of the Knights of Labor', in *Working-class America: essays on labor, community, and American society*, ed. Michael H. Frisch and Daniel J. Walkowitz (University of Illinois Press, Urbana, Ill., 1983), pp. 104–22; Herbert G. Gutman, *Work, Culture, and Society in Industrializing America* (Knopf, New York, 1977).

the New Deal, and the Second World War – saw a dramatic revival of claims for 'the people'. The reversal of the anti-democratic tendencies of the post-Civil War years entailed, in part, a rethinking of the old republican category of dependence. Economic dependence on government, long the mark of disgrace, no longer seemed so critical once millions of bread-winners were thrown out of work. Though timid by the standards of European social democracy, the New Deal's experimental programmes fostered the idea that all Americans deserved certain basic rights, to be secured by government aid if necessary – including that 'one-third of a nation' whom Franklin Roosevelt described as 'ill-clad, ill-housed, and ill-fed'. The war against fascism further emboldened claims that ethnic or racialist distinctions ought to play no part in American democratic life (although these distinctions remained far sturdier in people's hearts and minds than they did in official rhetoric). Throughout American life, in its burgeoning mass culture as well as its politics, a new kind of populism coloured American political talk and a new iconography infected its imagery of a diverse people locked in arms against adversaries and adversity – however sentimental or illusory these were in their depiction of American realities.[45]

The populism of the 1930s and early 1940s gave way, after 1945, to the more hard-headed, but ultimately no less optimistic, rhetoric of 'liberal pluralism'. The term became the catch-phrase of political scientists and political intellectuals evoking a polity in which every interest would have equally legitimate access to power and in which the old inequalities of race and class would be swept away by unending economic growth and judicious government intervention. Encouraged by straws in the wind like the *Fortune* poll, not a few observers now believed that the institutions were in place finally to eradicate class resentments and the language that went along with them. Such language, Daniel Bell argued in his tone-setting work, was a genre of 'ideology' – and hence irrelevant to the pursuit of public ends.[46]

It did not take long, however, for this brave new liberal pluralist confidence to collapse in a heap, in yet another massive struggle over

[45] William E. Leuchtenburg, *Franklin D. Roosevelt and the New Deal, 1932–40* (Harper and Row, New York, 1963), p. 231; Richard H. Pells, *Radical Visions and American Dreams: culture and social thought in the Depression years* (Harper and Row, New York, 1973).

[46] Daniel Bell, *The End of Ideology: on the exhaustion of political ideas in the fifties* (Free Press, Glencoe, Ill., 1960); Robert A. Dahl, *Who Governs? Democracy and power in an American city* (Yale University Press, New Haven, 1961).

the identity and rights of the people in which the terms of class, race, and politics all converged once more. Part of the price of the New Deal and what passed for the nascent American welfare state had been non-interference with the political power of established white Southern elites, including their local autonomy in preserving segregation and black disfranchisement. By the mid-1950s, however, Southern blacks, encouraged by the growing social power of the black colleges and black churches, as well as by the anti-racist rhetoric of the Second World War, made it clear that they would stand outside the mainstream of rights no longer. Once again a social movement pressed its demands, its outrage against the yoke of caste, into the political terms of rights and sovereignty; once again, the old, legitimate language of 'the people' resurfaced to challenge exploitative dependencies. Early on civil rights organizers declared that theirs was a 'people's' fight for the soul of American democracy, and not simply the orderly mobilization of an interest group. 'The peoples wants freedom,' the young Stokely Carmichael wrote on the blackboard of a Mississippi 'freedom school' in 1964. Before the decade's end, that language had turned into the still more defiant 'Power to the People!'[47]

Not since the 1860s and 1870s had the United States witnessed such a nationwide outburst of democratic radicalism as the one that grew out of the civil rights movement and the later crusade against the Vietnam War. Something approaching a rights revolution seemed in the offing, as feminists, gay activists, native Americans, and others all demanded that the polity be recast once again and ancient discriminations dissolved at the altar of equal rights. Reaction was not long in coming. Building on widespread resentments stirred up by the uprising of those who had once been dependent (and the *Kulturkampf* which accompanied it), conservatives found their voices again, and called for a restoration of the 'traditional' values of family, flag, unity, and church. After living through the economic doldrums of the 1970s, corporate elites pressed for a dramatic scaling down of liberal commitments to social services; groups once considered as essential blocs of American pluralist democracy were now stigmatized as greedy and corrupt 'special interests'; in

---

[47] Saul Landau and Paul Jacobs, *The New Radicals: a report with documents* (Random House, New York, 1966), p. 131; James Miller, *'Democracy is in the Streets': from Port Huron to the siege of Chicago* (Simon and Schuster, New York, 1987); Todd Gitlin, *The Sixties: years of hope, days of rage* (Bantam Books, New York, 1987).

some corners of the political world, there was revived talk of the need for 'virtue', 'consensus', and 'classical order', married to a defence of unregulated capitalism as the surest arbiter of human justice.[48]

So, it would seem, the claims of domination and inequality, injected into the language of popular right, have been negated once more by the very malleability and indistinctness of that language, and swept behind the veil of a conservative, consensual image of the people. At his most elegiac, even the great spokesman of modern American conservatism waxes eloquent in the phraseology of popular sovereignty. 'We the People': this was the rhetorical anchor of Ronald Reagan's speeches to his countrymen in his second administration, a language that borrowed from the sentimental populist imagery of the 1930s but tied it to his own restorationist cause.[49] Thus the unifying, classless metaphors in the language of American politics serve a venerable purpose once more.

Yet the relationship between the languages of dominance and common right in America is no simpler in the 1980s – despite the slickly merchandised political imagery and junk-mail hucksterism – than it was in the 1780s. The common wisdom (particularly among European observers of the curious political behaviour of Americans) holds that the language of American politics was drained long ago of all social significance – that it has served to blunt whatever limited sense of class or social conflict Americans have been willing to put into words. It is far wiser, however, to recognize that the terms of politics have encouraged, and been the carriers of, social conflict. From the Revolution, through successive periods of democratization and reaction, the terms of class and politics, of dominance and common right, shifting with specific historical context and battles, have never proved permanently separable. Nor is there reason to believe that this will cease.

Even a casual listening to the utterances of George Bush, Michael Dukakis, and Jesse Jackson in the 1988 presidential campaign should have confirmed the point. If all three mouthed some of the same words – if they all claimed to be champions of 'the people' – their respective meanings, their rhythms, their very sense of who 'the people' are, were quite distinct, set off from each other by carefully considered (and often

---

[48] For example, George F. Will, *The Pursuit of Virtue and other Tory Notions* (Simon and Schuster, New York, 1982).

[49] Ronald Reagan, 'State of the Union Message', *New York Times*, 28 Jan. 1987, p. 16.

none-too-subtle) codes and gestures. At the heart of those differences, deeply implicated in every line of every speech, were those other languages of power, supposedly alien to Americans, the languages of dominance.

12

Language and interpretation: Paul Robeson before the House Committee on Un-American Activities

William Downes

The aim of this essay is to examine the role of language in historical inquiry. I will also explore some possible contribution that can be made to the understanding of history by pragmatics, the theory of language use.[1] The essay considers the problem both generally and specifically, in a brief illustrative analysis of a text: the testimony of Paul Robeson before the House Committee on Un-American Activities (HUAC) on 12 June 1956.

The problem of language

There is a *prima facie* case that language is central to the activity of historians. Documentary or literary evidence is arguably the most complete and explicit kind of historical evidence. Texts are also the tangible result of the practice of historians. Linguistic activity figures as both evidential input and explanatory output.

I would like to thank Richard Crockatt and Jacqueline Fear for discussion and references to McCarthyism and the Cold War, Roger Fowler and David Houghton as regards issues in linguistic criticism and philosophy, and especially Penelope Corfield for our long ongoing dialogue on language and history.

[1] There are a variety of definitions of pragmatics. It can be thought of as the theory of interpretation, which includes communication as a special case. See Stephen C. Levinson, *Pragmatics* (Cambridge University Press, Cambridge, 1983); Dan Sperber and Deirdre Wilson, *Relevance: communication and cognition* (Blackwell, Oxford, 1986); William Downes, *Language and Society* (Fontana, London, 1984), esp. pp. 231–364.

Language is central to the historical problematic, because the twentieth century has made language itself both central and problematic. The historian's practice implicitly takes for granted certain culturally given meta-linguistic views. But this is an area where it is dangerous to trust common sense unquestioningly. Language faces at least two ways, towards the world which it represents and towards other persons as interlocutors in social contexts. The common-sense view is that language is a transparent window on the world. The world can be represented, its objects and events discussed, without attention to the words in which it is done. Similarly, common sense regards the relation between speakers and hearers as a usually reliable 'conduit' in which mental objects like thoughts or ideas are unproblematically put into words, and hence literally conveyed to the minds of hearers through the medium of language as a kind of receptacle for thoughts.[2] I argue, to the contrary, that, in both these situations, language is problematic.

The use of language opaquely interposes itself between subject and object. And when the object is the human world, the role of language becomes even more acute, because linguistic practices are not only necessary for that world's intelligibility but, intertwined with non-linguistic practices, in many cases themselves constitute social events. Indeed the subject-object terminology, with its orientation to a perceiver viewing an object of nature, is inappropriate.

Since the positions adopted here are controversial, these points need further examination. The first claim is that the world is not 'given' to us directly. There is no knowledge that is free from a point of view. There may be a kind of direct knowledge of 'what it is like' to have a certain experience, such as pain. But what is consciously judged to be an experience of one sort of thing rather than another is possible only in terms of a representational system.

Language constitutes the primary representational system.[3] It is the

---

[2] The 'conduit' metaphor originated with Michael J. Reddy, 'The conduit metaphor: a case of frame conflict in our language about language', in *Metaphor and Thought*, ed. Andrew Ortony (Cambridge University Press, Cambridge, 1979), pp. 284–324.

[3] The term 'language' is used broadly here. What is essential to a representational theory of the mind is that the mental representations have a syntax and a semantics. In other words, 'mental' representations or 'thoughts' are language-like, either theoretical constructs from language, which are said to underlie sentences and be expressed by them, or sentences themselves regarded from a logico-semantic point of view. For a discussion of the alternatives, see David Hills, 'Introduction: mental representations and languages of thought', in

only public means of representing the way a subject believes the world to be – a means that allows for the truth and falsity of beliefs and that is objective because co-ordinated in overt practices with the behaviour and thus the beliefs of others.[4] If language is the primary system of representation, then the very intelligibility of observation is given to us by our language. This resolves the relation between subject and object, between knower and the world, into a matter of semantics, the issue of how language is directed outwards to the world.

A first objection to this position is that it appears to permit a radical relativism. All we can believe are representations, and their objectivity is guaranteed not by experience alone, but by a community of agreement in behaviour and belief. If our knowledge of the world is mediated through language, then not only might it be language-relative, but also merely 'projected' onto the world. But this assumes that there is a world which is made up of determinate objective facts and which can be truly represented only in one way. Putnam argues that objective states of affairs or facts are 'real', but nevertheless also relative to the conceptual framework in which we represent them.[5] We take realism seriously, but it is an 'internal realism', internal because of the representational system we use. It is not a 'metaphysical' realism.

In such realism, the referring expressions, such as 'photons' or 'quarks' – even if they are very theoretical and in practice and in principle inaccessible to direct experience – can be construed as referring to really existing entities. However, the theoretical superstructure is an 'edifice', and is under-determined (that is, less than fully sustained) by what we

---

Readings in Philosophy of Psychology, ed. Ned Block (2 vols, Methuen, London, 1981), vol. 2, pp. 11–20, and other articles in pt 1 of vol. 2; Jerry Fodor, *The Language of Thought* (Harvester, Hassocks, Sussex, 1976).

[4] The public nature of language as the source of its objectivity derives from Wittgenstein's 'private language argument': Ludwig Wittgenstein, *Philosophical Investigations*, tr. G. E. M. Anscombe (Blackwell, Oxford, 1953), pp. 243–315, 348–412. His anti-mentalist argument that a language must be public suggests that natural language is the primary representational system. For a mentalistic critique, see Jerry Fodor, *Representations* (Harvester, Brighton, 1981).

[5] The position on 'cultural versus conceptual relativism', 'projection', and 'internal realism' which I am adopting is that of Hilary Putnam. See H. Putnam, *The Many Faces of Realism: the Paul Carus lectures* (Open Court, LaSalle, Ill., 1987), esp. pp. 1–40; idem, *Meaning and the Moral Sciences* (Routledge, London, 1978), esp. pp. 123–38. The deep conceptual schemes upon which the realism of our representations are founded are manifestations of 'forms of life' in Wittgenstein's sense.

can observe.[6] Alternative and equally realistic 'equivalent descriptions' can be true, given different assumptions and reflecting different interests.[7] Because of such under-determination, there must be other than observational reasons for the strength of our beliefs. These are pragmatic.[8] This is so because we also agree that in principle our beliefs can be abandoned in the face of a better theory. This pragmatic acceptance of a theory and its realistic interpretation is embedded in practices such as experimentation, as well as instrumentalities such as technological success and socio-economic benefits. Internal properties such as simplicity and consistency relative to the overall system of belief and the availability of alternative theories combine with practicalities to yield social criteria for assenting to representations true 'to the best of my knowledge', 'in the opinion of experts', and 'for the time being', and which are currently indispensable.[9] Credibility increases as the indispensable and unrefuted theory satisfies pragmatic criteria over time, until it is absorbed into common sense and even into those beliefs which appear indubitable and are criteria for being and behaving as a rational member of a community.

A second objection would be to accept mental representations but to query their relationship to language. The job of psychology is the explanation of behaviour, including linguistic behaviour. In common sense or folk psychology interpretations of what we do and say, mentalistic, or 'intentional', terminology predominates. Behaviour is explained in terms of such propositional attitudes as desires, beliefs, and intentions.[10] These mental states are viewed as causally efficacious with respect

[6] W. V. Quine, 'Two dogmas of empiricism', in idem, *From a Logical Point of View* (Harvard University Press, Cambridge, Mass., 1953); idem, *Word and Object* (MIT Press, Cambridge, Mass., 1960); and idem, *Ontological Relativity and Other Essays* (Columbia University Press, New York, 1969).

[7] Putnam, *Meaning and the Moral Sciences*, pp. 41ff. and 50.

[8] Pragmatism, as a philosophical tradition that traces its origins to C. S. Pierce, William James, and John Dewey, must be distinguished from pragmatics as a branch of linguistics and the philosophy of language (see fn 1). For an introduction to pragmatism, see Bruce Aune, *Rationalism, Empiricism and Pragmatism: an introduction* (Random House, New York, 1970).

[9] Realism raises the issue of 'convergence' as one scientific theory is replaced by another. Compare Putnam, *Meaning and the Moral Sciences*, pp. 18ff., and the incommensurability of theories propounded in T. S. Kuhn, *The Structure of Scientific Revolutions*, 2nd edn (University of Chicago Press, Chicago, 1970).

[10] Propositional attitudes are relations to representations, and are central to psychological statements and theories, both folk and scientific: see Fodor, *Language of Thought*.

to behaviour. This is certainly true in historical explanations, which employ the terminology of folk psychology. For example, Collingwood argues that the task of the historian is essentially to reconstruct rationally the intentional states that are alleged to lie behind actions.[11]

The issue here is the 'reality' of the mental states referred to in such linguistic accounts of behaviour. For example, if an agent believes that such-and-such truly accounts for what he or she did, then do the meanings of the expressions employed refer to real states in his or her head? The problems raised by this are undeniably complex.[12] Both Cartesian dualism, that the mind is immaterial, and behaviourism, that mental terms refer merely to dispositions to behave, must be rejected.[13] We can focus on the relation between mind, the terms in our interpretative discourse, and brain-states described at the neurophysiological level, the level at which physical causality operates.

This essay argues for an 'internal realism' of the mind, as it also opts for a conceptually relative 'internal realism' as regards other aspects of the world.[14] Thus, it rejects a non-realist option, such as Dennett's purely instrumental position, in which mind-talk is merely an 'intentional stance' adopted towards behaviour.[15] A subtle position termed 'anomalous monism' has been defended by Davidson and Putnam.[16] Although

[11] R. G. Collingwood, *The Idea of History*, ed. T. M. Knox (Clarendon Press, Oxford, 1946), esp. p. 217: 'Unlike the natural scientist, the historian is not concerned with events as such at all. He is only concerned with those events which are the outward expression of thoughts. At bottom, he is concerned with thoughts alone; with their outward expression in events he is concerned only by the way, in so far as these reveal to him the thoughts of which he is in search.'

[12] For a survey of various possible realist and anti-realist options about propositional attitudes and mental representations, see J. A. Fodor, 'Fodor's guide to mental representation: the intelligent auntie's *Vade-Mecum*', *Mind*, 94 (1985), pp. 76–100.

[13] A summary of arguments against these positions may be found in Peter Smith and O. R. Jones, *The Philosophy of Mind: an introduction* (Cambridge University Press, Cambridge, 1986); for critiques of behaviourism, see Bloch (ed.), *Readings in Philosophy of Psychology*, vol. 1, pt 1; and J. A. Fodor, *Psychological Explanation* (Random House, New York, 1968).

[14] Putnam, *Meaning and the Moral Sciences*, pp. 48–9.

[15] Daniel Dennett, 'Intentional systems', in idem, *Brainstorms* (Harvester, Hassocks, Sussex, 1978), pp. 3–22.

[16] See Donald Davidson, 'Mental events' and 'Psychology as philosophy', in idem, *Essays on Actions and Events* (Clarendon Press, Oxford, 1980), pp. 207–44; 'Mental events' is also found in Block (ed.), *Readings in Philosophy of Psychology*, vol. 1, pp. 107–18; Hilary Putnam, 'Computational psychology and interpretation theory', in idem, *Realism and Reason*, Philosophical Papers, vol.

every particular instance of a mental state is tokened in a brain, the relationship between mind and brain is anomalous, and there are no psycho-physical laws. A given belief can be tokened differently in different brains at different times, and indeed even in different organisms or artefacts. Thus, mind cannot be simply reduced to brain. The mind is 'compositionally plastic'.[17] Furthermore, anomaly arises because of how mental states, which are meaningful representations, are interpreted. We have the possibility of alternative interpretations that are all equally objective. In addition, therefore, mental states are 'computationally plastic'.[18] A given belief may be represented and semantically interpreted in an indefinite number of ways.

This shifts our attention to the issue of interpretation, of both linguistic and non-linguistic behaviour. Our mentalistic description makes interpretative statements that 'X *wants* O,' 'X *believes* that Y *owns* O,' and 'X *intends* to *buy* O from Y,' and so on for every relevant discrimination provided by English sentences. At the level of the brain, all that is individuated are analogues of tokens of these particular sentences. But the key issue is how the meaning of these statements, and hence of the activity, is interpreted. Each interpreter has to employ his or her own beliefs in order to do this. As we shall see below, this has to be done 'holistically'.[19] Utterances require reference to an inter-related web of the interpreter's background beliefs to obtain a relevant interpretation in a given context. The attributions aim to co-ordinate the whole set of beliefs of interpreter and one interpreted, to maximize mutuality, so that the behaviour of others is rational: that is, it makes sense in terms of what the interpreter believes. In other words, interpretation is incorrigibly inter-subjective, relative to each interpreter's conceptual assumptions about how human beings are, and systematic. It does not deal with sentences or actions taken one by one in isolation.

Because of this, alternative empirically adequate interpretations are always available. Quine would argue that any account is 'objectively

---

3 (Cambridge University Press, Cambridge, 1983), pp. 139–54; also Putnam, *Meaning and the Moral Sciences*, p. 41.

[17] Putnam, *Many Faces of Realism*, p. 14. The notion that the same functional state can be instantiated in a variety of physical systems is a central tenet of functionalism in psychology; see Block (ed.), *Readings in Philosophy of Psychology*, vol. 1, pt 3; and for a popular discussion, J. A. Fodor, 'The mind-body problem', *Scientific American*, 244 (1981), pp. 124–32.

[18] Putnam, *Many Faces of Realism*, p. 15.

[19] Davidson, 'Mental events', p. 217; 'Psychology as philosophy', pp. 238–9; Putnam, 'Computational psychology', p. 149; Quine, *Word and Object*, pp. 12–13; Downes, *Language and Society*, pp. 266–97.

indeterminate' – that is, that there is no objective 'fact of the matter' as regards intentional states which would make one alternative true rather than another.[20] No alternative is what a speaker or actor 'really' believed or intended. Putnam, interpreting Quine, would hold, rather, that these alternatives are equally 'objective'. But this objective truth or reality holds only internally within the particular explanation space that embodies and practically enables an interpreter's interests.[21]

Folk psychology is a discourse we have evolved to interpret ourselves publicly and objectively. The 'rational' is the objectivity that arises from the regular co-ordination of both behaviour and accounts of behaviour that is required for social practices. This discourse postulates minds as part of the common-sense theory of what it is to be a competent person. Persons with minds can be as complex and as various as the available and possible discourses about them, consistent with their linguistic and non-linguistic behaviour. Since these discourses are reflexive, we can predict that persons in different socio-historical contexts can have different self-conceptions and thus different mentalities within the physical constraints imposed by the possible behavioural output of a human nervous system, including constraints on language behaviour.[22] At the same time, interpretative discourses are social, and therefore relatable to human interests. A consequence of this conception of mind is that behaviour and inner experience can slip through the available nets of interpretation and be unintelligible – that is, 'mad' or 'irrational' or otherwise mysterious even to the subject. Even so, the way remains open for new discourses to render it intelligible.

---

[20] Quine, *Word and Object*, esp. pp. 68–79.

[21] Putnam, *Meaning and the Moral Sciences*, pp. 41–5, 132; Putnam, *Many Faces of Realism*, pp. 20ff. For another scholar who relates language and interests, see J. Habermas, *Knowledge and Human Interests*, tr. J. J. Shapiro (Heinemann, London, 1978). Note that Putnam's 'interest relativity of explanation' most emphatically rejects the anti-realist cultural relativism that 'reality' is only and simply constructed through discourse – a view that is so characteristic of post-structuralist thought. 'Our concepts may be culturally relative, but it does not follow that the truth or falsity of everything we say using those concepts is simply "decided" by the culture. But the idea that there is an Archimedean point, or a use of "exist" inherent in the world itself, from which the question "How many objects *really* exist?" makes sense, is an illusion': Putnam, *Many Faces of Realism*, p. 20.

[22] There are limits to 'plasticity' and possible interests and conceptual schemes 'heavily determined by innate and constitutional factors': Putnam, *Meaning and the Moral Sciences*, p. 56. See also D. Davidson, 'On the very idea of a conceptual scheme', in idem, *Inquiries into Truth and Interpretation* (Clarendon Press, Oxford, 1984), pp. 183–98. The door is here possibly opened to Chomskyan

The role of pragmatics, and of cognitive science generally, is to study the general representational properties and social practices of the languages of interpretation and the development of new interpretative discourses. It operates at the level of those features that apply to all interpretation. But there is a great diversity of alternative interpretative discourses available, embodying different models of the person: for example, those of deconstruction and other literary-critical practices, psychoanalytic interpretation, critical sociology, analytical philosophy, historical writing, and so on.[23] These are all discourses through which a society enacts its interest in self-interpretation and self-postulation within the constraints imposed by the physical world.

That has clear implications for the study of history, where close attention to people as 'intentional systems' (in Dennett's phrase) is necessary. Interpretation applies not only to the subject, but also to the object of inquiry. Clearly, human history is about both collective and individual action; but the intelligibility of action, the articulable reasons that can be given to explain action, presupposes linguistic representations.

The problem of history

The primary problem for historians, then, is the interpretation of the behaviour of the people of the past, who are the objects of history, including the language that makes it intelligible.

There are two central issues. Even if the denizens of the past ostensibly spoke the historian's own language, we can assume that past sentences both had different inferential connections and were applied to different ranges of experience in ways that cannot be pre-judged beforehand. This 'hermeneutic circle' is akin to a translation problem.[24] The key is that

---

universals: see N. Chomsky, *Rules and Representations* (Blackwell, Oxford, 1980), esp. pp. 185–216.

[23] Different theories of interpretation presuppose different conceptions of the person. Compare the interpretative theories and practices available in literary criticism, A. Jefferson and D. Robey (eds), *Modern Literary Theory: a comparative introduction*, 2nd edn (Batsford, London, 1986); Catherine Belsey, *Critical Practice* (Methuen, London, 1980); Terry Eagleton, *Literary Theory: an introduction* (Blackwell, Oxford, 1983). For language, society, and the person, see Rom Harré, *Personal Being* (Blackwell, Oxford, 1983).

[24] For hermeneutics, see R. J. Howard, *Three Faces of Hermeneutics: an introduction to current theories of understanding* (University of California Press, Berkeley, 1982); P. Ricoeur, *Hermeneutics and the Human Sciences: essays on language action and interpretation*, tr. J. B. Thompson (Cambridge University

the same issue arises in the interpretation of any language, even that of our own contemporaries.

But there is a second, deep difficulty, peculiar to history. The temporality of history means that the events it interprets do not now exist, and therefore cannot be observed. Nor does the language which conceptualized those events exist. The historian's empirical contact with the evidence is uniquely problematic. The evidential base has to be the remains of past activity. Given the centrality of language, direct textual or literary evidence of this activity provides a primary basis for its interpretation. Some small portion of this will be direct relic of a speech-event, such as a transcript or a documentary record which was an integral part of that event. It may be in the form of one of a multitude of perhaps archaic discourses, each of which relates to the non-linguistic component of the event in a different way. Contrast, for example, account books directly recording estate transactions according to a given accounting practice unfamiliar today and the radically different purpose of a body of late-medieval sermons which are didactic and normative.

Both represent fragments of the intelligibilities of the past. Interpreting each of these would require differing and extensive inferences to the non-linguistic events of which they were a direct part. The bulk of literary evidence is even more indirect. Much comes to us already interpreted in prior accounts. Or an event may be only briefly referred to or implicitly alluded to in other contexts. Two simultaneous interpretative activities will be required of the historian, and, with an inevitable multiplicity of perhaps conflicting secondary sources of varying reliability, the effort required will multiply. The chain of evidence can be very complex.

Furthermore, interpretation of what was said and done is a problem not only of history. It was also in principle problematic at the time it was done. The participants may or may not have behaved unreflectingly, and may or may not have overtly rationalized their activities. But to others, it was not always clear that was really happening or why, however the matter was made overtly intelligible at the time – if it was. That can be seen from the conflicting claims that surround contemporary events and contemporary language. This was as true in the past as it is now. It is the conjecture that 'things are not always what they seem to be.' There are reasons for this. If theories are just under-determined by experience, then the correct account of what happened is available,

---

Press, Cambridge, 1981); and R. Hollinger (ed.), *Hermeneutics and Praxis* (Notre Dame University Press, Notre Dame, Ind., 1985).

although open to dispute in everyday life, as it is in history. But this assumes there *is* a unique correct account of intentional behaviour. Alternatively, consider the case if Quine is correct, and in these cases there is no 'fact of the matter'. In principle, interpretation deals with the objectively indeterminate. Alternative accounts, consistent with linguistic and other behaviour, are not decidable in relation to the facts. No interpretation is privileged, because it is what participants say that they 'really' meant in some mental arena. The same conclusion also follows if we take Putnam's view of objectivity discussed above.[25]

The consequences for history would be that we might find a pattern of assent and dissent to sentences that we conjecture people from the past might agree with as an account of what they meant when they spoke and acted. But alternative and equally valid accounts could be constructed, both by others in the past or by historians today. Historical discourse is itself, therefore, a continuing dialogue about successive reinterpretation in such matters, just as is contemporary political or personal discourse.

Historians, of course, observe and use non-linguistic evidence: for example, archaeological remains, artefacts, art, and architecture, the layout of settlements or transport systems, effects on landscape and flora and fauna, and so on. Yet these evidential objects are also the relics of intentional activity, and judgements about them will therefore also be a form of interpretative discourse. It ought to be clear that the observations involved will be theory-laden.

Similarly with historians' practices that involve quantitative techniques. Statistical information is based on enumeration of instances as instances of categories. This is so, whether the historian compiles the data-base from primary materials where control can be exercised or in the more problematic case where the statistical information is itself a primary source. Consider categories drawn from any sophisticated network of terminology: demography, criminal statistics, or economics. The terms employed in recording causes of mortality for example, are embedded in whole explanatory theories in medicine, as well as in the practical discourses of diagnosis and bureaucratic procedures. The terms

[25] The reports which speakers or agents give about what they meant is *not* privileged with respect to being the sole correct account. If it has a special historical status, it is because it is the interpretation the participants recommend, and, if sincere, is some evidence of their self-interpretation; see Putnam, *Meaning and the Moral Sciences*, pp. 46–8. For sincerity, cynicism, and self-presentation, see E. Goffman, *The Presentation of Self in Everyday Life* (Penguin, Harmondsworth, 1971).

are theory-laden, whether used in the past or today. It is this body of theory, which is presupposed in the very activity of counting instances 'as' a member of a category, which is the basis of aggregated scores.

Indeed, historical inquiry itself has its own language. How do historians represent the past in their writings? In this perspective, history itself is another kind of interpretative discourse, one that gives intelligibility to past intelligibilities. This practice itself has a history. The historian confronts the language of the past not only in terms of the current context, but in terms of the interposed texts which make up the history of historical scholarship. Such texts have already established putative facts and interpretations which define a historian's beliefs about his or her domain, both in general and for the particular historical problem under study. In both areas, an internal dialectic has been established which sets forth the issues to which contemporary historians respond. In the case of a particular historical topic, the evidential base has usually been interpreted already. The present community of historians is engaged in a cooperative dialogue and debate within the parameters set by the history of 'history'. It is also important to realize that 'history' in its present form is an institutionalized social practice, a 'discipline' in the strictly nineteenth-century sense, and therefore is itself historically constituted by methodological norms, techniques, and criteria of adequacy for interpretation and explanation. These norms govern the multiplicity of discourses that count as 'history' produced by professional historians.[26] Implicit in such norms is a philosophy of history. It follows that every historian has such a philosophy. And this and the languages of its method inform his or her conceptualization of the past. This is an 'interest' in Putnam's sense, and creates a characteristically historical 'explanation space' and its own criteria for truth and reference.[27]

Within the philosophy of history there is a tradition relevant to the above view of language and history which can be broadly called hermeneutic. It claims that there is a fundamental discontinuity of method between natural science and the sciences of man, based on the intentional nature of the object of inquiry in the latter. The contrast is often drawn between scientific explanation and hermeneutic 'understand-

---

[26] The language employed by historians thus has its own form and meaning. It is a 'register' in the sense to be defined below, and amenable to sociolinguistic analysis (see fn 34).

[27] Putnam, *Meaning and the Moral Sciences*, pp. 43ff.

ing', with its method of *verstehen*.[28] We can consider all hermeneutical traditions, broadly conceived, to pose as a central problem the method of interpretation of intentional behaviour – in particular, texts as a primary kind of social practice.[29] For example, in Dilthey's terms, 'expressions' are the means of access to the 'life-structure' (or mind) of the persons in the social context of a culture's 'objective mind'.[30]

Until recently, the dominant competing philosophical position was a positivistic view of history, the *locus classicus* of which can be found in Hempel and Nagel.[31] The influence of this stance in formulating 'the problem of history' can be readily seen by glancing at either of the Gardiner volumes of readings in the philosophy of history.[32] Interestingly, this positivistic approach to history arose in part in response to the hermeneutic claim of a divergence of method, and kind of knowledge available, between humanistic and natural science, and in part in response to speculative and idealistic views of history. It attempted to resolve history into science.

But now, with the subsequent collapse of positivistic empiricism under

[28] See fn 24 above. The term *Verstehen* is often translated as 'empathetic understanding'. It originated in nineteenth-century thought regarding 'the sciences of man', as, for example, in Comte, Dilthey, and Weber: see T. Abel, 'The operation called *verstehen*', *American Journal of Sociology*, 54 (1948–9), pp. 211–18, for references.

[29] The hermeneutic tendency has many strands and alternative approaches. In the English-speaking world, the main strands are found in philosophers influenced by Wittgenstein, e.g. von Wright and Winch, and in the social sciences. See G. H. von Wright, *Explanation and Understanding* (Routledge, London, 1971); Peter Winch, *The Idea of a Social Science and its Relation to Philosophy* (Routledge, London, 1958); Anthony Giddens, *New Rules of Sociological Method: a positive critique of interpretative sociologies* (Hutchinson, London, 1976); William Outhwaite, *New Philosophies of Social Science* (Macmillan, London, 1987). Independently, Collingwood's philosophy of history is also hermeneutic in orientation.

[30] Wilhelm Dilthey, 'The understanding of other persons and their life-expressions', tr. J. J. Kuehl, in *Theories of History*, ed. Patrick Gardiner (Free Press, Glencoe, Ill., 1959), pp. 213–25.

[31] Carl Hempel, 'The function of general laws in history', *Journal of Philosophy*, 39 (1942), pp. 35–48; repr. in idem, *Aspects of Scientific Explanation* (Free Press, New York, 1965), pp. 231–43; Ernest Nagel, *The Structure of Science: problems in the logic of scientific explanation* (Routledge, London, 1961), pp. 547–606.

[32] Patrick Gardiner (ed.), *Theories of History* (Free Press, Glencoe, Ill., 1959); idem (ed.), *The Philosophy of History* (Oxford University Press, Oxford, 1974), esp. pp. 90–105, 187–215.

the sceptical critiques of Quine, Kuhn, Feyerabend, Hesse, and post-Wittgenstein thinkers such as Winch, von Wright, and Rorty, it is possible to argue that the language of natural science is itself holistic, and its empirical observations theory-laden and thus embedded in social and historical practices and interests.[33] Quine's claim that there is no 'fact of the matter' in intentional matters drives a large wedge between science and humanistic studies. The critique, in fact, involved subjecting scientific paradigms to a sort of hermeneutic.

The empiricist is preoccupied with how empirical knowledge is derivable from experience, in history as in science. The hermeneuticist is also preoccupied with the epistemological question. But both what happened in history, actions and events, and the evidential base for historical knowledge are intentional and therefore, as we have shown, involve representations, primarily linguistic ones. The epistemological question thus resolves itself into the hermeneutic question; how is intentional activity to be interpreted? I have argued above that the interpretative discourse which is used to understand language and action is one and the same, and involves the global 'holistic' attribution of beliefs and other psychological propositional attitudes to the persons interpreted. It attempts to rationalize the behaviour of the one interpreted by maximizing mutuality of belief, on the assumption that the interests, and hence explanation space, of the two participants coincide. But as interests do vary, alternative and equally objective interpretations are consistent with what people say and do. The self-interpretation of the speaker or agent is no more objective than that of anyone else. This points to another central claim of this essay, that contemporary pragmatic and sociolinguistic techniques of analysis can help in explicitly revealing both processes: that is to say, the reconstruction of what people 'meant' and, in addition, a range of alternative interpretations of what they said and did that go beyond what they 'meant'.[34]

---

[33] See Harold Morick (ed.), *Challenges to Empiricism* (Methuen, London, 1980); Winch, *Idea of a Social Science*; von Wright, *Explanation and Understanding*; Richard Rorty, *Philosophy and the Mirror of Nature* (Princeton University Press, Princeton, 1979).

[34] We have distinguished two traditions in the philosophy of history, empiricism and hermeneutics, but have not considered a third, narrativism. For a similar, three-fold analysis, see F. R. Ankersmit, 'The dilemma of contemporary Anglo-Saxon philosophy of history', in *Knowing and Telling History: the Anglo-Saxon debate*, History and Theory, vol. 25 (Wesleyan University Press, Middletown, 1986), pp. 1–27. The key figure who has developed narrativist philosophy of history is Hayden White, *Metahistory: the historical imagination in nineteenth-*

A case-study: Paul Robeson before the House Committee on Un-American Activities

This approach can help to elucidate a specific text: the testimony of Paul Robeson before the House Committee on Un-American Activities (see Appendix). Although there are many varieties of interpretative discourse, we can distinguish three general types. First, a text can be interpreted as an act of intentional communication. In this case, the task of analysis reproduces that of an addressee. The other two types of interpretation can, and usually do, *transcend* what the speaker plausibly could be said to have intended to convey, but are nevertheless acceptable, arguably true, accounts of the text. I shall call these latter two types critical and explanatory interpretation.

In intentional communication, the interpreter attributes intentions to the speaker, an intention to communicate and an intention to convey a specific message. Successful communication occurs when the hearer comprehends the speaker's message – that is, assigns the correct intentions to the speaker. The hearer has understood the 'speaker meaning', what the speaker intended to convey.[35] The hearer will give evidence compatible with this in replies and/or subsequent behaviour. There will

---

century Europe (Johns Hopkins University Press, Baltimore, 1973). This approach recognizes that historical writing itself has its own particular linguistic and discourse structures (see fn 26 above). White's radical move is to treat historian's narrative within a literary-critical framework, developing a trope-based theory of universally possible forms of historical narrative. A possible critique of White's position would be that his system is 'structuralist'. It does not take account of the fact that historians' varieties of writing are dynamic social practices. The features which make such texts 'history', as opposed to any other kind of writing, are social and contextual, not formal. A parallel debate about formal versus social criteria for 'literariness' is taking place within literary theory itself. It is arguable that there are no underlying or formal linguistic criteria for historians' texts. Nevertheless, the linguistic study of the various rhetorical structures and modes of representation employed by historians themselves will be a most fruitful direction for a future interaction of linguistics and history. For discussions of narrativism, see *Metahistory – Six Critiques*, History and Theory, vol. 19 (Wesleyan University Press, Middletown, 1980). For a view of literature as discourse and a technique of linguistic criticism which could be applied to historians' representations of the past, see Roger Fowler, *Literature as Social Discourse* (Batsford, London, 1981), esp. pp. 1–45, 180–200; Roger Fowler *et al.*, *Language and Control* (Routledge, London, 1979); and Roger Fowler, *Linguistic Criticism* (Oxford University Press, Oxford, 1986).

[35] H. P. Grice, 'Meaning', *Philosophical Review*, 66, no. 3 (1957), pp. 377–88; see also Levinson, *Pragmatics*, pp. 16–18.

be general, observable evidence that both participants assent to the same interpretative statements as regards speaker meaning.

The problem with intentional communication arises because the literal 'core' meaning of the expressions the speaker utters are no more than skeletal clues to what the speaker intends to convey. Content has to be interpreted in context. The key to understanding communication involves contextual implications, or 'conversational implicatures' in the terminology of H. P. Grice.[36] This is a class of inference which can be drawn only in context and which the interpreter attributes to the intentions of the speaker. The point is that the intended meaning, the one required for communication to take place, is not *coded* in the utterance. It must be inferred.[37]

This process can be illustrated from our text. Consider the remark by Gordon H. Scherer, a member of the Committee, in which he interrupts the main line of questioning to ask:

27 'When was the subpoena served on you, Mr Robeson?'

The literal content of (27) is not difficult to establish; the subpoena and its service has just been identified. Scherer is requesting that the time of the service be provided. But this is not sufficient to determine what Scherer probably intended to convey. The further intended meaning has to be inferred. Robeson has just given an account of why he was unable to produce the subpoenaed documents. Scherer puts at issue the time which Robeson had to locate them. He could imply in this context that he finds Robeson's excuse unpersuasive without further information about the time elapsed between now and the service of the subpoena.

By raising this issue, Scherer perhaps also implicates that he suspects that Robeson did not attempt to comply with the subpoena diligently enough. This interpretation is corroborated a moment later in (29), when he explicitly asks whether Robeson made the effort of looking for the documents. We can move further out into the inferential network in interpreting (27). Relative to the premise that Robeson may not have been diligent in compliance, and that such lack of compliance counts as being an uncooper-

---

[36] H. P. Grice, 'Logic and conversation', in *Syntax and Semantics, vol. 3: Speech Acts*, ed. Peter Cole and Jerry Morgan (Academic Press, London, 1975), pp. 41–58; see Levinson, *Pragmatics*, pp. 97–166.

[37] The form of inference employed in utterance interpretation may be both inductive and deductive; H. Putnam, 'Reference and understanding', in *Meaning and Use*, ed. A. Margalit (Reidel, Dordrecht, 1976), pp. 199–217; T. Moore, 'Reasoning and inference in logic and in language', in *Reasoning and Discourse Processes*, ed. T. Myers, K. Brown, and B. McGonigle (Academic Press, London, 1986), pp. 51–66, and other articles in this volume; Sperber and Wilson, *Relevance, Communication and Cognition*, pp. 65–117.

ative and therefore a hostile witness, Scherer may be implicating that Robeson is a hostile witness. Furthermore, since Robeson had earlier provided an excuse for non-compliance, the questioning of that excuse could imply in this context not only its lack of credibility in Scherer's eyes, but the belief that Robeson is being evasive and disingenuous, if not untruthful. None of this is conveyed literally by the words on the page.

A theory of communication must provide an account of which of these context-dependent inferences Scherer intended to convey. According to Sperber and Wilson, the key to understanding this process is the concept of relevance.[38] In their view, relevance is a matter of degree. And the degree of relevance of any stimulus, verbal or non-verbal, to an observer is a function of the number of contextual effects that the former has upon the latter relative to the amount of effort required to derive those effects.[39] A contextual effect is the effect which the stimulus has on the observer's beliefs. For example, the contextual implication that Scherer finds Robeson's excuse unpersuasive as it stands is new information, and is therefore a contextual effect.

For communication, we need to find out what information the speaker intended to convey to the addressee. Sperber and Wilson argue that this is just what is derivable if we presume that speakers aim to be optimally relevant. This means that speakers aim to produce utterances which have an adequate number of contextual effects and to produce them in the least costly way possible. Sperber and Wilson argue that it is just these effects that the speaker intended to produce.[40] Thus, to understand a speaker's intended message, we derive contextual effects until the information we obtain seems adequate or appropriate to the situation. By definition, the first such set of contextual effects we arrive at that satisfy us will have cost us the least effort. Therefore, we conclude it is just those that the speaker intended us to derive. Intentional communication has occurred. According to the Sperber and Wilson view, the above implicature, that Scherer found Robeson's excuse unpersuasive, would be his intended message, since it was easy to derive, if it was also adequate to this communicative situation.

The trouble is, what constitutes an adequate number of effects in a given situation? It is clear that further implications and other effects can be derived through further processing and expansion of the context. If a very accessible belief is that both the audience and Robeson himself already believe that he is a hostile witness, if for no other reason than that he

[38] Sperber and Wilson, *Relevance*.
[39] Ibid., pp. 118–37.
[40] Ibid., pp. 155–71.

has been subpoenaed, then Scherer's suspicions about the excuse would strengthen this belief in the audience, and be interpreted by Robeson as a charge that he is being uncooperative. The point is that, since the notion of optimal relevance depends on the adequacy of effects in a given situation, the way is open for what is optimally relevant – and therefore intended – to vary from interpreter to interpreter (and from situation to situation) depending on how many effects they require for adequacy.

This property of variability also opens the way for critical interpretation. Sperber and Wilson distinguish 'strong' from 'weak' implicatures.[41] The former are those which seem absolutely unavoidable and for which the speaker takes responsibility. The latter are those that require more work and for which the hearer takes progressively more responsibility. It becomes relatively less sure that we can attribute them to the speaker's intentions. This latter kind of processing characterizes critical and explanatory interpretation. Because of the problem of exactly determining adequacy relative to a situation, the boundary between the strong and the weak is variable and unclear. History involves a considerable amount of the sort of interpretation I have called 'transcendent'. It quickly transcends even the disputable area of adequacy of effects, and derives implications which more and more resist the attribution of conscious intention. On the other hand, speakers often accept transcendent interpretations of their behaviour. The implications were 'implicit in their remarks' or 'unconsciously intended'.

These distinctions between types of interpretation are reflected in ambiguities in the words 'intention' and 'belief'. On the one hand, common sense construes an intention as a conscious, determinate mental act which aims at achieving a preferred goal and figures in a teleological explanation of an action. If this was the case, only Scherer can tell us whether he intended to convey that Robeson is perhaps being uncooperative, evasive, or untruthful. On the other hand, the use of intentional idiom sometimes refers to the overall teleological intelligibility of the act, irrespective of the conscious formulability of an intention by the agent. There is an exactly parallel range of ambiguity in the attribution of beliefs and motives. These two uses of the word 'intention' correspond to our distinction between reconstructive and transcendent interpretation.

The principle of relevance accounts for the interpretation of any phenomenon, not just linguistic behaviour.[42] A large chunk of theory is involved in any observation: immediately, via the core sentences

---

[41] Ibid., pp. 199ff.
[42] Ibid., pp. 151–5.

entailed, and more remotely, via the various routes through the inferential network of background knowledge. Relevance gives us a way to explain exactly what parts of this set of background beliefs are involved in the comprehension of the phenomenon. It is precisely those without which the phenomenon would be irrelevant to the observer and context.

We have seen that the interpretation of speech and behaviour is very much broader than simply reconstructive attributions of intention to speakers or actors. There are meanings that are weakly implicated, where the responsibility shifts by degrees towards the observer and attribution of intention to the speaker or actor become progressively less plausible and 'deniability' increases. In the two types of transcendent interpretation, the speaker or agent is factored out, as it were, and the evidence is placed in a context in which its relevance is determined by the interests of an interpreter. Contextual effects are derived which could not have been plausibly intended.

In critical interpretation, the interest is in explicating the behaviour or the text in terms of social structure. We reveal how social power relations are enacted of which participants were unaware.[43] In broader explanatory interpretation, the behaviour or the text is transformed into evidence for some particular explanatory hypothesis. The institution of history and the interests it defines create new contexts for explanatory interpretation. These may differ greatly from the contexts in which the behaviour originated. These new explanatory contexts set the parameters of adequate relevance for the historian. The evidence is optimally relevant to the historian as evidence for an explanation – a premise which may utterly transcend the horizons of the original participants.

Why is it possible to make true interpretative statements, which transcend the beliefs or intentions of the one being interpreted? The possibility exists because there are regularities of belief in a society which are autonomous of the particular pattern of any one individual. The same is true of the regular social practices which the beliefs render interpretable. Critical interpretation interprets individual behaviour in terms of such social regularities or 'transpersonal' meanings. The possibility of true attributions of mentalistic predicates to individuals in terms of such autonomous 'social facts', of which the individual is not consciously aware and might either accept or deny, is a strong argument that persons with minds are socially constructed.

This autonomy of the forms of discourse practice can be illustrated by viewing the interrogation of Paul Robeson in institutional terms. In the

[43] Fowler *et al.*, *Language and Control*.

sociolinguistic theory of M. A. K. Halliday, each text realizes a *register*.[44] This is a delimited range of potential contextual effects which make up a given social situation. Institutionalized situations relate to their meaning potential along three contextual dimensions which define the register: *field, tenor,* and *mode* of discourse. 'Field' refers to the type of social activity constituting the situation; 'tenor' is the range of interpersonal relations enacted in the situation; and 'mode' includes both the medium of the discourse (spoken, written, written to be spoken, monologue, dialogue) and the symbolic forms and social meanings of its genre – for example, the characteristic rhetoric of a sermon or political advertisement. The Robeson text is the realization of a register, one of the inventory of such functional forms of discourse which constitute a society. To study the registers of a society is to gain access into one aspect of what Dilthey termed 'objective mind'.[45] A register analysis of the Robeson text is given in figure 1.[46]

The linguistic patterns exhibited by the text as 'the linguistic form of social interaction' realize the social and semantic choices woven together on these three dimensions.[47] Thus, the field generates much technical legal vocabulary: *subpoena* (6), *served upon you* (7), *litigation* (52), *application . . . for certiorari* (57, 59), *affidavit* (66), and so on. Both the field and mode select a sequencing pattern of questions and answers which superficially structures the exchanges of the text and simultaneously enacts the roles specified by the tenor.

From a critical point of view, the generic structure of the text is important. The words are from legal genres, and conventionally convey the formal authority-laden nature of the situation. Thus:

19 The subpoena which requires your presence here today contains
20 a provision commanding you . . .

The documents 'require' and 'command': human beings do not. Systematic depersonalization and suppression of overt mention of agency is a feature of legal and bureaucratic language.[48] We see this again in:

---

[44] M. A. K. Halliday, *Language as Social Semiotic* (Arnold, London, 1978). 'Registers' are discussed from a historian's point of view by J. G. A. Pocock, 'The concept of a language and the *métier d'historien:* some considerations on practice', in *The Languages of Political Theory in Early-Modern Europe*, ed. Anthony Pagden (Cambridge University Press, Cambridge, 1987), pp. 19–38.
[45] Dilthey, 'Understanding of other persons', p. 216.
[46] Walter Goodman, *The Committee* (History Book Club, London, 1969), p. 16n. for the Dies Resolution cited in Fig. 1.
[47] Halliday, *Language as Social Semiotic*, p. 122.
[48] Fowler, *Literature as Social Discourse*, pp. 30–2.

89 Mr. Chairman, I respectfully suggest that the witness be
90 ordered and directed to answer that question.
91 You are directed to answer the question.

and,

41 I respectfully suggest, Mr Chairman, this document be
42 incorporated by reference in this record marked as 'Robeson exhibit
43 No. 1' and filed in the files of the Committee.
44 It will be so incorporated.
45 My counsel suggests it may not be completed.

Note that the pleonastic phrases such as 'ordered and directed' (90) or 'true and correct' (37, 38) are purely symbolic markers of the genre. They indicate the impersonal authority of the institution, and have no other meaning. Authority relations are also conventionally implicated by the address term, title only, used by counsel to chairman and by the formula 'respectfully suggest'. The acts requested rest with the authority of the chair. But the passive voice is employed to refer to the acts themselves in: 'be ordered and directed' (89–91); 'You are directed' (91); 'be incorporated by reference . . . and filed . . .' (41–3); 'will be . . . incorporated' (44), and elsewhere in the text. The agent is not specified in the interventions of the chair. The contextual effect of this is to locate the source of authority in some impersonal locus, of which the role of chairman is merely the medium.

Linguistic depersonalization, by enacting relationships defined only on legal, institutional grounds, excludes personal appeals on non-legal grounds against such authority. Note that Robeson's objection in (45) is couched in the same register, although he sometimes chooses slightly inappropriate words as, in (92–5):

92 I stand upon the Fifth Amendment . . .
94 Do you mean you invoke the Fifth Amendment?
95 I invoke the Fifth Amendment.

This exchange shows Arens invoking the linguistic authority of the register and both Robeson's position outside the framework and his unwilling submission to it. His 'political' and 'semantic' answers to the central question, 'What do you mean by that?' (78–9) and 'Would you like to come to the ballot box . . .? (87) merely invoke the reassertion of the legal register from his questioners (89–91). There is a pattern throughout the text of power and resistance to it on Robeson's part, that parallels the contrast between personal-informal and impersonal-formal language. The pattern of question and answer reflects the power

---

FIELD OF DISCOURSE

The type of social activity performed

A Hearing of the United States House of Representatives
Committee on Un-American Activities, set up under
the Dies Resolution, 1938.[a]

TENOR OF DISCOURSE

The types of interpersonal relations involved

a) Social-situational roles: chairman, director of staff,
witness, counsel representing witness, etc.

b) Conversational roles: addressor, addressee, audience, etc.

c) Speech-act roles: questioner, answerer, etc.

MODE OF DISCOURSE

The medium and symbolic organization of discourse

a) Regularized transcript of spontaneously spoken
dialogue

b) Genre: examination of witnesses
(related to, but differing from, 'legal' genres)

---

[a]The resolution reads, 'Resolved, that the Speaker of the House of
Representatives be, and he is hereby, authorized to appoint a special
committee to be composed of seven members for the purpose of conducting
an investigation of (1) the extent, character, and object of un-American
propaganda activities in the United States, (2) the diffusion within the
United States of subversive and un-American propaganda that is instigated
from foreign countries or of a domestic origin and attacks the principle
of the form of government as guaranteed by the Constitution, and
(3) all other questions in relation thereto that would aid Congress in
any necessary remedial legislation.'

Figure 1 Register of the Robeson text

differential. The superior questioner role is in the hands of Arens, in
his role as counsel. Meanwhile, Robeson is compelled by the authority
of the institution to enact the role of witness, and therefore the inferior
role of respondent. Although he sometimes attempts to reverse the roles
(8–9), (78–88), the attempts are, perhaps ironically, submissive: 'Do I
have the privilege of asking . . .?' (8); or openly ironic and rhetorical
as in (11–18), trying to escape the power of the questions.

Consider now the questions which open the Robeson text. Arens says,

1   Paul Robeson, will you please come forward?
6   Are you appearing today in response to a subpoena which
7   was served upon you by the House Committee on Un-American Activities?

The grammar of these utterances literally mark them as questions. But are they questions? Line 1 is clearly a request. Lines 6 and 7 are more problematic. Consider what it means to ask a genuine question.[49] One sincerely seeks information from the one to whom one put the question, something one does not already know and which one believes the respondent can provide. In this context, these conditions are pretty clearly not satisfied. So in spite of its grammar, (6–7) is not a genuine question. To determine what is going on here, further inferencing is necessary.

The HUAC hearings form a very complex type of situation. The tenor of the discussion is mapped in figure 2. The role of participants like Arens is not personal but institutional. He is the director of staff, as Robeson is a witness. These define rights and obligations to perform certain linguistic acts. Moreover, the proceedings are transcribed for the record which, along with reporting back to the House, is their main textual output. The record may provide grounds or evidence for subsequent prosecution. The institutional roles of participants suggests that speeches, especially on the committee side, may have a group or collective source, in which individuals like Arens speak not for themselves but as part of a public institutional mechanism. In this case, individual intentions are subsumed into a collective intentionality and institutional purpose: the aims of the enquiry. Arens is 'speaking for' the committee. This clearly changes the significance of attempts to reconstruct his intentions.

Finally, the complex audience is very important. The hearing is performed for this diverse public audience. It is transmitted to a further audience through the media, and interpreted via them. It will have political effect, in Congress and in wider political discourse. It affects the audience by adding new beliefs and information, strengthening

---

[49] The term 'question' characterizes the utterance as a speech-act. See J. Austin, *How to Do Things with Words* (Clarendon Press, Oxford, 1955); J. Searle, *Speech Acts* (Cambridge University Press, Cambridge, 1969); J. Searle, 'Indirect speech acts', in *Syntax and Semantics*, ed. Cole and Morgan, vol. 3, pp. 59–82; Levinson, *Pragmatics*, pp. 226–83. For a discussion of the relationship between such action descriptions of utterances and inferences, see Downes, *Language and Society*, pp. 322–3; Sperber and Wilson, *Relevance*, pp. 243–54; and Searle, 'Indirect speech acts', pp. 73–4.

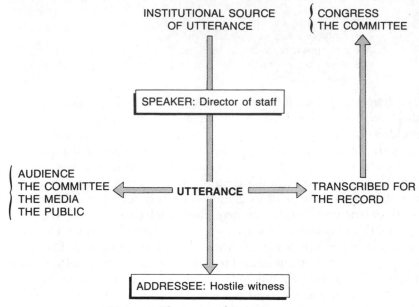

Figure 2 The tenor of Aren's utterances

already held beliefs, or revising previously held beliefs – that is, by having contextual effects.

Now consider Aren's remark in (6–7). It is not a question aimed at Robeson, although he is the addressee. Rather, it is done for the audience. It implies that if subpoenaed, Robeson has been legally compelled to appear. This information is put on the record and conveyed to the audience, to whom it may be news. There are further implications. If Robeson has been compelled to appear, it is likely that he would not have attended otherwise, and it follows that he is in all likelihood hostile to the proceedings. We will see later that in this context it also can weakly implicate that he has something to hide. Thus, in action language, we might term (6–7) a public demonstration, or coerced self-display of Robeson's status as hostile witness for the audience and the record. It follows his formal identification for the audience and the record in (1–5). It also suggests that the question and answer format of the hearing may only be superficial. This act of 'public demonstration', then, is one of the acts of this field of discourse. As such it is backed by the authority of Congress, as interpreted by the Committee.[50]

[50] Supreme Court decisions reflect alternative interpretations of the committee's activities. See A. H. Kelly and W. Harbison, *The American Constitution*, 4th

When Scherer intervenes with his questions in (27) and (29) he can now be seen to be joining in with the pattern of Arens's utterances. This places the earlier implications in a rather different context. The implication that Robeson may not have strenuously attempted to comply with the subpoena and is therefore uncooperative is now seen as not intended primarily as a message for Robeson, but instead as strongly directed to and for the wider audience and the record.

Turning to the central part of Robeson's testimony, lines 75ff., it appears to consist of a sequence of questions and answers. This befits what is superficially an investigative activity, to ascertain the degree of subversion in American life. Consider now the central question addressed to Robeson,

75   Are you now a member of the Communist Party?

This again has interrogative form. But it is most implausible that it is a genuine information-seeking question. We can take it as assumed by the Committee that they have adequate evidence that Robeson is indeed a communist, and that Arens is neither really attempting nor expecting to get that information from Robeson here. We can then ask, what is the optimally relevant interpretation of the utterance? If the proposition is considered true, then the most obvious implicature is that Committee believes, or has very good reason to think, that Robeson is a communist. But that, in itself, would not explain his reply,

76   Oh please, please, please.

Rather, we have further to assume that to the Committee being a communist is bad, and that therefore Robeson is being publicly accused or charged with communism. He is having it 'put to him that' he is a communist. In this light, all the preceding discourse has been building up evidence for the benefit of the audience and record, leading to this central charge.

Faced with an accusation, very few strategies are open in reply. One such strategy is to deny or dispute the turpitude of the charge. The success of the accusation ultimately depends, as Robeson says, on what is *meant* by 'the Communist Party'. His replies to the repeated commands to 'answer the question' corroborates the view that (75) is, in fact, an accusation:

78   What is the Communist Party? What do you mean by

---

edn (Norton, New York, 1970), esp. pp. 885–900, 1001–10; regarding HUAC, 'inquiries of this kind all too often had only a nominal legislative purpose; they were, instead, inquisitorial "trials", freed from most of the restraints of procedural due process of law.'

79		that?

. . .

81		What do you mean by the Communist Party? As far as
82		I know it is a legal party like the Republican Party and the Democratic
83		Party. Do you mean a party of people who have sacrificed for my people,
84		and for all Americans and workers, that they can live in dignity?
85		Do you mean that party?

In other words, if what Robeson says about the Communist Party is true, then being a communist cannot be the object of an accusation.

The importance of the background assumption that it is bad to be a communist again directs us into a web of belief and reveals its crucial role. Badness is not part of the literal meaning of 'X is a communist'. While this particular belief might be generated by itself to satisfy the requirements of optimal relevance in this context, for critical interpretation it is necessary to elaborate the beliefs about communism held by the Committee. We do not yet know the implicit content of the accusation. For critical interpretation, more is at stake than merely the badness of communism as an isolated assumption, although that is all we minimally need to assume to understand the question as an accusation.

There is an element of pretence here, both on Robeson's part perhaps – and on our own. Of course, we are aware of the set of beliefs of which 'Communism is bad' is a part. The set of beliefs is systematic. Its constituent assumptions are not viewed in isolation. This suggests that to the degree that a hearer is familiar with the discourses, in any register, in which any part of the belief system is required for optimal relevance, the whole system becomes more readily accessible, and therefore context-defining. This is a factor in ease of processing the rest of the text as its topics move around inside the system. The notion that background information is organized into large-scale networks or representational structures, sometimes termed 'frames' or 'schemata', which are accessed both in visual and verbal comprehension, has been proposed in cognitive science.[51] We need to study such systems of belief which seem to be 'in the air'. In doing so, we replicate the method of

---

[51] M. Minsky, 'A framework for representing knowledge', in *The Psychology of Computer Vision*, ed. P. H. Winston (McGraw-Hill, New York, 1975); Downes, *Language and Society*, pp. 295–7; T. Winograd, 'A framework for understanding discourse', in *Cognitive Processes in Comprehension*, ed. M. Just and P. Carpenter (Erlbaum, Hillsdale, N.J., 1977), pp. 63–88; R. C. Schank and R. Abelson, 'Scripts, plans, and knowledge', in *Thinking: readings in cognitive science*, ed. P. Johnson-Laird and P. Wason (Cambridge University Press, Cambridge, 1977), pp. 421–32; Putnam, *Meaning and the Moral Sciences*, p. 57; and also Sperber and Wilson, *Relevance*, p. 138.

the historian who exploits 'intertextuality' by using information derived in the comprehension of one text to understand another.[52]

'The Cold War frame' can be seen clearly in another very important text of the period, Senator Joseph McCarthy's opening statement before the Army–McCarthy hearings in 1954.[53] In this text, McCarthy makes unusually explicit the inferential connections involved in his beliefs. The most striking thing about his 'Cold War' mentality is that it is based on a war analogy. He makes this explicit a number of times; for example: '. . . of this war which we're in and it's a war.' The analogy provides the basic polarized structure of conflict between America and 'the communist organization'. According to McCarthy, it is a war which can end only 'by victory or death for this civilization', a war in which he and his colleagues 'man the watchtowers of the nation', a war which America is always in danger of losing. Communism in this theory is viewed as a mental force akin to a religion, which operates on minds to destroy freedom through a conversion of its victims into slaves. A communist 'is not a free agent . . . he has no freedom of thought . . . no freedom of expression.' McCarthy quite explicitly gives us a necessary condition for the use of the word 'communist', and thus stipulates an analytic definition or literal meaning for the term: '. . . he must take his orders from Moscow or he will no longer be a member of the Communist party.'

If we now combine McCarthy's definition of a member of the Communist Party with the concept of a war between Moscow and America, we get an inference that an American communist must be a 'traitor' and 'subversive', since he takes his orders, by definition, from the enemy in war. The Cold War frame makes it semantically impossible, because contradictory, to be both a loyal American and a member of the Communist Party. Furthermore, since we are dealing with the 'Communist conspiracy', it follows deductively that any communist accused of being just that will deny it, since secretive collusion for bad purposes is the meaning of the term 'conspiracy'. It is possible to see very clearly how these beliefs lock together in a network of inferential relations. This tightly organized and extreme Cold War frame system is also quite clearly related both to pre-war patterns of anti-communist

---

[52] 'Intertextuality' originates with Julia Kristeva, *Sémiotiké: recherches pour une sémanalyse* (Seuil, Paris, 1969); see T. Hawkes, *Structuralism and Semiotics* (Methuen, London, 1977), p. 144.

[53] U.S. Congress/Senate Special Sub-Committee on Investigations of Committee on Government Operations, *Special Investigation*, 83rd Congress, 2nd Session, 1954: opening statement by Senator Joseph McCarthy.

belief, to other systems of 'radical right' belief, and to more subtle and moderate versions of the same system – for example, in the original Cold War conceptualization of international relations by George Kennan which formed the basis for the consensus in post-war US policy.[54]

A deeper understanding of the implications of line 75 of the Robeson text is now possible. His initial reply, that since communism is not bad, therefore he cannot be accused of being a communist, fails, because by definition a communist is under the orders of the enemy in a war, is therefore subversive, and therefore bad. The optimal relevance of Robeson's reply to the Committee, and to anyone who shares the Cold War frame in its McCarthy form, would be that his response to the charge is predictable from his role in the conspiracy, and is evidence of that role. His statement that communists have helped his people merely confirms his mental enslavement. All Robeson's replies, including his repeated invocation of the Fifth Amendment, serve merely to demonstrate his communism. If one already affirmed the belief system, Robeson's replies would simply strengthen one's assumptions. If one did not, the demonstration might lend it credibility.

The content of the accusation in line 75 can now be spelled out. Because he is a communist, Robeson is charged with being a subversive in the Cold War. The overall structure of Robeson's testimony can be seen as a repeated process of accusation, reply, and reaccusation, in which Robeson's strategies of reply serve as an inexorable repetitive demonstration of his guilt relative to the Cold War frame, for the audience and the record. This demonstration is, of course, unintentional. He is being forced against his will by the discourse structure to demonstrate his guilt. The question-answer investigative pattern is only superficial. It is in this sense that discourse is opaque. The discourse-enacted power of the Committee traps Robeson like an insect displayed on a pin.

We have arrived at a critical interpretation in which we see that the purportedly investigative question-answer structure of the discourse is only superficial. Rather, the outcome of the Committee proceeding is

---

[54] For Kennan's 'Long telegram' and the Riga axioms, see D. Yergin, *Shattered Peace* (Penguin, Harmondsworth, 1977), pp. 17–41; George Kennan, 'The sources of Soviet conduct', in Walter Lippmann, *The Cold War* (Harper and Row, New York, 1972); originally published in *Foreign Affairs*, July 1947. For discussions of American anti-communism, see Alan Harper, *The Politics of Loyalty* (Greenwood, Westport, Ct, 1969); R. Griffith and A. Theoharis (eds), *The Specter* (Franklin Watts, New York, 1974); R. Freeland, *The Truman Doctrine and the Origins of McCarthyism* (New York University Press, New York, 1985).

that Robeson 'stands accused' or 'publicly charged' with being a communist, and therefore subversive, in the eyes of the audience and for the record. This practice of unwilling self-demonstration is the central social activity of the field of discourse of the Committee, at least when a hostile witness is involved.[55]

On a more abstract explanatory level, we can propose that Robeson is enmeshed in a social and linguistic practice in which the Committee attaches stigma to him. We could then consider the function of stigma-attachment in the McCarthy period and in general in US politics. Henceforth, Robeson bears the stigma of being a communist in all public situations. The discourse has actually transformed his status, much as if he bore the stigma of mental illness or a criminal record. As is well known, appearance before or being named by the Committee had a real and profound effect on people's lives and their subsequent careers.[56] The bad attribute, the source of the stigma, becomes the most accessible background information in determining the relevance of what that person subsequently says and does. Of course, stigma-attachment or its milder form, 'smearing', is a general strategy in political discourse. Note that it is not achieved, *pace* Winch, by following a rule.[57] It is an automatic result of the application of a term from a system of belief to one who stands over and against it, as the 'other'. It is relative to the beliefs one holds. Since political discourse is the institutional linguistic form of social conflict which involves implicit divisions of beliefs in a community, stigma arises naturally in this context.

The above interpretations transcend any communicative intentions of the participants in the hearings. It is unlikely that they would be acceptable to Arens or Scherer as an account of what they consciously thought they were doing. Members of the Committee would in all likelihood refer to its investigative brief: to establish 'the facts' and aid Congress in establishing the need for any remedial legislation or to reveal to the American public what is really taking place. It is clear that transcendent interpretations, although objective and true within the explanation space created by our interests and values, cannot readily be said to be going on in the minds or brains of Committee members. This is one way in which there is an objective indeterminacy in

[55] There are different patterns with different types of witness. Repentant witnesses are invited to 'name names', and this attaches the charge of communism to those thus named in an ever-expanding web of suspected subversion.

[56] Martin Bauml Duberman, *Paul Robeson* (Bodley Head, London, 1989); and see review by Eric Bentley, *Times Literary Supplement*, 12–18 May 1989.

[57] Winch, *Idea of a Social Science*, esp. pp. 51ff.

interpretation. All these equivalent construals can be true within their varying frames of reference.[58] If intentional terms are to be used at this level, it would appear that they refer to the 'intents', 'beliefs', and 'motives' of the institution – in other words, the social *functions* realized by its linguistic practices – which individuals, wittingly or unwittingly, enact with various degrees of self-consciousness. They are 'caught up in an historical process larger than themselves', and 'only doing their jobs'.

We can now see clearly the limitations of Collingwood's view of the distinctiveness of the historian's task. He seems to restrict historical interpretation to intentional action, the linguistic guise of which would be intentional communication. *Verstehen*, from this point of view, can be construed as simply the normal inferential way in which informative intentions are comprehended.[59] Presumably, such reconstructive interpretation aims to produce intentional accounts that are limited to what participants themselves would assent to, if they were able. But this is clearly wrong as a description of historians' practice. Historians are just as likely to interpret their subject-matter in an explanatory way. Discourse analysis also gives a fairly rigorous way of making analytically visible those fragments of the subject's web of belief that are required for interpretation, and of studying the structure and dynamics of belief systems in general, in individuals and in societies.

Belief systems are also the product of public discourses. This raises further interesting problems for historians, such as the possible constraints on the way belief systems change or resist change in terms of their dual role of comprehending stimuli and rationalizing social practices. Do belief systems evolve or change catastrophically? I have argued elsewhere that the wave theory of language change may be applicable to those revisions in background belief which necessarily

---

[58] It is possible that the best 'rational reconstruction' of a person's behaviour, in the light of a global overall picture, need not be the one that they would offer themselves. A person's rationalization of his or her own pattern of behaviour contains inconsistencies. If this is true, some 'transcendent' interpretation may be the *best* account; but, nevertheless, the mental states it ascribed to a participant would not be inscribed in their brains at all. See H. Putnam, 'Computational psychology', pp. 153–4; and Davidson, 'Mental events'. Note the differences on the 'evaluative' dimension in the interpretations in this case.

[59] *Verstehen* signifies the 'holistic' global nature of interpretation and also its non-demonstrative or inductive uncertainty. It remains problematic in that these processes resist explicit formalization. There are strategies, but no mechanical procedures, for hypothesis formation: see Putnam, *Meaning and the Moral Sciences*, pp. 67–8, 73–5.

precede semantic change.[60] And, finally, what is the specific relation of belief to material and other interests of a personal, social, or ideological nature?

It would seem to be impossible to talk about objective historical facts in the sense that there is only one correct account of what *really* happened in history. We cannot provide a secure epistemological foundation for the subject in the positivist sense. Rather, the process of interpretation itself, in the normative context of historians' practice, provides a hermeneutic basis for history. Empirical facts in history are hermeneutical. Historical explanations range over aggregates of interpreted intentional activities of the people of the past. The relevant lowest-level accounts of these activities usually employ mentalistic language; they are psychological. Since we have said that there are no psycho-physical laws, if only the physical has causal power, then it also follows that there will be no general laws in history.[61]

[60] Downes, *Language and Society*, pp. 291–3. The importance of the structure of belief systems (frames, schemas) in interpretation opens the door to a sympathetic reappraisal of nineteenth-century idealist views of history.

[61] 'Scientific' laws can be stated in formal terms, and are causally interpreted: Davidson, 'Mental events', pp. 222–5. However, this does not mean that interpretation in humanistic and social studies does not yield genuine knowledge: Putnam, *Meaning and the Moral Sciences*, pp. 57, 66–94.

Appendix to chapter 12

Subcommittee of the House Committee on Un-American Activities, convened at 10 a.m., 12 June 1956.[a]

1   MR ARENS: Paul Robeson, will you please come forward? Please identify
2   yourself by name, residence and occupation.
3   MR ROBESON: My name is Paul Robeson. I live at 16 Jumel Terrace,
4   New York City, and I am an actor and singer by occupation, and law on
5   the side now and then.
6   MR ARENS: Are you appearing today in response to a subpoena which
7   was served upon you by the House Committee on Un-American Activities?
8   MR ROBESON: Just a minute. Do I have the privilege of asking whom
9   I am addressing and who is addressing me?
10   MR ARENS: I am Richard Arens.
11   MR ROBESON: What is your position?
12   MR ARENS: I am Director of the Staff. Are you appearing today in response
13   to a subpoena served upon you by this Committee?
14   MR ROBESON: Oh, yes.
15   MR ARENS: And you are represented by counsel?
16   MR ROBESON: I am.
17   MR ARENS: Counsel, will you kindly identify yourself?
18   MR FRIEDMAN: Milton H. Friedman.
19   MR ARENS: The subpoena which requires your presence here today contains
20   a provision commanding you to produce certain documents, including
21   all the United States passports issued to you for travel outside the
22   continental limits of the United States. Do you have those documents?
23   MR ROBESON: No. There are several in existence, but I have moved
24   several times in the last year, and I could not put my hands on them.

[a] E. Bentley (ed.), *Thirty Years of Treason: excerpts from hearings before the House Committee on Un-American Activities, 1938–68* (Thames and Hudson, London, 1972), pp. 770–4.

25 They probably could be produced. I lived in Connecticut and we have got
26 a lot of stuff still packed. If they are unpacked I will be glad to send them
to you.
27 MR SCHERER: When was the subpoena served on you, Mr Robeson?
28 MR ROBESON: I have forgotten. It was about a couple weeks ago.
29 MR SCHERER: Did you look for the documents?
30 MR ROBESON: I have looked a great deal, and Mrs Robeson, who has charge
31 of all of this, has looked and we have not been able to put our hands
32 upon them. There is no reason not to produce them, certainly, if I could
33 find them.
34 MR ARENS: Did you file a passport application on July 2, 1954?
35 MR ROBESON: I have filed about twenty-five in the last few months.
36 MR ARENS: I lay before you a photostatic copy of a passport application
37 bearing a signature, Paul Robeson, and ask you if that is a true and
38 correct reproduction of the passport application which you filed on
39 July 2, 1954.
40 MR ROBESON: That is true.
41 MR ARENS: I respectfully suggest, Mr Chairman, this document be
42 incorporated by reference in this record marked as 'Robeson exhibit
43 No. 1' and filed in the files of the Committee.
44 THE CHAIRMAN: It will be so incorporated.
45 MR ROBESON: My counsel suggests it may not be completed.
46 MR FRIEDMAN: May I make a statement, please?
47 THE CHAIRMAN: Counsel is permitted to accompany his client for the
48 purpose of advising his client and not for the purpose of making statements.
49 MR FRIEDMAN: I am familiar with the rules, that is why I asked your
50 permission. May I make this statement to you, sir? I wish to make
51 a protest against questioning Mr Robeson with respect to his passport
52 application, in view of the fact that there is litigation now pending
53 concerning his passport application and Mr Robeson's right to a passport.
54 The litigation was tried in district court and it was the subject of a
55 decision in the court of appeals in the circuit last week. There may be
56 further hearings in the State Department and there may be a further appeal.
57 THE CHAIRMAN: Was an application made for *certiorari*?
58 MR FRIEDMAN: No, the time has not yet elapsed for an application for
59 *certiorari* but there may possibly be. I am not his counsel in that case,
60 and I am not speaking for counsel, but there may be a hearing somewhere
61 with respect to this matter.
62 THE CHAIRMAN: That is too nebulous.
63 MR FRIEDMAN: The procedure now calls for it, and it is not nebulous.
64 MR ARENS: Now, during the course of the process in which you were
65 applying for this passport, in July of 1954, were you requested to
66 submit a non-Communist affidavit?
67 MR ROBESON: We had a long discussion – with my counsel, who is in the
68 room, Mr [Leonard B.] Boudin – with the State Department, about

69 just such an affidavit and I was very precise not only in the application
70 but with the State Department, headed by Mr Henderson and Mr McLeod,
71 that under no conditions would I think of signing any such affidavit,
72 that it is a complete contradiction of the rights of American citizens.
73 MR ARENS: Did you comply with the requests?
74 MR ROBESON: I certainly did not and I will not.
75 MR ARENS: Are you now a member of the Communist Party?
76 MR ROBESON: Oh please, please, please.
77 MR SCHERER: Please answer, will you, Mr Robeson?
78 MR ROBESON: What is the Communist Party? What do you mean by
79 that?
80 MR SCHERER: I ask that you direct the witness to answer the question.
81 MR ROBESON: What do you mean by the Communist Party? As far as
82 I know it is a legal party like the Republican Party and the Democratic
83 Party. Do you mean a party of people who have sacrificed for my people,
84 and for all Americans and workers, that they can live in dignity?
85 Do you mean that party?
86 MR ARENS: Are you now a member of the Communist Party?
87 MR ROBESON: Would you like to come to the ballot box when I vote
88 and take out the ballot and see?
89 MR ARENS: Mr Chairman, I respectfully suggest that the witness be
90 ordered and directed to answer that question.
91 THE CHAIRMAN: You are directed to answer the question.
   (The witness consulted with his counsel.)
92 MR ROBESON: I stand upon the Fifth Amendment of the American
93 Constitution.
94 MR ARENS: Do you mean you invoke the Fifth Amendment?
95 MR ROBESON: I invoke the Fifth Amendment.
96 MR ARENS: Do you honestly apprehend that if you told this Committee
97 truthfully –
98 MR ROBESON: I have no desire to consider anything. I invoke the
99 Fifth Amendment, and it is none of your business what I would like
100 to do, and I invoke the Fifth Amendment. And forget it.
101 THE CHAIRMAN: You are directed to answer that question.
102 MR ROBESON: I invoke the Fifth Amendment, and so I am answering
103 it, am I not?
104 MR ARENS: I respectfully suggest the witness be ordered and directed
105 to answer the question as to whether or not he honestly apprehends,
106 that if he gave us a truthful answer to this last principal question,
107 he would be supplying information which might be used against him
108 in a criminal proceeding.
   (The witness consulted with his counsel.)
109 THE CHAIRMAN: You are directed to answer that question, Mr
110 Robeson.
111 MR ROBESON: Gentlemen, in the first place, wherever I have been in

112 the world, Scandinavia, England, and many places, the first to die
113 in the struggle against Fascism were the Communists and I laid many
114 wreaths upon graves of Communists. It is not criminal, and the
115 Fifth Amendment has nothing to do with criminality. The Chief
116 Justice of the Supreme Court, Warren, has been very clear on that
117 in many speeches, that the Fifth Amendment does not have anything
118 to do with the inference of criminality. I invoke the Fifth Amendment.
119 MR ARENS: Have you ever been known under the name of 'John
120 Thomas'?
121 MR ROBESON: Oh, please, does somebody here want – are you suggesting –
122 do you want me to be put up for perjury some place – 'John Thomas'!
123 My name is Paul Robeson, and anything I have to say, or stand for,
124 I have said in public all over the world, and that is why I am here
125 today.
126 MR SCHERER: I ask that you direct the witness to answer the question.
127 He is making a speech.

Select bibliography

Language

The study of language has endless ramifications, including its physiology and psychobiology, its grammar, syntax, lexicology, and phonetics, its conceptual structures, its cultural and distributional geography, its social applications, its verbal and literary output, the critical interpretation of its forms and meanings (in both speech and text), and its role in human cognition and expression – let alone the history of all these aspects. There are also instructive parallels with other systems of communication such as mathematical notation and music, as well as non-verbal communication via body language, dress, sign language, and visual representation.

Linguistics/sociolinguistics

To augment this brief listing, see bibliographies in Cameron, Crystal (plus glossary), Devitt and Sterelny, Lyons, and Ong (listed below).

Aarsleff, H., *From Locke to Saussure: essays on the study of language and intellectual history*, Athlone Press, London, 1982.

Bynon, T., *Historical Linguistics*, Cambridge University Press, Cambridge, 1977.

Cameron, D., *Feminism and Linguistic Theory*, Macmillan, London, 1985.

Chase, S., *The Tyranny of Words*, Methuen, London, 1938.

Chomsky, N., *Rules and Representations*, Blackwell, Oxford, 1980.

Crystal, D. (ed.), *The Cambridge Encyclopaedia of Language*, Cambridge University Press, Cambridge, 1987.

Culler, J., *Saussure*, Fontana, London, 1976; revised, 1988.

Devitt, M. and Sterelny, K., *Language and Reality: an introduction to the philosophy of language*, Blackwell, Oxford, 1987.

Downes, W., *Language and Society*, Fontana, London, 1984.

Eco, U., *A Theory of Semiotics*, Macmillan, London, 1977.

Fasold, R., *The Sociolinguistics of Society*, Blackwell, Oxford, 1984.

Fowler, R., *Linguistic Criticism*, Oxford University Press, Oxford, 1986.

Gazdar, G., *Pragmatics: implicature, presupposition, and logical form*, Academic Press, New York, 1979.

Grace, G. W., *The Linguistic Construction of Reality*, Croom Helm, London, 1987.

Habermas, J., *Communication and the Evolution of Society*, tr. T. McCarthy, Heinemann, London, 1979.

Harris, R., *The Language Myth*, Duckworth, London, 1981.

Lyons, J., *Language and Linguistics: an introduction*, Cambridge University Press, Cambridge, 1981.

Ong, W. J., *Orality and Literacy: the technologizing of the word*, Methuen, London, 1982.

Quine, W. V. O., *Word and Object*, MIT Press, Cambridge, Mass., 1960.

Robins, R. H., *A Short History of Linguistics*, Longmans, London, 1967.

Romaine, S., *Socio-historical Linguistics: its status and methodology*, Cambridge University Press, Cambridge, 1982.

Saussure, F. de, *Course in General Linguistics*, tr. W. Baskin, Peter Owen, London, 1960; McGraw-Hill, New York, 1966; Fontana, London, 1974.

Silverman, D. and Torode, B., *The Material World: some theories of language and its limits*, Routledge, London, 1980.

Stubbs, M., *Language and Literacy: the sociolinguistics of reading and writing*, Routledge, London, 1980.

Trudgill, P., *Sociolinguistics: an introduction to language and society*, Penguin, Harmondsworth, 1974; revised, 1983.

Textual analysis/literary theory

In addition to this introductory listing, there are detailed bibliographies in Culler, Hawkes, and Howard (listed below).

Bakhtin, M. M., *Speech Genres and Other Late Essays*, tr. V. W. McGee, University of Texas Press, Austin, 1986.

Barthes, R., *Elements of Semiology*, tr. A. Lavers and C. Smith, Cape, London, 1967.

Belsey, C., *Critical Practice*, Methuen, London, 1980.

Culler, J., *Structuralist Poetics: structuralism, linguistics, and the study of literature*, Cornell University Press, Ithaca, 1975.

Derrida, J., *Writing and Difference*, tr. A. Bass, Routledge, London, 1978.

Eagleton, T., *Literary Theory: an introduction*, Blackwell, Oxford, 1983.

Foucault, M., *The Archaeology of Knowledge*, tr. A. M. Sheridan Smith, Tavistock, London, 1972.

Goodheart, E., *The Skeptic Disposition in Contemporary Criticism*, Princeton University Press, Princeton, 1984.

Hartman, G. H., *Criticism in the Wilderness: the study of literature today*, Yale University Press, New Haven, 1980.

Hawkes, T., *Structuralism and Semiotics*, Methuen, London, 1977.

Howard, R. J., *Three Faces of Hermeneutics: an introduction to current theories of understanding*, University of California Press, Berkeley, 1982.

Jackson, J. R. de J., *Historical Criticism and the Meaning of Texts*, Routledge, London, 1989.

Jameson, F., *The Prison-House of Language: a critical account of structuralism and Russian formalism*, Princeton University Press, Princeton, 1972.

Jefferson, A. and Robey, D. (eds), *Modern Literary Theory: a comparative introduction*, Batsford, London, 1982.

Lentricchia, F., *After the New Criticism*, Athlone Press, London, 1980.

Macherey, P., *A Theory of Literary Production*, tr. G. Wall, Routledge, London, 1978.

Newton, K. M., *Interpreting the Text: a critical introduction to the theory and practice of literary interpretation*, Harvester Wheatsheaf, London, 1990.

Norris, C., *Deconstruction: theory and practice*, Methuen, London, 1982.

Pettit, P., *The Concept of Structuralism: a critical analysis*, Gill and Macmillan, Dublin, 1975.

Ricoeur, P., *Hermeneutics and the Human Sciences: essays on language, action and interpretation*, tr. J. B. Thompson, Cambridge University Press, Cambridge, 1981.

Said, E. W., *The World, the Text and the Critic*, Faber, London, 1984.

Veeser, H. A. (ed.), *The New Historicism*, Routledge, New York, 1989.

Wellek, R., *A History of Modern Criticism, 1750–1950*, vols 1–4, Cambridge University Press, Cambridge, 1981–3; vols 5–6, Yale University Press, New Haven, 1986.

Williams, R., *Marxism and Literature*, Oxford University Press, Oxford, 1977.

Young, R. (ed.), *Untying the Text: a post-structuralist reader*, Routledge, London, 1981.

History

There is a significant specialist literature on historiology, or the philosophy and history of the study of the past, which analyses theories, methodologies, and the work of past and present historians. For a massive 48 pp. bibliography, see Lloyd (listed below). The following brief list focuses upon debates about the nature of historical interpretation, including recent overviews of language and history.

Anderson, P., *In the Tracks of Historical Materialism: the Wellek Library lectures*, Verso, London, 1983.

Aron, R., *Introduction to the Philosophy of History: an essay on the limits of historical objectivity*, tr. G. J. Irwin, Weidenfeld, London, 1961.

Bloch, M., *The Historian's Craft*, tr. P. Putnam, Manchester University Press, Manchester, 1954.

Burke, P., 'Introduction', in *The Social History of Language*, ed. P. Burke and R. Porter, Cambridge University Press, Cambridge, 1987, pp. 1–20.

Butterfield, H., *The Whig Interpretation of History*, Bell and Sons, London, 1931, 1950.

Callinicos, A., *Making History: agency, structure and change in social theory*, Polity Press, Cambridge, 1987.

Carr, E. H., *What is History?* Macmillan, London, 1961; Penguin, Harmondsworth, 1964.

Collingwood, R. G., *The Idea of History*, ed. T. M. Knox, Clarendon Press, Oxford, 1946.

Gardiner, P., *The Nature of Historical Explanation*, Oxford University Press, Oxford, 1952.

Gardiner, P. (ed.), *The Philosophy of History*, Oxford University Press, Oxford, 1974.

Hexter, J. H., *The History Primer*, Basic Books, New York, 1971; Allen Lane, London, 1972.

Koselleck, R., *Futures Past: on the semantics of historical time*, tr. K. Tribe, MIT Press, Cambridge, Mass., 1985.

Lloyd, C., *Explanations in Social History*, Blackwell, Oxford, 1986.

Marwick, A., *The Nature of History*, Macmillan, London, 1970.

Parker, C., *The English Historical Tradition since 1850*, John Donald, Edinburgh, 1990.

Pocock, J. G. A., 'The concept of a language and the *métier d'historien*: some considerations on practice', in *The Languages of Political Theory in Early-Modern Europe*, ed. A. Pagden, Cambridge University Press, Cambridge, 1987, pp. 19–38.

Popper, K. R., *The Poverty of Historicism*, Routledge, London, 1957.

Ricoeur, P., *Time and Narrative*, tr. K. McLaughlin and D. Pellauer, 3 vols, University of Chicago Press, Chicago, 1984–8.

Schlöttler, P., 'Historians and discourse analysis', *History Workshop Journal*, 27 (1989), pp. 37 65.

Stone, L., 'History and the social sciences in the twentieth century', 1976, in idem, *The Past and the Present Revisited*, Routledge, London, 1987, pp. 3–44.

Thompson, E. P., *The Poverty of Theory and Other Essays*, Merlin Press, London, 1978.

Unger, R. M., *False Necessity: anti-necessitarian social theory in the service of radical democracy*, Cambridge University Press, Cambridge, 1987.

Walsh, W. H., *An Introduction to Philosophy of History*, Hutchinson, London, 1951; revised, 1967.

White, H., *The Content of Form: narrative discourse and historical representation*, Johns Hopkins University Press, Baltimore, 1987.

Wright, G. H. von, *Explanation and Understanding*, Routledge, London, 1971.

Class

The concept of 'class' has generated much debate: some argue for its existence; some refute it; many vaguely assume it. This listing introduces some historic systems of social classification. For a detailed bibliography, see Calvert (below).

Abbott, P. and Sapsford, R., *Women and Social Class*, Tavistock, London, 1987.

Amussen, S. D., *An Ordered Society: gender and class in early modern England*, Blackwell, Oxford, 1988.

Bendix, R. and Lipset, S. M. (eds), *Class, Status and Power: social stratification in comparative perspective*, Free Press, Glencoe, Ill., 1953; Routledge, London, 1967.

Bernstein, B., *Class, Codes and Control*, vol. 1: *theoretical studies towards a sociology of language*, Routledge, London, 1971.

Briggs, A., 'The language of "class" in early nineteenth-century England', in *Essays in Labour History: in memory of G. D. H. Cole*, ed. A. Briggs and J. Saville, Macmillan, London, 1960, pp. 43–73; reprinted in A. Briggs, *The Collected Essays of Asa Briggs*, vol. 1: *words, numbers, places, people*, Harvester, Brighton, 1985, pp. 3–33.

Calvert, P., *The Concept of Class: an historical introduction*, Hutchinson, London, 1982.

Cole, G. D. H., 'The conception of the middle classes', in idem, *Studies in Class Structure*, Routledge, London, 1955, pp. 78–100.

Cox, O. C., *Caste, Class, and Race: a study in social dynamics*, Monthly Review Press, New York, 1948.

Cressy, D., 'Describing the social order of Elizabethan and Stuart England', *Literature and History*, 3 (1976), pp. 29–44.

Duby, G., *The Three Orders: feudal society imagined*, tr. A. Goldhammer, University of Chicago Press, Chicago, 1980.

Dumont, L., *Homo Hierarchicus: the caste system and its implications*, tr. M. Sainsbury, Weidenfeld, London, 1970.

Furbank, P. N., *Unholy Pleasure or the Idea of Social Class*, Oxford University Press, Oxford, 1985.

Inden, R. B. and Marriott, M., 'Caste systems', *Encyclopaedia Britannica*, 15th edn, Chicago, 1974.

Jones, G. Stedman, *Languages of Class: studies in English working class history, 1832–1982*, Cambridge University Press, Cambridge, 1983.

Lukács, G., *History and Class Consciousness: studies in Marxist dialectics*, tr. R. Livingstone, Merlin Press, London, 1971.

Marwick, A., *Class: image and reality in Britain, France and the USA since 1930*, Collins, London, 1980.

Mohl, R., *The Three Estates in Medieval and Renaissance Literature*, Columbia University Studies, New York, 1933.

Mousnier, R., *Social Hierarchies: 1450 to the present*, tr. P. Evans, Croom Helm, London, 1973.

Neale, R. S., *Class in English History, 1680–1850*, Blackwell, Oxford, 1981.

Ossowski, S., *Class Structure in the Social Consciousness*, tr. S. Patterson, Routledge, London, 1963.

Rosen, H., *Language and Class: a critical look at the theories of Basil Bernstein*, Falling Wall Press, Bristol, 1972.

Sewell, W. H., *Work and Revolution in France: the language of labor from the Old Regime to 1848*, Cambridge University Press, Cambridge, 1980.

Thompson, E. P., 'Eighteenth-century English society: class struggle without class?', *Social History*, 3 (1978), pp. 133–65.

Wallech, S., ' "Class versus rank": the transformation of eighteenth-century English social terms and theories of production', *Journal of the History of Ideas*, 47 (1986), pp. 409–31.

Williams, R., *Keywords: a vocabulary of culture and society*, Fontana, London, 1976.

Notes on contributors

Penelope J. Corfield is Reader in History at Royal Holloway and Bedford New College, University of London. She is author of *The Impact of English Towns, 1700–1800* (Oxford University Press, Oxford, 1982) and writes on urban, social, and cultural history.

Geoffrey Crossick is Reader in History at the University of Essex. He has edited collections of essays on European shopkeepers and on Britain's lower middle class, and is author of *An Artisan Elite in Victorian Society: Kentish London, 1840–80* (Croom Helm, London, 1978).

William Downes is Lecturer in Linguistics at the School of English and American Studies at the University of East Anglia. He writes on sociolinguistics and belief systems, and is author of *Language and Society* (Fontana, London, 1984).

Philip A. Kuhn is Professor of History and of East Asian Languages and Civilizations at Harvard University. He is author of *Rebellion and its Enemies in Late Imperial China: militarization and social structure, 1796–1864* (Harvard University Press, Cambridge, Mass., 1970) and other studies of East Asian history and culture.

James Van Horn Melton is Associate Professor of History at Emory University, Atlanta, Georgia. He writes on the eighteenth-century German states, and is author of *Absolutism and the Eighteenth-Century Origins of Compulsory Schooling in Prussia and Austria* (Cambridge University Press, Cambridge, 1988).

Roger Mettam is Reader in History at Queen Mary and Westfield

College, University of London. He has edited a collection of documents on seventeenth-century French government and society, and is author of *Power and Faction in Louis XIV's France* (Blackwell, Oxford, 1988).

Daniel T. Rodgers is Professor of History at Princeton University. He is author of *The Work Ethic in Industrial America, 1850–1920* (University of Chicago Press, Chicago, 1978) and *Contested Truths: keywords in American politics since Independence* (Basic Books, New York, 1987), and he writes on modern American cultural and social history.

Farzana Shaikh is a former Fellow of Clare Hall, Cambridge and works in publishing. She writes on Indian Islam, and is author of *Community and Consensus in Islam: Muslim representation in colonial India, 1860–1947* (Cambridge University Press, Cambridge, 1989).

I. A. A. Thompson is a Fellow of the University of Keele in the Department of History. He is author of *War and Government in Habsburg Spain, 1560–1620* (Athlone Press, London, 1976) and writes on Spanish imperial history.

David Washbrook is Senior Lecturer in History at the University of Warwick. He writes on modern Indian history, and is author of *The Emergence of Provincial Politics: the Madras Presidency, 1870–1920* (Cambridge University Press, Cambridge, 1976).

Sean Wilentz is Professor of History at Princeton University. He is author of *Chants Democratic: New York City and the rise of the American working class, 1788–1850* (Oxford University Press, New York and Oxford, 1984) and writes on modern American labour, social, and cultural history.

Keith Wrightson is a Fellow of Jesus College, Cambridge, and University Lecturer in History. He writes on early modern British society and culture; and is author of *English Society, 1580–1680* (Hutchinson, London, 1982) and (with D. Levine) *Poverty and Piety in an English Village: Terling, 1525–1700* (Academic Press, New York and London, 1979).

Index